Advertising
Principles and Practice

(FOR STUDENTS OF B COM, M COM, BBA, MBA AND OTHER PROFESSIONAL COURSES)

Ruchi Gupta

Assistant Professor
Department of Commerce
Shaheed Bhagat Singh College
University of Delhi
Delhi

S Chand And Company Limited

(ISO 9001 Certified Company)

S Chand And Company Limited

(ISO 9001 Certified Company)

Head Office: D-92, Sector–2, Noida – 201301, U.P. (India), Ph. 91-120-4682700

Registered Office: A-27, 2nd Floor, Mohan Co-operative Industrial Estate, New Delhi – 110 044, Phone: 011-49731800

www.**schandpublishing.com;** e-mail: **info@schandpublishing.com**

Marketing Offices:

Chennai	:	Ph: 23632120; chennai@schandpublishing.com
Guwahati	:	Ph: 2738811, 2735640; guwahati@schandpublishing.com
Hyderabad	:	Ph: 40186018; hyderabad@schandpublishing.com
Jalandhar	:	Ph: 4645630; jalandhar@schandpublishing.com
Kolkata	:	Ph: 23357458, 23353914; kolkata@schandpublishing.com
Lucknow	:	Ph: 4003633; lucknow@schandpublishing.com
Mumbai	:	Ph: 25000297; mumbai@schandpublishing.com
Patna	:	Ph: 2260011; patna@schandpublishing.com

© S Chand And Company Limited, 2012

All rights reserved. No part of this publication may be reproduced or copied in any material form (including photocopying or storing it in any medium in form of graphics, electronic or mechanical means and whether or not transient or incidental to some other use of this publication) without written permission of the copyright owner. Any breach of this will entail legal action and prosecution without further notice.

Jurisdiction: *All disputes with respect to this publication shall be subject to the jurisdiction of the Courts, Tribunals and Forums of New Delhi, India only.*

First Edition 2012
Reprints 2015, 2016, 2018, 2019, 2020, 2021, 2022, 2023

Reprint 2025

ISBN: 978-81-219-4001-6 **Product Code:** H8ADV48MKTG10ENAA12R

PRINTED IN INDIA

By Vikas Publishing House Private Limited, Plot 20/4, Site-IV, Industrial Area Sahibabad, Ghaziabad – 201 010 and Published by S Chand And Company Limited, A-27, 2nd Floor, Mohan Co-operative Industrial Estate, New Delhi – 110 044.

Preface

The book, **Advertising: Principles and Practice**, broadly covers the principles on the basis of which advertising industry functions as well as how the same has been applied and used by corporates and advertising professionals in India. It is aimed at catering to the needs of both students as well as professionals in the advertising arena.

The book has been structured in the following parts.

- **Unit I – Basics of Advertising**, discusses the meaning of advertising, role of advertising in the marketing mix of a firm, advertising as a communication tool, different types of advertising and designing an advertising campaign. This part contains 5 chapters and 4 case studies in all.
- **Unit II – Advertising Management**, covers different steps of an advertising campaign, viz. advertising objectives, advertising budget, advertising message decisions, advertising media decisions and evaluation of advertising effectiveness. It also includes a chapter on advertising agencies. This section contains detailed discussions on topics like celebrity endorsements, mascots and online advertising in the form of separate chapters. This part contains 12 chapters and 5 case studies in all.
- **Unit III** – discusses the **Legal and Ethical Aspects of Advertising in India**. In addition to discussing the advertising law in India and various ethical issues in the field of advertising, the role of Advertising Standards Council of India (ASCI) in regulating advertising in India, and the concepts of surrogate advertising and comparative advertising have been discussed in this part. The recent Indian cases and decisions made thereunder have also been covered as part of the analysis in this section. There are 5 chapters, with 1 case study in this segment of the book.

In addition to this, the book also has a separate section '**Additional Case Studies**' which discusses 7 recent Indian case studies in advertising. These include Pepsi's *Youngistaan* Campaign, Tata Sky Plus launch campaign, *"Atithi Devo Bhavah"* campaign and Volkswagen Vento launch campaign, to name a few.

At the end is the **Advertising Glossary** for ready reference of advertising terms.

The book also includes many exhibits which provide real life examples from the Indian advertising industry. Since the book has many recent Indian case studies and exhibits, the users will be able to identify and relate to the advertising principles much easily. Discussion of various case studies in detail keeps the students well versed with the latest advertising techniques used by professionals in the industry.

The book has been written keeping in mind the curriculum requirements from academic perspective as well as intended at true knowledge addition for students.

RUCHI GUPTA

email: ruchigupta.sbsc@gmail.com

Disclaimer : While the author of this book has made every effort to avoid any mistake or omission and has used her skill, expertise and knowledge to the best of her capacity to provide accurate and updated information, the author and S. Chand does not give any representation or warranty with respect to the accuracy or completeness of the contents of this publication and are selling this publication on the condition and understanding that they shall not be made liable in any manner whatsoever. S.Chand and the author expressly disclaim all and any liability/responsibility to any person, whether a purchaser or reader of this publication or not, in respect of anything and everything forming part of the contents of this publication. S. Chand shall not be responsible for any errors, omissions or damages arising out of the use of the information contained in this publication.
Further, the illustrations used in the book are being used for purely academic purposes. Thus, the same should in no manner be termed as defamatory to any individual or organisation.

Acknowledgements

My love for the subject encouraged me to pen down my knowledge, learning and experience on the subject in the form of this book. By God's grace, I am happy to present this book to you and hope that the book will help the readers in their academic and professional pursuits.

Writing a book requires support and encouragement from a lot of people. I would be failing on my part if I do not thank all these people.

First and foremost, I want to thank my parents Mr. Ajit Kumar Kakkar and Mrs. Usha Kakkar for the education they have given me and the faith that they have shown in me which gave me the confidence to write this book. I would also want to thank my family, especially my husband, for his untiring support and encouragement in completing this book. My sincere thanks goes to the entire team of S.Chand, especially Mr. Navin Joshi and Mr. Shishir Bhatnagar for giving a wonderful shape to this book. I would also want to thank Prof. D.P.S.Verma, Former Professor, Delhi School of Econommics for the guidance and support that he has given to me right from my M.Com. days till date.

Case studies and exhibits form an integral part of the book. I want to thank all the companies and advertising agencies for coming up with such excellent and meaningful ads, the inclusion of which will provide excellent learning in the field of advertising to the readers of the book.

I have tried to use my experience in teaching advertising subject, as well as my learnings from various interactions with professionals and learned professors at seminars, conferences and other interactive discussion forums, to write this book. I am sure the book will be a good read for all those for whom it is intended.

This book is a gift from me to my husband, Sahil, and my son, Siddhant, the two most important people in my life.

RUCHI GUPTA

email: ruchigupta.sbsc@gmail.com

Contents

Unit I: Basics of Advertising

Unit–I
Basics of Advertising

CHAPTER 1

INTRODUCTION TO ADVERTISING

CONTENTS

Advertising is a promotional activity for marketing a commodity. In the present day world of mass production and distribution, advertising serves as a powerful tool in the marketing machinery. Different producers manufacture similar types of goods. They face tough competition in the market. Every producer is trying to create demand for his product. Advertising helps the manufacturer to increase his sales or maintain his market. It is only through proper advertising that a new product can be introduced in the market.

Advertising is the means of informing as well as influencing the general public to buy products or services through visual or oral messages. A product or service is advertised to create awareness in the minds of potential buyers. Some of the commonly used media for advertising are T.V., radio, newspapers, magazines, bill-boards, internet, etc.

Advertising plays a significant role in today's highly competitive world. Whether it is brands, companies, personalities or even voluntary or religious organisations, all of them use some form of advertising in order to be able to communicate with the target audience. As a result of economic liberalization and the changing social trends, advertising industry has shown rapid growth in the recent past.

MEANING AND DEFINITION OF ADVERTISING

The term 'advertising' is derived from the Latin word 'adverter' which means 'to turn' the attention. Every piece of advertising attempts to turn the attention of the readers or the listeners or the viewers or the onlookers towards a product or a service or an idea. Therefore, it can be said that anything that turns the attention to an article or a service or an idea might be called as advertising.

The most widely accepted definition of advertising is the one which is given by the American Marketing Association, according to which advertising is ***"any paid form of non-personal presentation and promotion of goods, services and ideas by an identified sponsor."***

This definition highlights the following features of advertising:

- Advertising is a paid form of communication.
- It can take any form-visual, audio, oral, written etc.
- It involves a non-personal presentation.
- Goods, services and/or ideas are promoted and presented.
- The sponsor is identified.

However, the definition given by the American Marketing Association suffers from some limitations. First, it has been argued that the definition does not talk about the persuasion aspect of advertising, without which it is very difficult to achieve advertising objectives. Keeping in mind this important aspect of persuasion, the following definition of advertising was proposed:

"Advertising is paid, non-personal communication of information from an identified sponsor using mass media to persuade or influence an audience so as to maximize profits."

The aforesaid definition though talks about the persuasion aspect of advertising but lays emphasis on the commercial side of advertising. However, it must be remembered that all ads are not commercial. For instance, advertisements giving messages like quit smoking, save water, drive safely, save the girl child, etc. do not have a commercial side attached to them. Thus, even this definition does not seem to be an adequate definition of advertising. Thus, yet another definition of advertising was proposed, according to which "advertising is controlled, identifiable information and persuasion by means of mass communication". This definition of advertising not only includes the persuasion aspect ignored by the definition given by the American Marketing Association but also goes beyond the 'paid form' and thus, includes even the non-commercial ads within its purview. In addition, the definition also states that advertising is 'controlled', which means that the time, space and direction of advertising can be controlled by the identifiable sponsor which is not there in publicity.

Some other definitions of advertising are given in Box 1.1.

Box 1.1: Some More Definitions of Advertising

- According to William J. Stanton, "advertising consists of all the activities involved in presenting to the audience a non-personal, sponsor identified, paid for message about a product or organisation."
- C.H. Sandage defines advertising as "a form of communication in which the communicator can control the character of his message and have it delivered to either a select or a mass audience at a very low cost."
- According to John J. Myers, "advertising is dissemination of information concerning an idea, service or product to compel action in accordance with interest of advertiser."
- According to Wright Winter, "advertising is controlled, identifiable information and persuasion to purchase the advertiser's product by means of mass communication media."
- In the words of Bay and Wheeler, "advertising is any form of paid, non-personal presentation of ideas, goods or services for the purpose of inducing people to buy them."
- In the words of J Thomas Russel and W Ronald Lane, "advertising is a message paid for by an identified sponsor and delivered through some medium of mass communication. Advertising is persuasive communication."
- The definition given by Houghton Miffin Company (1998) says, "Advertising is the non-personal communication of marketing related information to a target audience, usually paid for by the advertiser, and delivered through mass media in order to reach the specific objectives of the sponsor."
- In the words of C.H Sandge and V. Fryburger, advertising is "multi-dimensional; a powerful marketing tool; a component of economic system; a means of financing the mass media; a social institution; an art form; an instrument of business management; a field of employment and paying profession."

FEATURES OF ADVERTISING

A study of the aforesaid definitions helps us to understand the features and nature of advertising.

1. *Any Paid Form:* Advertising may take 'any' form-visual, audio, oral or written. Irrespective of the form of advertising, an advertiser needs to buy some time and space in some advertising medium like newspaper, magazine, radio, television, etc. The 'paid aspect' of advertising reflects the fact that the space or time for an advertising message generally must be bought. However, there are occasional exceptions to this and that is why one of the aforesaid definitions uses the words 'usually paid for' in defining advertising. For

instance, many T.V channels show ads to promote their own image among the audiences (e.g. 'Aaj Tak-Sabse Tez') and increase the popularity of their programmes among viewers. Although there would be costs involved in production of such ads, but such an advertising situation shows that all ads are not paid for.

2. *Non-personal Presentation and Promotion:* Advertising involves no direct face-to-face interaction between the prospect and the advertiser. It is, therefore, referred to as impersonal method of promotion. This is exactly opposite to personal selling where there is face-to-face presentation and promotion of product or service by the salesperson.
3. *Goods, Services and Ideas:* Advertising, being a powerful mass communication tool, is used not only to present and promote goods and services; it is also increasingly used to further the goals of public interest and social causes. We are exposed to thousands of ads everyday which present and promote various types of goods, services and ideas to us. Some examples of these ads are given in Table 1.1.

Table 1.1: Examples of ads of Goods, Services and Ideas

Goods	Services	Ideas
Colgate Toothpaste	Airtel Communication	Family Planning
Lux Soap	Vodafone Customer Care	Save the Girl Child
Surf Detergent Powder	Idea Communication	Prevention of AIDS
Cadbury Diary Milk Chocolate	Insurance plans by Metlife, UTI	HIV Awareness Programme
Soft drinks like Pepsi, Coke, Limca, Mirinda	Banking Services by ICICI, HDFC, HSBC	Save Water
Health drinks like Horlicks, Boost, Complan, Milo	Beauty/Personal Care Services by VLCC, Kaya Skin Clinic	Save Electricity
Nokia Mobile Phones	NIIT Education	Save Petrol
LG Refrigerators	Makemytrip.com	Quit Smoking
Sony Television	Kingfisher Airlines	Drive Safely
Levis Jeans	PVR Cinemas	*Atithi Devo Bhava*

4. *Identified Sponsor:* Advertising is undertaken by some identified individual or company, who makes the advertising efforts and also bears the cost of it. The words 'identified sponsor' clarify the difference between advertising and publicity. Just like advertising, publicity attempts to present certain ideas and opinions which may influence the attitudes and action of people. However, the source of publicity mostly remains unknown. As opposed to this, in case of advertising, the sponsor of ideas or opinions is known.
5. *Means of Mass Communication:* Advertising can be used to reach a large number of buyers at the same time. It is, therefore, a medium of mass communication.

6. *Controlled:* The advertiser/identified sponsor controls the content of advertising message, time and direction. Advertisers say what they want to say (they can decide the content of advertisement), and by selecting the appropriate medium (newspaper, TV, radio etc.), direct the message to their target audience.

7. *Persuasion:* The major objective of advertising inherent in the presentation and promotion of ideas, goods or services is to achieve predetermined objectives through persuasive communication, precipitating the change or reinforcement of desired attitude or behaviour.

8. *Advertising is a Science and an Art:* Advertising is a science as it has a systematized body of knowledge which can be taught and learnt in classrooms. Advertising is also an art as it involves practical application of the theory of advertising in designing ad campaigns.

9. *Advertising is a profession:* Advertising now is practiced as a profession. The advertising industry consists of the advertising agencies with billing running into crores of rupees per annum. Then we have a body of advertisers, mostly manufacturers, distributors, large retailers; service institutions etc. who sustain the advertising activity. We have the media consisting of the press, broadcast media (radio, TV), outdoor publicity etc. In all these three components, there are trained professionals like the Advertising Manager, the Media Manager, the Accounts Manager, the Space Selling Manager, the Art Director etc.

10. *Creative:* Advertising employs creativity to design an advertising campaign. Various stages in designing an ad campaign calls for creativity. Be it writing a slogan, or composing good jingles, or thinking of a good storyline for the ad, all demand a good amount of creativity from all the people involved in designing the campaign.

11. **Investment:** Some people consider advertising as a wasteful expenditure having a short-term effect. They believe that the money spent on advertising is charged to the customers by raising the price of the product. However, it should be remembered that advertising is an investment towards the building of goodwill and brand image of the product/organisation in the market. It should be sustained over a period of time; otherwise its message will be forgotten.

12. *Goal-oriented:* Advertising is a goal-oriented or purposeful activity aiming to achieve something. It may aim at increasing the sale of the product, increasing awareness among the target audience about a new product or new uses of a product, changing the habits of consumers, increasing usage, improving corporate image etc. Thus, advertising is directed towards the achievement of one or more goals or objectives and the advertising campaign is accordingly formulated to enable the achievement of these goals.

ADVERTISING – SCIENCE, ART OR PROFESSION?

Advertising has evolved, over the years as a systematized body of knowledge. It has its set principles and the rules and regulations framed out of both experiments and experience. There are certain principles that one should know if he is to enter the fascinating world of advertising. Advertising is a science as it has existence of a systematized body of knowledge. A lot of advertising literature is available on topics like setting advertising objectives, determining ad budgets, using advertising appeals, copywriting, layout designing, taking media decisions and evaluating the results of advertising, to name a few. The existence of vast literature in these areas makes advertising a science. However, advertising is a social science and hence not exactly like chemistry or mathematics. It deals with the human mind, to be very specific. Advertising is also a science as it draws heavily from sociology, psychology and economics.

Advertising is also an art. Art is the knowledge made efficient by skill. There is a considerable factor of creativity in advertising and it is essential to know when and how to use advertising principles for greater effect. One may study the science of advertising but one should go beyond this and develop through practice and experience the art of using it. Advertising is accepted more as an art because the principles and techniques available in advertising literature are not static. Moreover, advertising involves a lot of creativity in the areas of copywriting, use of humour and fear appeals, jingles, message execution styles and in overall design of advertising campaign. It is this creative aspect of advertising which makes it an art.

Of late, advertising is worthy of being considered as a profession as it is a specialized service for which personnel with rich experience and total training are required. It is an area that involves definitive and predictive work. It has become now a profession fulfilling the significant requisite of having a high degree of general and specific knowledge derived from experience, experiments and empirical analysis. The very growth and development of advertising agencies is a clear indication of advertising having emerged as a profession.

KEY PLAYERS IN THE ADVERTISING INDUSTRY

The advertising industry is complex because it has a number of different organisations involved in making decisions and executing advertising plans. The key players in the advertising industry include the advertiser (or the client), the agency, the media, the vendor and the audience. They all have different perspectives and objectives and a great advertisement is produced only when they come together as a team with a common vision. Let us now discuss about the various players in the advertising industry.

1. ***The Advertiser:*** Advertising begins with the advertiser, the person or the organisation that uses advertising to send out a message about its products. The advertiser initiates the advertising effort by identifying a marketing

problem that advertising can solve. The series of advertisements by Pepsi and Coca Cola after the pesticide issue explains how an advertiser struggles to maintain his position in times of crisis and how an agency helps the advertiser (its client) in developing a communication strategy to address a problem.

The advertiser makes the final decision about the target audience and the size of the advertising budget. The advertiser also approves the advertising plan, which contains details outlining the message and media strategies.

Finally, the advertiser hires the advertising agency, in other words, the advertiser becomes the agency's client. As the client, the advertiser is responsible for monitoring the work and paying the bills for the agency's work on its account. The use of the word 'account' is the reason agency people refer to the advertiser as "the account" and the agency person in charge of that advertiser's business as "the account manager".

2. ***The Advertising Agency:*** The second player in the advertising world is the advertising agency which creates the advertisement. Advertisers hire independent agencies to plan and implement part or all of their advertising efforts. This working arrangement is known as the agency-client partnership. It is very important to build a strong bond of trust between these two parties.

   An advertiser uses an outside agency because he believes that the agency will be more efficient in creating an advertisement or a complete campaign than the advertiser would be able to create on his own. Successful agencies such as Ogilvy & Mather, Lowe Lintas, McCann Erickson, FCB Ulka and Mudra have strategic and creative expertise, media knowledge, workforce talent, and the ability to negotiate good deals for clients. The advertising people working for the agency are experts in their areas of specialization and passionate about advertising.

3. ***The Media:*** The third player in the advertising world is the media. The media is composed of the channels of communication that carry the message from the advertiser to the audience. The development of mass media has been a central factor in the development of advertising because mass media offers a way to reach a widespread audience. We refer to these media as channels of communication. Each media vehicle (a particular newspaper, radio station or TV station, etc.) has a department in place that is responsible for selling ad space or time. Each medium tries to assist advertisers in comparing the effectiveness of various media as they try to make the best choice of media to use. Some of the media organisations assist advertisers in the design and production of advertisements. This is particularly true in case of local advertisers using local media, such as a retailer preparing an advertisement for the local newspaper.

   The primary advantage of advertiser's use of mass media is that the costs for time in broadcast media (television and radio), for space in print media (newspapers and journals), and for time and space in interactive media (internet), are spread over the tremendous number of people that these media reach. Thus, one of the advantages of mass media is that it can reach a lot of people with a single message in a very cost-efficient form.

4. *The Vendor (the Suppliers):* The fourth player in the world of advertising is the group of service organisations that assist advertisers, advertising agencies, and the media in creating and placing the ads: the suppliers, or vendors, who provide specialized services. Members of this group include artists, writers, photographers, directors, producers, printers, as well as self-employed freelancers and consultants, among the others. The array of suppliers mirrors the variety of tasks that it takes to put together an advertisement. Other examples of vendors include freelance copywriters and graphic artists, photographers, song-writers, printers, market researchers, direct-mail production houses, telemarketers and public relations consultants.

   Now the question is why to hire a vendor? The advertiser may not have expertise in that area, they may be overloaded, or they may want a fresh perspective. Another reason to rely on vendors is cost because services of vendors are often cheaper than the services of some in-house people.

5. *The Target Audience:* The formulation of an advertising strategy starts with the identification of the customer or prospective customer - the desired audience for the advertising message. The character of the target audience has a direct bearing on the overall advertising strategy, especially the creative strategy and the media strategy. For instance, if majority of the target audience of a detergent bar that sells in the rural market is illiterate, the advertiser might think of using an advertising medium like a local radio station where oral messages can be given rather than getting an advertisement printed in a local newspaper.

   Purchasers are not always the product users. In case of a children's cereal like Kellogs Chocos (Cornflakes), for instance, parents may purchase the product but kids consume it and definitely influence the purchase. Thus, Kellogs may actually have two target audience for a children's cereal, and would therefore, design one ad for the kids target audience and another for the parents target audience. It is critical, then, that advertisers recognize the various target audiences they are talking to and know as much about them as possible. The task of learning about the target audience is laborious and may take much time and cost to accomplish.

SIGNIFICANCE OF ADVERTISING

Advertising serves as an important promotional tool not only for manufacturers and traders but also holds substantial importance for consumers and society at large. The following points discuss the significance of advertising for these different groups.

Benefits to Manufacturers

1. ***Introduction of New Product:*** Advertising is helpful in introduction of new products in the market. Advertising achieves this by creating awareness about the new product and gaining its acceptance. By providing information about the new product, advertising stimulates the interest of the consumers and persuades them to buy it. Advertisements of Santro car featuring Shahrukh Khan were quite effective in creating awareness about this brand and gaining acceptance of people, when it was introduced in the Indian market.
2. ***Steady Demand:*** Advertising helps the manufacturers to create regular demand by smoothening out seasonal and other fluctuations. For instance, manufacturers of coffee advertise both hot and cold uses of the product to maintain a steady demand throughout the year. Steady demand enables regular production.
3. ***Promotes New Uses of the Product:*** Advertising helps in expanding the consumer base by promoting new uses of the product. For instance, advertisement of Dabur Honey shows that the product can be used for maintaining a good figure, to remain healthy and can be put on bread slices and ice creams. By promoting different uses of the product, advertising enables consumption of the product at a variety of occasions, thereby increasing product usage and thereby achieving increased sales of the product. Similarly, advertisement of Dettol shows that it can be used not only as an antiseptic lotion but also at other occasions- it can be mixed in water to do manicure and pedicure, it can be mixed in bathing water in summers to fight prickly heat, etc.
4. ***Economies of Scale:*** Advertising helps in maintaining a steady demand for products throughout the year. It also helps in expanding the customer base by entering new markets and by promoting new uses of the product. All this helps in maintaining regular production throughout the year. As a result, several economies of scale become available and cost of production per unit is reduced.
5. ***Meeting Competition:*** Advertising helps a firm in facing competition in the market. Advertising helps in attracting customers towards a brand by highlighting the strong points of the brands vis-à-vis the competing brands. By creating brand loyalty, it helps a firm to maintain sales and market share.
6. ***Corporate Image:*** Advertising helps in creating a good image of the firm and reputation for its products. A favourable image enables a firm to fight competition in the market and secure repeat order from customers. It is through effective advertising that names like Reliance, ICICI, Airtel, etc. have become household names.

Benefits to Customers

1. ***Education of Customers:*** Advertising provides information to the consumers about new products and their diverse uses. Consumers are educated about the proper use of the product, the prices at which they are available, various

promotional offers on the product, etc. Some ads increase the knowledge of public in general. For instance, the ads of water purifiers educate the public about the benefits of safe drinking water.

2. *Convenience in Shopping:* Advertising makes shopping convenient for the customers by reducing the time and effort involved in shopping. Customers are made aware about availability of different brands in the market and their specific features. This helps them in making their preferred choices much before they actually go to a shop and purchase the product.

3. *Lower Prices:* Effective advertising leads to reduced costs due to large scale production and economies of scale. The benefit of the reduced cost per unit is available to the consumers in the form of reduced prices of the products.

Benefits to the Salesmen

1. *Supports Salesmen:* Advertising provides great support to salesmen. If the brand is popular, it becomes easy for the salesmen to take entry in the door of prospective customer and convince him to purchase the product. Advertising prepares the necessary ground for the visit of salesmen by familiarizing the customers with the product and its uses. Thus, it becomes easy for the salesmen to convince the buyers. The salesmen can sell the product with much more ease if the product is well advertised.

Benefits to the Society

1. *Employment Generation:* Advertising provides direct employment to a large number of people engaged in designing, writing and issuing advertisements. These include copywriters, graphic designers, media planners, production houses, and advertising agencies. Indirectly, advertising increases employment opportunities by increasing the sales volume of production and distribution.

2. *Standard of Living:* Advertising improves the standard of living of people by providing new and improved products at reasonable rates. It educates people about these products and provides information for developing better ways of life. For instance, advertisements of microwave ovens show how a working couple can cook the food quickly by using the product.

3. *Sustains the Press:* Advertising provides an important source of revenue to the press. As a result, newspapers are available to the public at a lower cost. This helps in increasing their circulation. Without advertising, it will be difficult for the press to sustain itself as majority revenue comes through advertising, and not through sales revenue.

4. *Helps to solve Social Problems:* Social advertising helps to fight social problems like drug addiction, gender bias, female feticide, illiteracy, etc. Of late, Idea has designed its advertisements to fight social problems like casteism and illiteracy. Some social ads also motivate the public for eye donation, communal harmony and national integration.

CRITICISM OF ADVERTISING

The following points have been raised against advertising and people sometimes call it a social waste. The main points of criticism are as follows.

1. *Higher Prices:* It is argued that large amounts spent on advertising are transferred to the customers in the form of higher prices. But the defense says this is not true because advertising makes possible mass production, which in turn reduces prices through the economy of scale.

2. *Artificial Needs:* It is argued that advertising creates artificial needs and encourages wasteful consumption. By exploiting human sentiments, it persuades people to buy products which they do not need or cannot afford. Advertising promotes artificial living and creates demand for unwanted goods. The counter argument that the defense gives is that if there is no need for a product then people will not buy it. Advertising does not create needs; it helps the consumer decide which among the various brands to purchase. Marketers have found that the way to advertise and sell products is to satisfy genuine needs and wants, rather than to invent needs.

3. *Not Productive:* It is argued that advertising does not produce any tangible goods and thus, is a wasteful expenditure. However, defense says that all productive work need not result in tangible goods. Advertising, on the other hand, renders a very valuable service of providing information about the products to the customers. This important service rendered by advertising is extremely useful when consumers have to choose from among a variety of products.

4. *Deceptive:* It is argued that advertising is often deceptive and misrepresents facts to the consumers. Exaggerated claims and flowery language are used to deceive the customers. They are induced to buy goods through bogus testimonials and false claims. However, the defense argues that a few people misusing advertising does not mean that advertising itself is bad. Moreover, advertisers must know that continued deception would be self-defeating because it causes consumers to turn against a product. Thus, it is in the interest of the advertiser to stay honest.

5. *Offensive:* Sometimes advertising is found to be offensive and in bad taste. What is "offensive" is often subjective, determined by time and culture. For instance, ads using sex appeal, like Kamasutra Condoms, can be offensive for some, and not for others. Often the products themselves are not offensive, but the advertising offends in order to gain attention. For instance, the much criticized ad of Tuff Shoes featuring Milind Soman and Madhu Sapre used sex appeal to sell shoes!!!

6. *Creates Monopoly:* It is argued that advertising creates brand preferences and restricts free competition. Large firms which can afford huge amount of money on advertising eliminate small firms by creating brand monopoly. However, the counter argument given is that it is the age of the survival of

the fittest. If the brand which is advertised extensively is not able to perform or meet the expectations of the people, it will be forced out of the market. Also, brands continuously face competition from each other, a situation where monopoly cannot be created.

7. *Consumption of Harmful Products:* Advertising makes people consume products like alcohol and cigarettes which might affect their health. In India, inspite of a ban put on advertising of such products, manufacturers still are able to remind the consumers about their brands and such products in many indirect ways, for instance, Manikchand Filmfare Awards, Haywards soda, Kingfisher mineral water, Smirnoff cassettes and CDs, Teacher's Achievement Awards, etc. Through these advertisements, people are reminded of the liquor and tobacco products time and again, and the consumption of such products undermines their health.
8. *Discontented Society:* Advertising affects our value system by suggesting that the means to a happier life lie in the acquisition of goods and more materials things. Advertising leaves a section of the society discontented as people with less purchasing power cannot afford to buy goods even though advertisements create a strong urge in them for the same.

It is because of these points of criticism that it is often said that advertising is a social waste. Despite its drawbacks, advertising is a necessary marketing activity in the present business environment. It is not a social waste. It enables a manufacturer to introduce his products in the market and sell them. Advertising helps in educating the people regarding new uses of various products. It also strengthens the freedom of choice of the people. It sustains the press and gives employment to people. Advertising increases the standard of living of the people by informing them about the availability of new products. Thus, we can say that advertising is a useful marketing activity. Its drawbacks could be removed if the people and the Government keep a watch on the advertisers. People should satisfy themselves about the claims made by a producer before they purchase his products. The manufacturers or the advertisers should also avoid wasteful advertising and keep advertising expenditure within limits. They should also follow the ethical standards while advertising their products.

CONCLUDING NOTE

Advertising is an important means of informing and influencing target customers to buy goods or services. It makes use of visual, written and oral messages communicated through media like newspapers, magazines, radio, television, internet, billboards, hoardings, etc.

Advertising is a science, art as well as a profession. It is a science as it has existence of systematized body of knowledge. A lot of advertising literature is available on topics like setting advertising objectives, determining ad budgets, using advertising appeals, copywriting, layout designing, taking media decisions and evaluating the results of advertising, to name a few. The existence of vast literature in these areas makes advertising a science. Advertising is also an art as it requires creative decisions to be taken in areas like copywriting, use of humour and fear appeals, jingles, message execution styles and in overall design of advertising campaign. With the emergence and rapid growth of advertising agencies, advertising has also emerged as a very important profession.

Advertising plays a significant role for manufacturers, customers and the society at large. It helps the manufacturers in introducing new products, maintaining the demand of the existing products and attracting new customers. The consumers gain useful information about products, quality, terms of sales etc. It helps them to make a comparative analysis and make their best choice. Advertising generates huge revenue, employment opportunities in the country. It increases competition and motivate the producers to produce better alternatives of the existing products by utilizing the findings of research and development.

Advertising also has certain limitations. It multiplies the wants of the consumers. It adds to the cost of the product which ultimately increases the sales price. It may lead to creation of monopoly in the market. In real sense it does not increase the overall demand but simply shift the demand from one brand to other. Sometimes people feel tempted by seeing the advertisements and then get addicted to different harmful products like alcohol and tobacco. Advertising may also have adverse effect on our social, moral and ethical values. Nonetheless, the importance of advertising cannot be undermined. It has assumed a lot of importance in recent years.

QUESTIONS FOR DISCUSSION

1. Define advertising. What are the various features of advertising?
2. Advertising is a science, art and profession. Comment.
3. What are the key players in the advertising industry? Discuss briefly their roles in the advertising process.
4. Explain how is advertising important to manufacturers, consumers, salesmen, and the society in general.
5. What are the various criticisms levied against advertising?
6. Money spent on advertising is a waste. Do you agree?

Appendix 1.1

HISTORY OF INDIAN ADVERTISING

The primitive history of advertising can be dated back to the word-of-mouth advertising by hawkers announcing their articles for sale, merchants roaming from town to town spreading awareness about their goods and messengers of the kings announcing their messages. Advertising in India, in true sense, started in the 18th century with the birth of classified advertising. Advertisements appeared for the first time in print in 1780 in 'Bengal Gazette'- India's first newspaper. Initially, advertisements were imported from studios in England. But later, local ad development commenced in India with the setting up of newspaper studios. A lot of British retailers and medicine manufacturers were the major clients of these studios in those times. The medicine manufacturers used to advertise their medicines and retailers advertised their catalogues containing product information and promotional offers thereon. Advertising progress was gradual till the 20th century. But with India emerging a noteworthy market for products, ads for products of many multinational companies, like Lux, were designed for the Indian audience in the 1940s. Let us see some of the major milestones in Indian advertising since then.

1940-50

- In 1941, **Lux** signed Leela Chitnis as the first Indian film actress to endorse the product.
- In 1946, Air India's Bobby Kooka along with JWT's (ad agency) Umesh Rao created our own hospitable Maharaja. The *Maharaja* was a polished and courteous man with moustaches, in red imperial clothes, a striped turban and pointed shoes. The *Maharaja* made Air India the first Indian brand to have its own mascot.

1950-60

- P&G got **Vicks Vaporub** in India in 1952 and positioned it as a one stop solution for all cold symptoms. As opposed to this, the market leader at that time, Amritanjan, was positioned as an all-purpose ointment meant for cold, aches, pains, sprains, etc.
- The All India Radio's *Vividh Bharti Vigyapan Sewa* was started by AIR on October3, 1957. Among the first jingles heard were the ones for Hamam, Lifebuoy and Vicco Vajradanti.
- 1959 saw the marketing of India's first detergent powder **'Surf'** by Alyque Padamsee, an advertising guru.

1960-70

- The **Muscle-man of MRF** was created by Alyque Padamsee. For MRF tyres, durability was a key issue. Alyque and his gang dreamt up of a muscleman who was to be the company's public face - mascot who represented the essence and soul of the product promise - Strength. This gave it an instant identity and definition of what the brand stood for.
- 1964 saw Lifebuoy go through a major re-launch campaign. In the early 1960s, Lifebuoy was being sold as a body-odour soap. The marketing team at Lintas (ad agency) believed that the same strategy should be adopted in India. However, Alyque Padamsee, who was with Lintas at that time, convinced them that the health factor would work better for Lifebuoy in India. Thus, came up the famous jingle, *"Lifebuoy hai jahan tandaroosti hai wahan."*
- **Amul's** cute and bubbly **'Utterly Butterly Delicious' mascot** was created. The first Amul hoarding sporting the 'Utterly Butterly Delicious' Girl in a polka dot frock came up in 1967, in a hoading in Mumbai. The Amul Girl has made its way into the Guinness Book of World Records as the longest running outdoor advertising campaign.

1970-80

- Liril's positioning as a bathing soap made Alyque Padamsee a legend in the advertising fraternity. The landmark idea came in 1975 and what we saw was the **Liril girl** drenched under the falls wearing only a bikini. The ad was all about waterfalls, abundant water and the girl splashing about in total abandon singing "la…la la la laaa...". The first Liril ad was a masterpiece in itself. It was shot in Kodaikanal at a waterfall, a little beyond Guna caves.
- In 1977, Coca-Cola was virtually driven out of India. Eager to cash into the space left behind, companies started launching the domestic colas including Double 7, followed by Campa Cola, ThumsUp and McDowell's Thrill. While the other became popular in some local markets, Campa Cola dominated the Delhi market and ThumsUp ruled in Mumbai.
- 1970s saw the emergence of National Readership Surveys that fast started providing relevant data on consumer reading habbits.
- The birth of television in India in 1978 radically transformed the way advertising industry presented itself.

1980-90

- The soft drink concentrate concept was introduced in India. First launched as *Jaffe* in 1976, Pioma, an Ahmedabad based company, changed the name to Rasna in 1979. The company, along with the Mudra group launched the **'I Love You Rasna' campaign** in 1983. Rasna launched a soft drink concentrate with a range of nine flavours on a platform that offered both taste and economy. In 1986, Rasna became India's largest selling soft drink concentrate.
- Charms, the cigarette brand, initiated the trend for colour ads in newspapers.
- In 1983, Voltas came up with a huge corporate ad in the Times of India, laced with enticing body copy and starkling visuals. No one did two-page ads at that time, Voltas took the plunge and spent their annual advertising budget on this one ad.
- In 1982, the Asian Games virtually brought a whopping change in the lives of millions of Indians, when colour TV made debut in India. **Colour TV** brought with it a new medium of advertising.

- In 1980s, when Surf was facing a tough battle from Nirma, an economically priced detergent, Lintas came up with a bargain-oriented housewife *'Lalitaji'*, who with her remark *"Surf ki kharidari mein hi samajhdari hai"* won the battle for the brand fair and square.
- Persis Khambatta became the new **Garden woman** in 1985. Persis' uninhibited attitude in the Garden commercials represented the new urban Indian woman of the 1980s.
- Nestle came up with its 2-minute snack food, **Maggi Noodles**, and the brand has never looked back since then.
- Hero Honda rolled out its first motorcycle, the CD 100, in 1985 with the memorable **'Fill it, Shut it, Forget it'** campaign.
- The *'Hamara Bajaj'* campaign helped Bajaj to establish an emotional connect with consumers and also sustained Bajaj's sales which was experiencing a slump prior to the campaign.

- The **Onida's Devil** was born in the 1980s. Swishing his green tail and evil eyes in style, he positioned Onida as a television which is "Neighbour's envy, owner's pride".
- Men finally got a soap when Vinod Khanna was signed for Cinthol soap in 1986.
- Pepsi's ad campaign *"Yehi hai right choice baby, aha"* featuring Remo Fernandes using a combination of Hindi and English made its way into the hearts of teenagers of India.

1990-2000

- The 1990s stand witness to a radical transformation in the Indian TV industry. Breaking the monopoly of *Doordarshan,* the 1990s saw the satellite TV hit India. Star Plus was the first satellite TV channel to be aired in the Indian subcontinent. This was followed by Zee TV, India's first private satellite channel.

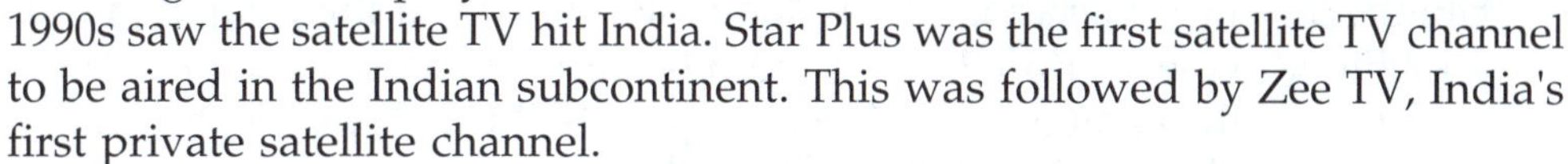

- 1990s marked the beginning of a new medium-**Internet**. Advertising agencies opened new media shops and went virtual with websites and Internet advertising.
- In 1998, Pepsi Co. came up with the first animated mascot, **Fido Dido**, for their lemon flavoured fizz drink, 7 Up. The mascot was first of its kind as it sang, danced, joked, laughed and cried with an equally enthralled audience.
- The Tuff shoes TV and print campaign released in 1998 flaunted models Milind Soman and Madhu Sapre, clad in nothing but a python and Tuff shoes. The ad led to a lot of public protest.
- In the early 1990's, chocolates were seen as 'meant for kids', usually a reward or a bribe for children. In the mid 1990's the category was re-defined by the very popular **'Real Taste of Life' campaign by Cadbury** shifting the focus from 'just for kids' to the 'kid in all of us'. The 'Real Taste of Life' campaign had many memorable executions, which people still fondly remember. However, the one with the "girl dancing on the cricket field" has remained imprinted in everyone's memory, as the most spontaneous & natural expression of happiness.

The New Millennium

- The Government of India launched the **'Incredible India'** campaign in 2003 to attract more tourists into the country. The campaign highlighted the geographical, historical and traditional glory of India.
- Hutch came up with its cute little mascot - the pug. Hutch's slogan "Wherever you go our network follows" was closely tied up with the **Hutch-Pug campaign**. The Hutch network was personified as the adorable pug dog following the owner, who was a very cute kid.
- Social Advertising received a boost in 2003 with the *'Do Boond Zindagi Ke'* campaign. The association of Amitabh Bachchan with the campaign brought credibility to the **National Pulse Polio Immunisation Programme**. The main objective of the campaign was to urge people through public interest ads to get their children vaccinated against polio.
- The metrosexual male arrived with Shahrukh Khan sitting proudly in a bath tub decorated with rose petals and surrounded by four Bollywood beauties - Hema Malini, Sridevi, Juhi Chawla and Kareena Kapoor, for Lux Soap in 2006.

- In 2007, Idea Cellular came up with its **"What an idea, sir ji"** campaign. The first ad in the series where mobile numbers were used as replacements for people's name in a village, was well received by the audience. The basic theme was to focus on treating everyone as equals. The social message was well delivered and what followed was a number of ads in this series - 'Education for all', 'Walk and talk', 'Save Paper, Save Tree', etc.
- In 2007, **Tata Tea's** *"Jaago Re"* campaign aimed at awakening the masses and alerting them to their responsibilities as citizens. The campaign thus, positioned the tea as a means of truly awakening people.
- **Vodafone Zoozoos** were created and the ads were aired during the IPL season in 2009. Zoozoos created an instant buzz both in traditional media as well as the social networking sites like Facebook, Twitter and Youtube.
- **Volkswagen** created a history in 2010 when in association with The Times of India and The Hindu, the company came up with a **'Talking Newspaper'** for the launch campaign of Volkswagen Vento.

CHAPTER 2

Role Of Advertising in Marketing Mix

CONTENTS

Marketing mix refers to the combination of four elements of marketing-Product, Price, Place and Promotion (4 P's). According to W.J. Stanton, "Marketing mix is the term used to describe the combination of the four inputs which constitute the core of advertising company's marketing system: the product, the price structure, the promotional activities and the distribution system". Philip Kotler defines marketing mix as, **"the set of marketing tools that the firm uses to pursue its marketing objectives in the target market"**.

Marketing mix represents the total marketing programme of a firm. It involves decisions with regard to product, price, place and promotion. These four elements constitute the core of a firm's marketing efforts and are called as the 4 P's of marketing by E.J. McCarthy. Every business firm must determine its marketing mix in an appropriate manner so as to meet the requirements of the customers.

ELEMENTS OF MARKETING MIX

The four major elements of marketing mix are described below.

1. **Product:** A product is anything that can be offered to satisfy a need or a want. Product component of the marketing mix involves decisions related to product size, product quality, product features, product packaging, labelling, branding, trademark, warranties and after-sales services. All these activities

are usually directed at a specific group of customers (target market) rather than consumers at large. The product should be such that it meets the requirements of the target market.

2. **Price:** Price is an important factor affecting success of a firm. Pricing decisions and policies have a direct influence on sales volume and profits of business. Price mix involves decisions regarding base price, discounts and other quantity rebates, allowances, credit terms, freight payments and resale price maintenance. The marketers pay attention to many factors before fixing the price of the product. These include competition from rival firms, how much the target customers will buy at various prices, how much it costs to produce and market the product, how much of the price can be allowed as discounts, the profit margins to be maintained etc.

3. **Place:** Place mix involves distributing the product from the place of production to the place of consumption. This category of decisions include the following-

   (*i*) **Distribution channels:** Whether to distribute the goods through wholesalers and retailers or directly selling them to the final buyer.

   (*ii*) **Intensity of distribution coverage:** Whether to provide intensive distribution, selective distribution or exclusive distribution for the product.

   (*iii*) **Warehousing:** Deciding number and location of warehouses to be owned/ hired

   (*iv*) **Inventory to be maintained**

   (*v*) **Modes of transport to be used**

4. **Promotion:** Promotion component of the marketing mix is concerned with bringing products to the knowledge of customers and persuading them to buy. It is the function of informing and influencing the customers. Promotion mix involves decisions with respect to advertising, personal selling, sales promotion and publicity. No single method of promotion is effective alone and therefore, a promotion campaign usually involves a combination of one or more promotional methods.

   Marketing mix is a very important concept in the marketing literature. It helps in determining the most optimum combination of the 4 P's and thus, in achieving the marketing objectives.

   All the marketing mix elements are inter-related. Decisions in one area affect decisions in other areas. How advertising would affect decisions in these four areas is explained in the rest of the chapter.

Advertising and Marketing Mix

Advertising is an element of promotion, which in turn is an element of marketing mix. Let us now study how advertising affects other elements of the marketing mix.

ADVERTISING AND PRODUCT

Advertising makes buyer aware of the product at the time of its introduction. Advertising in later stages informs the buyers about its features and attributes and the benefits it offers. Advertising facilitates the growth of the product, and also helps it when its sales decline. Advertising also makes the people favourably inclined towards products.

Product decisions cover various areas like branding, packaging, product life cycle stages, product planning etc. The relation of advertising to these areas is explained below.

Advertising and Product Life Cycle

The main factor that determines the use of advertising and promotion over the longer term is the stage in the product life cycle (PLC). As shown in Figure 2.1, the product life cycle consists of four major stages: introduction, growth, maturity and decline.

Advertising and promotion expenditures in the ***introduction*** stage typically are both high. A high level of advertising is needed to make people aware of the newly introduced product and to communicate its benefits for prospective buyers' consideration. A high level of promotion is also needed to further build awareness and induce people to try the new product.

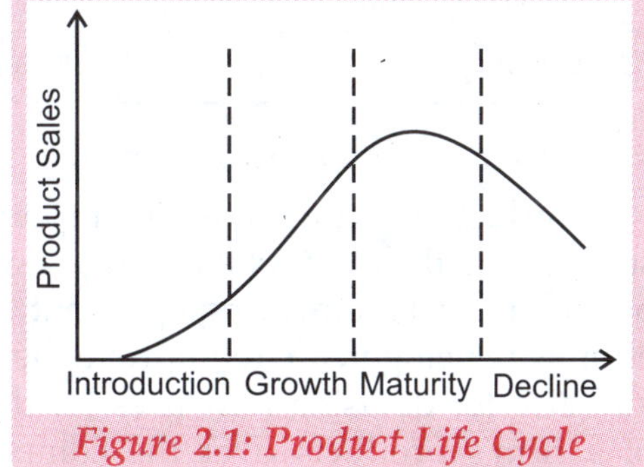

Figure 2.1: Product Life Cycle

Advertising and promotion strategy in the ***growth*** stage may differ depending on whether the brand is (a) either the market share leader or well differentiated from other brands in the product category, versus (b) an imitative "me-too" brand. In the former instance, advertising is emphasized as a means of maintaining brand identity and differentiation. In the latter instance, with a me-too product or brand, advertising can be lower because the imitator can capitalize on the leader's advertising. Correspondingly, promotion is higher so as to induce trial of, and switching to, the me-too brand. Thus, the relative roles of advertising and promotion may be reversed depending on the brand's positioning in the growth stage of the PLC.

Advertising and promotion strategy in the ***maturity*** stage may also differ, depending on whether the brand has managed to create (a) high brand loyalty, or (b) low brand loyalty. Brands with high brand loyalty usually will emphasize advertising to maintain the successful brand image. Brands with a low degree of loyalty, on the other hand, will usually have to emphasize promotion as a means of attracting and holding buyers.

Advertising and promotion in the ***decline*** stage of the product life cycle are phased out as the manager tries to minimize marketing costs. Advertising is discontinued. Promotion, however, is continued at a low level to the distributors, to keep the product in stock while the manufacturer's inventory is reduced to zero.

The relative roles of advertising and promotion according to PLC stages have been shown in Table 2.1.

Table 2.1: Relative roles of Advertising and Promotion according to PLC stages

PLC Stage	Advertising	Promotion
1. Introduction	High	High
2. Growth (a) Leader or Differentiated (b) Me-too product	HighLow	LowHigh
3. Maturity (a) High Brand Loyalty (b) Low Brand Loyalty	HighLow	LowHigh
4. Decline	None	Low (distributors)

Advertising and Product Planning

Product planning has an important place in the marketing mix. Recent strategies in the product planning area have been directed towards manufacturing better products and bringing about improvements in existing ones. Consistent efforts are being made to improve the quality of products, increasing their variety and also for devising new uses for them. Advertising highlights the superiority of a firm's products over the competing products and also seeks to enhance awareness and knowledge of new uses.

Advertising and Product Positioning

Advertising helps the advertiser to position his product/service in the minds of the customers in the desired way. For instance, advertisements of Airtel Digital TV have helped to position the product as one which promises high quality in terms of picture quality. Similarly, advertisements of Big Bazaar have helped to position itself in the customers' mind as a good quality product available at the lowest price.

Advertising and Packaging

Packaging is an important part of the marketing mix. Decisions taken in the packaging area determine to a great extent the designing of advertisements. For instance, the colour used on the product package is sometimes used extensively or prominently in the advertisements. We see a prominent use of purple colour in the ads of Cadbury's Diary Milk Chocolate, which is also the colour of its package. Similarly, we see the models dressed up in green and white colours in Dettol Soap ads.

The products also get an advantage of easy recognition by consumers if the advertisements prominently focus on the product packages. Thus, a consumer can easily recognise a packet of Maggi noodles lying on the shelf of a retailor from a distance because its advertisements prominently focus on the package.

Advertising and Branding

The brand provides to the customer a certain guarantee and assurance that the quality of the products is satisfactory as the brand name connotes accountability. To the manufacturer, it represents a means of gaining customer loyalty by building a consumer franchise around his particular brand. Advertising decisions are affected by a company's branding policy. For instance, a company may use a family brand name or an umbrella brand name under which it produces various products. Sony produces various products-music systems, DVD players, Televisions, Home theatre systems, Laptops etc. under the same brand name. Such a policy gives an option to the company to advertise all its products in one advertisement or individually advertise each of its products. On the other hand, some companies may choose to give a different brand name or individual brand name to its various products. For instance, Hindustan Unilever uses a different brand name for different bathing soaps it produces. Thus, we see different advertisements for Lux, Dove, Lifebuoy, Liril, and Pears.

ADVERTISING AND PRICE

Price is an important consideration in buying decisions. Many customers are price conscious and would like to know the price of a product for comparison purposes before finally deciding to buy. Price is also indicative of quality. Many people equate price with quality. The costlier the product, the better the quality. The reverse is also true. If a product costs less, customers may feel that it cannot be of good quality. Pricing a product is thus, an important and critical activity. If a lower price is fixed, it will affect the profitability of a business; and if a higher price is fixed, the product will not be able to stand in competition and may have to go out of the market. Therefore, the right price has to be fixed. Advertisements sometimes carry the price tag of the product. For some products, when many identical products are competing with each other for consumer preference, the price may be an important influencing factor. The other purpose of giving the price in advertisements is to discount the possibility of higher prices being charged by the retailer from the ignorant customer. The price of a product is sometimes made the theme of its advertisement to inform the prospects that the total product offering is economical. Advertising highlights the price, price-and-quality relationship, economical nature or premium nature of the product and changes in prices. For instance, the advertising campaign *"Paanch matlab chota coke"* highlighted the price of the small Coke bottle and did wonders for Coke's rural positioning.

ADVERTISING AND PLACE

Place refers to physical distribution, that is, the various channels through which products are made available. It is through advertising that the 'pull' effect may be created amongst potential buyers i.e. consumers start demanding the advertised products from retailers or walk into their stores. This, in turn, will motivate the channel members (wholesalers and retailers) to stock the product in anticipation of demand for the product. The advertisements by retailers like Shopper's Stop announcing upto 50% off on products results in many customers walking into their stores.

ADVERTISING AND PROMOTION

A marketer needs to balance the promotion mix consisting of advertising, personal selling, sales promotion and publicity. There should be co-ordination between all these elements of promotion.

Advertising and Personal Selling

Personal selling is the process of assisting and persuading a prospective buyer to buy a product or service in a face to face situation. It involves direct and personal contact between the prospective buyer and the seller or his representative.

Advertising and Personal Selling are very closely related to each other. Personal Selling is called oral advertisement while Advertising is called Salesmanship in print.

Advertising facilitates the role of salesmen. If the potential buyers are aware of the products because of advertising, salesmen can easily persuade them to buy the products. On the other hand, if a salesman contacts a potential buyer and introduces his product about which the potential buyer does not know, he may totally ignore the plea of the salesman. Moreover, the potential buyer might feel why should he stop using the product of the present brand all of a sudden. Advertising gives exposure of the products to the potential buyers. It explains to them the uses and advantages of the product/brand. It thus, helps in reducing the resistance of the consumers and makes the job of the salesman easier.

On the other hand, salesmanship picks up from where advertising leaves. Advertising creates demand and salesmanship converts the potential demand created by advertising into sales. Advertising in various media like newspapers, television, etc. just make the consumers aware about different products and brands. But still the consumer may be in a stage of indecisiveness. The salesman explains to the consumer how a product can satisfy his needs. He will list out the advantages of buying the given product. He may even give demonstration of the same, if required, and finally may be successful in selling it to the customer.

Inspite of being closely related to each other, there are some important differences between advertising and personal selling. These differences are listed in table 2.2.

Table 2.2: Differences between Advertising and Personal Selling

Advertising	Personal Selling
1. Advertising is an impersonal form of communication.	Personal selling is a personal form of communication.
2. Advertising involves transmission of standardized messages i.e., same message is sent to all the customers in a market segment.	In personal selling, the sales talk is adjusted keeping in view customers needs and background.
3. Advertising is inflexible as the message cannot be adjusted to the needs of the buyer.	Personal selling is flexible as the sales presentation can be adjusted according to the needs and background of the customer.
4. Advertising is a form of mass communication i.e., a large number of people can be reached.	Only a limited number of people can be contacted because of time and cost considerations.
5. In advertising, the cost per person reached is very low as it reaches a large number of people.	The cost per person is relatively high in case of personal selling.
6. Advertising can cover the market in a short time.	Personal selling efforts take a long time in covering the entire market.
7. Advertising makes use of mass media such as newspapers, magazines, radio and television.	Personal selling makes use of sales staff which has limited reach.
8. Advertising lacks direct feedback. Marketing research efforts are needed to judge customer's reactions to advertising.	Personal selling provides direct and immediate feedback. Salesmen come to know about the customers' reactions immediately.
9. Advertising plays a tremendous role in attracting the attention of the prospects and moving them to the interest stage.	Personal selling plays an important role in bringing about sales.
10. Advertising uses a wide choice of channels for transmission of messages-audio as well as visual, such as, radio, television, internet, etc.	In personal selling, there is only one channel for transmission of messages-personal talk of the salesman with the prospective customer.

Advertising and Sales Promotion

Sales promotion consists of all promotional activities other than advertising, personal selling and publicity that help to increase sales through short-term incentives. According to American Marketing Association, sales promotion includes "those marketing activities other than personal selling, advertising and publicity that stimulate consumer purchasing and dealer effectiveness, such as point of purchase displays, shows and exhibitions, demonstrations and various non-recurring selling efforts not in the ordinary routine".

The ultimate aim of sales promotion is increasing the sales and profits but it is different from advertising and personal selling in approach and techniques. Personal selling involves face to face contact with specific individuals while advertising is directed at a large number of potential customers. Sales promotion serves as a link between the two by focussing selling effort on selected small groups of people. Sales promotion usually involves non-recurring and non-routine methods, in contrast to the routine and recurring nature of advertising and personal selling. Under advertising, the media is not owned and controlled by the advertiser except in direct mail advertisements but sales promotion methods are controlled by the advertiser. Advertising and personal selling are essential or basic ingredients of promotion mix while sales promotion is a supporting or facilitating element of promotional strategy. Sales promotion bridges the gap between advertising and personal selling. It supplements and reinforces the personal selling and advertising efforts of the firm.

The differences between advertising and sales promotion are listed in Table 2.3.

Table 2.3: Differences between Advertising and Sales Promotion

Point of Distinction	Advertising	Sales Promotion
1. Meaning	Any paid form of impersonal presentation of a product, service or idea by an identified sponsor	Marketing activities which stimulate consumer buying and dealer effectiveness
2. Time horizon	Long-term perspective	Short-term perspective
3. Aim	To build image of producer and his product	To increase immediate sales
4. Scope	Television, radio, newspaper, magazines, films and other media	Free samples, coupons, contests, premiums, displays, exhibitions etc.
5. Regularity	Regular and recurring	Limited period, non-recurring
6. Emphasis	Informs, persuades and reminds buyers, attracts customers towards the product	Supplement to advertising and personal selling; pushes products towards buyers

Advertising and Publicity

Publicity is any form of commercially significant news about an organisation, a product or service carried by the press, radio, television, etc. that is not paid for by the sponsor. Thus, publicity is basically an information about the product, service or business organisation, which is communicated voluntarily by the media and is of commercial significance to the firm.

Advertising is different from publicity in the following ways.

1. Advertising is paid for by its sponsor whereas publicity is not paid for.
2. Advertising is done by an identified sponsor but in publicity, the sponsor is not identified.

3. Advertising is always impersonal whereas publicity may be both personal and impersonal.
4. In advertising, the sponsor exercises direct control over the size and frequency of the message. But in publicity, control lies with the news media.
5. Publicity has greater versatility than advertising. News, stories, editorials and special write ups about a company or its products appear more authentic to the readers than advertisements sponsored by a company.
6. Publicity is off guard because the news can reach even those who otherwise avoid advertisements. Advertising is not off guard in this way.

The basic differences between advertising and publicity can be summarized in table 2.4.

Table 2.4: Differences between Advertising and Publicity

Point of Distinction	Advertising	Publicity
1. Payment	Advertising is a paid form of dissemination of information. The firm has to pay for the use of space and time.	No payment is made to the media as the information is published voluntarily.
2. Identified	There is an identified sponsor, that is, the firm which wants to advertise its products or services.	There is no identified sponsor. Media communicates the information as it considers it newsworthy.
3. Control	The advertising firm has full control over the content, type, size, duration and frequency of the message.	The concerned firm has no control over the contents, type and size of information.
4. Purpose	Advertising is intended to give favourable and positive impression about the company and its products.	Publicity may generate favourable or unfavourable impression on the public about the company and its products.
5. Authenticity	Advertising is considered less authentic by people.	Publicity is considered more authentic.

CONCLUDING NOTE

Advertising as one of the elements of the promotion mix affects decisions in all the areas of marketing mix, be it product, price or place. It also affects decisions taken in other areas of the promotion mix, that is, personal selling, sales promotion and publicity. Advertising having such an important influence in all these decision areas implies that the firm cannot afford to take advertising lightly. At the same time, a marketer must not forget that no matter how good the advertising is and how much money is spent on it; the brand's success will also depend on other elements of the marketing mix such as pricing, packaging, product quality and positioning. Thus, we can say how effective advertising will be is dependent upon how well the promotion mix has been arranged and how well the total marketing mix is managed.

QUESTIONS FOR DISCUSSION

1. Discuss the importance of advertising in the product area of marketing mix.
2. How does advertising change with the different stages of a product in its life cycle?
3. Explain how advertising and personal selling are related to each other.
4. Distinguish between advertising and personal selling.
5. Distinguish between advertising and sales promotion.
6. Distinguish between advertising and publicity.
7. Explain how advertising affects various decisions in different areas of the marketing mix.

Case Study

BIG BAZAAR

Parent group: Future group
Owner: Kishore Biyani (CEO)
Founded: 2001
Headquarter: Jogeshwari, Mumbai
Industry: Retail
Tagline: *Is se sasta aur accha kahin nahi*!

Big Bazaar is a retail chain of hypermarket in India that reaches to customers with daily needs of a family at a reasonable price. This retail store is a subsidiary of Future group. Big Bazaar began its journey in October, 2001. Young entrepreneur, Kishore Biyani introduced India's first hypermarket retail outlet in Calcutta. In the same month, two more stores were added in Hyderabad and Mumbai. Now Big Bazaar is spread in more than 60 cities in India with more than 120 stores spread across India. It has already achieved a unique milestone to fastest rollout in very few years.

Though Big Bazaar was started in a format of garments, cosmetics, accessory and general merchandise, soon it evolved much more. Its product mix consists of clothing and accessories for all - men, women and children. It offers clothes, stationary and toys, footwear, plastics, home utility products, cosmetics, crockery, home textiles, luggage, gift items, and also food products and grocery. The added advantage for the customers shopping in Big Bazaar is that there are many attractive schemes and promotional offers going on in the Big Bazaar stores always.

This shopping store mainly attracts middle class and lower-middle class with the discounted pricing and lucrative offers at different products. Shopping in the Big Bazaar is a great experience as one can find almost everything under the same roof.

Big Bazaar has no doubt made a big name in the retail industry of India. This case study discusses how the pricing and promotional strategies of Big Bazaar are very much reflected in its advertisements.

Pricing Strategies of Big Bazaar

Pricing is a crucial strategic variable due to its direct relationship with a firm's goal and its interaction with other marketing elements. The importance of pricing decisions is growing because today customers are looking for a good value when they buy merchandise and services.

The pricing objective at Big Bazaar is to get "Maximum Market Share". Pricing at Big Bazaar is based on the following techniques:

- *Value Pricing:* Value pricing refers to charging a fairly low price for a high quality offering. Big Bazaar ensures that no other *kirana* store / departmental store are offering considerable discount compared to its own price. This helped Big Bazaar in being the "value for money" store. It promises consumers the lowest available price without coupon clipping, waiting for discount promotions, or comparison shopping.
- *Promotional Pricing:* Big Bazaar offers financing at low interest rate. The concept of psychological discounting (Rs. 99, Rs. 49, etc.) is also used to attract customers. Big Bazaar also caters on Special Event Pricing like close to Diwali.
- *Differentiated Pricing:* Differentiated pricing i.e. difference in rates based on peak and non-peak hours or days of shopping is also a pricing technique used by Big Bazaar. For example, Wednesday Bazaar by Big Bazaar.
- *Bundling:* The practice of joining related products together for the purpose of selling them as a single unit is known as bundling. This is generally carried out when the seller thinks that the characteristics of two or more products or services are such that these products might

appeal to many consumers more as a package than as individual offerings. Bundling arrangements usually feature special pricing arrangements which make it cheaper to buy products and services as a bundle rather than separately. Thus, bundling refers to selling combo-packs and offering discount to customers. The combo-packs add value to customer and lead to increased sales. Big Bazaar lays a lot of importance on bundling. For example,

3 Good Day family packs at Rs 60(Price of 1 pack = Rs 22)

5kg oil + 5kg rice + 5kg sugar for Rs 599

Buy any 20 items, Get 20 items free

Promotional Offers Run by Big Bazaar

Big Bazaar believes in advertising its brand and offers. The various promotional schemes undertaken by Big Bazaar are as follows:

- The punch line of Big Bazaar says *"is se sasta aur accha kahin nahi"*. This line gives the feeling that Big Bazaar gives merchandise which is cheapest in the market or, in other words, the value for money which a customer will be getting here will be more than anywhere else.
- Wednesday is the cheapest day. This is done to divert some of the crowd coming on weekends to a relatively free day. This offer targets housewives and encourages them to do their purchases of groceries and vegetables on a weekday.
- In 2005, Big Bazaar introduced a totally new sales-campaign – *"Sabse Sasta Din"* - means "The Cheapest Day". In just one day millions of consumers descended to Big Bazaar around the country and gradually this became their favourite shopping destination. Later, *"Sabse saste char din"* became quite popular in January 2010 (23rd-26th). A record 6.5 million walk-ins was achieved.
- Big Bazaar had also announced a unique exchange offer 'Bring anything old and take anything new'. Under the exchange offer, old garments, utensils, furniture, plastic ware, newspapers or just about anything would be weighed and valued and customers were given exchange coupons. There is also often a direct exchange on mobile and electronic goods during the period with attractive discounts on new purchases.
- Big Bazaar usually runs a full page advertisement on Saturdays and Sundays in all the leading dailies communicating various offers. This is done to attract

crowds on weekends because most of the people usually shop during weekends.

- Brand endorsements by M.S.Dhoni and Asin.

Thus, we see that advertising has a definitely important role to play in positioning the products of Big Bazaar in customers' minds (high quality products available at lowest cost). Advertisements of Big Bazaar also help it to achieve its pricing objectives. Also, its advertisements are quite effective in getting a lot of walk-ins in the stores of Big Bazaar across the country.

CHAPTER 3

ADVERTISING AS A COMMUNICATION TOOL

CONTENTS

Advertising has emerged as a very important communication tool in recent years. It is considered as the most effective way of communicating to the customers about the availability of the product, new variants of the product available in the market, new uses of existing products, new products available in the market and new prices at which the products are available. It is also an important tool used to influence and persuade the customers to buy particular products/services. This chapter seeks to explain how advertising becomes a very important part of the marketing communication process and how advertising through its influence and persuasion moves the consumers through various stages in the buying process. Let us first start with explaining the meaning of communication.

MEANING OF COMMUNICATION

Communication can best be summarized as the transmission of a message from a sender to a receiver in an understandable manner. According to Hudson, **"Communication in its simplest form is conveying of information from one person to another"**. In the words of Allen, "Communication is the sum of all the things one person does when he wants to create understanding in the mind of another". Thus, communication is an attempt to share understanding by two or more persons. It is a two-way process and is completed when there is some response from the receiver of information.

- Communication involves at least two persons - one who sends the message and the second who receives the message. In advertising terms, the sender of the message is the advertiser of the product and the receiver to whom the message is intended is the target customer.
- The basic purpose of communication is to create an understanding in the mind of the receiver of the information. Thus, an advertiser aims to put across his message to the consumer in such a way that he understands it.
- Communication may take several forms-oral, written, though visuals etc. Thus, advertising may use radio to send oral messages to customers, television for visual messages, newspapers and magazines for written messages, outdoor billboards, posters and internet for a combination of written and visual messages.
- Communication is a persuasive function. Thus, an advertiser uses advertising communication i.e. advertisements through various media to persuade the prospective customers to act favourably towards the product/service/idea advertised. This favourable response from the customers might mean an increase in sales, or improved brand loyalty, or favourable attitude towards the advertised brand.
- Communication is a two-way traffic. The process of communication is not completed until the message has been understood by the receiver. Effective communication leads to understanding.

PROCESS OF COMMUNICATION

The process of communication can be explained with the help of a communication model. The following figure shows a communication model with nine elements. Two represent the major parties in a communication - sender and receiver. Two represent the major communication tools - message and media. Four represent major communication functions - encoding, decoding, and feedback and response. The last element in the system is noise.

Figure 3.1 shows a model of communication process with these nine elements.

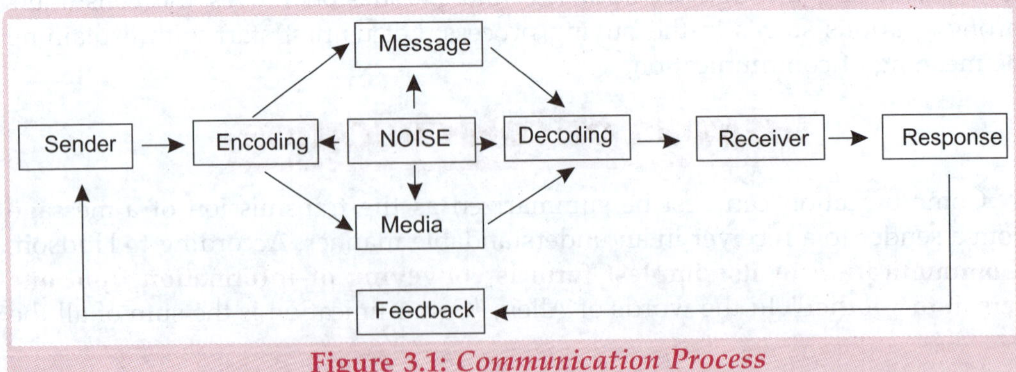

Figure 3.1: *Communication Process*

Let us now discuss these elements of the communication model in detail.

1. *Sender:* The sender is an individual, group, or organisation who initiates the communication. This source is initially responsible for the success of the message. The sender's experiences, attitudes, knowledge, skill, perceptions, and culture influence the message. The written words, spoken words, and nonverbal language selected are paramount in ensuring that the receiver interprets the message as intended by the sender. All communication begins with the sender. In case of advertising, the sender is the advertiser of a product/service.

2. *Encoding:* The first step that the sender is faced with involves the encoding process. In order to convey meaning, the sender must begin encoding, which means translating information into a message in the form of symbols that represent ideas or concepts. This process translates the ideas or concepts into the coded message that will be communicated. The symbols can take on numerous forms such as, languages, words, or gestures. These symbols are used to encode ideas into messages that others can understand.

3. *Message:* When encoding a message, the sender has to begin by deciding what he wants to transmit. This decision by the sender is based on what he believes about the receiver's knowledge and assumptions, along with what additional information he wants the receiver to have. It is important for the sender to use symbols that are familiar to the intended receiver. A good way for the sender to improve encoding his message is to mentally visualize the communication from the receiver's point of view.

   The encoding and message decisions are taken simultaneously. For instance, in case of advertising, the advertiser may want to inform (message) the target customers about the price of the product. Encoding of this message may then take place by putting this message in these words-"Ab aapki manpasand Nestle Munch sirf paanch rupay mein". Also, the advertiser would like to choose that type of message which will create attitude and feelings most likely to precipitate the desired action. The message content can focus on rational or emotional approach. Humourous messages attract consumer attention and put the person in a pleasant mood. Music can add emotion and make the consumers more inclined towards the message. The marketer may favour using fear or sex appeals or may like to use brand comparison approach. There is a wide choice in developing an appropriate message for the target audience.

4. *Media:* To begin transmitting the message, the sender uses some kind of channel (also called a medium). The channel is the means used to convey the message. Most channels are either oral or written, but currently visual channels are becoming more common as technology expands. The effectiveness of the various channels fluctuates depending on the characteristics of the communication. For instance, in case of marketing communications, most popular channels are television, radio, internet, newspapers, magazines, etc. Even within a particular medium, the advertiser as a lot of options. For

instance, in case of televisions, an advertiser can make a choice between various television channels depending on his product and the interest area of target market. Thus, an advertiser may advertise sports shoes on a sports channel like Ten Sports, educational kits for children can be advertised on channels like Cartoon Networks, FMCGs like soft drinks, potato chips, toothpaste, soap, detergents, etc. can be advertised on popular television channels like Sony, Star Plus, Zee etc. A marketing manager might also use more than one medium i.e. a combination of various media to put his message across to the target audience.

5. ***Decoding:*** After the appropriate channel or channels are selected, the message enters the decoding stage of the communication process. Decoding is conducted by the receiver. Once the message is received and examined, the stimulus is sent to the brain for interpreting, in order to assign some type of meaning to it. It is this processing stage that constitutes decoding. The receiver begins to interpret the symbols sent by the sender, translating the message to his own set of experiences in order to make the symbols meaningful. Successful communication takes place when the receiver correctly interprets the sender's message.

6. ***Receiver:*** The receiver is the individual or individuals to whom the message is directed. In case of advertising, the message is directed at the target market but it might be received by other customers also. The extent to which the receiver comprehends the message will depend on a number of factors, which include the following: how much the individual or individuals know about the topic, their receptivity to the message, and the relationship and trust that exists between sender and receiver. All interpretations by the receiver are influenced by their experiences, attitudes, knowledge, skills, perceptions, and culture. It is similar to the sender's relationship with encoding.

7. ***Response:*** Response refers to the set of reactions that the receiver has after being exposed to the message. In case of advertising, a response may mean developing a favourable attitude towards the product as a result of an advertising campaign. However, in many cases, measuring such responses in case of advertising is not easy.

8. ***Feedback:*** Feedback is the final link in the chain of the communication process. It is that part of the receiver's response that the receiver communicates back to the sender. After receiving a message, the receiver responds in some way and signals that response to the sender. The signal may take the form of a spoken comment, a long sigh, a written message, a smile, or some other action. Without feedback, the sender cannot confirm that the receiver has interpreted the message correctly.

9. ***Noise:*** Noise refers to the random and competing messages that may interfere with the intended communication. The element of noise in the communication process also refers to any type of unplanned disruption or interference that

may hinder the communication. Thus, for Pepsi, a Coke ad (competing message) is noise. Also, any other ad, even of products other than soft drinks, are noise for Pepsi as it makes it difficult for Pepsi to make its ad stand out and attract attention when the customer is bombarded with a number of advertisements these days. Sometimes, the selected channel may itself be the source of noise, such as distortion in a radio or television signal.

We have already said that the target customer may not receive the intended message because of the element of noise (random and competing messages that may interfere with the intended communication) in the marketing communication process. In addition to this, one also needs to know about the following three factors because of which the target customer may not receive the intended message.

a. *Selective Attention* -A person may be exposed to hundreds or thousands of ads or brand communications in a day. Because a person cannot possibly attend to all of these, most stimuli will be screened out. This process is called selective attention. Thus, selective attention means that marketers have to work hard to attract consumer's notice. The real challenge is to explain which stimuli people will notice. Generally, people are more likely to notice stimuli that relate to a current need. Thus, a person who is motivated to buy a car is most likely to notice car ads. The process of selective attention explains why advertisers go to great lengths to grab the audience's attention through, fear, music, or bold headlines.

b. *Selective Distortion* Selective distortion is the tendency to interpret information in a way that fit our preconceptions. Consumers often distort information to be consistent with prior brand and product beliefs. Thus, the target audience will hear what fits into their belief systems. As a result, receivers often add things to the message that are not there and do not notice other things that are there. The advertiser's task is to strive for simplicity, clarity, interest and repetition to get the main points across.

c. *Selective Retention* - People retain in long term memory only a small fraction of the messages that reach them. If the receiver's initial attitude towards the brand is positive and he rehearses support arguments (that is, tells himself things such as the product is in fashion or that it is reasonably priced or that it delivers good value, etc.), the message is likely to be accepted and have high recall. If the initial attitude towards the brand is negative and the person rehearses counter arguments (that is, tells himself that the product is highly overpriced or that the competing products offer more value to customers or that the brand is not doing well in the market, etc.), the message is likely to be rejected but to stay in long-term memory. Thus, the advertiser's task is two-fold here. He not only has to create an initial favourable attitude towards the brand but also through his ads communicate to the audience strong points about the brands so that the customers can rehearse the same and the brand is positively placed in the long-term memory of the customers. However, an advertiser must also remember the initial brand response could be created not just by advertising but by other things also. Thus, if a customer has had a previous bad experience with a brand or his friends and acquaintances are dissatisfied with the brand, the customer may develop an initial unfavourable attitude towards the brand.

Thus, the process of communication should start with keeping a specific audience in mind. The target audience critically influences the communicator's decisions regarding what has to be said, how, when and where it has to be said, as well as who has to say it. The prime objective of the sender is to get the message across to the receiver. The objective may not be achieved due to inattention, distortion, or even selective retention. The communicator must take into consideration characteristics of the audience and use these traits to guide message across.

MARKETING COMMUNICATION (MARCOM)

Marketing communications are the means by which firms attempt to inform, persuade and remind consumers, directly or indirectly, about the products and brands that they sell. Marketing communications perform many functions for the consumers. Consumers can be told or shown how and why a product is used, by what kind of person, and where and when. Consumers can learn about who makes the product and what the company and brand stand for; and consumers can be given an incentive or reward for trial or usage. The marketing communications mix consists of the following elements - advertising, sales promotion, personal selling, public relations and publicity, events, and direct marketing. Advertising is a very important element of the marketing communications mix.

ADVERTISING AS A COMMUNICATION TOOL

Advertising essentially is a tool of communication for marketing. In communication process, the sender sends a message through some medium so that it reaches the receiver. The transmission of message from a sender to a receiver is the backbone of any communication process. The end result of the communication process is the understanding of the message. In communication, we are trying to share information, ideas or an opinion. The message is sent through certain channels or media. The response to the message is known by receiving the feedback from the receiver.

When we are talking about advertising communication it is basically marketing communication. The sender is the advertiser. The message is the printed advertisement or brochure of a TV commercial or a radio spot. The media used are newspapers, magazines, TV and outdoors. The receivers are the target audience of the product. The favourable response to a product is the feedback. The sales reports also form the feedback.

Thus, the following elements are involved in advertising communication:

Advertiser: An advertiser could be an individual or an organisation, which wants to communicate with a target audience. The communication is about the products and services offered by the advertiser.

Advertisement: An advertisement message is meant for information. It goes beyond it, and tries to make people favourably inclined towards the product/service/idea. It may ask people to act on the message. To do so, an advertisement uses the persuasive power of appeals -both rational and emotional and sometimes, moral.

Media: The channels of communication are the media. They convey the ad message to the target audience. The most commonly used media are newspapers, magazines, radio, TV and outdoors. Each medium has its own strengths and weaknesses.

Target Audience: The readers of print media, or the listeners of radio or the viewers of TV make the audience. The product may be for mass consumption or for a targeted audience of the total consumers. Audience could be of users, non-users and potential users.

RESPONSE HIERARCHY MODELS

Much has been written and researched about how advertising works and the effects it produces. Exposure to an advertisement can result in a number of responses/effects on the target customers. It may result in creating awareness and a feeling of familiarity about the brand. Exposure to an ad may also lead to relevant information about the product's attributes, and, more importantly, the resulting benefits to the customers. An exposure can often generate feelings - positive or negative - which consumers begin to associate with the brand. Ad exposure can also create an impression that the brand is in fashion and favoured by some celebrities. These effects can lead to liking, preference, conviction, and finally, purchase of the brand. Understanding the response process that the consumers may go through in moving towards a desired behaviour as a result of exposure to advertising, is perhaps the most important aspect in developing an effective advertising programme.

Response hierarchy models of marketing communications concentrate on consumer's specific responses to communications. A number of models have been developed to explain how consumers may pass through various stages in eliciting some behaviour. The stages are as follows:

- *Cognitive:* This stage basically involves communication that deals with cognition or knowledge. It deals with creating knowledge, perception, ideas and awareness in the minds of people. Before people can be moved to action in terms of purchase, they must be informed about the same.
- *Affective:* This stage deals with the emotions or the affections. Thus, this is the stage that determines whether a person develops positive perception

about the product or simply dislikes it. At this stage, interest may further strengthen to take the shape of strong desires or preference.

- *Conative:* This mainly deals with the final buyer behaviour. In this case, the person on the basis of his preference or dislike for the product would either purchase it or reject the product.

We will discuss here some models (primarily, AIDA and Lavidge and Steiner's Hierarchy of Effects Model) to understand what response advertising can evoke from target customers. All of these models assume that the buyer passes through a cognitive (learn), affective (feel), and conative/behavioural (do) stage, in that order.

- In these models we assume that the buyer has a high involvement with the product category and passes through a "learn-feel-do" sequence. Thus, these models are also known as **High-Involvement Learning Models.**
- These models describe the stages individuals go through when making a purchase, or consumption decision.
- Advertising cannot induce immediate behavioural response; rather a series of mental effects must occur with the fulfilment at each stage before progress to the next stage is possible.
- Promotional activities are designed to move the potential buyer through the stages.
- The models provide the means of analysing promotional activities.

AIDA

The AIDA Model was presented by Elmo Lewis to explain how personal selling works. It is one of a number of models that analyse the customers' journey from ignorance of a product/service to its purchase. AIDA is an acronym for attention, interest, desire, action. The stages- Attention, Interest, Desire, and Action, form a linear hierarchy. It demonstrates that consumers must be aware of a product's existence, be interested enough to pay attention to the product's features/ benefits, and have a desire to benefit from the product's offerings. Action, the fourth stage, would come as a natural result of movement through the first three stages.

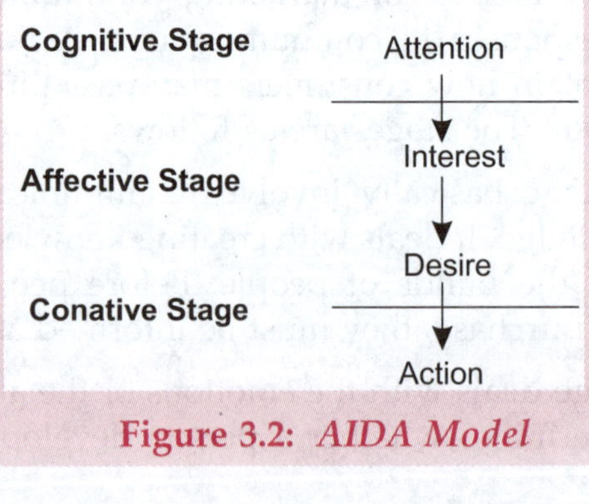

Cognitive Stage — Attention
↓
Affective Stage — Interest
↓
Desire
↓
Conative Stage — Action

Figure 3.2: *AIDA Model*

AIDA is a sequential model showing steps that marketing communications should lead potential buyers through. Promotion seeks to -Attract attention, Create interest, Develop desire, and Prompt action. The first stage is cognitive - it involves thinking, the next two stages are affective - they are about feelings, the last stage is conative - it is about action. Figure 3.2 shows different stages of AIDA model.

Specific characteristics of these four stages are discussed below.

1. *Attention*

- Grab the attention of the audience.
- Inform potential buyers about the product.
- Establish customer awareness about the product.
- At this stage, advertising is the key ingredient in the promotional mix.
- The promotional objective at this stage is to get the product seen and talked about.

2. *Interest*

- Create and stimulate buyer interest.
- This is achieved by creating an understanding of the benefits of the product in relation to the needs of the customer.
- At this stage, the promotional message focuses on how the product meets these needs.
- Move the potential buyer from passive awareness to a more active consideration of the product's merits.

3. *Desire*

- Create desire.
- Induce a favourable attitude to the product especially in relation to competing products.
- Arouse a desire for the product above any desire for competitors' products.

4. *Action*

- To prompt customer action.
- The action sought is for the customer to purchase the product.
- Induce a purchase by stressing the immediate desirability of the product.
- Personal selling and sales promotion play a major role at this stage.

Box 3.1: AIDA and the Promotional Mix

- Grab attention by means of publicity and advertising
- Excite interest by advertising
- Develop interest by sales promotion and selling
- Prompt action by selling and point of sale displays
- Customers will not buy unless marketers first grab their attention, gain interest and make the product desirable

Box 3.2: AIDA and Promotional Tasks

A- Establish customer awareness. Inform customers about the product.
I- Create buyer interest. Stimulate interest in the product.
D- Create desire. Induce a favourable attitude especially in relation to competing products.
A- Sell the product. Induce purchase by stressing the immediate desirability of the product.

LAVIDGE AND STEINER'S HIERARCHY OF EFFECTS MODEL

In this model, consumers pass through six stages. However, the stages are not the same in length of time and can occur simultaneously. For an innovative and expensive product, the process might take months; for impulse purchases, the stages can be completed in minutes. The effectiveness of promotion should be measured in terms of progress through the stages.

Among advertising theories, the hierarchy-of-effects model is predominant. It shows clear steps of how advertising works. Hierarchy-of-effects Model can be explained with the help of a pyramid. First the lower level objectives such as awareness, knowledge or comprehension are accomplished. Subsequent objectives may focus on moving prospects to higher levels in the pyramid to elicit desired behavioural responses such as associating feelings with the brand, trial, or regular use etc. It is easier to accomplish ad objectives located at the base of the pyramid than the ones towards the top. The percentage of prospective customers will decline as they move up the pyramid towards more action oriented objectives, such as regular brand use.

Stages in Lavidge and Steiner's Hierarchy of Effects Model

1. Awareness - Potential customers become aware of the existence of the product
2. Knowledge - Information about the features and benefits of the product
3. Liking - The development of a favourable attitude towards the product
4. Preference - The product is now the preferred choice of the customer
5. Conviction - The customer is now convinced that his preferred choice is right
6. Purchase - Preference and conviction translated into action

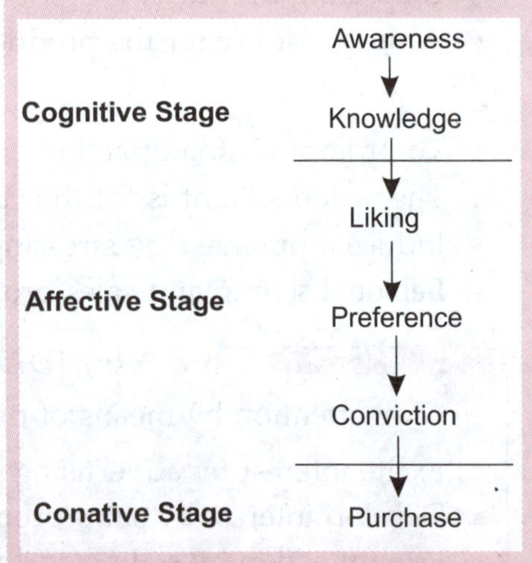

Figure 3.3: ***Hierarchy-of-Effects Model***

The first two stages are cognitive - they involve thinking, the next three stages are affective - they are about feelings, the last stage is conative - it is about action. Figure 3.3 shows various stages of Hierarchy-of-Effects Model.

Lavidge and Steiner believed that advertising has long term effects rather than immediate effects. But to move people to the action stage, there has to be shorter term action to build conviction. An explanation of the various stages of the model is given below.

1. *Awareness:* If most of the target audience is unaware of the object, the communicator's task is to build awareness, perhaps just focussing on name recognition, with simple messages repeating the product name. Consumers must become aware of the brand. This isn't as simple as it seems. Capturing someone's attention doesn't mean they will notice the brand name. Thus, the brand name needs to be made focal to get consumers to become aware. Magazines are full of ads that will capture your attention, but you'll have trouble easily seeing the brand name.

2. *Knowledge:* The target audience might have product awareness but not know much more; hence this stage involves creating brand knowledge. This is where comprehension of the brand name and what it stands for become important. What are the brand's specific appeals, its benefits? In what way is it different than competitor's brands? Who is the target market? These are the types of questions that must be answered if consumers are to achieve the step of brand knowledge.

3. *Liking:* If target members know the product, how do they feel about it? If the audience looks unfavourably towards the product, the communicator has to find out why. If the unfavourable view is based on real problems, a communication campaigns alone cannot do the job. For product problem it is necessary to first fix the problem and only then one can communicate about its renewed quality.

4. *Preference:* The target audience might like the product but not prefer it to others. In this case, the communicator must try to build consumer preference by promoting quality, value, performance and other features. The communicator can check the campaign's success by measuring audience preference before and after the campaign.

5. *Conviction:* A target audience might prefer a particular product but not develop a conviction about buying it. The communicator's job is to build conviction among the target audience.

6. *Purchase:* Finally, some members of the target audience might have conviction but not quite get around to making the purchase. They may wait for more information or plan to act later. The communicator wants these consumers to take the final step, perhaps by offering the product at a low price, offering a premium, or letting consumers tried out. This is where consumers make a move to actually search out information or purchase.

Thus advertising is thought to work and follow a certain sequence whereby the prospect is moved through a series of stages in succession from unawareness to the purchase of the product.

SOME OTHER MODELS

In addition to AIDA and Lavidge and Steiner's Hierarchy of Effects Models, we also have the following two models where the buyer has a high involvement with the product category and passes through a "learn-feel-do" sequence.

Innovation-Adoption Model : According to Everett M Rogers, this model evolved from work on diffusion of innovations. The model depicts various sequential steps and stages that the consumer moves through in adopting a new product or service. Marketers face the challenge of creating awareness and interest in the product or service among target audience and evaluate it favourably. The best way to persuade consumers to evaluate a brand is by inducing product trial or sometimes product-in-use demonstration. Figure 3.4 shows various stages in Innovation-Adoption Model.

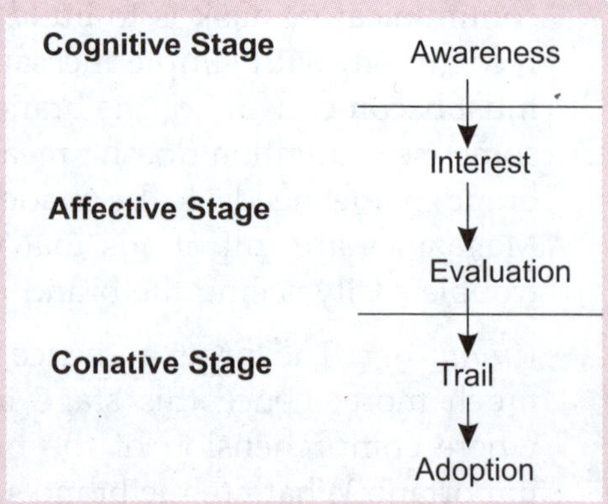

Figure 3.4: Innovation-Adoption Model

Information Processing Model : William McGuire developed this model which assumes that advertising audience are information processors and problem solvers. The first three stages in the model - presentation, attention and comprehension - are similar to awareness and knowledge, and yielding means the same as liking. Up to this point there is similarity with Lavidge and Steiner's Hierarchy of Effects model. The next stage, retention, is unique to this model and is not present in any other model. Retention refers to the ability of the consumer to accept and store in

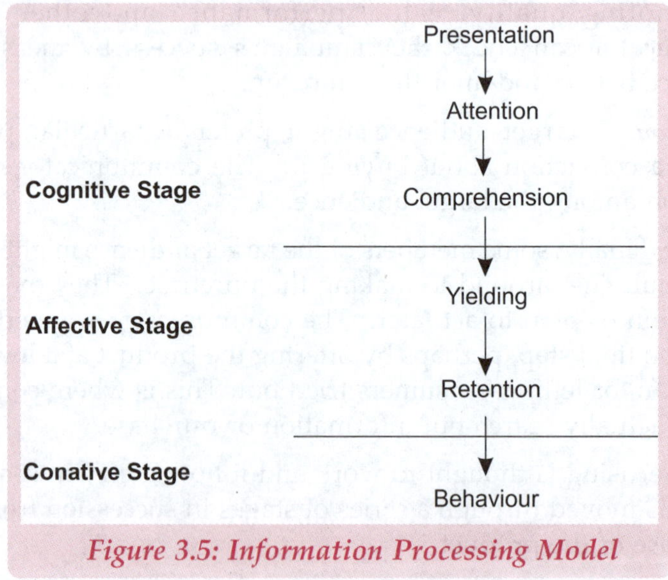

Figure 3.5: Information Processing Model

memory the relevant information about the product or service. Retention of information is important because most advertising is designed to motivate and precipitate action not just immediately and the retained information is used at a later time to make purchase decision. Figure 3.5 shows various stages in Information Processing Model.

HIGH AND LOW INVOLVEMENT LEARNING MODELS

All the four models discussed above indicate that the starting stage is cognitive, leading to affective stage and finally to conative or behavioural stage. This progression shows the following sequence:

Learn ⟶ Feel ⟶ Do

(Cognitive) (Affective) (Conative)

These Hierarchy of Effects Models are sometimes referred to as **standard learning models or high-involvement learning models.** The consumer is considered an active participant and gathers information through active learning. This type of learning is usually more relevant when the consumer is highly involved in the purchase situation and perceives much differentiation among competing brands. Advertising for these types of products or services usually is detailed and attempts to furnish great deal of meaningful information to the audience. Thus, this "learn-feel-do" sequence is appropriate when the audience has a high-involvement with a product category perceived to have high differentiation, as in purchasing an automobile or a house.

Research has shown that this high involvement sequence may not hold true in case of different product categories. Some convenience products that are consumed daily and purchased routinely do not require high involvement of consumers. Thus, some researchers have proposed a low-involvement learning model.

Low-Involvement Learning Model: Michael L Ray and colleagues at Stanford University have conducted much work on low-involvement learning. They say that when the products concerned are of low-involvement category (low risk, inexpensive, or of low interest) for the consumer, and ads are shown on television, advertising does not lead to an information based change in consumers' attitude to induce product trial. Instead, the ads are successful in inducing trial because of top-of-mind recall or awareness. The low-involvement sequence of advertising effect is different from Lavidge and Steiner's Standard learning model.

Learn ⟶ Do ⟶ Feel

(Cognitive) (Conative) (Affective)

Instead of active learning, the customer engages in passive learning and random information-catching under low involvement situations. Thus, the sequence "learn-do-feel" is relevant when the audience has low involvement and perceives little differentiation within the product category, for instance, when purchasing salt. The consumer learns about a particular brand of salt available in the market, buys it without much of information processing and on the basis of his experience with the brand bought, may attach a feeling of liking or disliking towards the brand.

THE FCB MODEL OF ADVERTISING STRATEGY

The FCB model of advertising strategy was developed in 1980 by Richard Vaughn, who researched how advertising works, and how best to establish communications objectives. The model introduced the Foote, Cone, Belding (FCB) strategy matrix, suggesting that advertising works differently depending on the product involved. Vaughn's work allows advertisers to select the communication method based on the type of product they are advertising, and the attitudes that consumers are likely to have towards the product. Vaughn suggested:

Not all advertising works in the same way. Sometimes communication of key information and salient emotion will be needed to get a sale; at other times, consumers will need one, but not both; and often, a purchase may occur with little or no information and emotion. The purpose of strategy planning is to identify the information, emotion or action leverage for a particular product, build the appropriate advertising model and then execute it. These differences are summarized in the popular FCB Matrix reproduced in Figure 3.6.

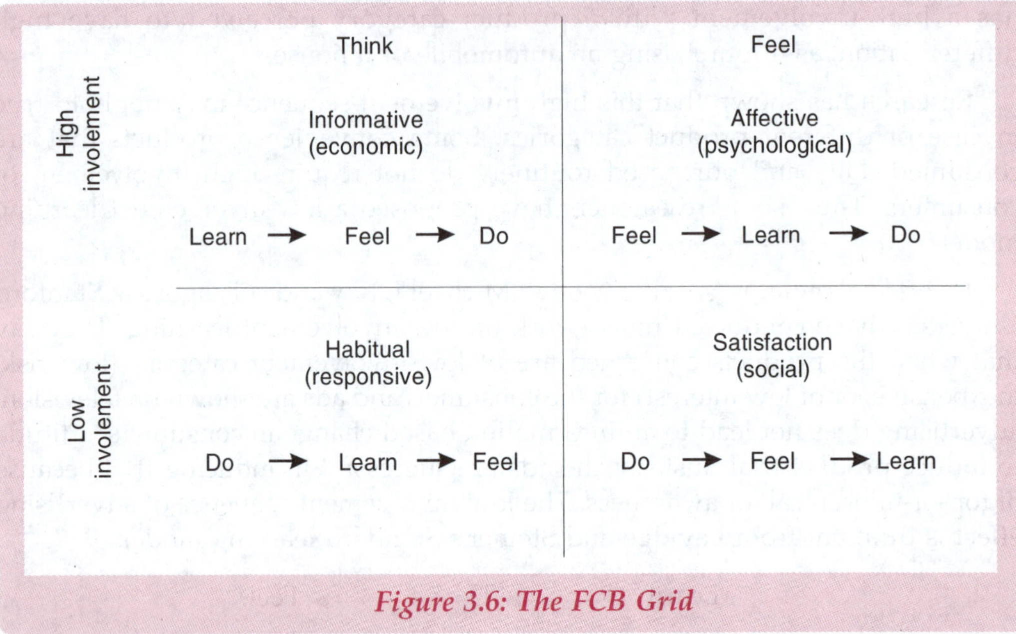

Figure 3.6: The FCB Grid

The matrix divides advertising strategy into two dimensions based on thinking versus feeling, and low involvement versus high involvement. Vaughn pointed out "this suggests there are purchase decisions where thinking is most involved and others where feeling dominated; there are situations that require more involvement and those that require less."

The model is powerful because it accommodates different versions of the learn-feel-do sequence and suggests different advertising strategies for each of the four quadrants.

This grid delineates four primary advertising strategies - "informative", "affective", "habitual" and "satisfaction" - with their most appropriate traditional and variant hierarchy-of-effects models. Vaughn identified 250 product categories for recently purchased products on the basis of involvement and the think-feel dimensionality. The grid suggests a different advertising strategy based on the level of thinking/ feeling and involvement associated with each of the four quadrants. Vaughn is careful to point out that the dashed line separating the quadrants should not be interpreted as a black and white distinction between thinking and feeling or high involvement and low involvement. Rather, it simply represents a guideline. The strategy for each quadrant is discussed separately below.

Quadrant 1 - High involvement / Thinking (Informative)

This quadrant implies that a large amount of information is necessary because of the importance of the product. Many major purchases qualify, (cars, homes, electronic equipment), and these are likely to include almost any product which needs to convey what it is, its function, price and availability. The basic strategy model is to adopt the Learn - Feel - Do sequence where information is designed to build attitudinal acceptance and subsequent purchase. Vaughn suggested, "consumers may be thought of as thinkers. Creatively, specific information and demonstration are possibilities. Long copy format and reflective, involving media may be necessary to get through with key points of consumer interest".

Quadrant 2 - High involvement / Feeling (Affective)

This product decision has high involvement but requires less specific information, therefore and attitude or feeling towards the product is more important. This is a psychological model, because the importance of the product is connected to the consumers' self esteem. Perfume, expensive watches, and sports cars are product examples that might fall into this quadrant. The advertising strategy requires emotional involvement on the part of the consumers so that they become connected with the product being advertised and subsequently become "feelers". Therefore, the proposed model is Feel - Learn - Do. Vaughn suggested "Creatively, executional impact is a possible goal, while media considerations suggest dramatic print exposure or "image" broadcast specials."

Quadrant 3 - Low involvement / Thinking (Doer)

Products in this category (including many common household items such as razors, insect repellents, and household cleaners) involve little thought and a tendency to form buying habits for convenience. The hierarchy model is a Do - Learn - Feel pattern suggesting that simply inducing trial (through coupons or samples) can often generate subsequent purchases more efficiently than "undifferenting copy points", leading in turn to increased brand loyalty. According to Vaughn, the most effective creative strategy is to stimulate a reminder for the product.

Quadrant 4 - Low involvement / Feeling (Self-satisfaction)

This product decision is emotional but requires little involvement, and is reserved for those products that satisfy personal taste (for example, cigarettes, candy, beer or snack food). This is a Do - Feel - Learn model where imagery and quick satisfaction are involved, and the consumer is considered a reactor whose interest will be hard to hold. Vaughn argued that the creative objective is to get attention with some sort of consistency, and suitable methods may include billboards, point-of-sale or newspaper advertising.

CONCLUDING NOTE

The communication process is the perfect guide towards achieving effective communication. When followed properly, the process can usually assure that the sender's message will be understood by the receiver. Although the communication process seems simple, in essence, it is not. Certain barriers present themselves throughout the process. Those barriers are factors that have a negative impact on the communication process. The advertiser's task is to overcome such barriers and get his message across to the target customers.

The Response Hierarchy Models also have implications for the advertisers. These models describe the stages individuals go through when making a purchase, or consumption decisions. Any stage in the response hierarchy may serve to establish advertising objectives and the effects can be measured. The target audience may be at any stage in the hierarchy and the advertiser's tasks may be different in each stage. For instance, if advertising research reveals that a significant number of target customers have low level of awareness about the brand and its benefits then the advertising task is to increase awareness of the brand, its attributes and the resulting benefits. In a situation where the target audience has product awareness but does not know much about the product, product knowledge must be imparted through communications. In cases where target audience has product knowledge but is not fully convinced to buy the product, consumer conviction should be built by promoting quality, value, performances and other features. Still if some consumers do not make a purchase or plan to act later, they must be led to take the final step perhaps by offering the product at a lower price, offering a premium, or coming up with an exciting sales promotion scheme.

Thus, the models reveal that advertising cannot induce immediate behavioural response; rather a series of mental effects must occur with the fulfilment at each stage before progress to the next stage is possible. The advertiser's task is to move the target customer to that next stage.

The FCB model of advertising strategy developed by Richard Vaughn suggests that advertising works differently depending on the product involved. The model guides advertisers to select the communication method based on the type of product they are advertising, and the attitudes that consumers are likely to have towards the product. The purpose of planning a communication strategy is to identify the information, emotion or action leverage for a particular product, build the appropriate advertising model and then execute it. Advertisements based on such a communication strategy can then help the advertisers in achieving advertising objectives.

QUESTIONS FOR DISCUSSION

1. What do you mean by communication? What are the various elements in the communication process?
2. Describe the various stages defined in the AIDA model to understand a consumer's journey from ignorance of a product to its purchase.
3. What are the various stages that a consumer goes through as per the Lavidge and Steiner's Hierarchy of Effects Model?
4. Write short notes on:

   (a) Innovation-Adoption Model

   (b) Information Processing Model
5. Discuss the FCB Model of Advertising Strategy.
6. "The target customer may not receive the intended message because of the perceptual processes of selective attention, selective distortion, and selective retention." Explain.

CHAPTER 4

TYPES OF ADVERTISING

CONTENTS

- Classification of Advertising on the basis of
  - Geographical Spread
  - Target Audience
  - What is being Advertised
  - Advertising Objectives
- Some Other Types of Advertising
- Case Study: Idea Cellular "What an Idea, Sir Ji"

Advertising is the promotion of a company's products and services carried out to achieve certain objectives. Advertising has become an essential element of the corporate world and hence the companies allot a considerable amount of revenues as their advertising budget. There are several reasons for advertising some of which are: increasing the sales of the product/ service, creating and maintaining a brand identity or brand image, communicating a change in the existing product line, introduction of a new product or service, increasing the buzz-value of the brand or the company etc. Thus, there are several reasons for advertising and similarly there exist various media which can be effectively used for advertising. Without effective and targeted advertising, a business cannot succeed. There are many types of advertising a business can utilize in effort to increase its sales and they can be classified into different categories.

CLASSIFICATION OF ADVERTISING

Advertising may be classified according to:

1. Geographical Spread (National/Local/Global)
2. Target Audience (Consumer/Trade/Industry)
3. What is being Advertised (Product/Service/Idea/Organisation/Place)

4. The Objective Sought (Stimulation of Primary/Secondary Demand, Direct/Indirect Action, Cooperative Advertising, Public Service Advertising)
5. Others

ACCORDING TO GEOGRAPHICAL SPREAD

1. *National Advertising:* National advertising refers to the fact that a company has a national target market and does not imply that the advertisement per se is nationwide. The company, thus, selects media with a countrywide base. Generally large, established firms belong to this category. Products like Lux soap, Sunsilk Shampoo, Taj Mahal Tea, Colgate Toothpaste etc. are nationally advertised.
2. *Local Advertising:* Small firms may like to restrict their business to State or regional level. Some firms first localize their marketing efforts and once success has been achieved, they spread out to wider horizons. A classic example is Nirma washing powder, which initially was sold only in Gujarat and subsequently entered the other markets. Retail stores also undertake local advertising. The area to be covered would generally be a city or a town and media would be selected which principally relates to that area. For example, a store of Big Bazaar in Gurgaon (Haryana) may give its ad in a newspaper which has its circulation in Delhi and NCR. Sometimes large firms may also go in for local advertising, e.g., when they undertake pre-testing of a product especially consumer products in selected areas before embarking promotional campaign on a national level.
3. *Global Advertising:* Multinational firms treat the world as their market. Firms such as IBM, Sony, Pepsi, Coke, etc. advertise globally, i.e. in different media categories across the world. The Coca-Cola Company rolled out its global integrated marketing campaign, "Open Happiness" in late January 2009, in the United States of America. Following this, it decided to roll out the campaign in India. The sub-continent was among the first few strategic markets for the campaign. 2009 saw Coca-Cola's long-time brand endorser, Aamir Khan 'Opening' happiness for the brand in India. Aamir Khan, who has been endorsing Coke for over a decade, was seen as a messenger of optimism in the campaign, where a bottle of Coke brought people together in their joy. Taking the message further, in 2010, Bollywood actor, Imran Khan, joined his uncle, Aamir Khan as an endorser for Coca-Cola.

ACCORDING TO TARGET AUDIENCE

1. *Consumer Advertising:* Consumer advertising is one which is directed to end consumers. This type of advertising takes place for those products which are used by the consumers. Advertisements of soaps, detergents, tea, coffee, soft

drinks, washing machines, televisions, refrigerators, cosmetics are all examples of consumer advertising. Such type of advertising generally appears in mass media like television, radio, magazines and newspapers.

2. *Trade Advertising:* This refers to consumer-product advertising designed to stimulate wholesalers or retailers to purchase products for resale to their customers. An example of trade advertising would be a Coca-Cola advertisement placed in a trade magazine such as 'Franchising', in order to promote Coca-Cola to food store managers. The primary objective of trade advertising is to promote greater distribution of the advertised product.

   An important form of trade advertising is retail advertising.

   Retail Advertising: Retail advertising may be defined as all advertising by the stores that sell goods directly to the consuming public. It includes, also advertising by establishments that sell services to the public, such as beauty shops, petrol pumps and banks.

   Retail advertising has a number of objectives. The primary one is to build store traffic, and advertising does that by emphasizing a reduced price on a popular item or by promoting the store image by focussing on unusual or varied merchandise, friendly and knowledgeable clerks, or prestige brands. Other objectives are:

   - Build store brand awareness
   - Sell a variety of products and brands by creating consumer understanding of items or services offered
   - Deliver sales promotion messages
   - Create and communicate a store image or personality
   - Create consumer desire to shop at this particular store

   The case study of 'Big Bazaar' (discussed at the end of chapter 2 of the book) is a classic example of Retail Advertising in India.

3. *Industrial Advertising:* Industrial advertising is directed at business firms and other organisations which purchase and use industrial products such as raw material, machinery, tools and equipment, etc. For instance, an advertisement for electric motors may be directed at manufacturers of washing machines, an advertisement for certain types of tools may be directed at manufacturers of tractors, etc. As compared to consumers, industrial buyers are few in number. Trade and technical journals are the main media used in industrial advertising.

WHAT IS BEING ADVERTISED ?

The modern definition of 'product' in marketing is "anything that can be marketed is a product". In that sense, it is not only a tangible product which can be advertised, but also services, ideas, organisations and places are advertised.

On the basis of what is being advertised, advertising may be classified as follows:

1. ***Product Advertising:*** Such advertising is done to promote the sale of a tangible product. For example, Colgate toothpaste, Lux soap, Ariel detergent powder, Cadbury Diary Milk Chocolate, Nokia Mobile Phones, Ruffles Lays, Harvest Gold Bread, Maruti A-star car, LG Refrigerators, etc. Product advertising may be direct action or indirect action advertising (explained later).

2. ***Service Advertising:*** This type of advertising attempts to promote the sale of services which are intangible, inseparable and perishable. Advertisements by banks, insurance companies, hotels, airlines, health care services, mobile phone service providers etc. fall in this category.

3. ***Idea Advertising:*** Advertising, being a powerful mass communication tool, is used not only to present and promote goods and services but also to further the goals of public interest and social causes. This is achieved through what is known as idea advertising. Advertisements like quit smoking, family planning, save the girl child, HIV awareness programme, Pulse Polio Immunization, save water, save electricity, etc. are all examples of idea advertising.

4. ***Institutional Advertising:*** Institutional Advertising is done by business firms and institutions to build their image. Such advertising does not attempt to sell anything directly. The objective is to improve the goodwill or the organisation as a whole, not focusing on any one product or service of the organisation. Institutional advertising is also known as corporate advertising. An example of institutional advertising is Superstar Amitabh Bachchan promoting Reliance, Anil Dhirubhai Ambani Group.

5. ***Place Advertising:*** Advertising of places is done to promote tourism to such places. Advertisements like Go Goa, Dubai Shopping Festival, Kerala-God's Own Country etc. are all examples of place advertising.

WHAT ARE THE OBJECTIVES ?

1. ***Primary Demand Advertising:*** Primary demand advertising is that type which is designed to stimulate the demand for a generic category of a product, rather that emphasizing on a particular brand of a product. For example, the *"piyo glassful doodh"* advertisement by Mother Diary emphasizes that it is good to drink milk, without emphasizing on the brand Mother Diary.

   Primary demand advertising is used in two situations. The first is when the product is in the introductory stages of its life cycle. This is called pioneering advertising. Under this, an individual firm may be run an ad about its new product, explaining the product's benefits, not emphasizing the brand name. The objective of pioneering advertising is to inform, and not to persuade the market.

   The second use of primary demand advertising is by trade associations to stimulate the demand for their industry's product which is in competition with other product categories. Thus, the national Egg Co-ordination Committee urges us to eat eggs when it says, *"Sunday ho ya Monday, Roz Khao Ande"*, and the *"piyo glassful doodh"* by Mother Diary urges us to drink milk. Here, the *"piyo glassful doodh"* ad, tries to meet competition that it faces from other product categories like soft drinks, juices, etc.

2. ***Secondary Demand Advertising:*** Secondary demand advertising is intended to stimulate demand for individual brands such as Amul Milk, Sony Television, etc. Selective demand advertising is essentially ***competitive advertising.*** This type of advertising is used when a product has gone beyond the introductory stage of its life cycle. The product is then sufficiently well-known, and several individual brands are competing for a market share. The

objective of competitive advertising is to persuade the potential customers, and it emphasizes the particular benefits of the brand being advertised.

Comparative advertising is also one type of selective demand advertising that has been used for a wide variety of products. In comparative advertising, the advertiser directly or indirectly points out towards a rival brand and states that the advertised brand is better than the other. (It should be remembered that in India law does not permit taking the name of the rival brand directly for the purpose of comparative advertising.)

3. *Direct Action Advertising:* With direct action advertising, sellers seek a quick response to their advertisements. For instance, an advertisement in the newspaper with a coupon, which when redeemed will give the person a free sample of the product, may urge the reader to send immediately for a free sample. Harvest Gold Bread had used this technique where they inserted a coupon in the newspaper on the redemption of which the buyer would get a pack of Harvest Gold Buns free with the bread. This helped Harvest Gold to secure a quick response to the brand in the initial period of launch of the bread.

4. *Indirect Action Advertising:* Indirect action advertising is designed to stimulate demand over a longer period of time. Such advertising is intended to inform customers that the product exists and to point out its benefits. The idea is that when customers are ready to buy the product, they will look favourably upon the seller's brand. Thus, an advertisement for a brand of car may not immediately result in sale but can place the car favourably in the minds of prospective customers. When these people are ready to buy a car, three months later, or six months later or one year later, it might lead to sale.

5. *Cooperative Advertising:* Cooperative advertising involves the sharing of the cost of advertising by two or more sponsors. Cooperative advertising may be vertical or horizontal.

   Vertical Cooperative Advertising involves firms on different levels of distribution - such as manufacturers and retailers. The manufacturer and the retailer share the retailer's cost of advertising the manufacturer's product. Another type of vertical cooperative advertising involves an advertising allowance - also called a promotional allowance. This allowance is an off-invoice or cash discount offered by a manufacturer to a retailer to encourage the retailer to advertise or prominently display the product. The arrangement provides added incentive for the retailer to advertise the manufacturer's product.

   Horizontal Cooperative Advertising involves a group of firms on the same level of distribution - such as a group of retailers. All stores in a shopping mall, for instance, may run a joint ad weekly in the newspaper.

6. *Public Service Advertising:* Public Service Advertising refers to those advertising efforts which are done as a part of social responsibility by such entities as advertising agencies, Government, NGO's as well as other business organisations. The main objective behind Public Service Advertising is to

spread social consciousness among the masses and promote important social issues which generally go unnoticed. Such advertisements may range from being subtle to direct, and practical to ironic. Some of the issues discussed through Public Service Advertising campaigns over the years include Female Feticide, Blood Donation, AIDS Awareness, Use of Condoms, Polio Eradication, Family Planning and National Integration.

Today, Public Service Advertising has become very popular and is considered to be one of the most effective means to create social awareness and bring about a change / shift in the mindsets of people. Recent time has seen a change in the way major companies have started advertising with a social message. Whether it is Idea's "What an idea Sir *ji*", Aircel's "Save our Tigers" campaign (refer Exhibit 4.1) or Tata Tea's "*Jaago Re*", every major giant is trying to discharge its social responsibility by given a social message to consumers. The intention is to make every Indian aware of some inevitable responsibilities, wake up and ACT - be it for their own good or for a common cause.

Exhibit 4.1: Advertisements with Social Messages- "Save our Tigers" Campaign

AIRCEL, one of India's leading GSM mobile service provider initiated the campaign towards a social cause in association with WWF-India to help save our tigers. Aircel's "Save Our Tigers" campaign intended to draw attention towards dwindling numbers of tigers across the planet and to bring forward the seriousness of losing tigers from our planet.

Cricket Player and Aircel's brand ambassador Mahendra Singh Dhoni, footballer Bhaichung Bhutia and South Indian actor Surya were part of this campaign. Apart from TV and print advertising, a website www.saveourtigers.com, was launched, which was instrumental in propagating and disseminating information about saving tigers. It urged people to be informed and create buzz across all forums like blogging, writing on facebook, twitter and writing letters to the editors of newspapers. The campaign also created a platform where people could donate money to NGOs working relentlessly for the cause.

There are a few benefits that public service advertising gives to the brand which cannot be overlooked. Firstly, such campaigns help the brand come across as socially responsible and mature. It helps them prove that they are beyond just selling their products to the consumers. Secondly, the brand creates a lasting impression on the mind of the consumer and is in the consumers mind for all the right reasons which is a definite plus.

OTHERS TYPES OF ADVERTISING

1. *Political Advertising:* Political advertising is created either by political parties or candidates. Mostly we come across such advertising at the time of elections. Election advertising either lists the achievements of the party of candidate or propagates their ideological basis. Sometimes, they are provocative too. Such advertising may become comparative, where the weaknesses of the opposition are highlighted to show their party or candidate in favourable light. An example of political advertising is the "India Shining" campaign during the 2004 elections, which aimed at highlighting the progress India had made during the tenure of Atal Bihari Vajpayee as the Prime Minister.

2. *Financial Advertising:* When public limited companies invite the general public to subscribe to the share capital of the company, it is called financial advertising. In a broader sense, it includes all advertising by financial industry such as banks, car loan companies, insurance companies, non-banking financial companies etc.

   The copy of financial ad gives highlights of the project, details of the issue, crisis rating, management's perception of the risk factors, closing date of the issue, lead manager's name and address, promoter's name and address, name of the company and its address. Apart from these routine things the investing public is motivated to invest by suitable copy matter - a slogan, a promise of returns, profile of the product etc. The media used for financial advertising are mainly the print media, especially the press and to some extent magazines. Mega-issues are promoted even on TV.

3. *Speciality Advertising:* Specialty advertising refers to the special form of advertising on various merchandise such as t-shirts, pens, mugs, diaries, calendars, mouse pads, caps, stickers, mobile phone accessories, car and bike stickers, key rings, sign plaques, bookmarks, bathroom accessories, toys, glassware, luggage tags and many more. With specialty advertising, the advantage is that anything you can think of is a good mode for advertising your company name, its logo, or even its message, can be used.

   For example, if a company wants to give out a t-shirt with your message and logo on it as a special promotional offer to subscribers of a particular scheme, it will obviously want to order t-shirts in bulk. The logic is that the more such ads that it releases in the market, the more the visibility for its product.

QUESTIONS FOR DISCUSSION

1. What are the various ways in which advertising can be classified?
2. Distinguish between primary demand advertising and secondary demand advertising, giving examples of each.
3. Distinguish between direct action advertising and indirect action advertising, giving examples of each.

4. Write a short note on cooperative advertising.
5. What do you mean by public service advertising?
6. Write short notes on:
   (a) Speciality Advertising
   (b) Political Advertising
   (c) Trade Advertising
7. Give examples of how some companies in the recent past have used social messaging in advertising.
8. Identify under what category/categories will the following advertisements fall.
   (a) Pepsi's *Youngistaan* Campaign
   (b) Lux Soap
   (c) Go Goa
   (d) An advertisement of Maruti Alto mentioning its various dealers in Delhi and NCR in the Hindustan Times.

Case Study

Advertisements with Social Messages

IDEA CELLULAR

About Idea Cellular

IDEA Cellular, a leading telecom service provider in India, is an Aditya Birla Group Company. IDEA Cellular is a public listed company, listed on the Bombay Stock Exchange (BSE) and the National Stock Exchange (NSE. Idea is one of the leading mobile services operators in India, in revenue terms. It recorded a subscriber base of over 78 million as on end November 2010. It became a pan-India integrated GSM operator covering the entire telephony landscape of the country, and expanded its NLD and ILD operations in the financial year 2010. During the year, Idea increased its revenue market share by over 1%, despite stiff tariff war in the market.

Brand Initiatives

The aim of IDEA Cellular is to strengthen the brand and to place it as a reliable and trustworthy brand in the minds of the customers. The company not only uses creative advertising campaigns but also works with strategic communication partners on campaigns like sponsorship of the Idea International Indian Film Academy awards and the television programs "Idea Rocks India", "Idea Star Singer" and "Idea Andhra Idol". The company seeks engagement with subscribers on a variety of levels, from major celebrity fashion shows to small local events timed to coincide with new product offerings.

Since August 2003, IDEA Cellular has commissioned a Brand Track Index Study to evaluate the health of its brand. The Brand Track Index Study is a monthly study conducted by TNS, a marketing consultant engaged by IDEA Cellular to evaluate its brand using face-to-face interviews on a random sample of mobile users as well as those intending to purchase mobiles within the next three months. According to the study the brand - 'Idea' is perceived as "reliable/ trustworthy" and one that "offers cheaper and good promotional offers". The company has improved its rating in the Brand Track Index calculated by the study over these years which reflects the growing strength of the brand - 'Idea'.

The main communication medium for the brand is television, where it seeks strategic coverage of the brand 'Idea' in various formats. Billboards and hoardings are used as a secondary medium, customized for specific regional preferences to communicate effectively at the local level. The company also uses other mass communication media such as the press and radio to communicate price plans and other tactical and customer information.

All the key initiatives are subject to a rigorous testing to ensure accountability for all the money spent on advertising and to improve the chances of success.

The present case examines the advertising strategies of IDEA Cellular, particularly, the "What an idea, Sir ji" series of advertisements, which used mobile telephony to solve social issues.

Advertising Objective

To elevate the brand above transactional stories of network, reach and tariffs and instead demonstrate and claim the real power of mobile phone technology.

Idea's Advertising Campaigns (What an Idea, Sir ji" series)

Idea had not hired any celebrity to promote its services till late 2007, in contrast to its competitors. However, when Idea expanded its geographical presence to cover several telecom circles in India, it hired film star Abhishek Bachchan to endorse its brand in October 2007. Idea's focus in its ads also changed from highlighting its tariff plans and network coverage to using mobile telephony to solve social issues.

Idea's initial advertising campaigns were based on the theme 'An Idea can change your life'. In 2007, Idea started its attempt of giving a social message through its advertisements. The first one which became a hit with the audience touched on the caste system prevalent in the society.

Proposing a world without caste

IDEA Cellular took the guts to take the politics of caste and religion and came up with an ad wherein mobile numbers are used as replacements for people's name in a village. In the commercial, Abhishek Bachchan, the *sarpanch* of the village decides that all names should be replaced by numbers to avoid caste conflicts. The concept seems to work in the end, with Junior B's crony praising the boss with "What an idea, sir ji". The ad was well received by the audience, the social message delivered and the audience seemed to agree with the tagline **"What an idea, Sir ji"**.

- **The TVC:** Riots break out between two communities in a village. Villagers approach the sarpanch for a settlement. Something strikes the sarpanch as he gets a call on his Idea phone. He rules, *"koi bhi apne naam se nahin jaana jayega."* People get known by their cell phone numbers instead of their caste. Impressed by the solution, a man praises the sarpanch, "What an idea, Sir *ji* !"

According to Nikhil Rao, Group Creative Director, Lowe (advertising agency), "We've amplified the baseline, 'An Idea can change your life', and tried to focus a little harder on it instead of producing a heavy ad. The mobile firm uses numbers extensively, so we projected the same in a nice manner associating people with their phone numbers. The basic theme was to focus on treating everyone as equals." Junior B's big 'Idea' clicked and the company started with a series of advertisements carrying social messages.

Proposing a world in which no one suffers from the disability to communicate

The TVC opens on a guide of Taj Mahal introducing himself to a couple of foreigner ladies. Giving his card to one of them he tells that he is known for giving "full story at best price". He walks off on not getting any reply from her as she stands still with a puzzled look on her face. He realises that the two of them are deaf-mute when he sees them talking in sign language. He is pleasantly surprised on receiving a message on his Idea phone from her Idea phone saying, "Need a guide". Showing her the Taj Mahal he messages back saying, "Symbol of love". The girl breaks into a smile and replies back with "What an Idea". The guide reads the message and concurring with her announces, "What an Idea!" The ad ends with: *"Ek Idea jo badal de aapki duniya"*.

'Education for all' Campaign

Idea launched another campaign in 2008 with a spotlight on 'education for all'. The campaign highlighted the power of mobile telephony in Indian social context.

Developed by Lowe Lintas (ad agency), the thought-provoking ad campaign had Abhishek Bachchan playing the head of an educational institution. When challenged by the traditional, physically bound classroom methodology that prevents reaching out to many more who are in need of education, he uses mobile telephony to overcome the barrier.

Mr. Sanjeev Aga, Managing Director, IDEA Cellular, said: "Idea is redefining mobile telephony standards through its reach, connectivity and value-added features. We believe strongly that new ideas can change our lives, a thought that has been central to our brand promise from the beginning".

Mr. Abhishek Bachchan, brand ambassador, Idea, said: "Idea is power, and power is all about bringing in desirable social change. The creative messaging of Idea in the past campaigns has effectively addressed the caste issue and the need for communication without frontiers. The new campaign addresses a very relevant social theme - education for all, especially the girl-child. I am pleased to be playing a part in this campaign and contribute to making a difference through the power of the idea".

Mr R Balakrishnan, Chairman & Creative Officer, Lowe Lintas, explained: "Idea campaigns have been specifically tailored to bring mobile telephony closer to the Indian consumers. By integrating a social message into the new campaign, we are not only reinforcing the difference that can be made through the use of modern technology but also the power of a new idea".

Participative Governance

With 'What an Idea sir *ji*' campaign, the challenge was to strike on a big idea that can empower and transform consumers' life - 'An idea can change your life'. This time Lowe Lintas (ad agency) discovered an essential truth that it leveraged.

"Mobile provides a feeling of empowerment to people by enabling them to participate in a national contest/debate/discussion."

Thus, **the idea** which evolved was: If politicians used mobile to know citizens views on decisions that impact their lives, it would be a true victory of democracy.

The idea came to life when the agency hit on the fact that across reality shows today, consumers are playing judge by voting for the participant they like. Imagine using mobile phones for true democracy that empowers people to have a say in decision that impact their lives. It's about bringing to life the proverbial-Democracy for the people and by the people possible through mobile telephony. The agency, in fact, brought the idea to life by putting up issues that impacted people's life and asked them to SMS their views.

Media strategy was to concentrate on TV, since no other medium can build the reach and impact that was necessary to address the challenge. And with half the money that competition spends it was wise to not spread our resources thin. Outdoor advertising like billboards and radio was used as the surround medium to provide support to the campaign.

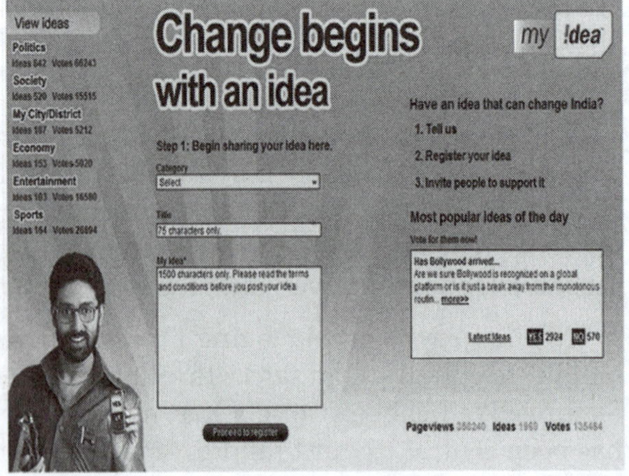

In December 2008, Idea also launched a website called http://bythepeople.in to take forward its TVCs based on democracy.

IDEA Cellular's campaign with brand ambassador Abhishek Bachchan was adjudged the 'Best Celebrity Endorsement of the Year' at the first edition of NDTV Tech Life Awards in May, 2009. The trophy was jointly received by Bachchan and IDEA Cellular chief marketing officer Pradeep Shrivastava.

Abhishek Bachchan said, "I am happy to associate with a brand which is young, humane and is a champion in its category. Idea's communication is simple, effective and appealing to the masses and classes. It has given me an opportunity to connect with my countrymen and offer simple solutions to complex issues prevalent in our society. It is encouraging to see that my role in this communication has inspired people, and is recognized by the industry."

Shrivastava added, "We are delighted to receive the NDTV Tech Life Awards in its very first year of inception. This recognition reflects the success of our campaign with our brand ambassador, which is aimed at demonstrating the power of an idea by looking at mobile telephony and what it can do, in a way that's fresh, imaginative and elevating".

Walk When You Talk

The next campaign in the "What an Idea, Sir *ji*" series was launched to bring forward people across different walks of life, age-groups and societies and get them to walk for fitness. IDEA planned to initiate a countrywide movement on Walking & Talking, and expected that *'Ek Idea pe chal padega India'*.

In the commercial Abhishek Bachchan played a doctor who quoted how people can get fit by simply Walking while Talking and provoked this idea to the general public.

The jingle "walk and talk, walk and talk, walk and talk" and "bol-chal, bol-chal, bol-chal, bol-chal, bol-chal, bol-chal, bol" played its part in making the ad appealing. Advertising gurus agreed that the rhyming words walk, talk, bol and chal added to the quirkiness of the campaign.

Save Paper, Save Tree Campaign

After long and unfruitful debates between the developed and developing nations, to save the Earth, came a very different advertising strategy by Idea Cellular in the year 2010. The campaign extended its concern over the issue at the same time successfully managed to make an impression on the audiences.

In the advertisement, Abhishek Bachchan, the brand ambassador of Idea, plays the role of an agonized 'Tree'. He strikes the idea of using mobile phone to save paper, and therefore, the greenery around him. More and more people switch to their mobile screens rather using paper. The tree regains life and leaves the audience with a simple message - 'Use Mobile, Save Paper'.

In another advertisement, a lady is shown bargaining for vegetables, she takes mobile number of the vendor and instantly transfers the amount to his account via mobile. This new campaign from Idea abided by the essential brand promise of providing a simple, fresh and imaginative solution to a complex problem of the society. The campaign was developed by Idea's creative agency, Lowe.

Speaking about the campaign, Mr. Pradeep Shrivastava, Chief Marketing Officer, Idea Cellular said, "Environment, as a subject, touches all, but gets attention only at strategic forums. The common man gets to contribute little towards the cause, due to lack of direction and ideas. Hence, IDEA Cellular has taken up the responsibility of educating the 500 million mobile phone users in the country. If they start using the mobile phone more judiciously, together we can make a significant contribution of saving paper, and therefore, the green cover necessary for the health of the planet".

As per the press release, "World over, millions of tonnes of trees get cut every day to produce paper, leading to alarming rates of deforestation. The new Idea TVC showcases how the mobile phone can be used as an efficient tool to read daily newspapers, generate e-bills, make payments and transactions, issue e-tickets and boarding passes; thereby saving tonnes of paper every day".

Break the language barrier with an Idea!

Idea's brand ambassador, Abhishek Bachchan, who, in the past, was seen in various avatars such as the *Sarpanch*, Tourist Guide, School Principal, Politician's

Assistant, Doctor, and even a Tree, was now seen in a completely different role. The Sir *ji* character who won millions of hearts with his smart ideas and witty comments gave a new idea to overcome the language barrier, without speaking a language!

The new ad from leading mobile brand unravelled an idea which aimed to help millions of Indians - who move out of their homes for career, education, travel and other prospects in life; or need to communicate with people talking different languages in their own surroundings - to easily adapt to the change in environment and communicate smoothly.

Speaking about the campaign, Ms. Anupama Ahluwalia, Vice President - Marketing, IDEA Cellular, said "Almost every Indian has gone through a situation where one has struggled to communicate with another fellow Indian just because of language. India's diversity lies in its languages, and rather than being intimidated by this barrier, we need to just find a simple solution to overcome it and easily adapt to different environments and people. The new Idea campaign offers a champion idea to address this concern of our society, through the power of mobile telephony. We are confident that the new brand campaign will build a strong connect with the audience and further grow Idea's 70 million subscriber base".

The TVC : The TVC opens with four friends sitting at a tea stall. They are all quiet and look sad. The vendor, a mute man asks his little help the reason for their silence. He tells them that all four of them have got new jobs. He continues by saying that they are all going away, "a Marathi is going to Kolkata, a Bengali to Kerala, Malayali to Haryana and a Haryanavi to Mumbai" and that they are worried, as they don't know the language of the places they are going to. On hearing this, the vendor gets an idea. Then we see all four friends one by one reach their respective destinations. They are shown speaking to each other on mobile phones, taking assistance and getting their way around. With an idea from a mute man their problems are solved and they go back to thank the vendor. The vendor through sign language tells them "to speak you don't need to know a language".

IDEA Cellular also launched a service to take forward the overcoming of the language barrier. Idea announced the 'Language Helpline' which offers conversational support to callers.

Idea's Language Helpline is available across all 22 telecom circles and in 16 Indian languages - Assamese, Bengali, Bhojpuri, English, Gujarati, Hindi, Kannada, Kashmiri, Malayalam, Marathi, Tamil, Telugu, Oriya, Punjabi, Rajasthani and Urdu. Language assistance is offered on the most spoken language(s) in the circle. The helpline number is the Idea customer care number of that circle. Callers seeking assistance on language are directed to the Language Helpline through the IVR menu in a user-friendly manner. A team of agents who understand and speak the local language have been deployed to assist callers.

Announcing the launch of Language Helpline, Anupama Ahluwalia, Senior Vice President - Marketing, IDEA Cellular said, "Our consumer research revealed an interesting insight that people struggle to communicate with other fellow Indians when they move out to other parts of the country where a different language is spoken. Idea's consumer oriented approach led us to the development of a unique and novel concept - 'Language Helpline', to offer real-time assistance on day-to-day conversations to those who need to communicate with local people in their preferred language. The Idea Language Helpline is a demonstration of the power of mobile telephony in bridging language barriers and will take the brand to a new level of consumer connect".

Concluding Note

The testimony of the success of these ads is reflected from the rapid growth of Idea's subscriber base in the country. Today the brand is perceived as one of the biggest national players. Idea's tagline 'What an idea, Sir *ji*' generated tremendous recall value for the brand and amongst the masses. Analysts felt that using Abhishek Bachchan, one of the leading movie actors in India who is extremely popular among youngsters, was one of the reasons for the significant improvement in Idea's brand recall. Analysts also attributed the success of Idea in improving its brand recall and subscriber base to the creative work done by Lowe Lintas (the ad agency). Idea's ads were in contrast to that of its competitors like Bharti, Airtel and Vodafone which focused on their value added services (VAS) and products. However, some experts felt that while Idea's ad campaigns were creative and improved its brand recall, there was nothing in the ads that would attract a customer of its competitors or a new subscriber. They felt that Idea should have promoted the unique selling points of its products and services in the ads rather than only projecting the uses of mobile telephony. Nonetheless, there is no denying the fact that Idea could effectively take up some social issues using mobile telephony through its "What an idea, Sir *ji*" series of advertisements.

CHAPTER 5

ADVERTISING CAMPAIGN

CONTENTS

An advertising campaign consists of all the tasks involved in transforming a theme into a coordinated advertising program to accomplish a specific goal. The campaign must be consistent with the advertiser's corporate and promotional strategies.

DEFINITION

According to Belch and Belch (2004), **an advertising campaign is a series of advertisement messages that share a single idea and theme which make up an integrated marketing communication (IMC)**. Advertising campaigns appear in different media across a specific time frame.

The critical part of making an advertising campaign is determining a campaign theme as it sets the tone for the individual advertisements and other forms of marketing communications that will be used. The campaign theme is the central message that will be communicated in the promotional activities. The campaign themes are usually developed with the intention of being used for a substantial period but many of them are short lived due to factors such as being ineffective or market conditions and/or competition in the marketplace and marketing mix.

Thus, an advertising campaign refers to a coordinated series of linked advertisements (broadcast usually through several media channels) that

1. focus on a common theme and one or few brands or products,
2. are directed at a particular segment of the population (target audience), and
3. are aimed at achieving a specific objective (such as awareness or market share).

Advertising campaigns may last from a few weeks and months to years. Though the campaign is conveyed through different media, it has a single theme and its unified approach. During the campaign period, a series of advertisements with identical message are published through different media in order to have positive impact on the people. The purpose of advertising campaign is to solve marketing problems with the help of extensive advertising. It may be treated as outcome of the overall marketing strategy. Advertising efforts through well planned campaign gives better results than regular advertising on a small scale. This is because buyers are forgetful of erratically appearing advertisements. However, repeated advertisements on the same theme give better response from the consumers.

CHARACTERISTIC FEATURES OF ADVERTISING CAMPAIGNS

- Advertising campaigns may be organized at the national, regional or local levels.
- Sometimes, they may be necessary for facing market competition.
- Direct mail, radio, TV and press are used for the execution of advertising campaigns.
- Advertising campaigns are costly due to increasing media rates.
- Advertising campaign is meant for the whole organisation and not for the advertising department alone. Thus, proper co-ordination between advertising campaign, production programme, sales and finance department is necessary for the successful execution of the advertising campaign.

DEVELOPING AN ADVERTISING CAMPAIGN

Planning advertising campaign is a lengthy process but is essential for successful execution of the campaign. Large companies prefer to hand over the entire work of planning advertising campaign and its execution to advertising agencies. During the planning process, the agency has to do lot of research and finalize various details of the advertising campaign. In general, the following broad steps are involved in the process of planning of advertising campaign:

1. *Review of Company's Marketing Position:* A company which desires to introduce advertising campaign may appoint an advertising agency for planning and execution of advertising campaign. In this case, a joint meeting

of executives of the company and advertising agency is arranged to review the present marketing position of the company, with reference to:

- The product
- The Consumers
- The Market Analysis
- The Competitive situation

In addition, special marketing problems faced by the company are reviewed. This type of study prepares a background for planning advertising campaign which is likely to give promising results. Detailed discussion on such items guides the agency experts in planning the advertising campaign.

2. *Defining target market:* While planning advertising campaign, it is important to work out who are the potential buyers and where are they located. The common criteria used to segment target markets are demographic, geographical, psychographic etc. This has been explained in detail later in this chapter.

3. *Determining the Objectives of Advertising Campaign:* An advertising objective is a specific communication task to be achieved with a specific target audience during a specified period of time. The objectives of advertising campaign need to be decided before finalizing other details. The objectives guide the entire planning process. Specific objectives are dictated by the firm's overall marketing strategy.

   Typical objectives include-

   - Introducing a new product or service
   - Expanding the use of the product
   - Attracting customers of competitors
   - Developing consumers loyalty
   - Making the brand image popular and
   - Motivating target customers to buy regularly and in larger quantities
   - Improve dealer relations
   - Support personal selling

4. *Budget allocation:* Budget allocation is a limiting factor in the advertising campaign. The selection of advertising media, frequency of the advertising message, attractiveness in advertising, etc. depend on the budget provided. The advertiser will provide substantial budget, if he feels that such campaign is likely to give substantial benefits.

5. *Creating the Message:* The message must first get the attention of the target audience. It must then influence the audience in the desired way.

   The message has two elements-

   - Appeal: the reason for accepting the message (rational, emotional, moral)
   - Execution: transforming the appeal into words and visuals

The advertising message must be carefully targeted to impact the target customer audience. A successful advertising message should have the following characteristics:

a. Meaningful - customers should find the message relevant

b. Distinctive - capture the customer's attention

c. Believable - a difficult task, since research suggests most consumers doubt the truth of advertising in general

6. *Media Selection:* It is necessary to decide the media to be used for communicating the message. Advertisers have to decide what type of media, which category, and which specific vehicles are to be used.

- Certain factors influence the media choice

  - The objectives of the ad

  - The audience to be reached

  - The requirements of the message

  - The time and location of the buying decision

- Major media- Newspapers, magazines, radio, television, internet

There are a variety of advertising media to choose from. A campaign may use one or more of the media alternatives. The key factors in choosing the right media include:

a. Reach - what proportion of the target customers will be exposed to the advertising?

b. Frequency - how many times will the target customer be exposed to the advertising message?

c. Media Impact - where, if the target customer sees the message - will it have most impact?

7. *Media Scheduling:* The advertising agency in consultation with the advertiser has to prepare a schedule for each media and insertion of each advertisement in the media. Media schedule will include time and frequency of each advertisement in the selected media.

8. *Execution of Advertising Campaign:* After the planning of advertising campaign, the next step is the execution of advertising plan in actual practice. This includes,

a. Preparation of advertising copy,

b. Arrangements with media for publication,

c. Booking time and space in media etc.

It is also possible to introduce the advertising campaign on a small scale in a test market and thereafter, at the regional or national level.

9. *Monitoring of the Advertising Campaign:* Proper supervision of the execution of advertising campaign is necessary in order to make it successful. It deficiencies are noticed suitable remedial steps should be taken so as to have orderly execution of the whole campaign. By conducting post campaign tests, it is possible to know the effectiveness of advertising campaign.

   The evaluation of an advertising campaign should focus on two key areas:

   a. The Communication Effects - Is the intended message being communicated effectively and to the intended audience?

   b. The Sales Effects - Has the campaign generated the intended sales growth? This second area is much more difficult to measure.

Unit II of the book talks in detail about planning and execution of advertising campaigns.

DEFINING TARGET MARKETS

Defining target markets is a very important step in planning of an advertising campaign.

Most of the companies design products which are suited not for the entire population or the entire market but for a particular group of people or certain segments of the market. For instance, a company manufacturing a pimple control cream tries to sell it basically to the teenage group and not the other age groups. Thus, for this company, its target market is the teenage group which is a segment of the entire market. Therefore, **the target market for a product can be defined as the group of people or market segment(s) to which the marketer wants to sell a product.** It also necessarily should represent that group of people who have the need for the product and the ability to pay for it.

As already said, the target market for a product is the group of people or market segment(s) to which the marketer wants to sell a product. In general, marketers segment their markets using five approaches, which have been discussed below.

- Segmentation on the basis of Demographics
- Segmentation on the basis of Geographics
- Segmentation on the basis of Psychographics
- Segmentation on the basis of Behavioural Characteristics
- Segmentation on the basis of Benefits Sought

The decision regarding which approach or combination of approaches is the best will vary with the market situation and product category.

1. *Demographic segmentation* means dividing the market on the basis of characteristics such as age, gender, ethnicity, religion, income, education, and household size. Thus, a company making lipsticks will divide the market on the basis of gender and then target the female segment.

2. *Geographic segmentation* uses location as a defining variable because consumer needs sometimes vary depending upon where they live - rural, urban, suburb, regional, national, etc. The most important variables are region, nation, state or city. Thus, a product which is meant for a particular region or state may be advertised in a local newspaper and not a national newspaper.
3. *Psychographic segmentation* is primarily based on studies of how people spend their money, their patterns of work and leisure, their interests and opinions, and their views of themselves. Thus, a girl who is young and independent might relate with the girl shown in the Scooty Pep ad.
4. *Behavioural segmentation* divides people into groups based on product category and brand usage. Thus, the marketer of a product category like insurance might feel that there are less people buying insurance policies. Through advertising, he might want to convince people that they need an insurance policy.
5. *Benefit segmentation* is based on consumers' needs or problems. The idea is that people buy products for different benefits they hope to derive from them. For example, car buyers might be grouped based on whether they are motivated by concerns for safety, mileage, durability or dependability, performance, luxury or enhancement of self image. Thus, ads of Maruti Alto car might talk about better mileage while ads of Mercedes Benz might talk about performance and luxury.

Once the target market is identified, the advertiser can mobilise all the forces viz., message strategy, media mix, media vehicles, etc. to reach it. For instance, the marketing and advertising strategies of the company manufacturing the pimple control cream are directed towards the teenage group. Here, the message appeal used may use a subtle fear appeal (advertising appeal) that girls who have pimples are a little conscious and use of the pimple control cream will make them look beautiful and more confident. Also, as far as the advertising media decision is concerned, the advertiser might choose to advertise on television on those television channels that are most viewed by the youngsters (media vehicles), like, MTV, UTV Bindaas, 9XM etc. The advertiser may also choose to advertise on other TV channels during specific programmes, which are popular with youngsters, for instance, during X-Factor on Sony TV. In addition to this, other advertising media can also be chosen, for instance, advertising in magazines like Femina which have basically a huge female readership. Thus, we see that **definition of a target market helps the advertiser in making decisions about the message and media, and of course, this has to be done keeping in mind the advertising budget in hand.** The role of target market in advertising message and media decisions has been discussed below.

Role of Target Market in Advertising Message Decisions

The target market for a product influences the following message decisions of the advertiser.

- *Advertising Appeal:* The target market for a product influences the advertising appeal used by the advertiser in the advertisements. For instance, in an advertisement for men deodorant, where the target market is males, fantasy may be used as the advertising appeal where the ad may show that a man who uses that brand of deodorant is being chased by beautiful females. To take another example, for a product like a baby oil or a baby shampoo where the target market comprises of all mothers of infants, the advertiser may use emotional appeal saying won't you give your baby the best?

- *Advertising Copy:* Advertising copy refers to the text of a print, radio, or television advertising message that aims at catching and holding the interest of the prospective buyer, and at persuading him or her to make a purchase. In case of a product like a radiation machine which is used in the treatment of cancer patients, the target market is the entire medical fraternity including all doctors, hospitals and nursing homes (i.e. the target market is industrial buyer). Therefore, the ad is given in a medical journal, a journal which has a good circulation in the entire medical fraternity. The advertising copy of this ad given in the medical journal can make use of all the technical terms used in the medical profession. However, a medicine like Vicks cough tablet which is aimed to be sold to the general public (i.e. target market is the consumer market), the advertising copy cannot use technical terms talking about the cough, but rather keep it simple by saying that in case of cough, use Vicks. In fact, jingles like *'Vicks ki goli lo, khich khich door karo'* can be used effectively to put across the message to the audience.
- *Message Source:* The target market for a product may sometimes also influence the choice of the message source, that is, the person delivering the message to the target audience. In 1980s, for the product Surf, where the target market for the product was all the housewives, a fictitious character Lalitaji was created to put across the message "Surf ki kharidaari mein hi samajhdaari hai".

Similarly, in case of a product like Kellogg's Chocos, where the target market comprises of kids and mothers, animated characters are created to give the message to the kids. The ad also uses a popular celebrity, Karishma Kapoor, as the mother of the kid. This message source was chosen because the celebrity has a high scoring on the likability factor and is herself a mother in real life.

Role of Target Market in Advertising Media Decisions

The target market for a product influences the following media decisions of the advertiser.

- *Media Mix:* An advertising medium is a channel of communication like newspapers, radio, television, etc. through which advertisement is transmitted to the target group of customers. In determining the media mix for his product, the advertiser chooses a particular advertising medium or media for advertising his product. For instance, a product which is meant for the rural market (target market) and where not many people are literate, choosing newspapers and magazines might not make much sense. Instead, these people may be reached out by giving ads on television and radio. The message should be put across to them in a very simple language and catchy music and jingles can be used to get their attention.
- *Media Vehicles:* The target market for a product also influences choice of media vehicles. For instance, a company manufacturing *agarbattis* identifies its target market as that group of people who have a religious bent of mind. The company decides to reach these people using television, magazines and radio. With the advertiser having chosen television, magazines and radio as the advertising media to be used, he now decides on the media vehicles. Thus, he might try to reach the target audience by advertising on television channels like Sanskar and Aastha, magazines like *Yog Shivir* and on radio during the time of *Bhakti Geet*.

FACTORS INFLUENCING PLANNING OF AN ADVERTISING CAMPAIGN

1. *The organisation:* The position of the company undertaking advertisement campaign needs proper consideration while planning advertising campaign. The production capacity of the organisation, its financial position, the sales force available, the product to be marketed are some factors which need proper consideration.
2. *Advertising Objectives:* An advertising campaign is well executed when its advertising objective is well defined. The campaign must use such headlines, slogans, illustrations which help to achieve the advertising objectives.
3. *Advertising budget:* Planning of advertising campaign depend on the budget provision made by the company for such campaign. For advertising agency, the main consideration is how much to spend on the campaign. The media used, frequency of advertisements in media, etc. depend on the budget provided for the campaign.
4. *The product:* Product or service is the base of entire advertising campaign. Such product may be consumer or industrial, direct usable or durable, high or low priced and finally facing high or low market competition. The planning of advertising campaign should be as per the features of the product.

5. *Consumers:* While planning ad campaign, it is important to take in to account composition of consumers, their buying habits, purchasing power, location etc. This will help the advertiser to select suitable advertising theme, media and frequency of advertisements.

6. *Language:* Most of the ads are initially conceived in English, Hindi and regional languages are better understood by the people. Bilingual advertising is sometimes more effective. This has been seen a lot in case of Pepsi's ads, for instance, "Yehi hai right choice baby, aha".

7. *Competitors:* Advertisement is normally influenced by the extent of market competition and the strong and weak points of competitors. Experts can plan the campaign properly after studying the position of market competition and the policies of competitors.

8. *The media:* Advertising campaign is influenced by the media available for advertising purpose. It is necessary to select media which are suitable for the product, target consumers, budget allocation and so on.

9. *Sales promotion efforts:* Advertising campaign should be properly adjusted with the plans of other departments of the company. It should be adjusted with the production schedule and the sales promotion plan prepared by the sales department.

10. *Identification of Current Problems:* Advertising campaign is basically meant for dealing with the current marketing problems of the company. The possible problems may be: sales are reducing, merits of the product are not brought to the notice of target consumers, the product fails to face market competition effectively, etc. It is necessary to give attention to such current problems while planning advertising campaign.

11. *Government Regulations:* In our country, government exercises control over the media. A number of restrictions have been imposed by the government. In order to plan an effective advertising campaign it is desirable that the advertiser is well-informed about government regulations and controls in various media. Unit III of the book discusses in detail the various laws which regulate advertising in India.

CONCLUDING NOTE

An advertising campaign is a series of advertisement messages that share a single idea or theme. Developing an advertising campaign involves a number of steps including review of company's marketing position, defining target markets, defining the objectives of the advertising campaign, determining the budget, creating the message, selecting the media, media scheduling, execution of the campaign and its monitoring. The advertising campaign developed must be consistent with the advertiser's corporate and promotional strategies.

QUESTIONS FOR DISCUSSION

1. What do you mean by an advertising campaign? What are the characteristic features of an advertising campaign?
2. What are the various steps involved in developing an advertising campaign?
3. Explain how the target markets influence the message and media decisions of the advertiser.
4. Explain the various factors that an advertiser must keep in mind while designing an advertising campaign.
5. Take an advertisement and analyse it from the point of target market, advertising objectives, advertising message and appeals used, advertising media used and the results of the campaign. (Refer case studies given at the end of the chapter).
6. A company wants to advertise its new brand of luxury cars. What should be its target market and on what basis should the company segment the market?

Case Study

TATA TEA "JAAGO RE" CAMPAIGN

Company: Tata Global Beverages Limited

About Tata Tea: Launched in 1985, Tata Tea was responsible for starting the polypack revolution in tea. The brand was built on the support of the garden fresh story, with the platform of *'Asli Taazgi'*. From a single variant, this brand today has 4 variants - Tata Tea Premium, Tata Tea Gold, Tata Tea Agni and Tata Tea Life.

Tata Tea Premium, the portfolio's flagship brand, is currently the largest packet tea brand in the country with an All India value share of 8.8% (March, 2011)

Tata Tea's Advertising: Earlier, the advertising of Tata Tea relied heavily on talking about maintaining the freshness of tea gardens in its pack and bringing to its consumers the same freshness. Later, this was changed to highlight the *'taazgi'* and physical and metal rejuvenation brought about by consuming a cup of Tata Tea.

The company then came up with this mega idea, where they moved from the premise of just mental and physical rejuvenation to intellectual awakening, hence, the *'Jaago Re'* campaign. The new communication attempted to migrate tea from being a physical and emotional revitaliser to becoming a catalyst for 'social awakening' with the message *'Har Subah Sirf Utho Mat, Jaago Re'*. This established thought leadership for the brand thereby reinforcing its market leadership.

Advertising Agency used for The ***'Jaago Re'*** campaign: Lowe Lintas

Target Market: The youth of urban India

Advertising Objective: To awaken the youth to cast their votes and make a difference in the political leadership of India.

The agency, Lowe Lintas decided to make tea younger by connecting with young India. To do this, it had to shift the standard category codes - from nurturing, bonding, and rejuvenating to provoking and awakening.

The New Positioning: A brand of tea that not only wakes you up but also AWAKENS the consciousness in you.

The Key Communication Message: *'Agar aap soyenge toh yeh desh kaise jagega?'*

The Campaign: *'Jaago Re'* began as a movement in 2007, with the aim to make tea a youthful drink. The Tata Tea campaign is about liberation and empowerment. The insight was to make tea more appealing to the young generation, who frequent the coffee joints. The whole idea of awakening is integral to tea, as that is how people look at it. This concept was made more relevant by using the awakening in a broader sense, thus, making the brand more interesting and relevant.

The campaign aimed at awakening the masses and alerting them to their responsibilities as citizens, one of which was to question the political leaders. Tata Tea used a number of interesting ads to engage the Indian youth into the *'Jaago Re'* campaign.

One of the TVCs showed that with the elections approaching, Bhawar Lal Bhandari, a politician, goes out asking for votes. Surrounded by his supporters he visits a guy with the request. Ordering tea for him, the guy asks his qualification. As Bhandari fails to answer that, our guy demands, *"Apna work experience bataiye."* The answer comes from the politician's assistant who says, *"Pachchis saal se hain is line mein"*.

With frustration showing on his face, the politician demands if he is being interviewed. The guy answers, *"Sir, itni badi job ke liye apply kiya hai apne."* Stunned by the reply the politician asks, "Kaunsa job?" The guy says, *"Desh ko chalane ka job, Sir."* He then offers the shocked man a cup of tea. The Voice Over says "*Har subah sirf utho mat* (Jingle: *Jaago re* !) Tata Tea."

After this, came the next phase of the campaign. In 2008, with elections round the corner, Tata Tea made an attempt to get the youth out of their homes to vote. The voter registration was driven through an interactive application on its website www.jaagore.com, which helped users identify their constituency, prepared a ready to print voter registration form in five minutes, guided them to the nearest voter registration centre and updated them via SMS when their names were added to the voting list.

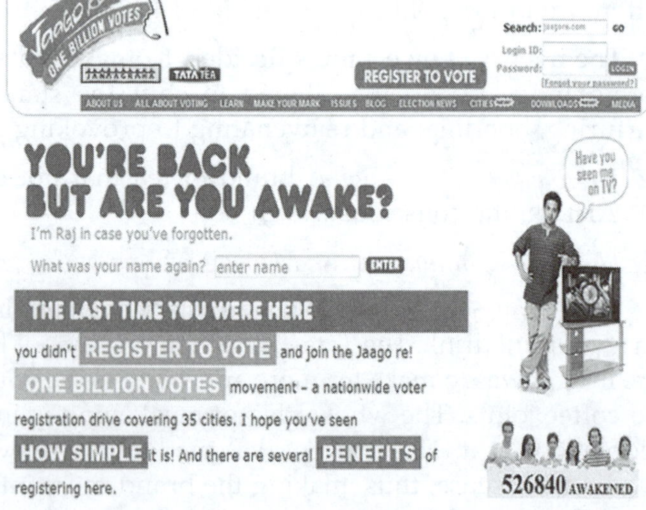

The initiative was launched in association with the non-profit organisation, *'Janaagraha'*, and the integrated media agency, Arc Worldwide. The focal point of the campaign is a website, www.jaagore.com, which was developed by the latter.

The *'Jaago Re'* website: At the *'Jaago Re'* site, visitors were led step by step through the process of registering to vote. A character, Raj, showed them how the voting list is prepared. Using conversational language, he also busted common myths related to voting.

Most important, the site allowed people to fill a voter registration form online and informed them about their constituencies. MapMyIndia pooled in for this part, with an interactive map displaying the constituencies and polling booths in 35 cities. Since the Government of India does not accept online registrations, visitors could take a printout of the filled form and submit it at the nearest Election Commission office. Further, once the form was submitted, the only thing the voter needed to do was to send an SMS to a short code. The *'Jaago Re'* team took up the responsibility to follow up on the status of the application and send mobile alerts to the voter.

Through www.jaagore.com, Tata Tea was able to bring citizen volunteers together with more than 70 NGOs to give their time for a range of good causes.

According to the traffic details received from Arc Worldwide, the site received 4,47,603 unique visitors and more than 1,00,000 users registered with the site, within 70 days of its launch. Around 85,000 users enrolled themselves for the voting process. ARC Worldwide (India) also revealed that ninety per cent of the 1,00,000 users, who enrolled for the election process through Jaagore.com, were in the age group of 18-30 years and were from the metros of Delhi, Mumbai, Hyderabad, Pune etc.

Advertising Media Used: Television, Radio and an Internet campaign, including virals, social networking sites like facebook and orkut, and online ads. An outreach programme for on-ground activities in college campuses and offices was also designed. The task of the media was to build awareness, connect with the youth of India, engage them, call to action (vote), and build brand equity for Tata Tea.

Result:

- Campaign recognition was 86.3%, as against the benchmark of 63. 4%.
- Brand association jumped to 98.8%, as against the benchmark of 39.5%.
- Over 600,000 people registered to vote at jaagore.com, a unique, non-profit initiative.
- *'Jaago Re'* campaign consistently won at the Effie Awards. In 2009, the campaign was awarded the Gold Effie, Consumer Products and the Bronze Effie, Integrated Marketing. In 2008, it was awarded the Silver Effie, Consumer Products and the Bronze Effie, Integrated Marketing.

Thus, Tata Tea, through its *'Jaago Re'* campaign, has acted as an activist beyond advertising. Also, the brand recall is very high and the platform of *Jaago Re* is appropriate as the name signifies what tea is supposed to do - awaken people.

Case Study

"THANDA MATLAB COCA COLA" CAMPAIGN

Company: Coca Cola India (CCI)

Advertising Campaign: "Thanda Matlab Coca Cola"

Target Audience: People in Rural India

Objective: CCI began focusing on the rural market in the early 2000s in order to increase volumes. The campaign *"Thanda matlab chota Coke"* was launched to support Coca Cola India's (CCI) rural marketing initiatives.

The Problem: The poor rural infrastructure and consumption habits that are very different from those of urban people were two major obstacles to cracking the rural market for CCI. Because of the erratic power supply most grocers in rural areas did not stock cold drinks. Also, people in rural areas had a preference for traditional cold beverages such as *lassi* and lemon juice. Further, the price of the beverage was also a major factor for the rural consumer.

The Strategy: CCI's rural marketing strategy was based on three A's - Availability, Affordability and Acceptability. The first A - Availability emphasized on the availability of the product to the customer by changing the distribution strategy; the second A - Affordability focused on product pricing (The company introduced 'Chota Coke' priced at Rs.5), and the third A - Acceptability focused on convincing the customer to buy the product through messages given in product advertisements.

Once CCI entered the rural market, it focused on strengthening its distribution network there. It realized that the centralized distribution system used by the company in the urban areas would not be suitable for rural areas. In the centralized distribution system, the product was transported directly from the bottling plants to retailers. However, CCI realized that this distribution system would not work in rural markets, as taking stock directly from bottling plants to retail stores would be very costly due to the long distances to be covered.

The company instead opted for a hub and spoke distribution system. Under the hub and spoke distribution system, stock was transported from the bottling plants to hubs and then from hubs, the stock was transported to spokes which were situated in small towns. These spokes fed the retailers catering to the demand in rural areas. CCI not only changed its distribution model, it also changed the type of vehicles used for transportation. The company used large trucks for transporting stock from bottling plants to hubs and medium commercial vehicles transported the stock from the hubs to spokes. For transporting stock from spokes to village retailers, the company utilized auto rickshaws and cycles.

Further it also distributed around 2,00,000 refrigerators to its rural retailers. It also purchased 5,000 new trucks and auto rickshaws for boosting its rural distribution. Through its rural distribution initiatives, CCI was able to increase its presence in rural areas from a coverage of 81,383 villages in 2001 to 1,58,342 villages in August 2003. Apart from strengthening its distribution network, CCI also focused on pricing in rural market.

The Launch of 'Chota Coke': A survey conducted by CCI in 2001 revealed that 300 ml bottles were not popular with rural and semi-urban residents where two persons often shared a 300 ml bottle. It was also found that the price of Rs10/- per bottle was considered too high by rural consumers. For these reasons, CCI decided to make some changes in the size of its bottles and pricing to win over consumers in the rural market. In 2002, CCI launched 200 ml bottles (*Chota Coke)* priced at Rs 5. CCI announced that it would push the 200 ml bottles more in rural areas, as the rural market was very price-sensitive.

It was widely felt that the 200 ml bottles priced at Rs. 5 would increase the rate of consumption in rural India. CCI also targeted the rural consumer aggressively in its marketing campaigns, which were aimed at increasing awareness of its brands in rural areas.

The initiatives of CCI in pricing were supported by extensive marketing in the mass media as well as through outdoor advertising. The company put up hoardings in villages and painted the name Coca Cola on the compounds of the residences in the villages. CCI also launched television commercials (TVCs) targeted at rural consumers. In order to reach more rural consumers, CCI increased its ad-spend on *Doordarshan*.

When CCI launched Chota Coke in 2002 priced at Rs. 5, it bought out a commercial featuring Bollywood actor Aamir Khan to communicate **the message of the price cut** and the launch of 200 ml bottles to the rural consumers. The commercial was shot in a rural setting. In the summer of 2003, CCI came up with a new commercial featuring Aamir Khan, to further strengthen the Coca-Cola brand image among rural consumers.

"Thanda Matlab Coca Cola": The commercial aimed at making coke a generic name for "*thanda*". Prasoon Joshi, national creative director - McCann Erickson, the creator of the commercial, said that the reason for picking up the word "*thanda*" is explained by the fact that "*Thanda* is a very North India-centric phenomenon. Go to any restaurant in the north, and attendants would promptly ask, "*thanda ya garam*?" "*Thanda*" usually means *lassi* or *nimbu pani, garam* is essentially tea. Because the character, in itself, represented a culture, we wanted to equate Coke with "thanda", since *thanda* too is part of the popular dialect of the north, thus making thanda generic for Coca-Cola. With the long-playing

possibilities of the thanda idea becoming evident, "*thanda*" became the central idea. Once we decided to work on that idea, the creative mind just opened up."

Between March and September 2003, CCI launched three commercials with the "*Thanda Matlab Coca-Cola*" tag line. All the three commercials aimed to make rural and semi-urban consumers connect with Coca-Cola. The first ad featured Aamir Khan as a *tapori* (street smart); in the ad he made the association between Coca-Cola and the word *thanda*. The second commercial in the series featured Aamir Khan as a Hyderabadi shop-keeper. Here again he equated the word thanda with Coca-Cola. The third commercial featured Aamir Khan as a Punjabi farmer who offered Coca Cola to ladies asking for Thanda.

One of the TVCs: In one of the TVCs, three girls explore the possibility of quenching their thirst. They approached a farmer tending his fields. Astonished, he blabbered in Punjabi "*Yeh ganne de khet wich tamatar kitho*?" "*Woh, actually pyas lagi thi*", is the answer. "*A ji, pyas di ki gal hai. Jado morniyan aa gayi hain kheta wich, bin badal barsat kara de hukum karo ji*". The girl coyly asked for '*thanda pani*'. "*Thanda!*", he shrieked and started drawing water from the well. "*Thanda peene de bahane aayi, kudi, thanda peene de bahane aayi, yara da tushan dekh lo*", sang the rustic farmer. The bucket came up with bottles of Coke. Quenching her thirst, the girl flirtatiously complimented, "*Tussi great ho*". "*O ji yaran da tushan*", the farmer replied.

Advertising Media Used: Along with TVCs, CCI also launched print advertisements in several regional newspapers and made extensive use of outdoor advertising.

Result: CCI claimed all its marketing initiatives were very successful, and as a result, its rural penetration increased from 9% in 2001 to 25% in 2003. CCI also said that volumes from rural markets increased to 35% in 2003.

Unit–II
Advertising Management

CHAPTER 6

ADVERTISING OBJECTIVES

CONTENTS

Every organisation should have objectives to provide a framework for action. Advertising is a part of the promotion mix and thus, advertising objectives should be in line with the overall promotional or marketing objectives of a firm which in turn, should be in line with the overall organisational objectives. Setting advertising objectives is the starting point in developing an advertising campaign.

CLASSIFICATION OF ADVERTISING OBJECTIVES

According to Philip Kotler, advertising objectives can be classified according to whether their aim is to inform, persuade, remind or reinforce.

1. *Inform:* Informative advertising, seeks to tell the market about the product, explain how the product works, and build awareness of both the product and the company. Such objectives are normally pursued at the launch of a new product, or on modification of an existing product.
2. *Persuade:* Persuasive advertising seeks to encourage the target audience to switch brands, make the purchase, and create a preference in the market for

the product as opposed to its competition. Advertising of this nature is required in highly competitive markets, where a range of products compete directly with each other.

3. *Remind:* Reminder advertising is used to maintain interest and awareness of a well established product in the market, often used in the latter stages of its product life cycle. It is also often used at the point-of-purchase to remind consumers of the brand.

4. *Reinforce:* Reinforcement advertising aims to convince current purchasers that they made the right choice. Automobile ads often depict satisfied customers enjoying special features of their car. Also, many consumer durable product ads often depict satisfied customers enjoying special features of their newly purchased brands. The purpose of reinforcement advertising is to maintain market share.

Box 6.1 lists possible advertising objectives according to the classification given by Philip Kotler.

Box 6.1: List of Advertising Objectives

To Inform

- Telling the market about a new product
- Suggesting new uses for a product
- Informing the market of a price change
- Explaining how the product works
- Describing available services
- Correcting false impressions
- Reducing consumer's fears
- Building a company image

To Persuade

- Building brand preference
- Encouraging switching to your brand
- Changing consumer's perception of product attributes
- Persuading consumers to purchase now

To Remind

- Reminding consumer that the product may be needed in near future
- Reminding consumer where to buy the product from
- Keeping product in consumer's mind during off seasons
- Maintaining 'top-of-mind' awareness

To Reinforce

- Convincing current purchasers that they made the right choice
- Highlighting the positive features of a product that satisfied the people who have already purchased it

Thus, it can be said that in general, that the objective of advertising is to inform, to persuade, to remind or to reinforce. However, an advertiser may choose one or more of the following specific advertising objectives as a starting point in developing his advertising campaign.

1. To create awareness about the product or brand.
2. To create customer interest in the product or brand.
3. To change customers' attitudes favourably towards the brand.
4. To deliver information about the product or brand.
5. To increase sales.
6. To increase market share.
7. To build brand loyalty.
8. To support the activities of the distribution channel.
9. To build the company or brand image.
10. To stimulate behaviour (buy, call, click, visit, etc.)
11. To remind about the brand.
12. To support the sales force.
13. To increase the usage of a product.
14. To introduce a price deal.
15. To develop overseas market.
16. To create buzz/word of mouth.

IMPORTANCE OF OBJECTIVES

Setting advertising objectives helps a marketer in the following ways.

- Objectives serve as *communication devices* and facilitate the coordination of the various groups working on the campaign, on both the agency and the client side. Problems can be avoided if all parties involved have a set of written and approved objectives to guide their decisions and actions.
- Good objectives provide the advertiser with guidance and direction for the development of the campaign. They provide *a framework for decision-making* in areas such as advertising budgets, media selection, creative strategy etc.
- Objectives also provide a *benchmark or standard against which success or failure of the campaign can be measured*. When specific objectives are set it becomes easier for management to measure what has been accomplished by the campaign.

SALES AS AN ADVERTISING OBJECTIVE

When an advertiser defines objectives in terms of sales, the objectives focus on increasing absolute sales in terms of rupees, increasing sales by a certain percentage, or increasing the firm's market share.

Evaluation of Sales as an Advertising Objective

Advertising objectives like any organisational objective must be operational. This means that advertising objectives should provide an effective criterion for decision-making and should provide standards with which results can be compared.

An immediate sale is one of the convenient and tempting advertising objectives. However, *objectives that involve an increase in immediate sales are not operational in many cases because of the following two reasons.*

1. **Advertising is only one of the many factors influencing sales, and it is difficult to isolate its contribution to sales.**

The other forces that influence sales include price, packaging, distribution, product quality and features, competition and changing consumers' tastes. It is extremely difficult to isolate the effect of advertising on sales. Figure 6.1 shows some of the factors influencing sales of a product.

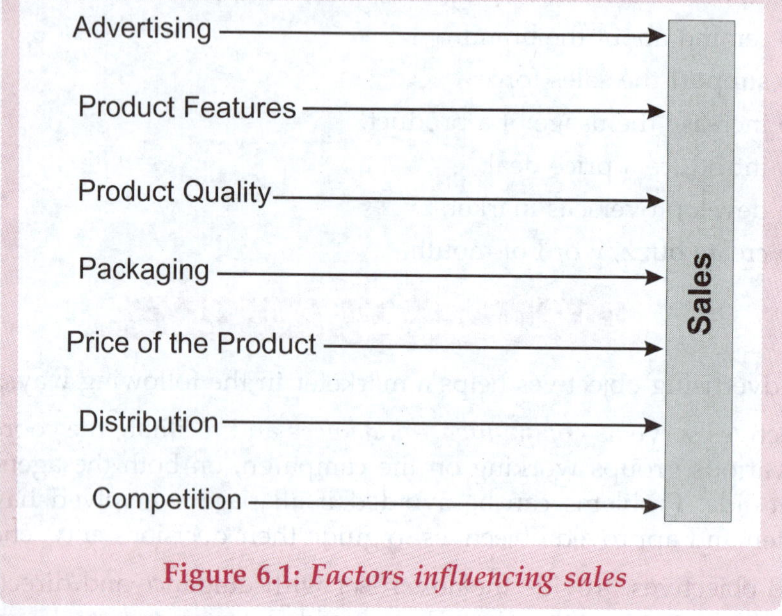

Figure 6.1: ***Factors influencing sales***

Let us suppose that a company manufacturing bikes runs a campaign for a new model, but not many bikes get sold. The problem may be due to a poor advertising campaign, or it is also possible that the advertisement did, in fact, attract a lot of target audience but due to some other reason like the quality of the bike, its price etc., not much sales took place. Thus, it would be wrong to hold the advertising campaign responsible for not achieving increase in sales. Similarly, it would be wrong to attribute an increase in immediate sales to advertising. In other words, sales cannot be an effective criterion for evaluating advertising effectiveness. It is because of this reason that sales cannot be considered as an operational advertising objective.

2. There is a long-term effect of advertising on sales.

The contributory role of advertising in achieving increase in sales often occurs primarily over the long-run. In other words, advertising generates a substantial lagged effect on sales. This means that the impact of an advertising campaign cannot be known for certain until a certain length of time has passed. For example, a prospective customer might be exposed to an advertisement today but the resultant purchase might take place six months hence.

Consider Figure 6.2. It shows that advertising may lead to immediate sales or may help in creating brand awareness or improving attitudes which will culminate into purchase much later.

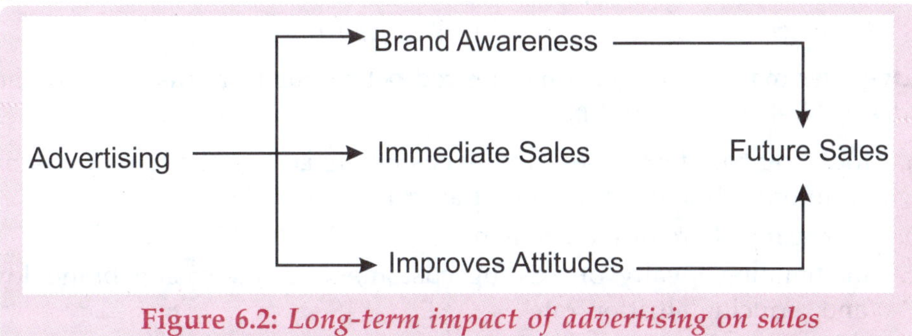

Figure 6.2: *Long-term impact of advertising on sales*

The above discussion reveals that advertising objectives that emphasize sales are usually not very operational because they provide little practical guidance to the decision-makers.

SETTING ADVERTISING OBJECTIVES

If immediate sales do not form the basis of operational advertising objectives, how should one proceed in setting advertising objectives? The solution lies in addressing a set of questions. Addressing the following three questions in a careful and systematic way will often yield useful and effective objectives.

1. Who is the target segment?
2. What is the ultimate behaviour within that segment that advertising is attempting to precipitate, reinforce, change or influence?

   (i.e. Is advertising trying to induce trial purchases of new customers, maintenance of loyalty of existing customers, increasing share of requirements or increase in the usage rate?)
3. How can advertising help in achieving the desired behaviour?

   (i.e. Should advertising be used to create awareness, communicate information about the brand, create a brand image or attitude, build long term brand associations, or associate feelings or a type of user personality with the brand?)

Let us try addressing these questions one by one.

Step 1: Identifying the Target Market

For identifying the target audience, the market needs to be segmented and then that segment(s) be selected in which the marketer wants to operate. Market can be segmented on various basis like age, gender, geographical location, income, family size, occupation, usage rate, loyalty status, lifestyle, etc.

To take an example, in case of marketing a pimple-control cream, the market may be segmented on the basis of age and then the teenage segment can be selected as the target segment. Once this is done an advertiser can plan his entire advertising effort towards this particular segment i.e. towards the teenagers.

Similarly, the target market for a car like Mercedes would be people who fall in the high income bracket. Thus, the total market would be segmented on the basis of income and the high income segment would be chosen as the target market for such a product.

Step 2: Analysis of Ultimate Desired Behaviour

An advertiser may like to get some desired behaviour from his target audience. This desired behaviour could be:

a. inducing trial purchases of new customers i.e. attracting new customers from other brands and from other categories
b. increasing share of requirements
c. maintaining loyalty of existing customers i.e. increasing brand loyalty and reducing attrition rate
d. increase in the usage rate

A. Inducing Trial Purchases of New Customers

One of the possible behaviours that an advertiser might attempt to achieve is inducing trial purchases of new customers. This can be achieved by attracting new customers from other brands or by attracting new customers from other categories.

Consider Figure 6.3 which shows a market divided into three segments.

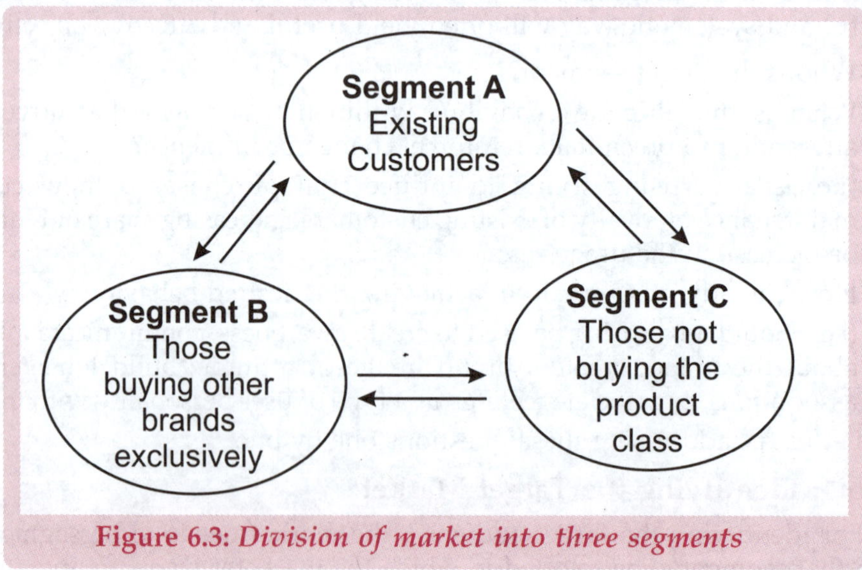

Figure 6.3: *Division of market into three segments*

Segment A includes those who are our existing customers. Some members of segment A will buy only our brand, but there might be some other members in this segment who, in addition to our brand, might be buying other brands too. For instance, for a product category like soups and understanding the behavioural dynamics from the viewpoint of an advertiser of Knorr Soups, some customers in the market might be buying only Knorr Soups while some of the existing customers of Knorr Soups might also be buying Maggi Soups besides buying Knorr Soups. Segment B contains people who buy other brands to the exclusion of ours. Continuing with the same example, segment B would thus, contain those people who buy a different brand of soup other than Knorr Soups. Segment C buyers are not buyers of any brand in the product category. Thus, segment C would include all those people who do not purchase any brand of soup. In an attempt to attract new customers, the advertiser can focus his efforts on segment B and/or segment C.

New customers from other brands (Attracting customers from segment B to segment A)

The focus here is to increase the size of segment A and the approach here is to attract members of segment B to get them try our brand. Thus, for mobile phone service providers, Airtel may try to attract customers of Vodafone or Idea may try to attract customers of Airtel. Attracting the customers of other brand to increase one's market share may be difficult if other brands are performing satisfactorily. It is, therefore, best to find out which existing users of the competing brand are the most dis-satisfied with it and target these "switchable" consumers. One could also try to target those customers who are most likely to influence others to switch too. Thus, the mobile phone service providers should try to figure out those consumers who are not happy with their current service provider, may be because of tariff rates or tariff plans or billing problems or poor network access etc. An effort should then be made to attract such customers to the segment of your existing customers and thus, increase the market share.

New customers from other categories (Attracting customers from segment C to segment A)

Another approach to increase the size of segment A is to attract people from segment C, i.e., those people who are currently not buying the product category. Thus, if players like Reliance can attract some people belonging to the lower income groups, who are not currently using a mobile phone, to buy a Reliance mobile phone and use its services at a rate which they can easily afford, they are able to increase the size of their existing customers segment.

B. Increasing Share of Requirements

Some customers may repeatedly switch among one brand and others. In many product categories (e.g., soap), customers may have more than one preferred brand, and they allocate their total category requirements over these few brands based on temporary price discounts, habits, etc. It may be possible to convince such customers to become more loyal. For instance, a customer might use three different brands of soap-brand X, brand Y and brand Z, in a month. A particular brand of soap, say brand X, can try to increase its "share-of-wallet", i.e. try that this customer buys more units of brand X soap as compared to the number of units purchased of brand Y and Z.

The advertising task here is not one of getting a new user but of increasing the existing user's share of requirements going to that particular brand.

C. Increasing Brand Loyalty and Reducing Attrition

If a brand suffers from high attrition rate (i.e. a low repurchase rate), a defensive strategy should be used. The marketer should not forget that he is not the only one advertising. All his competitors are constantly trying to steal his customers away or trying to increase their "share-of-wallet". It is, therefore, very important to recognize the effect that advertising has on reinforcing a present customer's existing preference for a brand. Researches have also indicated that actual experience with a product/brand is a bigger determinant of brand satisfaction and hence, brand loyalty.

D. Increasing Usage

It is also possible to increase the usage of existing customers in the product class. This is especially true for market leader brands in the food and beverage product categories and other consumable categories. For instance, the advertisements of products like Dabur Roohafza and Dabur Honey show how these products can be used in different and varied ways. In essence, the goal would be to increase the amount consumed per occasion, or to suggest new usage occasions and opportunities.

Step 3: Using Advertising to Achieve Action (Desired Behaviour)

Usually advertising is not well suited to directly precipitate action. Rather, it is better at conducting some communication, association, or persuasion task that will hopefully result in the desired action being precipitated.

For instance, when the desired action is trial purchase by the consumer, advertising should focus on creating brand awareness. This brand awareness will work as an intervening variable which will help in achieving the desired behaviour from the customers i.e. a trial purchase.

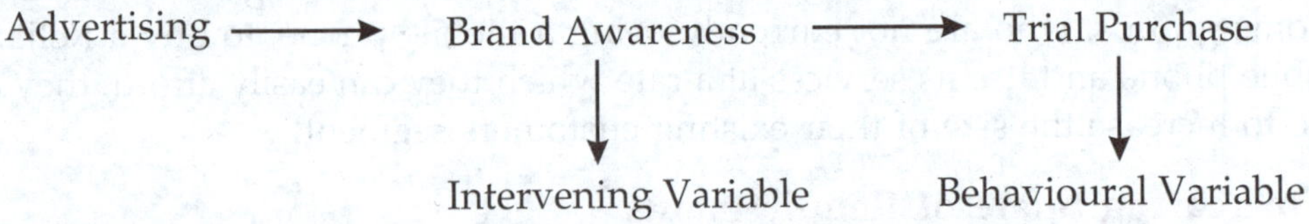

A trial purchase can also be precipitated by more than one intervening variables helping in generating the desired behaviour. This is exhibited in the following equation.

Advertising → Brand Awareness → Knowledge of Brand Attributes → Trial Purchase

The above two equations show that advertising can help in creating brand awareness which can lead to trial purchase (desired behaviour) either directly or through creation of brand attribute knowledge. In other words, advertising with the help of intervening variables can help in generating the desired behaviour.

Given below are some more examples of how advertising can achieve the desired action through intervening variables.

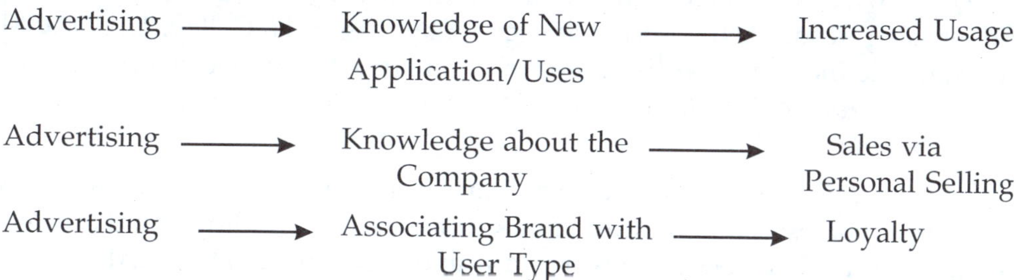

It is now clear that the desired action is achieved with the help of intervening variables. Thus, it makes sense for the advertiser to set intervening variables as the advertising objectives. If advertising can make these intervening variables work, the desired response/action will automatically be forthcoming.

Thus, in the foregoing analysis, the following can be cited as advertising objectives:

- Creating brand awareness
- Giving knowledge of new applications/uses of the product
- Providing knowledge about the company
- Associating brand with a particular user type

THE CASE OF MULTIPLE OBJECTIVES

A more complicated model would be one where advertising has more than one objective, that is, when advertising stresses on more than one intervening variables to achieve the desired action.

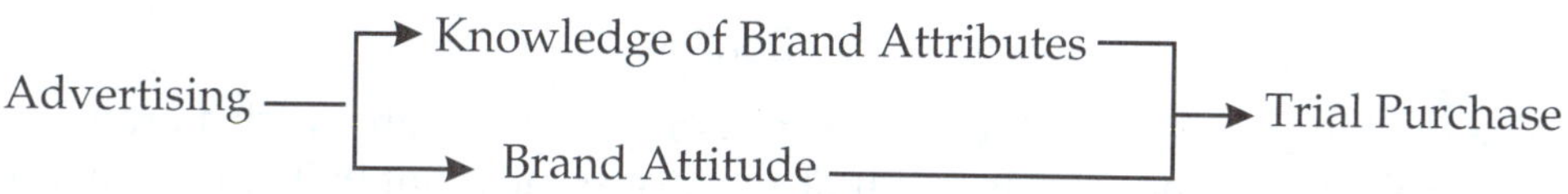

When the advertising campaign can focus upon a single well-defined objective, the communication task is made easier. When several objectives are introduced, there is always the danger that the campaign will become a compromise that will be ineffective with respect to all the objectives. Experts in the advertising industry suggest that simplicity in advertising objectives is vital. An advertisement that tries to say too much loses focus and becomes ineffective. In addition, research has shown that advertising that tries to maximize effectiveness with regard to one objective very often fails to be effective on the other objectives.

The approach in setting advertising objectives just outlined in the aforesaid discussion is an improvement and extension of the DAGMAR approach, which is discussed below.

THE DAGMAR APPROACH

DAGMAR is an acronym for Defining Advertising Goals for Measured Advertising Results. The concept was given by Russell H. Colley. The DAGMAR approach defines an advertising goal (i.e. an advertising objective) as *a specific communication task to be accomplished among a defined audience, in a given period of time.*

A Communication Task: As seen earlier in our discussion, an advertising objective involves a communication task (for example, building brand awareness, changing attitude of people towards a brand etc). In the DAGMAR approach, the communication task is based on a specific model of the communication process, as shown in the figure below.

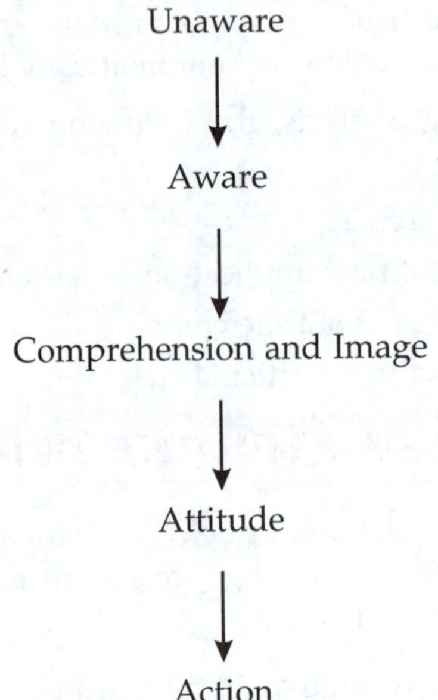

The model suggests that there is a series of steps through which a brand must climb to gain acceptance. An individual starts at some point by being unaware of a brand's presence in the market. The initial communication task that advertising is to do is increase consumer awareness of the brand. The second step of the communication process is brand comprehension. This involves the target audience learning something about the brand - in what way is it different from its competitors? Whom is it supposed to benefit? etc. Thus, at this stage of the communication model, the objective of advertising is to impart such knowledge to the target audience. The next step in the communication model is attitude or conviction. At this stage, advertising aims at developing a favourable attitude of the target customers towards the brand. The last stage, that is the action stage, involves some move on the part of the customer, such as, trying a brand for the first time, visiting the showroom etc. [1]

Thus, *as per DAGMAR approach, advertising objectives are nothing but communication tasks to be accomplished*. These communication tasks are nothing but the intervening variables discussed earlier (step 3 in setting advertising objectives) in our discussion. The DAGMAR approach assumes that focus on these intervening variables – awareness, comprehension and conviction (i.e. communication tasks) will lead to action.

A Specific Task: Another important concept of DAGMAR approach is that the advertising goal should be specific. It should be a written, measurable task involving a starting point, a defined audience, and a fixed time period. Thus, an advertising goal for a manufacturer of brand X of detergent could be set as follows:

To increase awareness (communication task) of brand X of detergent from 20% to 70% (amount of change) within two months (time period) among housewives (target).

To stimulate thinking about advertising objectives within the DAGMAR concept, Colley provided advertisers with a checklist of 52 advertising tasks and suggested that each task be evaluated in terms of its relative importance. The checklist is shown in Appendix 6.1 given at the end of the chapter.

Critical Evaluation of the DAGMAR Approach

The DAGMAR approach uses communication tasks like awareness, comprehension, attitude etc. in setting advertising objectives. It made a point that such goals are more appropriate for advertising as compared to some other measures like sales, which have multiple causes. The DAGMAR approach also focuses attention upon measurement, thus, encouraging marketers to create objectives which are specific, measurable and operational.

However, the DAGMAR approach has been criticized on the following grounds.

1. *Sales Goal:* The DAGMAR approach emphasizes on the intervening variables like awareness, comprehension, etc. which will ultimately lead to sales. Critics say that if there is a close relationship between these intervening variables and sales then why not measure sales directly and set sales as the advertising objective.
2. *Measurement Problems:* Intervening variables like awareness, brand comprehension, attitude etc. are difficult to measure as compared to sales.

---

[1] A communication model such as the DAGMAR model, which implies that the target audience will sequentially pass through a series of steps, is termed as a hierarchy-of-effects model. There are a number of hierarchy models which have been proposed. One such model is the AIDA model which explains an individual passing through four stages-attention, interest, desire and action. The model given by Robert Lavidge and Gary Steiner includes six stages- awareness, knowledge, liking, preference, conviction, and purchase. These models have been explained in Chapter 3 of the book.

3. *Noise in the System:* It can be argued that there might be many other factors besides advertising that determine awareness, brand comprehension etc. For instance, an adverse publicity might lead people to comprehend the brand in a particular way. It does not necessarily mean that the advertisement was ineffective.

4. *Inhibits Ideas:* The DAGMAR approach provides guidance to the creative team in designing the advertising campaign. By emphasizing intervening variables and not the final result, the creative talent of these people might be inhibited and there is a likelihood that they may not come up with great ideas.

COMMUNICATION OBJECTIVES OF ADVERTISING

It follows from the aforesaid discussion that an advertising objective involves a communication task to be accomplished. A marketer may, thus, focus on the following communication objectives of advertising.

1. *To create awareness:* One of the important objectives of advertising is to create awareness about the existence and availability of a product or a service. It also makes the target audience aware about any changes or modifications introduced in the product. For instance, when Hutch became Vodafone, its advertisements did a good job in creating awareness that "Hutch is now Vodafone".

The story was told by Hutch's brand ambassador-pug, the cute little dog. The ad opened with the famous "Hutch" pug resting in a pink kennel (Pink was the colour of brand "Hutch"). The pug left for a stroll. He came back and found a bigger red kennel instead of his pink one and the message that popped up was, "Change is good" followed by "Hutch is now Vodafone".

2. *To develop comprehension:* Another communication objective of advertising is to develop comprehension, that is, to create an understanding wherein, consumers are educated by providing knowledge about the product or service. Some advertisers have done a great job in imparting knowledge about their brands and their features to the target audience. For instance, advertisements by Saffola Gold have stressed on the fact that Saffola Gold refined oil helps

in reducing the cholesterol level. Similarly, advertisements of Aquaguard show how its three-stage purifying system helps in purifying water.

3. *To create conviction:* Advertising seeks to convince the target audience that they need the product and they will be benefited by the product if they purchase it. For instance, the advertisement of Dabur Chyawanprash tries to convince the target audience that they need the product.

The film opens on Amitabh Bachchan asking, "*Chintu ko Dabur Chyawanprash ki kya zaroorat hai? Toh chaliye aaj mummy ko hi bhej dete hain na school.*" We see the mother as a student struggling to manage a seat in the bus. Trying to carry on with the stressful timetable she finds the taekwondo classes back-breaking. The situation is no different in the playground where she struggles to keep pace with the kids. Bachchan lends his voice by saying, "*ab samajh mein aaya bachcha hona bachchon ka khel nahin? Isiliye Dabur Chyawanprash.*" The ad ends on Amitabh Bachchan as he says, "Dabur Chyawanprash. *Zaroorat hai.*"

4. *To secure action:* The last communication objective of advertising is to persuade target customers to respond. Such a response or action can be secured in the form of a purchase or by making enquiries about the product from the dealers or by walking into the showroom etc. For instance, an advertisement announcing Rs.5 off on purchase of Maggi Family Pack is expected to secure an action in the form of purchases by the target customers.

CONCLUDING NOTE

It is important to set clear objectives for an advertising campaign, whether it is intended to build awareness, develop brand comprehension or convince the consumers to purchase the brand. These communication objectives of advertising are measurable and, in turn, help in achieving the behavioural objectives of inducing a trial purchase, or increasing brand loyalty or increasing product usage. The advertisers should, thus, focus on communication objectives rather than using sales as an advertising objective.

The objectives should be in place well before a campaign begins, to ensure that each campaign has a specific task. The results should be measurable, in order to ensure the campaign is worth the marketing investment.

QUESTIONS FOR DISCUSSION

1. Advertising objectives can be classified according to whether their aim is to inform, persuade, remind, or reinforce. Explain and list some specific objectives that advertisers may work with under each of these heads.
2. Setting advertising objectives helps a marketer in many ways. Do you agree?
3. Evaluate sales as an advertising objective.
4. What are the various steps involved in setting advertising objectives?
5. Critically examine the DAGMAR approach in setting advertising objectives.
6. What are the various communication objectives of advertising? Explain with the help of some examples.
7. "The basic objectives of advertising is to increase sales and profits". Do you agree? Give reasons.

Appendix 6.1

ADVERTISING TASK CHECK LIST (DAGMAR)

This check list is a "thought starter" in developing specific advertising objectives. It can be applied to a single ad, a year's campaign for each product, or it can aid in developing a company's entire advertising philosophy among those who create and approve advertising.

Note: All the tasks defined in DAGMAR's check list are evaluated on the following importance scale.

Scale of Importance

Not Important					Very Important
0	1	2	3	4	5

List of Tasks

To what extent does the advertising aim at closing an immediate sale?

1. Perform the complete selling function (take the product through all the necessary steps toward a sale)?
2. Close sales to prospects already partly sold through past advertising efforts?
3. Announce a special reason for "buying now" (price, premium, etc.)?
4. Remind people to buy?
5. Tie in with some special buying event?
6. Stimulate impulse sales?

Other Tasks:

____

____

Does the advertising aim at near-term sales by moving the prospect, step by step, closer to a sale (so that when confronted with a buying situation the customer will ask for, reach for or accept the advertised brand)?

7. Create awareness of existence of product or brand?
8. Create "brand image" or favourable emotional disposition toward the brand?
9. Implant information or attitude regarding benefits and superior features of brand?
10. Combat or offset competitive claims?
11. Correct false impressions, misinformation and other obstacles to sales?
12. Build familiarity and easy recognition of package or trademark?

Other Tasks:

___

___

Does the advertising aim at building a "long range consumer franchise"?

13. Build confidence in company and brand which is expected to pay off in years to come?
14. Build customer demand which places company in stronger position in relation to its distribution (not at the "mercy of the market place"?
15. Place advertiser in position to select preferred distributors and dealers?
16. Secure universal distribution?
17. Establish a "reputation platform" for launching new brands of product lines?
18. Establish brand recognition and acceptance which will enable the company to open up new markets (geographic, price, age, sex)?

Other Tasks:

___

___

Specifically, how can advertising contribute toward increased sales?

19. Hold present customers against the inroads of competition?
20. Convert competitive users to advertiser's brands?
21. Cause people to specify advertiser's brand instead of asking for product by generic name?
22. Convert nonusers of the product type to users of product and brand?

23. Make steady customers out of occasional or sporadic customers?
24. Advertising new uses of the product?
25. Persuading customers to buy larger sizes or multiple units?
26. Reminding users to buy?
27. Encouraging greater frequency or quantity of use?

Other Tasks:

____

____

Does the advertising aim at some specific step which leads to a sale?

28. Persuade prospect to write for descriptive literature, return a coupon, enter a contest?
29. Persuade prospect to visit a showroom, ask for a demonstration?
30. Induce prospect to sample the product (trial offer)?

Other Tasks:

____

____

How important are "supplementary benefits" of end-use advertising?

31. Aid salesmen in opening new accounts?
32. Aid salesmen in getting larger orders from wholesalers and retailers?
33. Aid salesmen in getting preferred display space?
34. Give salesmen an entry?
35. Build morale of company sales force?
36. Impress the trade (causing recommendation to their customers and favourable treatment to salesmen)?

Other Tasks:

____

____

Is it a task of advertising to impart information needed to consummate sales and build customer satisfaction?

37. "Where to buy it" advertising
38. "How to use it" advertising
39. New models, features, package
40. New prices
41. Special terms, trade-in offers, etc.

42. New policies (guarantees, etc.)

Other Tasks:

____

____

To what extent does the advertising aim at building confidence and goodwill for the corporation among:

43. Customers and potential customers?
44. The trade (distributors, dealers, retail sales people)?
45. Employees and potential employees?
46. The financial community?
47. The public at large?

Other Tasks:

____

____

Specifically what kind of images does the company wish to build?

48. Product quality, dependability?
49. Service?
50. Family resemblance of diversified products?
51. Corporate citizenship?
52. Growth, progressiveness, technical leadership?

Other Tasks:

____

____

Source: Russell H. Colley, *Defining Advertising Goals for Measured Advertising Results* (New York: Association of National Advertisers, Inc., 1961), pp.62-68.

CHAPTER 7

ADVERTISING BUDGET

CONTENTS

Once the advertising objectives are set, the next step is to determine the advertising budget, that is, the total amount of money a marketer allocates for advertising during a specific time period.

"Half the money I spend on advertising is wasted; the trouble is I don't know which half..." said US merchant Jon Wanamaker. Ever since he spoke those golden words, millions of advertising minds across the world have been trying to work out 'which half' of their advertising budget works for them! Or better still, how to increase that half to a distinctly better figure; or gaining more bang for the buck.

MEANING OF ADVERTISING BUDGET

Budget is a quantitative expression of future plan of activities, that is, it is a future plan of activities expressed in terms of rupees. It is prepared for a fixed period of time. **Advertising budget is a financial document that shows the total amount to be spent on advertising and lists the way this amount is to be allocated.** It is a translation of advertising plan into money to be spent on advertising.

The advertising budget of a business grows out of the advertising goals and objectives of the company, which in turn grow out of the marketing goals and objectives of the company. According to William Cohen, "In some cases your budget will be established before goals and objectives due to your limited resouces. It will be given, and you may have to modify your goals and objectives. If money is available, you can work the other way around and see how much money it will take to reach the goals and objectives you have established."

The advertising budget is an estimate of the funds needed for meeting the advertising objectives of an organisation. It is a statement of proposed advertising expenditure which would enable meeting advertising objectives with planned strategies within a given period of time. **Advertising budget shows how much amount is to be spent on advertising promotional effort and how this amount will be allocated among different media, sales territories, products, selling activities, etc.**

Advertising budget is prepared by the advertising manager in consultation with the marketing manager of the company. It is then approved by the top management for its implementation. However, in small business organisations, which do not have a separate advertising department, the responsibility of preparing advertising budget lies on the marketing manager or the top management.

Box 7.1 gives lists down some definitions of advertising budget.

Box 7.1: *Some Definitions of Advertising Budget*

- Advertising budget is an estimate to meet the financial requirements of advertising plan so that advertising objectives can be achieved within specific time period.
- Advertising budget is the quantitative expression of future plan of advertising activities in monetary terms. It shows the total amount to be spent on advertising and its allocation among different advertising activities so that advertising objectives can be achieved in a specific period of time.
- Advertising budget is the translation of an advertising plan into monetary terms. It shows the amount of proposed advertising expenditure and its apportionment on various advertising activities of the company.

From the aforesaid discussion, the following points are clear about an advertising budget.

1. Advertising budget is a translation of an advertising plan into monetary units.
2. It helps in meeting advertising objectives of an organisation.
3. It is prepared for a specific future period of time.

4. Advertising budgeting is prepared by the advertising manager in consultation with the marketing manager and approved by the top management.
5. It shows the plan of allocation of available funds to various advertising activities.
6. It is a limiting factor which determines the size of the advertising campaign.

ADVERTISING BUDGET AS AN INVESTMENT

Traditionally, money spent on advertising was considered to be a waste. Also, advertising expenditure was considered an item of current expenditure whose benefits were assumed to accrue in the current period. However, now it is widely accepted that advertising expenditure is an item of capital expenditure and will provide benefits not only in the current period but also in the future periods. It is rather an investment whose returns will accrue in future. An effective advertising campaign is capable of producing lots of benefits including increase in sales, improved goodwill of the organisation, increase in market share, maintaining customer loyalty, etc.

Advertising budget differs from company to company. Some companies spend large amount on advertising, while some companies spend very less amount on advertising. Nonetheless, the growing importance of advertising in the recent past has resulted in massive spending on advertising by the companies in India and worldwide. Table 7.1 reveals the amount spent by the top ten advertisers in India during 2004-05.

Table 7.1: ***Top Ad Spenders in India (2004-05)***

	Companies	Ad Spend (in Rs. crore)
1.	Hindustan Lever	835.98
2.	ITC	220.53
3.	Ranbaxy Laboratory	201.72
4.	Tata Motors	172.37
5.	Dabur India	171.79
6.	Hero Honda	147.48
7.	Bajaj Automobiles	143.87
8.	Colgate Palmolive	136.84
9.	Reckitt Benckiser	124.41
10.	Nestle India	121.26
11.	ICICI Bank	116.26
12.	Reliance Industries	114.56
13.	GlaxoSmithline Consumer	101.45
14.	Britannia Industries	101.09

Source: http://ptpt502.wordpress.com/2007/12/29/top-ad-spenders-in-india

METHODS OF SETTING ADVERTISING BUDGET

There are several methods used in developing an advertising budget. The most common ones are listed below:

1. Affordable method
2. Percentage of Sales method
3. Competitive Parity method
4. Objective and Task method

Let us now discuss each of these methods in detail.

AFFORDABLE METHOD

Under this method, **advertisers base their advertising budget on what they can afford.** After all the allocations have been made to cover other relevant company expenditures, whatever is left is allocated to advertising, presuming that this is what the firm can afford to spend on advertising.

Advantages:

1. This is a very simple method of determining advertising budget.

Disadvantages:

1. The affordable method leads to an uncertain annual advertising budget which makes it difficult to prepare long range plans.
2. The method is not logical. It fixes advertising budget on the basis of what the company can afford instead of considering the advertising needs of the firm.

PERCENTAGE OF SALES METHOD

The percentage of sales method is a commonly used method of determining advertising budget. **Under the percentage of sales method, a fixed percentage of the sales figure is allocated as the advertising budget. This sales figure could be the *last year's sales figure* or the *average of the sales figures of last few years,*** say, last five years.

Let us assume that a company allocates 10% of the average sales figure in the last five years as its advertising budget. Let us also assume that the sales figures of this company during the five year period (2006-10) have been as follows.

Year	Sales (in Rs.)
2006	Rs.20,00,000
2007	Rs.25,00,000,
2008	Rs.22,50,000,
2009	Rs.27,50,000
2010	Rs.25, 00,000

Then, the average sales figure of the five years would be

= Rs.(20,00,000+25,00,000+22,50,000+27,50,000+25,00,000)/5

= Rs.120,00,000/5

= Rs. 24,00,000.

The company's advertising budget would then be determined as 10% of Rs.24,00,000 which is equal to Rs.2,40,000.

If the same company has a policy of allocating 10% of the last year's sales figure as the advertising budget of the current year then the advertising budget would be calculated as follows:

10% of Rs.25,00,000 (last year's sales figure)

= Rs. 2,50,000.

Under the percentage of sales method, a company may also use ***projected sales figure*** in determining the advertising budget. Thus, if the company in our example expects to achieve Rs. 27,00,000 of the sales in the coming year, then its advertising budget would be 10% of Rs.27,00,000 which is equal to Rs.2,70,000.

Yet another way of determining advertising budget under the percentage of sales method is to determine the budget amount by working out the selling price, profit per unit and advertising cost. Let us assume that a selling price of product A is Rs.500 and the seller has a profit margin of Rs.100 on it. Out of this Rs.100, he decides to fix Rs.15 as advertising expenditure on every unit of product sold. Also, let us assume that the projected sales figure of product A in the coming year is 1,00,000 units. Thus, the advertising budget for product A would be determined as Rs.15 x 1,00,000 = Rs.15,00,000.

Advantages:

1. The method is simple and easy to understand. Regardless of whether past sales or projected sales are taken as the basis for calculation, it is easy to arrive at the budget figure.
2. Advertising expenditures are directly related to the funds available. If a company sold more in the last year, presumably more funds are available to be spent on advertising this year.
3. The method satisfies the financial managers who believe that expenses should be closely related to the movement of corporate sales.
4. The method encourages the managers to fix up the budget in terms of relationship between advertising cost, selling price and profit per unit.

Disadvantages:

1. The method views sales as a factor determining advertising spending rather than viewing sales as a result of advertising.
2. The dependence of advertising budget on year to year sales fluctuations makes long range planning difficult.

3. This method does not provide a logical basis for choosing a specific percentage for determining advertising budget.
4. The method discourages experimenting with aggressive spending. Thus, the percentage of sales method might lead to underspending when the potential is great.
5. The method cannot be used if the advertiser introduces a new product in the market. For a new product, past sales figures are not available. Also, projected sales figure of a new product may not be realistic. Moreover, a new product requires a heavy advertising expenditure in the initial stages, that is, in the introduction stage of PLC, although sales in the introduction stage may not be high.
6. The method does not take into account the competition and market opportunities while setting advertising budget.

COMPETITIVE PARITY METHOD

Under this method, the advertising expenditures of competitors are taken as the guidelines for setting advertising budget. The logic behind this method is that collective wisdom of various firms in an industry cannot be too far from the optimal figure. The marketer believes that by having the same amount of advertising spending as his competitors, he will maintain his market share. Thus, this method is used as a defensive device by the advertiser.

Advantages:

1. The method recognizes competition as an important factor in determining advertising budget.
2. It enables a company to monitor the marketing and advertising strategies of competitors.
3. The collective wisdom of the firms in an industry generates advertising budgets that are close to optimal.
4. By determining advertising budget as an amount close to the competitors' spending on advertising, this method reduces the chances of promotional wars.

Disadvantages:

1. The reputation, resources, opportunities and objectives of various firms differ so much that following the competitors might not give a good estimate of what the company should be spending on advertising.
2. There is no guarantee that what firms in the industry spend on advertising is the optimal level. The market conditions and conditions within the company change overtime and there is a possibility that the firms may not be spending at the optimal level.

3. There is no ground for believing that budgets based on competitive parity discourage promotional wars from breaking out. Promotional wars are likely to break out when competitors respond to each other's increased advertising outlays.

4. The method ignores factors like the level of production, sales estimates and advertising objectives of a firm, which are important in determining a more realistic advertising budget.

OBJECTIVE AND TASK METHOD

This is the most logical way of setting advertising budget wherein the focus is on the advertising task that is to be achieved. Under this method, advertising objectives are fixed after intensive market research. For instance, for a new product launched in the market, the advertising objective might be to create brand awareness among 40 percent of the target consumers in a given period of time. After this, marketers identify the tasks which must be performed to achieve these objectives. These tasks may include advertising on television, radio, newspapers and magazines. The advertising cost of each relevant task is then calculated. This would mean calculating the costs of advertising on television, radio, newspapers and magazines. In addition to this the cost of hiring an advertising agency, designing the advertising copy, etc. also need to be considered. The aggregate cost of all these tasks is then set as the proposed advertising budget. These figures may be accepted if they are within the financial resources of the company.

Thus, **the objective and task method involves the following steps:**

a. Task Definition – The objective of the advertising programme have to be defined in the first place. These might include creating awareness, arousing interest, strengthening comprehension etc.

b. Determining the type of strategy, media and the amount of exposure required for efficient satisfaction of the task set.

c. Estimating the cost of various elements of advertising that have been considered.

d. Deciding whether the firm can afford the budget taking into account the financial constraint and availability of funds.

Advantages:

1. The objective and task method is more objective and logical as compared to other methods as it is based on advertising objectives and the tasks to be accomplished to achieve the objectives.

2. The method takes into account the business conditions and also the competition in fixing up the advertising budget.

3. The method does not rely on past sales figures or projected sales figure. Thus, this method is suitable for new products when advertising must be developed more or less from scratch.

Disadvantages:

1. The method fails to provide a basis for prioritizing advertising objectives.
2. If the objectives are not well defined, all efforts would go waste.
3. It is difficult to ascertain the specific tasks required to achieve the objective and costs associated with a particular task. For instance, if the objective is to create awareness among 40 percent of the target consumers, then it is difficult to determine what specifically are those tasks which need to be performed to achieve this level of awareness and what are costs of performing these tasks.

Affordable Method Based on what the company can afford	**Percentage of Sales** Based on a certain percentage of current or past or forecasted sales
Competitive Parity Based on competitors' advertising budget	**Objective and Task** Based on determining objectives and tasks, then estimating costs

Figure 7.1: ***Advertising Budgeting Methods***

Figure 7.1 sums up the various advertising budgeting methods available to an advertiser.

ADVERTISING BUDGETING PROCESS

The aforesaid discussion concludes that the objective and task method is the most logical way of setting an advertising budget. Let us now see what all steps will be required in advertising budgeting process when an advertiser follows the objective and task method of setting advertising budget.

The advertising budgeting process involves the following steps.

1. *Setting Advertising Objectives:* The first step in the advertising budgeting process is to set advertising objectives. The most common advertising objectives include increasing the level of sales, increasing the market share, creating awareness about the product, disseminating information about product's features and its uses, building brand loyalty, etc. The advertising objectives should be laid down clearly, and as far as possible in quantitative terms, so that they can help the advertising manager in determining and allocating advertising budget.
2. *Determining the Tasks to be Performed to Achieve Advertising Objectives:* After identifying the advertising objectives, the next step is to determine the tasks and activities to be performed to achieve these objectives. These tasks may include selection of an advertising agency, selection of advertising media like television, radio, magazines etc., designing of advertising copy, deciding on the frequency and timing of ad, etc. All this requires a good knowledge of various activities of an effective advertising campaign.

3. *Preparing Advertising Budget:* After identifying various tasks and activities to be performed to achieve advertising objectives, the next step is to find out the cost of all such tasks and activities. The total cost of these tasks and activities is the amount required for advertising budget. However, to keep the budget flexible and to take care of the contingencies, some amount is set aside in the form of provision for contingencies, and added to the total cost of tasks and activities to fix the amount of advertising budget.

4. *Approval of the Top Management:* The amount of advertising budget determined is sent through the marketing manager to the top management for necessary approval. Sometimes the advertising budget is scrutinized by a budget committee before placing it before the top management. If the top management feels that the budget is justified, need-based and within affordable limits, then it will pass the budget.

5. *Allocation of Advertising Budget:* Once the top management has approved the advertising budget, the next step is to allocate it. Advertising budget is allocated on various product lines, product items, sales territories, etc. It specifies the amounts to be spent on media, advertising research, administrative expenses, etc. Advertising allocation depends upon company's policies, stage of product life cycle, company's promotional policies, competitor's policies, etc. While allocating the advertising budget to different activities/territories/products, the budget should have the flexibility to accommodate sudden changes in the market, competitor's strategies and changes in other components of the marketing environment.

Let us assume that the amount of advertising budget determined is Rs.50 lakh for a year. The advertising manager may allocate this amount as shown in Table 7.2

Table 7.2: *Example of Allocation of Advertising Budget*

Expenses	Budget (2007) (Rs.) (1)	Actual Expenditure (2007) (Rs.) (2)	New Budget (2008) (Rs.) (3)	% increase or decrease over earlier budget {(3)-(1)}/(1) x 100
Expenses on advertising media	20,00,000	22,00,000	30,00,000	+ 50 %
Expenses on advertising research	2,00,000	1,70,000	2,00,000	No Change
Expenses of preparing ad copy	10,00,000	9, 80,000	12,00,000	+ 20 %
Administrative expenses of advertising dept.	5,00,000	5,00,000	6,00,000	+ 20 %
TOTAL	**37,00,000**	**38,50,000**	**50,00,000**	**+ 35 %**

6. *Monitor and Control:* After allocation of advertising budget, it is essential to have an adequate monitoring and control over it. Monitoring means keeping a constant check over the actual expenditure. Controlling requires comparing the actual expenditure with planned expenditure and taking corrective action to have necessary control over the costs. Monitoring and controlling are required to reduce wastage in advertising expenses and to increase efficiency in various advertising activities.

DETERMINING THE OPTIMUM ADVERTISING BUDGET

The optimum level of advertising budget is determined with the help of marginal approach to advertising budget. According to the marginal approach, advertising budget is decided on the basis of marginal cost and marginal revenue of advertising. Marginal cost here refers to the increment/increase in advertising spending. Marginal revenue refers to the additional revenue generated at each level of advertising spending.

According to the marginal approach, a firm should increase its advertising spending if the marginal revenue (MR) is more than the marginal cost (MC). The optimum level of advertising spending would be determined at a level where marginal revenue (MR) equals marginal cost (MC). Any further increase in the advertising spending after the level at which MR = MC will be unprofitable. This approach of determining optimum advertising spending (optimum advertising budget) can be explained with the help of Table 7.3

Table 7.3: *Determining Optimum Advertising Spending*

Advertising Expenditure (Rs. Lakhs)	Marginal Cost of Advertising (Rs. Lakhs)	Total Additional Revenue (Rs. Lakhs)	Marginal Revenue (Rs. Lakhs)	Effect on Profit (Rs. Lakhs)
(1)	(2)	(3)	(4)	(5)=(3) – (1)
20	—	10	—	-10
25	5	14	4	-11
30	5	20	6	-10
35	5	30	10	-5
40	5	45	15	5
45	5	65	20	20
50	5	75	10	25
55	5	80	5	25
60	5	84	4	24
65	5	85	1	20
70	5	85	0	15
75	5	83	-2	8

In Table 7.3, incremental marginal cost is Rs.5 lakh at each level. In the initial stages, MR < MC and the total profit is negative. When advertising expenditure increases to Rs. 40 lakh, total profit becomes positive (as indicated in column 5). Thus, if the firm wants to make profits, it must spend at least Rs.40 lakh on advertising. Any advertising spending less than this amount will only result in losses as the profit figure is negative. Thus, Rs. 40 lakh is determined as the minimum level of advertising spending. Also, optimum level of advertising spending is determined at a level where MR = MC i.e. when the firm spends Rs.55 lakh on advertising. This is because, at this level, total profits are maximum (i.e. Rs.25 lakh as indicated in column 5). After this level, increase in advertising spending is not worthwhile as incremental revenues cannot achieve an increase in the profit figure. The firm should ideally fix Rs.55 lakhs as the advertising budget. It can also fix its advertising budget between the minimum level and the optimum level.

The marginal approach to advertising budget is also known as the incremental approach to advertising budget. The method is rational, simple and easy to understand. However, it must be remembered that it is not easy to estimate marginal revenue generated by incremental advertising spending. Also, this method is based on the assumption that only advertising affects the incremental revenue, whereas, the fact is that there are various other factors like product quality, brand image, packaging, product price, etc. which affect incremental revenue.

FACTORS INFLUENCING THE ADVERTISING BUDGET

The following factors should be kept in mind while setting the advertising budget.

1. *The advertising tasks to be achieved:* The advertising spending depends on the advertising task that a marketer is trying to achieve. For instance, a large amount of advertising spending will be required if the task is to create brand awareness and brand persuasion to generate trial purchase in case of a new brand. However, in case of established brands, where the consumers have already tried and tested the brand and are satisfied with it, only reminder advertising will suffice.
2. *Stage in the product life cycle:* The introductory phase of a product's life cycle requires heavy spending to create brand awareness and generate trial purchases. The growth phase also requires a high spending as it is the time to take advantage of the growing demand, to invest in and build market shares. In the maturity stage, with an existing consumer base, the advertising spending is likely to be relatively less.
3. *Market share:* High market-share brands usually require less advertising expenditure as a percentage of sales to maintain market share. On the other

hand, firms with low market-share, attempting to increase their market share require larger expenditures.

4. ***Competition:*** The heavier the competition in the market, the greater is the choice of brands available to the consumers. This often leads to not just more advertising but also to more cut-throat advertising, thereby requiring more advertising expenditure. The trend is very much evident in case of soft-drink industry. The huge advertising spending by the soft-drink giants - Coke and Pepsi, in areas of new ad films produced, signing film stars and cricketers as their celebrity endorsers, and high repetition of ads in various media in an attempt to compete with each other makes their advertising budget exorbitant.
5. ***Frequency of advertising:*** If frequency of product purchase is high, then repetitive advertising will be required. This will mean a larger advertising budget. This is especially true in case of FMCGs (Fast Moving Consumer Goods) like toothpastes, tea, detergents, soaps, etc. whose purchase frequency is very high. It is probably, because of this reason that Hindustan Lever has emerged as the top spender in advertising in the last few years with an exorbitant advertising budget.
6. ***Product differentiation:*** The more similar the product to the competitive products, the greater the need to invest in brand differentiation through advertising. Here, advertising aims at establishing brand superiority over other competing brands by highlighting the brand's unique selling proposition (USP) and other distinguishing features.
7. ***Support from retailers:*** The lesser the support from retailers, the greater is the need to advertise and to 'pull' the consumer to the brand. If the brand enjoys good 'push' by the retailers, then the burden on advertisers gets reduced to some extent.
8. ***Financial resources:*** The level of advertising must be adapted to the availability of funds. If more funds are available, the organisation can afford to have a large advertising budget. However, if financial resources are limited, the size of the advertising budget will be small.

CONCLUDING NOTE

Marketers and advertisers must remember that none of the above factors can be considered in isolation in setting the advertising budget of an organisation. It is a mix of the aforesaid factors along with the circumstances of the organisaton, its policies and the market conditions of the economy that will finally determine the level of advertising spending of the organisation.

QUESTIONS FOR DISCUSSION

1. What do you mean by advertising budget?
2. Do you agree that advertising budget is an investment made by a company?
3. What are the various methods of setting advertising budget?
4. Critically evaluate the percentage of sales method of setting advertising budget.
5. Describe the objective and task method of setting advertising budget.
6. Which is the most logical method of setting advertising budget?
7. What are the various steps involved in advertising budgeting process?
8. How will you determine the optimal advertising budget for your company?
9. What are the various factors influencing the advertising budget of a company?
10. Write short notes on:

    (a) Affordable Method of setting advertising budget

    (b) Competitive Parity Method of setting advertising budget

CHAPTER 8

Advertising Message Decisions

CONTENTS

The message is considered as the most vital component in advertising communication process. The message is the thought, idea, attitude, image or other information that the advertiser wishes to convey to the target audience. How an advertising message is presented is critically important in determining its effectiveness. An ideal message should command and draw attention, hold the interest, arouse desire for possession of the product, and elicit action.

Formulating the message will require solving four problems:

1. What to say? – Message Content
2. How to say it logically? – Message Structure
3. How to say it symbolically? – Message Format
4. Who should say it? – Message Source

MESSAGE CONTENT

The effectiveness of a message depends to a large extent on its content. **The advertiser must locate an appeal, theme, idea or unique selling proposition.** An advertising appeal refers to the approach used by an advertiser to attract the attention or interest of consumers and/or influence their feelings towards the product, service or cause. Through the use of different kinds of appeals, advertising attempts to communicate and influence the purchase and consumption behaviour of existing and potential customers. Some ads may be designed with an intent to appeal to the rational and logical aspect of the consumers' decision-making process and others might try to evoke some desired emotional response. Broadly, there are three types of advertising appeals – rational, emotional and moral.

Rational appeals in a message capture audience interest by claiming that the product will produce certain advantages. For example, messages demonstrating quality, economy, value or performance. Generally industrial buyers are the ones who respond the maximum to emotional appeals. They are knowledgeable about the product, trained to recognize value and are accountable to others for the choices they make. When consumers purchase expensive goods, they have a tendency to gather much information as they can beforehand for estimating the advantages. Rational appeals work well for such consumers.

Emotional appeals in a message attempt to stir up negative or positive emotions that will motivate an individual to go in for the purchase of the product. Marketers must search for the right emotional selling proposition. The product may have similarities to a competitive product, but its unique associations should be promoted. Advertisers may use positive emotional appeals like humour, love, pride and joy woven into their messages. Advertisers may also use negative appeals like fear, guilt and shame to get people to stop doing things like drinking, smoking, or taking drugs.

Moral appeals in messages are directed towards the audience's sense of what is right or wrong, good, proper, or correct thing to do. Moral appeals may be used for the purpose of exhorting people to support social causes and issues, for example, eye donation, helping the aged. The topic of 'Advertising Appeals' is discussed in detail in Chapter 10 of the book.

MESSAGE STRUCTURE

Besides the message content, the effectiveness of a message also depends on its structure. The important aspects of message structure are: Drawing conclusions, repetition, one-sided versus- two-sided arguments, and the order of presentation.

Drawing Conclusions

It is important for the advertisers to decide whether the message should allow the audience to draw their own conclusions about the product /service or the message should draw a definite conclusion for the audience.

Some of the early advertising experiments supported stating conclusions for the audience rather than allowing the audience to reach their own conclusions. However, such consumers feel that the message which draws a conclusion is an attempt at forcefully influencing their choice. Also, this may have negative reactions in the following situations.

a. If the communicator is seen as untrustworthy, the audience members might resent the attempt to influence them.

b. If the issue is simple or the audience is intelligent, the audience may be annoyed at the attempt to explain the obvious.

c. If the issue is highly personal, the audience might resent the communicator's attempt to draw conclusion.

Recent research supports ads asking questions from the viewers and allowing them to form their own conclusions.

The advertiser should follow the following thumb rule when faced with the question of whether to draw conclusions for the audience.

- Complexity of the issue (more complex issue – draw conclusion)
- Level of education possessed by the receiver (less educated – draw conclusion)
- Whether immediate action required (Urgent action – draw conclusion)
- Level of involvement (low involvement – draw conclusion)

For instance, a soft drink like Pepsi (a low involvement product), when says, *"Yahi hai right choice baby"*, is obviously drawing a conclusion for the consumers that this is the soft drink that they should drink.

Repetition

Repeating an ad message is often beneficial, for it develops a continuity of impression in the minds of the target audience, and may increase the predisposition to think and act favorably towards the products advertised. Everything else being equal, a repeated message increases awareness and knowledge on the part of the prospect. Audience retention improves with repetition, and falls off quickly when repetition is abandoned.

One-sided vs. Two-sided Advertisements

This section discusses whether the advertiser should only praise the product or should also mention some of its shortcomings. The most common approach in sales and advertising is a one-sided approach where the advertiser talks about the benefits of the product. However, there are situations where two-sided messages which mention the shortcomings of the product turn out to be more effective as compared to one-sided messages. Listerine had a two-sided message which worked well. It said that Listerine tastes bad twice a day. One Canadian

Cough Syrup advertised "Relief is just a yuck away". These are examples of how an advertiser can intelligently put across a two-sided argument.

Some research findings indicate that

1. One-sided messages tend to work best with the audiences that are initially favorably inclined to the claims made in the ad message. Two-sided arguments go well when audiences have an unfavorable opinion about the communicator's position.
2. Two-sided messages tend to be more effective with educated audiences capable of sound reasoning.
3. Two-sided messages tend to be more effective with audiences that are likely to be exposed to counter propaganda.

However, it is the single-side communication or one-sided messages that are commonly used, because it is difficult for the advertiser to refer to the product's shortcoming and still effectively persuade prospects to buy it.

Order of Presentation

Whether to put the strongest argument first or last in the advertiser's presentation is equally important. Sometimes this is considered a part of copywriting strategy. In a one-sided argument, it is advisable to present the strongest point first, for it will result in better attention and interest. This is especially important in newspaper advertising where the audience often does not attend to the whole message.

In case of a two-sided message, the issue is whether to present positive argument first or in the end. If the audience is initially opposed to the product, the advertiser might start with the negative argument first and conclude with the strongest argument.

Climax versus Anticlimax Order: When the strongest message arguments are presented at the end of the message, it is called *climax* order. But when the most important message points are presented at the beginning of the message, it is referred to as *anticlimax* order. The main message points when presented in the middle are called *pyramidal* order. Figure8.1 shows the climax order, anticlimax order and pyramidal order in the presentation of advertising message.

Based on research findings, the following guidelines can help in deciding the message order.

- When the audience is likely to have low involvement in a product category, an anticlimax order tends to be most effective.
- In case of audiences having high level of interest in the product category, a climax order tends to be most effective.
- The least effective order of presentation is believed to be the pyramidal order.

Figure 8.1: *Climax, Anticlimax and Pyramidal Order in Message Presentation*

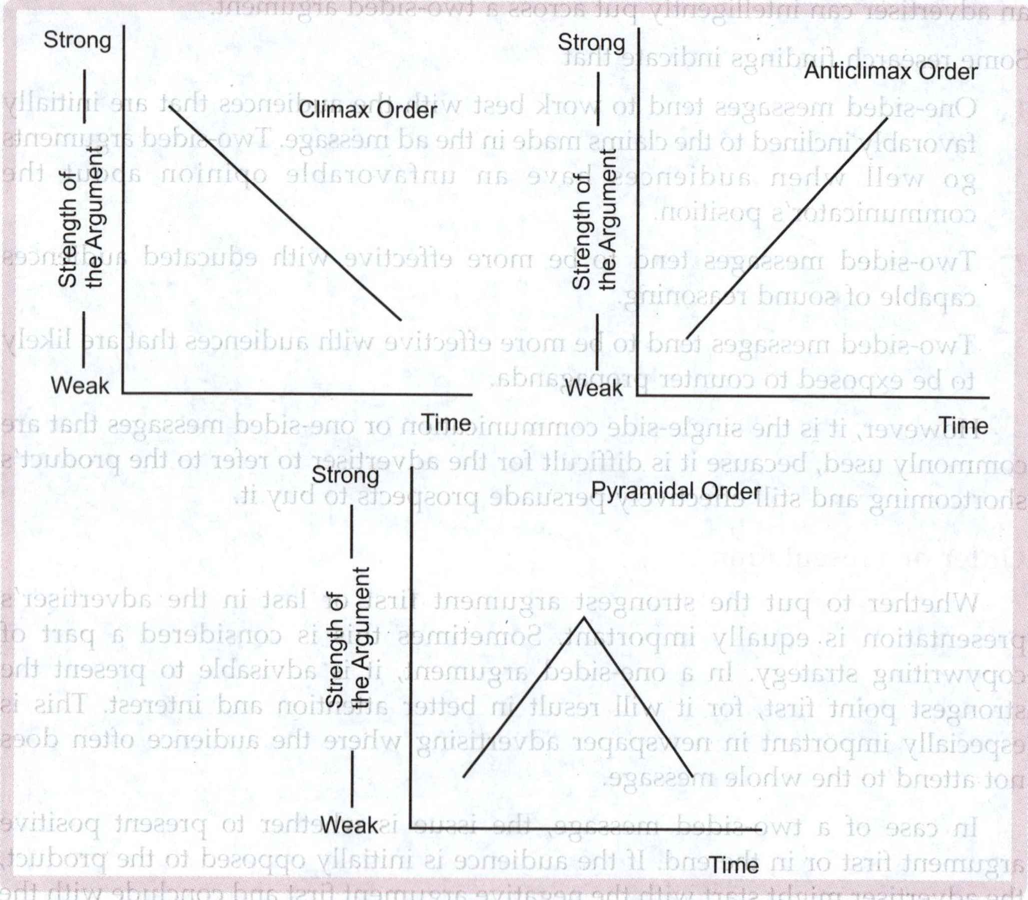

Primacy and Recency Effects: Primacy effect occurs when the information presented first in the message is most effective. Recency effect occurs when the last arguments presented are most persuasive. Most effective sales presentations and messages open and close with strong selling points and bury weaker arguments in the middle.

MESSAGE FORMAT

Decisions in this area involve deciding on the advertising copy, using illustrations and designing the layout of an ad. Advertising copy refers to the text of a print, radio, or television advertising message that aims at catching and holding the interest of the prospective buyer, and at persuading him or her to make a purchase. Illustrating is usually the work of an artist in case of television. Layout generally refers to the activity of deciding how various components of an ad are to be placed and positioned, specifically in case of a print ad.

Advertising brings concepts on a piece of paper to life in the minds of the target customer. In a print ad, the communicator has to decide on headline, copy, illustration and colour. For a radio message, the communicator has to choose words, voice quality and vocalizations. For instance, the sound of an announcer promoting an automobile (generally, male voice) has to be different from one promoting a new brand of moisturizing cream (generally, female voice). If the message is to be carried on television, all these elements plus body language (nonverbal clues) have to be planned. Presenters have to pay attention to facial expressions, gestures, dress, postures and hairstyles. Thus, in an ad promoting a new brand of detergent, a housewife using a different brand may be shown wearing a sari, sweating and washing clothes, her facial expressions are sad conveying that she is not happy with the brand that she is using. The ad may then show that on using the new brand of detergent (the brand being promoted), she is not sweating any more, looks more fresh, her facial expressions also change and she looks happy now. Thus, a lot can be communicated through these nonverbal cues.

Message format elements like ad size, colour, illustration and layout greatly affect a print ad's impact. A minor rearrangement of mechanical elements can improve attention-getting power. For instance, a larger ad in a newspaper might gain more attention. Attention should also be given to other message formatting elements. The picture (illustration) must be strong enough to draw attention. The headline must reinforce the picture and lead the person to read the copy.

Advertising copy, illustration and layout have a very important role in determining the success of an advertisement in drawing customer's attention. All three of these are essentially creative in nature. Chapter 9 of the book, 'Creative Side of Advertising', discusses in detail about these decisions.

MESSAGE SOURCE

Message source means the person involved directly or indirectly in communicating the advertising message. Companies take due care in selecting the message source. They are quite aware of the fact that source characteristics effect on the advertising message and thus, select individuals who will maximize the ad message influence on the audience. 'Source Credibility' and 'Source Attractiveness' are two important dimensions of message source.

Source Credibility

Source credibility means the extent to which the audience perceives the source as having relevant knowledge, expertise or experience and believes that the source will provide unbiased and objective information about the product or service. The element of credibility has two important dimensions – expertise and trustworthiness.

A person with more expertise in any field is considered more credible than the one with less expertise. For any reason if the audience thinks that a particular source, inspite of being knowledgeable, lacks honesty or may be biased, then the source would be less effective. A source that is portrayed as being similar to the audience in terms of background, social status, lifestyle, opinions, activities and attitudes could be liked and identified with. A source may be considered as high on one dimension of credibility (such as competence), but low on another. This might also have an impact on the effectiveness of the source in getting the desired response from the audience.

Expertise

Research findings show that expert and trustworthy endorsers are more persuasive than others who are considered less knowledgeable or trustworthy. A message coming from an expert influences beliefs, opinions, attitudes and behaviour because the audience believes that the information coming from such a source is accurate. For instance, a doctor may be considered as an expert in recommending a drug.

Trustworthiness

The consumers must also be convinced about the expert's trustworthiness. It often helps if trustworthy individuals say things that are not only favourable to the brand but also talk about some insignificant limitation of the product, as no product can be thought to be flawless.

Companies often use the following as message sources:

- Celebrity
- Expert
- Typical satisfied customer
- Announcer
- Company CEO

The selection of an appropriate spokesperson for a product or a service is an important, but a difficult decision.

Using a *celebrity* has the advantage of publicity and attention-getting power, regardless of the product type. Large segments of the audience can instantly recognize and identify with the famous celebrity and the attraction and goodwill associated with the celebrity can be transferred to the product. Local celebrities or actors or actresses who are not so well known can often be used in local or regional markets.

On the negative side, celebrities are not usually considered experts. It is not advisable to use celebrities for high-involvement products, especially when the consumers are looking for an expert advice or credible information. However, celebrities can also be experts in some situations. For instance, Sachin Tendulkar is not just a celebrity but also an expert in selecting sports shoes, and hence, the association with Adidas.

Furthermore, celebrities not only cost a lot but are hard to get as endorsers are usually contractually prohibited from endorsing similar or competing products. If some event happens to reduce the popularity of celebrity with the public, the publicity could backfire on the associated brand as well. For instance, when Ajay

Jadeja was allegedly involved in match fixing charges, Pepsi's ad featuring Jadeja was withdrawn. The advantages and limitations of using celebrities as endorsers are explained in detail in Chapter 11 of the book.

An ***expert*** is likely to be the best choice when the product is technical or consumers need to be reassured that the product is worth buying especially in case of high-involvement products. An expert can dispel fears in the audience concerning the product whether those fears arise from not knowing how something works, concern about side effects, health-related concerns about product-use or concern about fulfilling a role such as father, mother, housewife, and so on. Doctors, lawyers, engineers, and other kinds of experts can be chosen and at considerably less cost than a celebrity. For instance, a doctor recommending Colgate and announcing that Colgate has been approved by the Indian Dental Association puts to rest many fears and reinforces the belief of consumers in Colgate toothpaste.

A ***typical satisfied consumer*** is often the best choice when it can be anticipated that there will be strong audience identification with the role involved, the person is similar to many members of the target audience, and attributes of sincerity and trustworthiness are likely to come through. For instance, VLCC uses a typical satisfied customer for its weight-loss programme and, Harpic and Vim bar use a typical housewife to explain how these products can be helpful to a housewife. In 1980s, *Lalitaji* became a household name when she urged every Indian woman to trust only Surf with *"Surf ki kharidari me hi samajhdari hai"*.

Radio advertising uses an ***announcer*** spokesperson as the essential source component. The creativity uses in preparing the ad copy, the props used, and the announcer's special ability to bring about persuasive impact can make a radio ad successful.

Companies may sometimes also use *Company CEO* as the spokesperson. For instance, Anil Ambani seen in the ad of Reliance. A CEO may be used as the spokesperson when some important message is to be communicated, like enhancing the belief in the company (for instance, after the coke pesticide issue), or how a company has grown over a period of time (Reliance ad- *"Ek soch thi, ek sapna tha"*).

Research shows that the effectiveness of an endorser is related to the type of product being endorsed. In general, when the purchase is based more strongly on a brand's awareness and/or likability, like in many low involvement purchase decisions, a celebrity endorser is likely to be appropriate. A celebrity endorser may also be very useful when the consumers aspire to the lifestyle of that celebrity endorser. Aishwarya Rai's Lo'real campaign "...because I'm worth it" is an example here. In contrast, experts are likely to be more appropriate for more rational and highly involved purchase decisions. For instance, an expert fund-rating group is more effective in recommending a mutual fund as compared to a celebrity.

Source Attractiveness

Attractiveness of a source refers to similarity, familiarity and likeability. Similarity is an assumed resemblance between the source and the members of the audience. Familiarity means that customers have knowledge of the source through exposure. Likeability is the affection developed for the message source as a result of physical appearance (for instance, film stars like Katrina Kaif) and behavioural aspects (for instance, cricketers like Sachin Tendulkar who are a pride of the country).

Advertisers often use physically attractive people in their ads to attract attention. Attractiveness generates positive influence and can lead to favouable evaluations of product as well as ad. The relevance and suitability of the message source depends on the nature of the product. For instance, a celebrity like Aishwarya Rai is suitable for endorsing a beauty soap like 'Lux'. However, even an attractive celebrity like Shahrukh Khan might not be suited to endorse a 'Quit Smoking' campaign.

Celebrities like film stars and cricketers are popular message sources because of their attractiveness and likeability. The marketers use celebrities to endorse their products because of many other reasons too. At the same time, celebrity endorsements have their own disadvantages.

CONCLUDING NOTE

No matter how big the advertising budget is, advertising can succeed only if the ads gain attention and communicate well. The purpose of advertising is to get the consumers to think about or react to the product or a message in a certain way. The creative concept guides the choice of specific appeals, advertising copy, illustrations, layout and message source to be used in an advertising campaign. All these message elements along with ad repetition and order of presentation of arguments work together to gain target customer's attention and to get the message across to him.

QUESTIONS FOR DISCUSSION

1. What are the various message decisions that an advertiser has to take?
2. What precautions should be kept in mind as far as drawing conclusions (about the product advertised) for the target audience is concerned?
3. Distinguish between one-sided and two-sided messages.
4. Discuss the meanings of climax order, anticlimax order and pyramidal order in context of the order of presentation of arguments in an advertisement.
5. How do various qualities of a message source influence the target audience? Explain with examples.
6. What type of an endorser will you use for the following products?

   (a) Detergent Powder (b) Toothpaste

   (c) Beauty Soap (d) Health Drinks

CHAPTER 9

Creative Side of Advertising

CONTENTS

Advertising is an art and hence, it is creative. Creative advertising needs to be imaginative, intelligent, sharp, to the point and extremely catchy. Creativity should focus the attention of the people on the product. The message and appeal made should be able to make positive impact on the consumers. Creative strategy is used in conceiving, writing, designing and producing advertising messages.

Copywriting, illustrating and layout are different activities associated with the creative stage of advertising development. *Copywriting* in print is the activity of putting words to paper, particularly those contained in the main body of the text (the main arguments and appeals used), headlines and sub-heads. In broadcast, the copywriter is a script writer who develops the scenario or script to be used in radio or television medium. Writing a jingle, that is, the lyrics for music may also be involved. *Illustrating* is usually the work of an artist in case of television. *Layout* generally refers to the activity of deciding how various components of an ad are to be placed and positioned.

COPYWRITING

Copywriting is the art of writing selling messages. It is salesmanship in print. If it fails to provoke the desired attention, interest, desire and action, it has failed. Copywriting is likely to be assisted by other forms of creativity such as pictures, typography and perhaps, colour. The copywriter should think visually and direct these other elements to achieve his or her purpose.

The copywriter should work closely with the visualiser and typographer to obtain artistic and typographical interpretation of his or her copy. The copywriter cannot successfully work in isolation, merely writing the words, with artists working in similar isolation to create the physical appearance of the advertisement. Ideally, the complete advertisement should be a team effort. The design and layout should give effective presentation of the words, the illustrations should give emphasis and support, and the typography (choice of typefaces, and their size and weight) should make the copy legible and give emphasis where necessary. The copywriter should always try to write with the final appearance of the advertisement in mind.

ADVERTISING COPY AND ITS ELEMENTS

Advertising copy refers to the text of a print, radio, or television advertising message that aims at catching and holding the interest of the prospective buyer, and at persuading him or her to make a purchase. The major elements of copy are discussed below. All of them may not be necessary for most advertisements.

1. The Headline

The first and possibly the most important copy element is the headline. The headline of an advertisement will normally present a selling idea or will otherwise help to involve the prospect in reading of the advertisement. Most advertisements have headlines of one sort or the other and their primary function is to catch the eye of the reader. Experts have suggested various things to make headlines effective and capable of attracting the audience. For instance, use of contrasting colours, leaving a lot of blank space in a newspaper ad, etc.

David Ogilvy considers the headline as the most important element in most advertisements. He says that five times as many people read the headline as those who read the body copy. The headline in the print ad of State Bank of India (SBI) shown here gives the complete message to the reader as to why he should prefer SBI.

2. The Sub-head

Sometimes important facts have to be conveyed to the reader and it may require more space than what should be used for a headline. Such information can be put in smaller font size than the headline and is known as sub-head.

3. The Body Copy

The body copy refers to the text in the advertisement which contains details regarding the functions/benefits/features of the product/service. The body copy can be short or long depending on how much there is to say about the product.

4. Captions

Captions are small units of text used with illustrations, coupons and special offers. These are generally less important than the main selling points of the advertisement (set out in the body copy) and are usually set in font sizes smaller than the body copy.

5. Blurb

A blurb or a balloon is an arrangement where the words appear to be coming from the mouth of one of the characters illustrated in the advertisement.

6. Boxes and Panels

Boxes and panels are the captions placed in special display positions so as to get greater attention. It is a caption which is lined on all the sides and singled out from the rest of the copy.

7. Slogans and Logo Types (Signature)

A slogan may refer to the basic theme, or USP (unique selling proposition) of the product, or something with which the target audience would relate the product to. For instance, *Thanda Matlab Coca-Cola* for Coke, Nokia – Connecting People, etc.

A logo type is the symbol of the company, its seal or trademark, which is also referred to as signature. It is an important tool in quick recognition and identification of the company and for creating familiarity for the audience. Figure 9.1 shows the various elements of a print ad of Sunfeast Marie Light Oats.

Figure 9.1: *Elements of Print Ad of Sunfeast Marie Light Oats*

REQUIREMENTS OF AN EFFECTIVE COPY

A good copy must comply with the following guidelines.

1. It must be precise.
2. It must aim to sell.
3. It must be sincere.
4. It must be designed keeping in view the type of audience.
5. It must stimulate interest.
6. It must create desire.
7. It must create confidence.
8. It must influence the reader's thoughts/actions.

David Ogilvy points out some factors which can go into the making of an effective copy.

1. He strongly recommends the use of testimonials in the copy, especially from celebrities, to have a favourable impact.
2. The readers should be given helpful advice. Such copies are more popular than the ones that deal entirely with the product.
3. Another point which Ogilvy stresses is the use of such language in the copy with which the audience is familiar.
4. Every advertisement should be a complete sales pitch for the product because it is unrealistic to assume that the audience will follow a series of advertisements for the same product.

Ogilvy also warns against the temptation to entertain or to produce award winning campaigns as they might not meet advertising objectives.

TYPES OF ADVERTISING COPIES

The various types of advertising copies are discussed below.

1. *Scientific copy:* In this type of copy, technical specifications are specified. It is used in case of high involvement goods, durable goods and industrial goods. For instance, newspaper ads which talk about specifications of a laptop.
2. *Descriptive copy:* In a non-technical manner, the product attributes are described. The copy uses direct sentences. It looks very commonplace announcement. For instance, Cinthol talks about the lime freshness in its ads.
3. *Narrative copy:* Here a fictional story is narrated. The benefits of the product emerge from the story. Maybe, the narrative is humorous. Or else, it has strong appeal. It should make an imprint on the memory of the audience. For instance, the *"Daag achche hain"* campaign by Surf Excel.
4. *Colloquial copy:* Here informal conversational language is used to convey the message. It could even become a dialogue. Amul Chocolates-a gift for someone you love-follow a colloquial pattern. The woman says, "I am too old for mini-skirts, too young to be a grandma". And the man says, 'But I think you're just right for Amul Chocolates'.
5. *Humorous copy:* Humour has been heavily used in advertising, especially in TV commercials. For instance, Fevicol ads have been using humour to put across the message.
6. *Topical copy:* Such a copy is integrated to a recent happening or event. For instance, during the world cup days, Britannia's ad campaign – *'Britannia Khao, World Cup Jao'* and, during IPL, Idea's *'Ungli cricket'*.
7. *Endorsement copy:* Here a product is endorsed by an endorser – celebrity, or an expert or even a typical satisfied customer. Shahrukh Khan endorsing for Dish TV is an example.
8. *Questioning Copy:* In this copy, several questions are put forward not to seek answers but to emphasize a certain attribute. Such questions can be asked in a humourous tone or a serious tone depending on the product being advertised. For instance, Close-up used a questioning copy in asking *"Kya aap Close-up karte hain? Yah duniya se darte hain? Aap Close-up Kyon nahin karte hain?"*
9. *Prestige Copy:* Here the copy is used to build an image for the product. A distinguished and favourable atmosphere is created for the sale of the product.
10. *"Reason Why" Copy:* It is known as an explanatory copy where the reasons for a purchase are explained. Each reason illustrates a particular attribute, and its benefit to the consumer. One attribute may be chosen and repeated several times, each time an occasion is given to justify it. For instance, Santro used the 'total number of Santro buyers' figure to promote its product while Maruti emphasized on the 'service availability almost anywhere'.

11. ***Comparative copy:*** Here two brands are compared either in good light or in a way to belittle the other. The cola war can be an excellent example of this type.
12. ***Disruptive copy:*** This copy comes about when there is a disruption in the way of thinking or conventional thinking. A subtle form of such copy is the HDFC Standard Life ad where a girl buys a car for her father and the father says, *"beti badi ho gayi aur car bhi"*.

PRINT COPY PRINCIPLES

For print ads, one of the key elements is the headline, which must attract the attention of the reader and pull him down into the body copy.

John Caples has suggested the following rules for writing a good ***headline***.

1. Try to get self-interest into every headline, that is, suggest to the reader that here is something he wants.
2. If you have news, such as a new product or a new use for an old product, be sure to get that news into your headline in a big way.
3. Avoid headlines which are mere curiosity headlines. Curiosity combined with news or self-interest is an excellent way to pull the target audience. However, curiosity by itself is not enough.
4. Avoid headlines which paint the gloomy or negative side of the picture. Take the cheerful positive angle.
5. Try to suggest in your headline that here is a quick and easy way for the reader to get something he wants.

Since most people reading print ads never go beyond the headline, it is also extremely important that the headline and pictures complement each other so well and tell the story so easily that a reader who looks on headlines and pictures can get the message without having to read a word of the body copy.

As for the ***body copy***, the following points have been suggested.

1. Make it interesting: Interest should be captured with the first sentence or lead-in paragraph.
2. Make it specific: The specific word, phrase, or sentence communicates a much sharper image than does a general one.
3. Keep it simple: Simple language communicates best. Do not overwrite.
4. Make it concise: Get to the point quickly.
5. Make it believable: Believability and conviction are key goals of advertising communication.
6. Use language that sparkles: Avoid clichés and use language that is meaningful to the reader. Use dynamic words and concise adjectives.
7. Provide a surprise: Copy that is overly predictable tends to be dull. Inject something that will keep and hold the reader's attention.

RADIO COPY PRINCIPLES

1. For radio ads, a key principle is usually to write a copy that creates a picture in the minds of the listeners.
2. The radio ad must pull the listener in from whatever is being done into an imagined situation, through the use of human voice, sound effects, humour and music.
3. It is also important in radio advertising to mention the brand name and key selling benefit early and often.
4. Short words and short sentences are usually easier to understand in radio advertising.

TELEVISION COPY PRINCIPLES

1. Television scripts must be written to take advantage of the visual nature of the medium, by using demonstrations, close-up of the product and packages, etc.
2. Television ads get higher recall scores if they contain more frequent visual representation of the brand name, package and the key product attributes.
3. Television ads also get higher persuasion scores if the shots in the ads are more connected and better linked to each other.
4. If the message is to be carried on television then the communicator has to carefully choose words, voice qualities (speech – rate, rhythm, pitch, etc.), vocalizations (pauses, sighs, etc.).
5. Presenters also have to pay attention to the facial expressions, gestures, dress, postures, hair styles, etc. For instance, a model in an ad for Dettol soap, is seen wearing green and white clothes, the colour associated with the package of the brand.

TYPES OF TELEVISION COMMERCIALS

The advertiser has to turn the big idea into an actual ad execution that will capture the target market's attention and interest. Audio and visual elements can be combined to produce several types of television commercials, just as a story can be told in many different ways. Emphasis can be placed on the story itself, on the problem to be solved, or on special human emotions or storytelling techniques such as humour, fantasy, and so on. The creative people must find the best style, tone, words, and format for executing the message. Any message can be presented in different execution styles, such as the following.

- ***Slice of life:*** This style shows one or more "typical" people using the product in a normal setting. For instance, a family seated at the dinning table might be shown trying a new brand of soup.
- ***Lifestyle:*** This style shows how a product fits in with a particular lifestyle. For example, advertisements of Reid and Taylor suitings depict dressing for the elite class.
- ***Fantasy:*** This style creates a fantasy around the product or its use. For instance, many ads are built around dream themes. The ads of Axe deodorants are such ads where the guy who uses Axe deodorant is shown surrounded by girls.
- ***Mood or image:*** This style builds a mood or image around the product, such as beauty, love, or serenity. No claim is made about the product except through suggestion. Advertisements of products like Lux soap endorsed by popular film stars like Aishwarya Rai and Abhishek Bachchan build an image of beauty and love around the product.
- ***Demonstration:*** This style is designed to illustrate the key advantages of the product by showing it in actual use in advertisements. An advertisement of a fairness cream might use the demonstration style in showing how a girl having dark complexion becomes fair in 4 weeks by using the said cream.
- ***Musical:*** This style shows one or more people or cartoon characters singing about the product or the use of a product. For example, Airtel's ad where the college students are shown singing *"Jaise chai ke liye toast hota hai, vaise har ek friend zaroori hota hai"*, followed by VO "Airtel, *dil jo chahe pass laye*".
- ***Personality symbol:*** This style creates a character that represents the product. For instance, Fido-Dido of 7-up, the Amul girl and Vodafone's Zoo Zoos. Thus, the Fido-Dido of 7-up in an ad with actress Mallika Sherawat conveys that the bottle of 7-up now has a new shape.
- ***Technical expertise:*** This style shows the company's expertise in making the product. After the Coke pesticide issue, we saw ads demonstrating the expertise that Coke has, trying to ensure the consumers that much care is taken to ensure that the customers are delivered the best, and that there are no pesticides present in it.

- *Scientific evidence:* This style presents survey or scientific evidence that the brand is better or better liked than one or more other brands. For instance, Indian Dental Association certifying Colgate toothpaste.
- *Testimonial evidence or endorsement:* This style features a highly believable or likable source endorsing the product. Many companies use actors or sports celebrities as product endorsers. For instance, Sachin Tendulkar endorsing Adidas.
- *Patriotic:* This style uses a patriotic theme in the advertisements. For instance, Bajaj's *"Buland bharat ki buland tasveer, hamara Bajaj, hamara Bajaj"*. Even *"mile sur mera tumhara, toh sur bane hamara"* uses the patriotic theme to bind the people of the nation together.

JINGLES

A jingle is a memorable slogan, set to an engaging melody, mainly broadcast on radio and on television commercials. An effective jingle is constructed to stay in one's memory. The best jingles could stick with a consumer for their entire life. Creative people are able to weave the brand name of the product in the jingle so nicely that the consumer automatically remembers the brand name as he sings the jingle or gets reminded of one. How many of us can forget "*Vicks ki goli lo, khich khich door karo*" or "*Lifebuoy hai jahan, tandurusti hai wahan*". A well-crafted tune can do the wonders of people remembering the product and the jingle for many years.

Ad jingles are very challenging to create. The challenge is that you don't have the time for an elaborate musical piece. It has to be short and yet powerful.

Exhibit 9.1: Some Memorable Jingles of Indian Advertisements

Lifebuoy: *Tandurusti ki raksha karta hai Lifebuoy, Lifebuoy hai jahan, tandurusti hai wahan, Lifebuoy.*

Nirma: *Washing powder Nirma, washing powder Nirma, doodh si safedi, Nirma se aaye, rangeen kapda bhi khil khil jaye, sabki pasand Nirma.*

Vicks: *Gale mein khich khich gale gale mein... um kya karoon, Vicks ki goli lo khich khich door karo.*

Close-up: *Kya aap Close-up karte hain, ya duniya se darte hain, aap Close-up kyun nahin karte hain.*

Hutch: *You and I in this beautiful world, green grass blue sky in this beautiful world.*

Zandu Balm: *Zandu balm, Zandu balm peera hari balm, sardi sardard peera ko pal mein door kare, Zandu balm, Zandu balm.*

Nerolac: *Jab ghar ki raunak badani ho, deewaro ko jab sajana ho, Nerolac, Nerolac, rango ki duniya mein aao, rangeen sapne sajao, Nerolac, Nerolac.*

Bajaj: *Buland bharat ki buland tasveer, hamara Bajaj, humara Bajaj.*

Jingles appeal to the masses so much, because they directly hit the basic emotional as well as practical needs. They are simple but subtle, real but touching, you don't have to pay attention, because they are there, even if you do not like them to be there. You ignore the jingles, but they will find a way out, to haunt you, because they are designed to follow you wherever you go. They do control our minds, not just like that! The makers of jingles go through audience research and many rigorous tests. So the ad-effect is inevitable. Exhibit 9.1 shows some memorable jingles of Indian advertisements.

ILLUSTRATING

Illustrating means the use of pictures and photographs including visual contents, colours, art work and identification marks (company logo, trademark, etc.). Such decisions are a crucial part of print advertising.

Illustrations are usually the most important visual element in any print advertisement. Illustrations work to enhance the headline and body copy. They contribute to their effectiveness in one or more of the following ways:

(a) They attract the attention of the desired target audience.

(b) They communicate a relevant idea quickly and effectively – often one that is difficult or complicated to convey verbally.

(c) They interest the headlines in the headline and copy.

(d) They help make the advertisement believable.

The activity of illustrating is of crucial importance for many consumer non-durable products where pictures and photographs are used to convey a central idea, and there is little or no need for long explanations or a recitation of copy points. Normally, an artist will be involved in selecting materials or will actually draw original pictures for the advertising.

Creative professionals make specific decisions as to what will and will not be included in an illustration. At times, illustration can be found in more than one category. The following points highlight the ***different ways a product or service can be depicted in an illustration.***

1. ***Part of the product:*** Sometimes, the appeal rests with a particular part of the product, rather than the whole. In such a case, a particular feature may be emphasized by close-up illustration or photography.
2. ***Product ready for use:*** An illustration in a setting ready for use can make the product make alive. Kitchen appliances are usually placed in a setting ready for use.
3. ***The product being tested:*** At times, illustrations show the tests a product undergoes before it is sold. This is particularly applicable to business-to-business sale of products.
4. ***Differentiating features of the product:*** Many brands have a unique or differentiating feature that can be visualized. For instance, the ruggedness

and durability of an automobile may be depicted by showing the automobile being driven through on rocky roads.

5. ***Product itself:*** In many instances, such as appearance, style, or to help identify the product at the store, a picture is necessary. Generally, product pictures are rated highly in readership tests. The print ad of Nano car shown here uses the illustration of the product itself. The headline conveys that the smallest of cars can fit the entire family without a squeeze and the body copy talks about the various features of the car – tall seating position improves visibility, entry and exit, small turning radius of just 4 metres, powered by all new z-cylinder, 624 cc aluminium MPFI petrol engine, 4 speed gearbox, etc.

6. ***Product in use:*** In many cases, showing use illustrates benefits. For instance, a Lakme ad showing the model wearing Lakme lipstick and other products shows the product in use.

7. ***Consumer reward from using the product:*** Although every product ad shall offer a reward, some rewards are more visual than others. For instance, before and after illustrations of weight loss programme of VLCC.
8. ***Effect of not using the product:*** The illustration can also be used to illustrate the results of not using the product. Usually the results are negative, such as, the problem of grey hair that would otherwise not be visible if the product (hair oil, hair colour or hair dye) is used.

Figure 9.2: ***Illustration of a print ad of Colgate Toothpaste***

Artwork is equally important, if not more important than writing the copy, where the goals of advertising are attention getting or building awareness. Thus, in addition to writing the copy, pictorial materials should be developed that are tied into the self-interest and understanding of the audience, "tell a story" at a glance, are relevant to the product and copy theme, and accurate and believable in the context of the selling message. Another popular rule is to include pictures of at least a part of the product or the entire product. Illustrating also involves decisions as to what "identification marks" (company or trade name, brand mark, trade mark) to include.

In any case, the illustration should be such that the message is effectively put across to the audience. Figure 9.2 shows illustration used in the print ad of Colgate toothpaste. Figure 9.3 shows illustration of a print ad carrying a social message.

Figure 9.3: ***Illustration of a print ad carrying a social message***

Research studies have shown that:

1. Attribute information is recalled better when it is presented both in words as well as picture(s).

2. More imagery is created if the picture makes it easier for the consumer to imagine himself or herself in engaging in that behaviour.
3. The effects of pictures or brand attitudes seem to increase if they contain product relevant information especially for high involvement products.

In any case, pictures, headlines and body copy should be interrelated and should work together to communicate a unified message.

LAYOUT

A layout is a mock-up, or model, in the form of a sketch, drawing, or painting of what the proposed ad might look like. Physically, the layout is the plan that indicates where the component parts of the ad (headline, subheads, illustrations, and body copy) are to be placed for most effective communication. Thus, layout involves decisions as to how the various components of headline, body copy, illustrations, and other elements of a print ad are to be arranged and positioned on the page. The artist can experiment with alternative arrangements until he or she arrives at the most promising one.

The layout guides the copywriter in planning copy and the lettering specialists, typographers, and other production experts in their works. The layout also provides a guide for estimating costs.

Preparing the layout

Layout artists often work within certain space limitations. In newspapers and magazines, they are limited to certain standard sizes and shapes, typefaces, and so on. In designing outdoor ads like billboards, they are limited by standard billboard sizes.

The artist can do a better job of visualizing the ad if the copywriter has already done some visual thinking. Both should work toward the same basic goal: expressing the message idea in the most effective form. Most artists begin by making several thumbnail sketches, or miniature rough sketches, of possible layouts. Ordinarily, these rough sketches are one-eighth to one-fourth the size of the final product. A thumbnail sketch offers artist an opportunity to try out a variety of ideas. The *rough layout* will be the exact size of the final advertisement. Many artists make numerous roughs, other artists only a few. Some layouts are sent to the printer or to newspapers in very rough form, depending on how much service the media provide. In a rough layout, headlines are often hastily lettered in and body text indicated only in pencil. The layouts in more final shape can be used to help all concerned to visualize which of several alternatives provide the greatest promise of success. When a selection has been made among alternative roughs, the *finished layout* is composed. The artist may complete this layout or may instruct a commercial studio to do it. The illustration, lettering, and the logotype will be drawn the way they are to appear in the final advertisement. The text will be indicated by lines neatly written in blocks of varying lengths to stimulate paragraphs. A finished layout, then, is almost a facsimile of the finished advertisement. When the finished product is carried one step further, the ***comprehensive layout*** is the result. If, for example, the illustration is to be a painting or a drawing, the artist will probably be asked to make the final illustration for the comprehensive. The type will be set and proof of it pasted on the layout.

The basic **principles of preparing layout** which can be applied to advertisements are:

1. ***Law of Unity:*** All parts of a layout should unite to make a whole. This unity can be disturbed by an irritating border, too many different and conflicting typefaces, badly disturbed colour, disproportionate elements, or 'busy' layouts containing a confusion of parts. Thus, care should be taken to avoid all these mistakes.
2. ***Law of Variety:*** Law of unity is a basic principle of designing a layout. Nonetheless, there should be change and contrast as with bold and medium weight of type, or good use of white space. The advertisement should not be monotonous, and grey masses of small print need to be enlivened by subheadings. Variety can also be used with the help of pictures.
3. ***Law of Balance:*** It is essential that an advertisement should be well balanced. The *optical* balance is one-third down a space, not half-way. A picture or headline may occupy one-third and the text copy two-thirds, to achieve an optical balance. The *symmetrical* balance falls mid-way so that a design can be divided into equal halves, quarters and so on, but care should be taken not to divide an advertisement into halves which look like separate advertisements.
4. ***Law of Rhythm:*** Even though a printed advertisement is static, it is still possible to obtain a sense of movement so that the eye is carried down and through the advertisement. A simple device is to indent paragraphs of text (as in a book or newspaper report) so that the eye is led from paragraph to paragraph. But the general flow of the overall design should be pleasantly rhythmic.
5. ***Law of Harmony:*** There should be no sharp, annoying and jerky contrasts, unless perhaps there is a deliberate intention as in some kinds of direct response ads which use shock tactics. Normally, all the elements should harmonize, helping to create unity.
6. ***Law of Proportion:*** This applies particularly to the type sizes used for different widths of copy. The wider the column, the larger the type size and vice versa. A narrow advertisement needs small text type, but a wide advertisement needs larger text type. Wider columns and larger type also need larger size of the heading.
7. ***Law of Scale:*** Visibility depends on the scale of tones and colours, some appearing to recede, others appearing to advance. Pale pastel colours recede white bold, primary colours advance. Black looks closer to the eye than grey, and red is the most dominant colour. Black on either yellow or orange is very bold whereas, white on yellow is weak. The law of scale can be used with

typographical design when headlines and subheadings are made to contrast with grey areas of text type. Where colours are concerned, this principle can be applied whenever full colour is used in press advertisements, TV commercials, posters and packaging.

8. *Law of Emphasis:* The rule here is that 'all emphasis is no emphasis', which occurs if too much bold type is used, or there are too many capital letters. A sentence in upper and lower case lettering reads more easily than one wholly in capital letters. Yet emphasis is essential, and this links up with the other laws of variety and scale. An advertisement can be made to look interesting if there is emphasis such as bold type or if certain words are emphasized in a second colour. White space can also be an effective way of creating emphasis. Every inch of space does not have to be filled with words just because it has been paid for. Another form of contrast is to reverse white on black, a method often used with logotypes and name-plates. Reverse colour should not be overdone for it tends to reduce legibility. A bad mistake is to print a lot of text in white on a black or coloured background.

In addition to the above principles, the following *guidelines* are helpful in designing an effective layout.

1. The headline usually occupies about 10 to 15 percent of the total area. Headlines are usually placed below the illustration and above the copy.
2. Ideally, the picture should occupy slightly more than one-half of the entire space. The total area of all illustrations combined should occupy that amount of space.
3. Unless the name of the product is prominently displayed in the headline or shown in the illustration, the logotype should be emphasized and put in a prominent setting.
4. Borders are useful to keep readers from wandering away from the ad especially in newspaper advertisements.
5. Typographical consistency reassures readers that they are looking at one ad, not several.

CONCLUDING NOTE

The creative process involves the translation of a marketing proposition into verbal and visual devices that will communicate the essence of that proposition in ways that are attention getting and persuasive. Working in teams, copywriters and art directors try to come up with creative ideas that set their advertising apart from the clutter. Such idea generation is an extremely challenging task and the best ideas are those which meet the objectives and are very distinctive in execution.

QUESTIONS FOR DISCUSSION

1. What do mean by advertising copy? Explain the various elements of an advertising copy.

2. What is the purpose of a headline? How can headlines be made more effective?
3. What are the requirements of an effective advertising copy?
4. What are the various types of advertising copies? Give examples of each.
5. Discuss some print copy principles that an advertiser should keep in mind.
6. What points should an advertiser keep in mind while deciding about advertising copy for a radio ad and a television ad?
7. What are the various execution styles in case of a television ad? Explain with examples how an advertiser can effective use these styles in putting across his message to his target audience.
8. What do you mean by jingles? What purpose do they serve?
9. What is the meaning of illustrating? What are the various ways in which a product or service can be depicted in an illustration?
10. What is the meaning of layout in case of a print ad? What principles of preparing layout should an advertiser keep in mind while designing a print ad?
11. What makes an advertisement pull the attention of the target audience, and make them read the copy?
12. You are asked to prepare an advertising copy for a cell phone service provider to be inserted in the newspaper. Explain the points you will consider in preparing such a copy.
13. You are asked to prepare an advertising copy for a brand of shampoo to be inserted in a magazine. Explain the points you will consider in preparing such a copy.
14. Take any two print ads and identify its various elements (headline, body copy, etc.)

CHAPTER 10

ADVERTISING APPEALS

CONTENTS

One of the most critical decisions about creative strategy in advertising involves the choice of an appropriate appeal. Creating advertising appeal for a good or service begins with identifying a reason for people to buy it. Advertising agencies then build an advertising campaign around this appeal. The advertising agencies use different tricks and types of advertising appeals that influences the mind of people targeted in a particular group.

MEANING AND FEATURES OF AN ADVERTISING APPEAL

An *advertising appeal* refers to the approach used by an advertiser to attract the attention or interest of consumers and/or influence their feelings towards the product, service or cause. Through the use of different kinds of appeals, advertising attempts to communicate and influence the purchase and consumption behaviour of existing and potential customers. Some ads may be designed with the objective to appeal to the rational and logical aspect of the consumers' decision-making process and others might try to evoke some desired emotional response. A vast amount of time, money and energy goes into the creative work of developing advertising appeals to influence the buying behavior of consumers. Developing advertising appeals is a challenging task. It is typically the responsibility of the creative people in the advertising agency.

Box 10.1 discusses some features of advertising appeals.

Box 10.1: Features of Advertising Appeals

- Advertising appeals refer to the approach used to attract the attention of consumers.
- The purpose is to influence consumer feelings towards the product, service or cause.
- Advertising appeals attempt to influence the behaviour of consumers.
- They motivate the consumers to purchase the product.
- It is a challenging task.
- It is the responsibility of the creative people in the advertising agency.

TYPES OF ADVERTISING APPEALS

Advertising Appeals can broadly be classified into three categories – Rational, Emotional and Moral. Figure 10.1 shows a broad classification of advertising appeals used by the advertisers.

Figure 10.1: Types of Advertising Appeals

Retional Appeals

- Economy
- Convenience
- Quality
- Health
- Performance
- Efficiency
- Durability

Emotional Appeals

- Positive Emotional Appeals – Humour, Pride, Love, Joy
- Negative Emotional Appeals – Fear, Guilt, Shame, Anxiety

Moral Appeals

RATIONAL APPEALS

Rational appeals are those directed at the thinking process of the audience. They appeal to the audiences' self-interest. Rational appeals emphasize on the benefits of the product like quality, economy, convenience, comfort, health, performance, efficiency, durability and dependability. They attempt to show that the product would yield the claimed benefits.

Let us now discuss some examples of rational appeals.

Advertisements of Aquaguard and Aquafina highlight the "purity of water" aspect, giving consumers a rational reason to buy the products.

Advertisements of products like television, refrigerators, automobiles, music systems, washing machines and other consumable durables highlight the quality and features of their products. They may also emphasize on the brand's popularity and special offers which again are rational reasons for a consumer to buy the product.

Products like Women's Horlicks, Complan and Calcium Sandoz focus on the health and nutrition aspect in their advertisements.

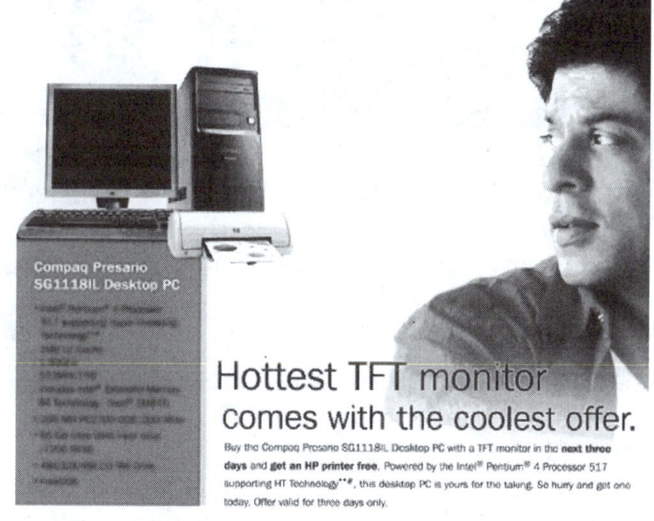

Advertisements of Lifebuoy and Pepsodent emphasize on protection from germs and cavities to sell their products.

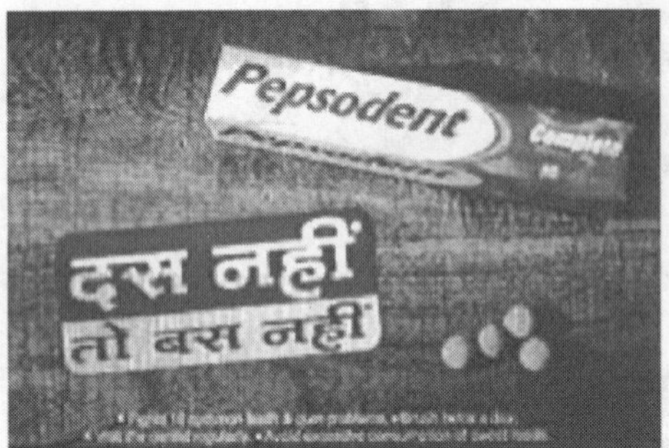

The advertisement of McDonalds which says "McDonald's *ka* Happy Price Menu Rs 20 only" emphasizes the economy aspect, thereby giving consumers a rational reason to buy the product.

Industrial buyers are most responsive to rational appeals. They make purchase decisions based on the technical specification of the product, product quality, features, performance etc. Most industrial buyers are knowledgeable about the product class and are responsible to others about their choice. Thus, industrial buying decisions are generally based on sound rational grounds. Consumer durables of high value are also often bought on the basis of rational appeals. Such consumer purchase decisions are also based on information about different brands available, a comparison amongst them and a rational choice made on the basis of product's quality, economy, convenience, comfort, health, performance, efficiency, durability or dependability.

EMOTIONAL APPEALS

Emotional appeals attempt to use negative or positive emotions that will motivate purchase. Emotions are those mental agitations or excited states of feeling which prompt us to make a purchase. Emotional motives may be below the level of consciousness, and may not be recognized by a person; or even if he is fully aware that such a motive is operating, he is unwilling to admit it to others because he feels that it would be unacceptable as a proper reason for buying among his associates and colleagues. Emotional appeals, unlike rational appeals, are not preceded by careful analysis of the pros and cons of making a buying.

An emotional appeal is related to an individual's psychological and social needs for purchasing certain products and services. Many consumers are emotionally motivated or driven to make certain purchases. Advertisers aim to cash in on the emotional appeal and this works particularly well where there is not much difference between multiple product brands and its offerings. Emotional appeal includes personal and social aspects.

Personal Appeal

Some personal emotions that can drive individuals to purchase products include safety, fear, love, humor, joy, happiness, sentiment, stimulation, pride, self esteem, pleasure, comfort, ambition, nostalgia etc.

Social Appeal

Social factors cause people to make purchases and include such aspects as recognition, respect, involvement, affiliation, rejection, acceptance, status and approval.

Emotional appeals can be studied under two broad categories – Positive Emotional Appeals and Negative Emotional Appeals.

POSITIVE EMOTIONAL APPEALS

Advertisers use positive emotional appeals such as humour, love, pride and joy to influence the behaviour of consumers. Humour appeals work best for low involvement and feeling-oriented products.

Most baby food products use a mother's love appeal. For instance, the advertisement of Johnson's baby products shows a mother's love for her baby and the tender care that a Johnson's baby product will provide just as a mother does.

The love appeal is also used by the advertisers during some special occasions like the Valentine's Day, Mother's Day, Father's Day etc. The print ad of Canon shown here uses the love appeal to promote its product on Valentine's Day.

Advertisers also use messages communicating the joy and thrill associated with using the product. The ad of Frooti with the jingle "Mango Frooti, Fresh and Juicy" is an example here. The same holds true for advertisements of soft drinks. For instance, in March, 2011, Coca-Cola India unveiled the *'Brrrrr'* campaign, the globally successful campaign for brand Coca-Cola. The communication is based on a spontaneous *Brrrrr* expression, an incomprehensible and spontaneous feeling of upliftment one derives after sipping an icy cold Coca-Cola. Other positive emotional appeals involving pride and prestige are also used by advertisers. For instance, Reid and Taylor suiting's "Bond with the Best" conveys the pride associated with the product.

Humour Appeals: Humour is one of the most common advertising appeals used by the advertisers. Humour appeals evoke the feelings of amusement and pleasure and thus help in-

a. Attracting attention
b. Improving memory of the brand name
c. Creating a good mood
d. Distracting the audience from counter arguing.

With the advertising clutter increasing and the audience being exposed to innumerable ads in a day, it becomes difficult to attract their attention. An ad which does not catch audience's attention cannot be expected to achieve its results. Humourous ads, by attracting the attention of the audience, make the job of the advertiser much easier. Humourous ads can be created by using an interesting and entertaining storyline. Humour is also reflected in the jingles, the satire and the puns used in the ads.

Fevicol ads have used humour to create ads that can convey the message to the audience in a very light and humourous way. The punch line *"Fevicol aisa jod lagaye, achche se achcha na tod paye"* is very interestingly conveyed in all its advertisements. For instance, one ad which shows a bus overloaded with people and none of them are falling apart. It rightly portrays *"Fevicol ka jod hai tutega nahi"*. Also look at exhibit 10.1 which shows how a Fevicol ad conveys its message in a humourous way. Mentos is yet another brand which uses humour in its advertisements. Consider Exhibit 10.2 which shows the use of humour by this brand in its ads.

Exhibit 10.1: Fevicol Ads Use Humour Appeal to Convey the Message

Pidilite has an amazing number of funny and creative ads for Fevicol, which is no doubt their flagship brand. Creativity is the art of good agency and Ogilv has always given Fevicol out of the box memorable moments. In fact, that's the reason why all Fevicol ads have not only been outstanding, but have also always clearly established the brand. The ads have used humour appeal in conveying the message *"Fevicol ka jod hai tutega nahi"*.

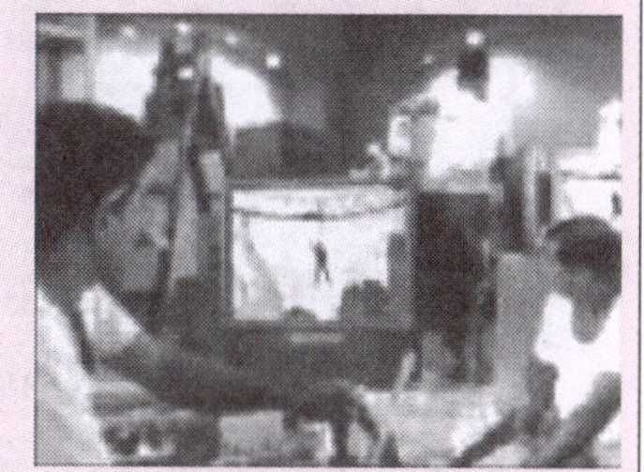

In one of the ads, a group of carpenters are at work. However, their attention is divided between their work and a TV set, where a man hanging over a chasm is clinging on to a woman for dear life. *"Pakde rehna"*, the woman screams. *"Chodna nahin"*, the man pleads. The workers watch as the couple on the screen keep up the *"Pakde rehna-chodna nahin"* strain for an incredibly long period. Fed up with the melodrama, one of the carpenters gets up in disgust. *"Arre, yeh bhi koi* film *hai!"* he exclaims. Wanting to continue with his work, he walks over to the TV and picks up a can of Fevicol placed on top of it. Instantly, the man on screen falls. Surprised, the carpenter peers at the can of Fevicol he has picked up. Slowly, he turns and eyes another TV, at the top of which a tub of Fevicol is perched. The man on screen is still dangling over the chasm. *"Chodna nahin..."*

Another ad which is in tune with the above ad; the carpenters are in the ad. One of them is busy scrambling eggs, while listening to the radio. He stumbles up on an egg which refuses to crack. The voice-over on the radio goes *"Dum lagakar ... haisha! Zor laga kar... haisha!"*. Inspired, the man decides that brute force is the only way he is going to get that egg to crack. He tries to hit it with a hammer. Much to his amazement, it slips from his hand, hits a pot, causes a hole in it and the water pours out! Surprised, he checks on the hen that laid the eggs; only to see that it was feeding from an old Fevicol box! And the voice-over simultaneously says, *"lagta hai yeh Fevicol ka kaamal hai.... tootega nahi!"*

Fevicol came up with *'Moochwaali'* ad to celebrate 50 years of the adhesive brand's bond with the ordinary Indian. This time Ogilvy & Mather developed an ad wherein a small girl is shown with moustaches while doing a stage play and it was stuck on her face with the help of a little dab of Fevicol. She is shown in various stages of her life - as a newly married bride, an eager mother, a middle aged woman, one nearing old age and the last, finally, on her death bed, all the while, sporting the moustache. Moustache remains on her upper lip throughout her life until she dies and then takes rebirth with moustaches. The message, of course, is that what is stuck with Fevicol remains so for life, and thereafter. The ad closes with the tag line, *'50 Saal Se Champion'*.

Exhibit 10.2: Use of Humour Appeal in Mentos Ad

A teacher is busy taking his class when a student enters the classroom. Expressing disapproval he scolds the latecomer, "*Ab aa rahe ho*? Get out!" VO: *Yeh hai aam zindagi*. Cut to the shot of the boy arriving late again for the class. Being smarter this time he enters the class taking back steps. Mistaking him for leaving the class the teacher says "*Kahan jaa rahe ho*? Sit down!" Having his way the clever boy takes his seat. VO: *Yeh hai* Mentos *zindagi*. Mentos. *Dimag ki batti jala de*.

The jingles used in the advertisements may themselves be quite effective in creating humour and attracting the attention of the audience. For instance, Close-Up toothpaste's jingle, *"Kya aap Close-Up karte hain"* is quite entertaining. Such jingles are also quite effective as far as brand recalls are concerned.

While humour can help the advertisers in getting attention and securing brand recall, it can also hurt the effectiveness of an ad. This can happen when humour overshadows the product or the brand. For instance, one may remember the lines, *"Wah Sunil babu, naya ghar, nayi car, Badiya Hai"*, but one might get a little confused as to whether the brand advertised was Asian Paints or Nerolac. Yet another problem in using humour in advertisements is that what strikes one person as humourous, another might consider it silly and irritating. Also, the probability of humour to irritate will increase with repetition. Nonetheless, researches have proved that humourous ads have higher recalls.

NEGATIVE EMOTIONAL APPEALS

An advertiser can work with negative appeals such as fear, guilt, shame etc. to get the desired response/behaviour from the target audience. Use of such appeals can get people to do things that they should do (for instance, brush their teeth regularly) or to stop doing things they should not (for instance, Quit Smoking).

Fear Appeals: One of the most important emotional appeals used by the advertisers is the fear appeal. Fear appeals are mostly used in those cases or those products that are designed to protect a person from loss of life or property or undermining of health. Advertisements issued in public interest for the use of seat belts while driving, against smoking, prevention of aids, and drug abuse have all focused on the fear of loosing one's life.

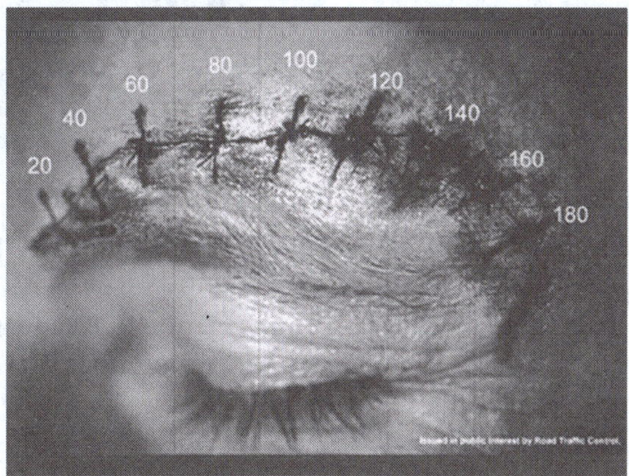

An advertisement pic shown here urges people to drive safely. The ad is issued in public interest by Road Traffic Control. Another print ad shown here carries a message that chewing tobacco causes mouth cancer and tries to use fear by showing a garlanded photograph of a dead person whose face can't be seen as he died of mouth cancer which was caused by chewing of tobacco.

Many insurance ads in the past have used the fear appeal to make the audience realize that they too need insurance. For instance, one of the advertisements of United India Insurance Policy shows a house burning in flames in a fire and says, "If you think you don't need insurance, think again!! You Need United India Fire Insurance Policy." By arousing such a fear, the ad tries to get the desired behaviour from the audience, that is, purchase of a United India Fire Insurance Policy. However, these days most of the insurance ads are using a positive emotional appeal to get the message across to the audience. For instance, ICICI's insurance ad with the tagline *"Jeetay Raho"* uses a positive emotional appeal instead of a negative one.

The use of fear appeal can also be seen in some products which might cause some concern related to health of a person. Consider Exhibit 10.3 which shows an advertisement of Saffola Gold. The advertisement shows how a wife is worried about the unhealthy state of her husband. The ad then talks about how Saffola

Gold oil helps in reducing the cholesterol level, soaks less oil while cooking and takes care of the heart. The ad uses the fear appeal to show that one must switch over to Saffola oil if one has to take care of the growing cholesterol level and prevent heart diseases.

Exhibit 10.3: Advertisement of Saffola Gold Uses Fear and Anxiety

Growing thoughtful, a lady thinks of a day her husband played cricket. Jingle: *"Dil mein Sehwag ke khwaab hai. Par saans deti jawab hai."* Husband slowly grows breathless as he tries to take his runs. He was forced to stop midway. Jingle: *"Na fit lage yeh janab hai, abhi to yeh jawan hain."* Next shot he is checking out his increasing paunch. Jingle: *"Ishtyle bhi bemisal hai, bekabu pait ka haal hai. Bas kuch kilo ka sawaal hai, abhi to yeh jawaan hai."* The wife rubs her hubby's expanding tummy. The hubby tries to woo his wife, when his cell rings and interrupts them. Jingle: *"Dil mein bhara romance hai. Na chain ka koyi chance hai. Tension bhi full advance hai. Abhi to yeh jawaan hai."* The wife worries for her stressed husband. MVO: *"Yehi ishare hain ki ab inka dil jawaan nahin raha."* MVO: *"Saffola Gold apnaye. Yeh cholesterol ghaatane mein madat kare, aur khaane mein kam tail sauke, taki unka dil bhi kahe.."* Jingle: *"Abhi to yeh jawaan hai."*

Some of the ad messages of toothpastes employ a subtle fear appeal. They present the fear of tooth decay or unhealthy gums or bad breath, and then suggest the use of a specific brand of toothpaste to get rid of such fears.

There are also more subtle fears associated with social and psychological motivations of the people. These include the fear of loss of friends, status or job, rejection, or a sense of failure to be a good parent or homemaker. Such fears, in turn, lead to the feeling of shame, guilt and embarrassment. For instance, there are ads which say that if you do not use a particular brand of deodorant, you will smell bad and you might lose your friends. The advertisement of Lizol floor cleaner shows that if you have not disinfected the floor with Lizol, you don't have protection from germs. When your baby crawls on the floor, he might catch some infection from the germs. Thus, the ad arises the guilt feeling of not being a good homemaker if you haven't used Lizol.

Similarly, in an ad of Godrej hair dye, a kid tells his mother that he doesn't want his father to come to the school as he feels embarrassed when the teacher addresses his father as "uncle" because of his grey hair. This is not just a feeling of embarrassment for the kid but for the father as well. By using such negative emotions, the ad tries to move the target audience towards the use of this product.

In advertisements of many fairness products, it is shown that a girl or a boy is rejected because of dark complexion. Such ads use the fear of rejection and use an emotional route to sell their products.

Read Exhibit 10.4 to see how the fear factor has been used in Indian advertising.

Exhibit 10.4: The use of 'Fear' Factor in Indian Advertising

Indian advertising uses fear in three ways.

Raise anxiety: This is the most popular form addressing mainly the woman, mother and wife, and her "care-giving" persona. The active concern for her near and dear ones gives advertising an opportunity to raise her anxiety levels towards unseen but existent enemies. So, Pepsodent is about *'dishum dishum'* against germs caused by food; Dettol and Lifebouy is about 'dirt' germs that can cause disease and Saffola is about today's stressful life in general that makes her husband susceptible to "lifestyle" diseases at an early age.

The anxieties may not necessarily be disease-related - Complan is based on a mother's normal concern of "is my child growing right". Interestingly, anxiety is raised either explicitly as in the case of Pepsodent and Dettol; or a little more implicitly as in Complan.

Demonstrate Danger: This is less frequently used because of the Indian cultural resistance to talk about death and illness openly and because marketing theory often states that you should sell benefits (positive stories) with brands rather than highlight fears. There is a hypothesis that people tune off negative emotions and visuals - and are unaccepting of dangers. Yet, when you want to break inertia, fear helps to be most dramatic. It just forces the viewer to notice and listen. Saffola did it very successfully in the early 90s with its visual of a husband being wheeled into an operation theatre with the background sounds of an ambulance siren. However, the fear of rejection for a dark girl has been a story for 'Fair and Lovely' cream and it has been considered by the society as advertising in bad taste.

A variation is about demonstrating danger "light-heartedly" - the way Anchor shock proof switches have done over the years. When the fear is known, it works; else it ends being taken up casually.

Arousing tension: This is perhaps the most difficult to do in advertising. One of the ads showed a woman leaving the gas stove on and then captured the visuals of people, ignorant of this, trying to light a fire in the house for different reasons. Tension builds as to when the house could explode.

Adapted from: "Indian advertising uses the 'fear' factor, www.rediff.com, February, 2008

Research studies have proved that for the preferred reaction to occur, fear needs to be at the right level. If the level of fear in the ad is too low, the emotional response will not be forthcoming. Therefore, a selection of the appropriate fear level is important. It should be strong enough to heighten the drive of the people to buy a particular product. On the other hand, if the level of fear is too high, people may exhibit a defensive behaviour, may try to avoid the advertisement, or may not accept the threat. They may even take the view that the solution recommended in the ad may be inadequate to deal with so great a fear.

An advertisement based on fear appeal needs three elements to elicit the desired response from the audience. It must convince the audience that

1. the depicted threat is very likely,
2. that it will have severe consequences,
3. that the advocated behavioural change will lead to removal of the threat.

For instance, an ad by Cancer Patients Aid Association shows that cigarette smoking may lead to cancer which might result in death, and that quitting smoking can remove this threat.

One of the ways of making fear or anxiety ads more effective is to depict as the object of threat not the person seeing the ad but instead some family member or friend close to the ad viewer. An ad for an education policy taken for a child, or an ad for a floor cleaner to provide your child with a germ free environment are appropriate examples here.

It is also said that fear appeal is most effective when source credibility is high. Thus, the pulse polio campaign, which warns people about the threat of polio to their kids if they do not get them the dosage in time, uses celebrities like Amitabh Bachchan and Shahrukh Khan for sending the message across to the people.

An advertiser may try to induce a particular behavioral change by emphasizing either positive or negative appeals, or a combination of both. Positive appeals use the strategy of reducing a person's anxiety about buying and using a product, while negative appeals use the strategy of increasing a person's anxiety about not using a product or service. In general, a positive appeal stresses the positive gains to a person from complying with the persuasive message; the negative appeal stresses his loss if he fails to comply. David Ogilvy, the guru of advertising said that it is better for advertising to sell hope rather than fear; highlight the solution rather than the problem; create amazement rather than shock.

MORAL APPEALS

Moral appeals are those appeals to the audience that appeal to their sense of right and wrong. They are often used to exhort people to support social causes, such as cleaner environment, adult literacy, equal rights for women, consumer protection, and aid to the disadvantaged.

The print ad of Agewell Foundation shown here has a headline "Since when did a useless piece of furniture have eyes that light up at the first kind word?". It ends with the baseline "Let's add life to their years". Similarly, TVCs of Help Age India invoke a moral responsibility where we ought to take care of the disadvantaged older people.

In the same league is the "Save the Girl Child" campaign which insists that it is our moral duty to stop female feticide and to save the girl child.

SEX APPEALS IN ADVERTISING

Sex and nudity have always sold well. Sexuality, sexual suggestiveness, over sexuality or sensuality raises curiosity of the audience and can result in strong feelings about the advertisement. It can also result in the product appearing interesting.

Sex appeals are being increasingly used in advertising to grab the attention of the audience. The use of sex appeals is justified in case of products like condoms and undergarments. But advertisers are increasing using sex appeal in case of many other products also. These products are mainly personal care products like cosmetics, deodorants, perfumes etc. For instance, consider Exhibit 10.5 which shows the use of sex appeal in an ad of Axe deodorant. However, there are advertisers who use the sex appeal even in case of those products where they are not needed at all. For instance, the much criticized ad of Tuff Shoes featuring Milind Soman and Madhu Sapre used sex appeal to sell shoes!!!

Exhibit 10.5: Use of Sex Appeal in an ad of Axe Deodorant

Three stunningly sensuous women talk about their men. "My guy is wicked", reveals the first. The second stunner, lets in on her secret, "My man is intense." "My man's rough", the third seductively croons about her man. "A tiger, teddy bear, party animal" is how they describe their men. But the men turn out to be one man enjoying the attention of the three gorgeous women. Voice Over: "For the men with many dimensions. The Axe dimension dome party. Buy Axe...Get to the dome."

The advertisers probably feel that sex is an easy way to attract the target audience. But is the sex appeal really effective in selling the product?

Research has shown that men remember the sexy illustration and forget the brand. Also, people who are favourably inclined towards sex, have higher brand recalls of brands that use sex appeals in their ads, while negatively inclined people to sex have a lower recall. Also, inappropriate sex appeals have lowest recall. Appeals that are consistent with the product, lead to a higher recall. There might also be gender-related responses to sex appeal. Females may find the sexual ad offensive and so if used for a feminine product, sex appeal may not work. For instance, a lipstick ad showing a female model that is seductive may grab the attention of the male-audience rather than the targeted female audience.

The use of sex in types of advertising appeals can have a boomerang effect if it is not used carefully. It can interfere with the actual message of the advertisement and purpose of the product and can also cause low brand recall. If this is used then it should be an integral part of the product and should not seem vulgar. The shift should be towards sensuality.

Sex appeals are interpreted differently from time to time, region to region, person to person, country to country, and society to society. Even the same person reacts to them differently at different stages of his life cycle.

SOME OTHER ADVERTISING APPEALS

Given below is a list of some other advertising appeals used by the marketers.

1. Music Appeal

Music can be used as a type of advertising appeal as it has a certain intrinsic value and can help in increasing the persuasiveness of the advertisement. It can also help capture attention and increase customer recall. The recent ad of Airtel with the jingle *"Hare ek friend zaroori hota hai"* uses music and tries to establish a positive emotional connect with its target audience, i.e. the youngsters, urging them to stay connected with their friends using Airtel and its services.

2. Scarcity Appeal

Scarcity appeals are based on limited supplies or limited time period for purchase of products and are often used while employing promotional tools including sweepstakes, contests etc.

3. Masculine/Feminine Appeal

Used in cosmetic or beauty products and also clothing. This type of appeal aims at creating the impression of the perfect person. The message is that the product will infuse the perfection or the stated qualities of muscularity or femininity in you.

4. Brand Appeal

This appeal is directed towards people who are brand conscious and wish to choose particular products to make a brand statement.

5. Snob Appeal

This appeal is directed towards creating feeling of desire or envy for products that are termed top of the line or that have considerable qualities of luxury, elegance associated with them.

6. Adventure Appeal

This appeal is directed towards giving the impression that purchasing a product will change the individual's life radically and fill it with fun, adventure and action.

7. Less than Perfect Appeal

Advertisements often try to influence people to make certain purchases by pointing out their inadequacies or making them feel less perfect and more dissatisfied with their present condition. These types of advertising appeals are used in cosmetic and health industries.

8. Romance Appeal

These advertisements display the attraction between the sexes. The appeal is used to signify that buying certain products will have a positive impact on the opposite sex and improve your romantic or love life. Fragrances, automobiles and other products use these types of advertising appeals.

9. Emotional Words/Sensitivity Appeal

These advertisements are used to drive at and influence the sensitivities of consumers.

10. Youth Appeal

Advertisements that reflect youth giving aspects or ingredients of products use these types of appeals. Cosmetic products in particular make use of these appeals.

11. Endorsement

Celebrities and well known personalities often endorse certain products and their pitching can help drive the sales.

12. Statistics

Advertisements also use statistics and figures to display aspects of the product and its popularity in particular.

13. Bandwagon Appeal

This type of advertising appeal is meant to signify that since everybody is doing something you should be a part of the crowd as well. It appeals towards the popularity aspect or coolness aspect of a person using a particular product or service.

ESSENTIALS OF AN ADVERTISING APPEAL

Given below are some essentials of an advertising appeal.

1. It should be interesting enough to hold the audience's attention.
2. It must be rightly used in conjunction with the product being advertised.
3. It must be believable. It should not make extravagant claims.
4. It must be exclusive or unique. Consumers must be able to distinguish the advertiser's message from the competitor's message.
5. It must contain truthful information. An ad that tries to deceive results in a bad reputation for the advertiser.

CONCLUDING NOTE

Advertising appeals can be rational, emotional or moral depending on the nature of the product, quality of the product, human needs and motives, the message to be conveyed and the advertising objectives to be met. The choice of appeals in advertising is an art and it requires a creative mind. Advertisers must try to strike the right link between their product and the appeal to get the desired behavioural response from the target audience.

QUESTIONS FOR DISCUSSION

1. What do you mean by an advertising appeal? Discuss the characteristics of advertising appeals?
2. What are the various kinds of advertising appeals used by an advertiser? Give examples of each.
3. What do you mean by rational appeals? Explain with examples the use of rational appeals in Indian advertisements.
4. What are the various kinds of emotional appeals used by an advertiser?
5. Write a short note on humour appeals in advertising. Why are humour appeals so popular with the advertisers?
6. Evaluate 'fear' as an advertising appeal.

7. What are the differences between rational and emotional advertising appeals? Which of the two should be preferred? Why?
8. Write short notes on:
   (a) Moral Appeals in advertising
   (b) Sex Appeals in advertising
9. What points should an advertiser keep in mind while deciding about the appeal to be used in advertisements?
10. Name five products which can be advertised using rational appeal.
11. Name five products which can be advertised using emotional appeals.
12. Identify the type of appeal used in the following advertisements.
    (a) *"Kya aap close-up karte hain" (Close Up)*
    (b) *"Aise hare ek friend zaroori hota hai"* (Airtel)
    (c) Save the girl child
    (d) *"Daag achche hain"* (Surf Excel)
13. Suggest an advertising appeal for the following.
    (a) Sports Shoes
    (b) Shampoo
    (c) Luxury Car
    (d) Fairness Cream
    (e) Television
    (f) Charity Organisation

Case Study

Use of Emotional Appeal

CADBURY DIARY MILK'S 'SHUBH AARAMBH' CAMPAIGN

About Cadbury

Cadbury, since 1948 is a leading global confectionery company with an outstanding product range of chocolates, gums and candy brands. With over 50,000 people employed, they have district operations in 60 countries and sell sweets around the globe. Cadbury enjoys a value market share of over 70% (as in March, 2011) and they are poised in a leap towards quantum growth.

Cadbury Dairy Milk has been the market leader in the chocolate category for years. It has participated and been a part of every Indian's moments of happiness, joy and celebration. Today, Cadbury Dairy Milk alone holds 30% value share of the Indian chocolate market.

Advertising Campaigns of Cadbury Diary Milk

In the early 90's, chocolates were seen as 'meant for kids', usually a reward or a bribe for children. In the mid 90's the category was re-defined by the very popular 'Real Taste of Life' campaign, shifting the focus from 'just for kids' to the 'kid in all of us'. It appealed to the child in every adult. Cadbury Dairy Milk became the perfect expression of 'spontaneity' and 'shared good feelings'.

The 'Real Taste of Life' campaign had many memorable executions, which people still fondly remember. However, the one with the "girl dancing on the cricket field" has remained etched in everyone's memory, as the most spontaneous & un-inhibited expression of happiness. This campaign went on to be awarded 'The Campaign of the Century', in India at the Abby (Ad Club, Mumbai) awards.

In the late 90's, to further expand the category, the focus shifted towards widening chocolate consumption amongst the masses, through the *'Khanewalon Ko Khane Ka Bahana Chahiye'* campaign. This campaign built social acceptance for chocolate consumption amongst adults, by showcasing collective and shared moments.

The *'Kuch Meetha Ho Jaaye'* campaign associated Cadbury Dairy Milk with celebratory occasions and the phrase *"Pappu Pass Ho Gaya"* became a part of street language. It has been adopted by consumers and today is used extensively to express joy in a moment of achievement and success.

The interactive campaign for *"Pappu Pass Ho Gaya"* bagged a Bronze Lion at the prestigious Cannes Advertising Festival 2006 for 'Best use of internet and new media'. The idea involved a tie-up with Reliance India Mobile service and allowed students to check their exam results using their mobile service and encouraged those who passed their examinations to celebrate with Cadbury Dairy Milk. The *"Pappu Pass Ho Gaya"* campaign also went on to win Silver for 'The Best Integrated Marketing Campaign' and Gold in the Consumer Products category at the Effies 2006 (global benchmark for effective advertising campaigns) awards.

Use of Emotions in Cadbury's Advertising

Cadbury has always come up with innovation and pleasing advertisements connecting chocolates to happiness. It has been successful in reaching the masses and capturing the consumers by maintaining quality, price and standards.

Cadbury ruled the 1990s in terms of TVCs and, as already said, many still recollect the 'Cadbury girl' dancing on the cricket field in delight after breaking the barricades to celebrate her boyfriend's century. This was not the only emotion that creative people at O&M portrayed. In order to change the whole concept of chocolate being a pampering agent for children to chocolate being "the real taste of life", the taste of happiness and a reflection of all the euphoric emotions in life, it portrayed moments that are so simple, yet, at the same time, they were so unique to Indian sensibilities and emotions.

There has been a constant drive behind Cadbury's advertisements – to include more Indian consumers in the target group. Resonating jingles like *"Kuch meetha ho jaye"*, *"Khush hai zamana aaj pehli tareekh hain"* and the *"Shubh Aarambh"* campaigns have made Cadbury so integral to the Indian culture, customs, emotions and sensibilities that one hardly remembers its British lineage or the fact that the company is now a part of the US-based Kraft Foods. Even though many are jostling for the chocolate space in India, Cadbury has firmly cemented its position as number one purely because of its emotional connect.

The Campaign *'Shubh Aarambh'*

In 2010, Cadbury came up with the *'Shubh Aarambh'* campaign which means an auspicious start. In the ***first TVC launched under the campaign,*** a boy sees a girl eating a Dairy Milk at a bus stop and asks her for a bite. The girl refuses saying that she doesn't know the boy. The boy continues saying that his mother has told him to have something sweet before starting any auspicious work. The girl gives in, gives him a piece and asks him what work he was about to start. The boy replies that he was planning to drop her home.

Shot in Pondicherry, the Bus Stop TVC was the first of the Shubh Aarambh campaign. This *'Shubh Aarambh'* TVC is targeted to the youth who have come of age but still have Indian values in their heart. Cadbury here is looking to exploit the tradition of India where people distribute and eat something sweet before starting any work or before any occasion of importance. It is also trying to portray itself as a substitute for the sweets we distribute among relatives and friends on festivals.

Overall, the concept and the execution of the advertisement were brilliant. Cadbury has always pulled the emotional and not the intellectual strings, to drive sales. *'Shubh Aarambh'* was driven by an effort to refresh the take on *'Kuch Meetha Ho Jaye'*. Specifically, there was a shift from the notion of celebrating happy occasions with chocolate to the concept of anticipating the occurrence of something good after consuming the chocolate.

The media mix for this campaign included television, radio, digital, outdoor and print. The campaign also included significant point of purchase (POP) activities. The creative duties for the campaign lied with Ogilvy India (advertising agency). The creative brief was to deliver the culture of sweet consumption - that leads to auspicious beginnings - in a manner that is not traditional.

The ***second commercial under the umbrella of the "Shubh Aarambh" campaign*** was set in a middle class housing society. The TVC opened with a couple stepping out of their house. But all of a sudden, the wife hid behind the door. The husband looked at her in astonishment, to which the nervous wife replied that she cannot step out wearing jeans, as she was worried about the neighbours and her mother-in-law as to what they would say. The husband offered her a cube of Cadbury Dairy Milk and told her that his mother would say, *"Shubh kaam karne se pehle meetha khalo, kaam acha hoga"*. The wife took a bite of the cube and reluctantly smiled at him. The husband then pointed towards the exit and she timidly stepped out with him. Just then, a young neighbour noticed her and said *"Arre Waah! Jeans!"* The commercial ended with the woman receiving the compliment with some degree of confidence and pride. The VO then stated, *"Shubh Aarambh. Kuch Meetha Ho Jaye."*

On the selection of situations for this campaign, Abhijit Avasthi, national creative director, Ogilvy & Mather India, said, "While unfolding the *'Shubh Aarambh'* theme, we were consciously looking for situations which have universal appeal, though they might connect a little better with certain age profiles. So while the 'Bus Stop' works better with youngsters, 'Jeans' might work a little harder with the adults."

A Cadbury spokesperson commented, "At Cadbury, we have always strived to give our patrons a reason to enjoy every little moment of happiness with a bar of Cadbury Dairy Milk. *'Shubh Aarambh'* as a thought creates an anticipation of happiness and gives the Indian tradition a refreshing new approach." Of the response to the campaign, the spokesperson added, "The campaign has been well received across the spectrum of our target audience and we are pleased by the initial response that the campaign has received. The advertisements have been especially appreciated for their simplicity and we are positive that this campaign will play a significant role in enhancing the brand-connect with the consumers."

Concluding Note

Shubh Aarambh is based on a specific cultural insight — the Indian tradition of eating sweets before a new beginning or embarking on a new journey. Although rooted in a strong cultural truth, the campaign has a contemporary and youthful twist to it that allows people to easily connect with it.

CHAPTER 11

Celebrity Endorsements

CONTENTS

The use of celebrity advertising for companies has become a trend and a perceived winning formula of corporate image building and product marketing. Associating a brand with a top-notch celebrity can do more than perk up brand recall. It can create linkages with the celebrity's appeal, thereby adding refreshing and new dimensions to the brand image. As existing media get increasingly cluttered, the need to stand out has become paramount and celebrities have proved to be the ideal way to ensure brand prominence. Sign on a celebrity and there is an instant buzz. The brand leaps out of the clutter. And if the chemistry between the celebrity and the brand is right, the buzz could well turn into a roar. But circumstances are not always as ideal. Unless accompanied by a powerful idea, there is a good chance that the communication could sink into another clutter of celebrity-endorsed advertising.

DEFINITION OF A CELEBRITY ENDORSER

Friedman and Friedman (1979) state that:

"A celebrity endorser is an individual who is known to the public (actor, sports figure, entertainer etc.) for his or her achievements in areas other than that of the product class endorsed".

McCracken (1989) defines a celebrity endorser as:

"any individual who enjoys public recognition and who uses this recognition on behalf of a consumer good by appearing with it in an advertisement".

Both these definitions encompass the general definition of a celebrity endorser. That is a celebrity is well-known and uses his or her fame to help a company sell or enhance the image of the company, products or brands.

However, it is to be remembered that celebrity endorsers are not only used for commercial purposes but also for moral purposes or for spreading general awareness about issues of concern to the society. We have seen icons like Amitabh Bachchan and Shahrukh Khan endorsing the Pulse Polio Campaign. Also, when Aishwarya Rai asks the nation to donate their eyes, it strikes a chord with millions of hearts and there is an overwhelming number of people who pledge their eyes for the cause.

CELEBRITY ENDORSEMENTS IN INDIA

Mostly by Film Stars and Cricketers

Advertisers point out to the 2 C's that enjoy mass adulation in India- Cinema and Cricket; and accordingly a majority of the endorsement deals are bagged in by film stars and cricketers. Advertisers believe that advertising messages delivered by these celebrities provide a higher degree of appeal, attention and recall.

Pepsi Co. has used a variety of celebrities including Shahrukh Khan, Aishwarya Rai, Hrithik Roshan, Amitabh Bachchan, Kareena Kapoor, Fardeen Khan, etc. Aamir Khan signed a huge Rs. 6 crore deal with Coca-Cola for the *'Thanda Matlab Coca-Cola'* campaign. Coke ads have also featured Hrithik Roshan, Aishwarya Rai and Vivek Oberoi. Hindustan Lever's 'Lux' has been using popular film actresses like Sridevi, Kareena Kapoor, Priyanka Chopra, Katrina Kaif etc. to endorse the soap.

Cricketers are not far behind in their popularity. Sachin Tendulkar, Rahul Dravid Virendra Sehwag and M.S. Dhoni are the darlings of advertisers. With cricket having a fanatic following in India, it has virtually become a religion. The cricketing stars have endorsed a host of products including Pepsi, Coke, health drinks, jams, sports shoes and even credit cards. Sachin Tendulkar, due to his immense popularity, has been used as a spokesperson for Pepsi, Boost, Adidas, Visa and Airtel, to name a few.

The Exceptions

The fact that film stars and cricketers rule the hearts of millions leaves less scope for other celebrities to try their hand in this field. Nonetheless, some advertising campaigns have used some celebrities who are neither film stars nor cricketers. NIIT signed Vishwanathan Anand, JK Tyre wanted to speed into the market with Narain Karthikeyan, Rotomac Pens wanted Javed Akhtar to pen down his script by using the brand, and of course, who can forget the *'Wah Taj'* campaign of Taj Mahal tea by Zakir Hussain.

ICONIC AND MOMENTARY CELEBRITIES

Iconic celebrities are those who have become icons and will have likeability for many years. On the other hand, momentary celebrities are those who are for the time being popular due to some recent achievement made. The persona of iconic celebrities is greater than their performance, and hence, they aren't easily tarnished by a bad performance-for instance, a bad game (cricketer), or a flop movie (film star). Thus, an iconic celebrity's poor performance does not affect the brand. However, this is not true in case of a momentary celebrity.

Companies use iconic and momentary celebrities for different reasons. Iconic celebrities are generally used for brand building. For instance, Shahrukh Khan for Hundai Santro, Amitabh Bachchan for Reid and Taylor and Sachin Tendulkar for Boost. Momentary celebrities are generally used to increase the short-term sales of the product. Examples are Zayed Khan for Pizza Hut and Vivek Oberoi for Coke.

REASONS FOR USING CELEBRITY ENDORSEMENTS

Companies use celebrity endorsers in their ad campaigns due to the following reasons.

1. *Ensuring High Recall Rates:* In the midst of the advertisement clutter, the ads that celebrities endorse achieve high recall rates. The theory of 'selective attention' states that people tend to pay more attention to what is important

and interesting to their beliefs. Therefore, when people see their favourite celebrities in the ads, they pay more attention to the ads. At the same time, the advertiser can be sure that the positive feeling towards the ad has got transferred to the product.

When Aishwarya Rai appears in an advertisement appealing with her beautiful fluttering eyes to the viewers to donate their eyes she instantly attracts attention, enabling retention of the message and possibly changing people's attitude towards eye donation as well.

Similarly, Munch commercial portraying Rani Mukherjee as a cheeky village girl who dons different characters just to steal a Munch, got incredibly good results in recall and was a big hit with the kids. Rani's likeability and mischief were well leveraged by the brand.

2. *Brand Building:* Celebrities can also help the corporates in brand building. Think Boost and you think energy and that's what probably made Boost look at Sachin Tendulkar. Research has shown that this association has consistently been successful in strengthening the brand's core values and building brand stature. Sachin's 'Boost is the secret of my energy' campaign was a hit among the kids. Consumer feedback has shown that kids look upto Sachin as a true hero, want to emulate everything that he does and can't seem to get enough of him. Later when Sehwag was emerging as a new cricketing hero, Boost strengthened its position by coming up with 'Boost is the secret of our energy' campaign.

3. *Improving Soiled Image:* When Cadbury India wanted to restore the consumer's confidence in its chocolate brands following the high-pitch worms' controversy, the company appointed Amitabh Bachchan for the job. The worm controversy of 2003 had eaten into Cadbury's credibility and market share alike. Cadbury responded promptly with strict quality control which included using a 'purity seal pack'. But Cadbury needed a voice of authority to take these facts to the consumer and there was just one person who fitted here- Amitabh Bachchan. The commercial showed a testimonial by Bachchan on a factory visit. Twelve weeks after the campaign was launched, sales reached 90 percent of the volumes prior to the worm crisis. Moreover, Bachchan's presence helped Cadbury in getting media coverage that added to the campaign's impact.

   Similarly, when the even more controversial pesticide issue shook up Coca-Cola and PepsiCo, both soft drink majors put out high-profile damage control ad films featuring their best and most expensive celebrities.

While Aamir Khan led the Coke fightback, Pepsi brought Shahrukh Khan and Sachin Tendulkar together once again in a television commercial which drew references to the safety of the product.

4. ***Likeability of the Endorser:*** People like ads more if they like the endorsers in the ads. When a person likes the endorser in the ad, he or she is more likely to believe what the endorser says about the advertised product and therefore will develop more positive feelings toward the ad and the brand itself. Celebrities are able to attract attention and retain attention by their mere presence in the advertisements.

   However, according to advertising experts, a celebrity does help in increasing brand sales, but only if he/she is selected carefully and used effectively. The personality of the brand and the celebrity have to complement each other and the selection of the celebrity is, therefore, very important. Also, a lot depends on how the celebrity is used.

5. ***Repositioning/ New Product Launches with Celebrities:*** Celebrities may also help reposition products having sagging sales. Cinthol, when it was introduced as New Cinthol, had Vinod Khanna to endorse it. Boost made use of the combined vigour of Kapil and Sachin to capture the minds of kids. Post Bachchan, Parker's sales increased tremendously. Dabur India roped in Amitabh Bachchan for an estimated Rs 8 crore.

   Introduction of a new product can also be done successfully with the help of celebrities.

   In 1998, when Hyundai entered India with the Santro, they faced a huge challenge. No one had heard of Hyundai, fewer knew how to pronounce it. Hyundai needed to strike an immediate connect with consumers and Shahrukh Khan seemed the best choice. The ad got attention, recall and what is more, in the crowded car market it got greater visibility.

6. ***Adding Glamour:*** Companies also use celebrities to add that extra bit of glamour in their ads, which they believe gets transferred to the brand as well. The Godrej-Preity Zinta association is an example here. Godrej was a solid brand but it lacked glamour. Godrej felt that Preity with her youthful, trendsetter image would be the right fit. And did Zinta magic work? Yes, the brand image was definitely lifted. Similarly, in products such as cosmetics, the glamour of the celebrities used gets transferred to the product as well.

7. ***PR Coverage:*** Corporates also use celebrities for the sheer PR coverage they generate. Most celebrity-company associations are covered by most media. When the Big B first starred in the ICICI commercials, tremendous media hype was created.

8. *Psychographic Connect:* Celebrities are loved and adored by their fans and advertisers use stars to capitalize on these feelings to sway the fans towards their brand.

THE 'MATCH-UP' HYPOTHESIS

Advertisers feel that the right celebrity is the one who is in sync with the product/service and is the perfect match for it. The 'match-up' hypothesis specifically suggests that the effectiveness of celebrity endorsements depends on the existence of a 'fit' between the celebrity spokesperson and the endorsed brand. McCracken in his 'Meaning Transfer Model' (1989) has explained the effectiveness of celebrity spokesperson by assessing the meanings consumers associate with the endorser and eventually transfer to the brand. Hindustan Lever's 'Lux' soap in India has been using popular film actresses to endorse the soap since its launch, implying that they owe their stunning looks to the brand. This consistent message, hence, reinforces the brand values and has been successfully able to position the soap rightly as the 'beauty soap'. The '*jhatka*' of Mirinda needs a personality with a sense of humour. That's Govinda and Amitabh for you. Let us now take up some more examples to understand how advertisers strive to find a celebrity who will rightly 'fit' with the brand's/product's core values.

Nakshatra Jewellery and Aishwarya Rai-Flawless beauty

DE Beers, India's first branded jewellery, when introduced Nakshatra Jewellery, wanted an Indian beauty to be the face of Nakshatra and it felt that there was just one flawless face-Aishwarya Rai. Aishwarya and the diamonds are flawless, example of a perfect fit.

Airtel (Hello Tunes) and Kareena Kapoor-Youth

When Airtel wanted to introduce a new service called 'Hello Tunes', for which the target audience was young people, Kareena Kapoor was chosen for her youthful appeal.

Titan and Aamir Khan-Perfectionist

When Titan signed Aamir Khan, everyone knew the brand. Titan's concern was to take the brand to the next level; it wanted to promote the idea of multiple watches. Titan felt that a celebrity would accelerate the process. It also felt that both Aamir and Titan are Indian icons, both have made a mark internationally, the obsession with detail is common to both, as also a sense of style.

Following are some more examples of the right Match-Ups.

Brand-Celebrity Association	*Common Characteristics*
1. Adidas-Sachin Tendulkar	Sports
2. Rotomac-Javed Akhtar	Excellent Writing Skills
3. Boost-Sachin Tendulkar	Energy
4. Lux-Kareena Kapoor	Beauty
5. JK Tyre-Narain Karthikeyan	Speed
6. Kenstar Microwaves-Sanjeev Kapoor	Excellent Cook

WHY CELEBRITY ENDORSEMENTS MAY NOT WORK

Using celebrity endorsers in ad campaigns may fail due to the following reasons.

1. *Improper Positioning:* Associating with a star, however big he or she may be, in itself does not guarantee sales. The most it can do is generate interest in the product or create a buzz around it. Take the case of Maruti Versa, which was launched amidst a lot of fanfare. In spite of Maruti signing up superstar Amitabh Bachchan and his son Abhishek Bachchan as brand ambassadors for Versa, the brand's sales remained sluggish. To be fair, the Big B magic did work and the ads created significant interest, drawing people into the showroom. But perhaps the positioning itself was faulty as people were expecting a larger than life car, just like the brand's ambassador.
2. *Brand-Celebrity Disconnect:* If the celebrity used in the ad represents values that conflict with the brand values and positioning, the advertising will create a conflict in the minds of the target audience who may reject the proposition. Take for instance, a brand of battery like Eveready using an old celebrity like the Big B might not make much sense. Also, the commercial showing Shahrukh Khan in a bath tub, endorsing Lux soap, is difficult to digest.
3. *Clutter:* In recent times, there has been such a flood of celebrity endorsements that it has led to the very clutter that it aimed to break. For instance, Amitabh Bachchan endorses or has endorsed Pepsi, ICICI, BPL, Parker pens, Nerolac, Dabur, Reid & Taylor, Maruti Versa, Cadbury and a few social messages too. Bollywood king Shahrukh Khan endorses Omega, Pepsi, Hyundai, Clinic All Clear and Airtel among other brands. This over-exposure can be bad for the brand. Unfortunately in India, we have too many brands chasing too few celebrities.

   The marketer must analyse that the law of diminishing marginal celebrity utility is at play no matter how larger-than-life a celebrity may be. A celebrity may become the spokesperson of many products and runs the risk of getting overexposed. When a celebrity is a spokesperson for one product, he may have high credibility but when he endorses a variety of products, his or her perceived credibility gets reduced due to overexposure. The economic motivation underlying the celebrities' endorsements may also become too apparent to consumers and they may take them for granted. Also, because of the diminishing marginal celebrity utility is at play, another Bachchan endorsement ceases to be a novelty.

4. *Dissatisfaction with Product Performance:* One cannot sell an ordinary product just by making a celebrity endorse it. A celebrity can only arouse interest of the consumers in the product/brand advertised. He cannot come to the rescue of the marketer if the product fails to deliver performance. Sachin Tendulkar's endorsement of Fiat Palio was quite a success initially but as word about the poor fuel efficiency of Palio spread, its sales took a beating. Thus, a celebrity endorsement does not, in itself, guarantee sales. At best, it can create a buzz and make consumer feel better about the product. But ultimately, the product is the real star and has to deliver on the promise.

5. *Vampire Effect:* The concept of a celebrity becoming bigger than the brand is known as the vampire effect. The customer ends up remembering the celebrity but not the brand. When Rahul Dravid was signed to endorse Sil jam, people could recall seeing the ad but they missed out on the brand name of the jam. Thus, it is a big challenge for the advertiser to not to allow the celebrity overshadow the product. An advertising campaign designed effectively can help the marketer in getting rid of this problem. For instance, when Titan had used Aamir Khan in its campaign 'watches meant for different occasions', despite the presence of Aamir, nowhere did the consumer miss out that it was a Titan commercial.

   In case of Nerolac Paints, which was endorsed by Amitabh Bachchan, around 80% of the respondents when asked to associate Bachchan with any paint, did so with Asian Paints, which is the biggest competitor of Nerolac.

6. *Skepticism towards Celebrity Endorsement:* Advertisers must realise that celebrity endorsement is not a definitive tool to achieve brand superstardom. The assumed acceptance of celebrity endorsement amongst an audience is the most common advertiser fallacy. Depiction of Hema Malini using a brand of detergent is unlikely to convince a housewife that the powder understands her plight. Similarly, Sonali Bendre's endorsement of Nirma beauty soap generated lot of skeptical reactions as people did not believe that the Bollywood heroine would be using the endorsed soap herself but was rather modeling for Nirma for money and money alone. In such cases, a celebrity can give rise to skepticism or disbelief because it might be a bit too much for the masses to believe that the celebrities who are rich and can afford the best in the world are actually using a mass product being advertised on television.

DISADVANTAGES OF CELEBRITY ENDORSEMENTS

Using celebrities has its own disadvantages.

- **Cost:** Celebrities do not come cheap and may cost the company a fortune. Often celebrities-in-the-making are signed by companies before they hit peak stardom because their endorsement deals are cheaper and corporates want to catch them young. Here it becomes important to study the life cycle of a star's career and ensure that he/she is signed up during his/her growth stage. Mostly, ad agencies and marketers work together as a team to arrive at the right choices as far as celebrity endorsement deals are concerned, given that the stakes sometimes run into crores.
- **Risk Factor:** Many risks are associated with celebrity endorsements. Companies like Parker, ICICI and Dabur have used Amitabh Bachchan remarkably well, while some others have been unable to exploit his 'Big B' status. The endorsement of Hyundai Santro or Airtel by Shahrukh Khan has worked well for the actor as well as for the brands. However, when Khan canvassed the image of a metro-sexual man when he was seen endorsing Lux soap, which was usually treated as a women's soap earlier, it was not much appreciated. Celebrity endorsement is, therefore, *capable of manifesting both favourable and adverse effects for the brands* with which they associate.

  Since celebrities may become targets of *negative publicity*, the risk factor could be high. Companies, which used some cricket stars in their advertisements, have been embarrassed and worried when the latter embroiled in match-fixing scandals and controversies and made headlines for the wrong reasons. Pepsi has suffered with three tarnished celebrities - Mike Tyson, Madonna, and Michael Jackson. Since the behaviour of the celebrities reflects on the brand, celebrity endorsers may at times become liabilities to the brands they endorse.

  When a celebrity is on the ascent it makes sense to hook the product to the star and derive maximum benefits before the *star status fades away*. The returns of celebrity endorsements, like any other advertising, are not easy to measure. The benefits accrue over a period of time, with the celebrity campaigns and other factors contributing to the overall increase in the brand value.

  Hedging the risk: The first thing to ensure before signing a celebrity is to try and choose some celebrity whose record is flawless. Also, it's best not to depend on one celebrity, because that can backfire. Instead, it is better to use many celebrities who represent the same values. Pepsi does this quite well. Capitalising on the popularity of cricket and films in Indian, Pepsi uses several cricketers and film stars in its ads. So when Azharuddin and Jadeja got embroiled in the match-mixing controversy, Pepsi's severed its association only with these stars, but its relationship with cricket continued. One should seriously consider the risks of associating with a well-known personality and hedge against a future scandal by not relying on just one celebrity and instead linking the brand's association with a broad theme represented by several celebrities.

If the marketer can't afford many celebrities, then he should get his thinking caps on and come up with a better, safer idea to ensure that he is in control of the brand's destiny - not the stars! In this context, one must not forget that the Amul girl, Ronald of McDonalds, Fido-Dido of 7-up and Vodafone's Zoo Zoos are no less than celebrities.

CONCLUDING NOTE

Celebrity endorsement is a serious business, and if used effectively could have a lasting impression on the brand, its activities and its image. For advertisers using celebrity endorsements, there is one very important thing to keep in mind - never let the celebrity become your brand. In doing so, one runs the risk of killing the brand no sooner the hype around the celebrity fades. A brand needs to have a strong identity of its own and it should ideally not piggyback on the identity of a celebrity and hope to achieve success. Marketers need to turn their brands into celebrities rather than celebrities into brands.

QUESTIONS FOR DISCUSSION

1. What do you mean by a celebrity endorser? What are the various celebrity endorsements that the Indian advertising industry has seen in the recent past?
2. Discuss with examples how the use of various celebrity endorsers can help a marketer meet his objectives.
3. What do you mean by the 'Match-up Hypothesis'? Give examples of how the concept of match-up hypothesis helps in finding the right celebrity for a product/service.
4. Do you think that celebrity endorsements are a sure shot way to achieve success? Why or why not?
5. What are the various circumstances under which celebrity endorsements may not bring desirable results?
6. Are there any precautions that a marketer should take before signing celebrities as their brand ambassadors?
7. Write short notes on:
   (a) Brand-Celebrity Disconnect
   (b) Law of Diminishing Marginal Celebrity Utility

Appendix 11.1

BRAND ENDORSEMENTS OF SHAHRUKH KHAN

Shahrukh Khan is a popular film star who scores high on 'likability' factor by the Indian public. He is a popular choice of many for endorsing brands. Shahrukh Khan earns crores of rupees every year through endorsements. In the recent years, he has endorsed a number of brands including Pepsi, Hyundai Santro, Videocon, Airtel, Compaq, Tag Heur, Pepsodent, Sunfeast Biscuits, Emami Fair and Handsome, Emami *Nav Ratna* oil, Clinic All Clear, Omega, Nerolac Paints, HP printers, Linc pens, Boro Plus, Emami *Sona Chandi*, Nokia, ICICI, HP Printers, Belmonte, Lux Cozi, Hundai i10, D'Décor and Dish TV.

Appendix 11.2

LUX-THE BEAUTY SOAP OF FILM STARS

Lux—derived from the word luxury— was launched in 1899 as a laundry soap in the UK. In 1925, the brand was extended to the toilet soap category. The brand, which is positioned as the favorite soap of film stars, has been consistent in terms of its communication and positioning. The brand is a classic example of successful celebrity endorsements.

Lux is positioned as a beauty soap in India, and Unilever has used successful film stars for its endorsement. The first ambassador Leela Chitnis featured in a Lux advertisement which flagged off the Lux wagon. She gave way to a galaxy of stars which included Madhubala, Nargis, Meena Kumari, Mala Sinha, Sharmila Tagore, Waheeda Rehman, Sairah Banu, Hema Malini, Zeenat Aman, Juhi Chawla, Madhuri Dixit, Sridevi, Aishwarya Rai Bachchan, Kareena Kapoor, Priyanka Chopra and most recently Katrina Kaif.

In 2005, Lux celebrated its 75th anniversary sparking of a controversy. Deviating from its tradition of roping in the Bollywood Divas, this time none other than Shahrukh Khan endorsed Lux. The ads created instant controversy with marketers discussing whether the brand has suddenly become MALE. Some argue that Unilever (then Hindustan Lever Ltd.) was testing a new positioning to appeal to male users while others say that it was a one time endorsement to break the clutter. For marking the 75th year, Lux also came out with a celebration range (including Chocolate Seduction) endorsed by Kareena Kapoor. These innovative products created lot of excitement and ensured that Lux remained in the top of the mind of the consumers.

LUX ADVERTISEMENTS THROUGH AGES

Lux campaigns have wooed millions of people over the decades. Popularly known as the beauty soap of film stars, Lux has been an intimate partner of the brightest stars on the silver screen for decades. An ode to their beauty and, an announcer of their stardom, advertising campaigns of Lux have featured film stars across the nation, promising their beauty and complexion to common women.

Appendix 11.3

CELEBRITY ENDORSEMENTS IN SOCIAL ADVERTISING

What is Social Advertising

Social Advertising is conceived as an application of advertising concepts and techniques to various socially beneficial ideas and causes. According to Kotler, social advertising means "The design, implementation, and control of programs calculated to influence the acceptability of social ideas, and involving consideration of products, planning, pricing, communications, and advertising research."

It is a process for influencing human behaviour on a large scale, using marketing principles for the purpose of societal benefit rather than for commercial profit (Bill Smith, 1999). It is about applying marketing and advertising principles to promote health and social issues and bringing about positive behavioural changes.

Examples of Social Advertising

Social Advertising is used in the advertisements of ideas like Water & Fuel Conservation, Family Planning, Use of Contraceptives, Domestic Violence, Consciousness about Voting rights, *Beti Bachao* Movement, *Jago Grahak Jago* etc. Social advertising also includes creating awareness about dieses like AIDS, TB, Breast Cancer, Malaria, Dengue, & Swine Flu and campaigns like Pulse Polio campaign and *Goli ke Hamjoli* campaign.

Social Marketing sells a behavioural change to a targeted group of individuals. The behavioural change sought could be accepting a new behaviour, rejecting a potential behaviour, modifying a current behaviour or abandoning an old behaviour.

1. *Accept a New Behaviour:* Don't drink and drive
2. *Reject a Potential Behaviour:* Stop female feticide
3. *Modify a Current Behaviour:* Water & Fuel Conservation
4. *Abandon an Old Behaviour:* Quit Smoking

Features of Social Advertising

1. Non-commercial (non-profit motive)
2. Promotes Health and Social Issues
3. Aimed for Societal Benefit (by bringing about a behavioural change)
4. Performed by Government (e.g. Pulse Polio Campaign), NGOs (like CRY, Cancer Patients Aid Association etc.) or Big Corporates (e.g. "*Jaago Re*" campaign of Tata Tea)

5. Generally promoted by Popular People (Celebrities). However, it should be remembered that not all social advertising campaigns make use of celebrities.

Social Advertising & Celebrity Endorsements

- Polio Drops- Amitabh Bachchan, Shahrukh Khan
- Vivek Oberoi- Quit Smoking
- Rahul Dravid-T.B. Dots.
- Eye Donation- Aishwarya Rai.
- Indian Tourism, Awareness about Voting, Patriotism- Aamir Khan.
- AIDS- Jacky Shrooff
- *Beti Bachao* Movement- Kapil Dev

CELEBRITIES IN SOCIAL ADVERTISING

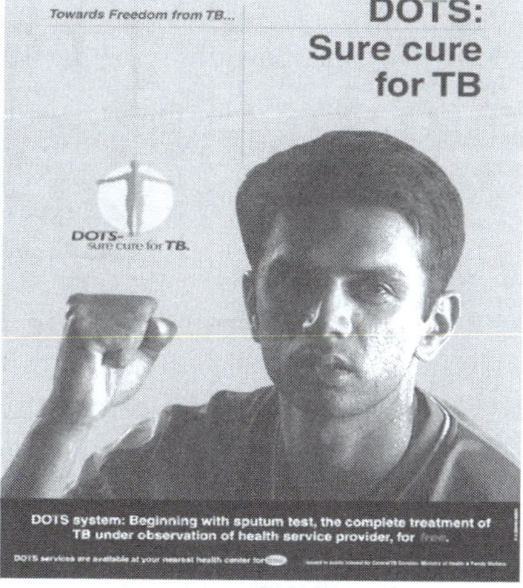

Important Aspects While Using Celebrities in Social Advertising

1. While selecting the celebrities for social advertising, there should not be any conflicts between the message or the product and the celebrity's personality. For instance, Shahrukh Khan is not suitable for 'quit smoking' campaign.
2. Only a popular celebrity can bring about the behavioural change desired in social advertising. This is exactly the reason why Amitabh Bachchan and Shahrukh Khan are used for the Pulse Polio Campaign. The outcome of the campaign has been tremendous with a large number of people turning up at the immunisation centres.

CHAPTER 12

MASCOTS

CONTENTS

Mascots refer to any fictitious character, person or animal used to represent a brand and communicate about the brand and its offerings to the consumers. Mascots are used as communication channels between the consumer and the product. It is the mascot that enters our living room everyday to inform us which brand of burger is the tastiest or which mobile service provider you should trust to ensure a good connectivity. Mascots have powers beyond what ordinary marketing can achieve.

ORIGIN OF THE TERM 'MASCOT'

The term mascot has a very strange origin. At the turn of the 20th century a French composer named Edmond Audran (1842-1901) wrote a series of operettas, the most famous being La Mascotte. This was a light hearted story of a virgin farm girl who brought good luck to whoever employed her. The English translation was called 'Mascot' and it could be anything – a person, an animal or a fictitious character, provided it brings good luck for that company.

USE OF MASCOTS IN INDIAN ADVERTISING

The success stories of Indian mascots date back to 1946 when Air India's Bobby Kooka along with JWT's Umesh Rao created our own hospitable *Maharaja*

The *Maharaja* was a polished and courteous man with moustaches, in red imperial clothes, a striped turban and pointed shoes. *Maharaja* became the face of the public sector aviation giant, Air India, for many years until Air India and Indian Airlines were merged and the *Maharaja* faded away.

One of the longest running mascots in Indian history is the **Amul Girl,** the chubby butter girl who warmed her way into the nation's heart in 1967. Sylvester daCunha of Advertising and Sales Promotion (ASP) Company was given the Amul account in 1966. He came up with what has been one of the longest running mascots in history, and has made its way into the Guinness Book of World Records as the longest running outdoor advertising campaign. Whether the hoardings were by the roadside, near the office building, over by the bus stop, one could find them anywhere, and they took the nation by the storm. The Amul girl with her innocent smile could be seen flaunting her favourite butter in her hands on the hoardings. One of the wonderful things about the campaign was that the hoardings always stayed fresh in the minds of the consumer, with an ever evolving topical message which reflected the latest events in the Indian society.

Emulating the Amul example, **Asian Paints** came up with *Gattu* designed by RK Laxman. The Little Boy with a paint brush in one hand and a bucket of paint in the other sent this message to Indian customers that it is only Asian Paints which can help them preserve their home sweet homes. Recently, *Gattu*, the boy mascot for Asian paints was quietly withdrawn. The brand was being given a contemporary look and was rejuvenated. In the process, the mascot was removed, being replaced by Saif Ali Khan and Big B as the brand ambassadors of the respective brands.

The **Bunny of *Lijjat Pappad,*** was a puppet designed by Ramdas Padhye. *Shri Mahila Griha Udyog* promoted this adorable mascot, which easily secured a place in every child's heart.

Not all mascots were gentle, cute and adorable. Creative minds have also come up with mascots whose devilish looks helped many brands regain their lost market share. The **green tailed Onida devil** took the onus of carrying forward the Rs.1500 crore company Mirc. Electronics, brand Onida, on his strong shoulders. All through the 26 years of its service, he left the competitors of Onida envious and green. With the appealing and complementing tagline, "Neighbours envy, owner's pride," this devil communicated too well for the consumer durable company. However, Onida's devil suddenly disappeared in 1998, a move considered as professional suicide by experts. In 2003, the devil was re-launched, but failed to deliver.

The **Muscle-man of MRF** was created by Alyque Padamsee. For MRF tyres, durability was a key issue. Alyque and his gang dreamt up of a muscleman who was to be the company's public face-mascot who represented the essence and soul of the product promise – 'Strength'. This gave it an instant identity and definition of what the brand stood for.

Created by Joanna Ferrone and Sue Rose in 1985, the imaginative caricature of a freaky young guy called **Fido Dido** has been the brand mascot of **7UP** ever since. It became extremely popular, with it being highlighted on television as well as other media. In fact there were lunch boxes, schoolbags, water bottles and many other kid items using the mascot because of its popularity. It is an easy name to pronounce and was young and trendy in its attire and outlook.

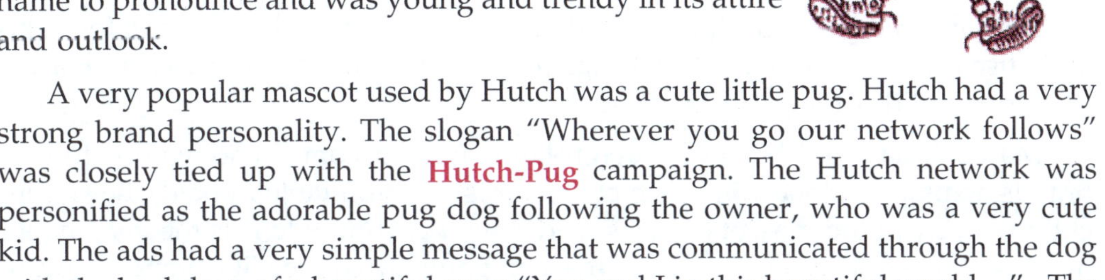

A very popular mascot used by Hutch was a cute little pug. Hutch had a very strong brand personality. The slogan "Wherever you go our network follows" was closely tied up with the **Hutch-Pug** campaign. The Hutch network was personified as the adorable pug dog following the owner, who was a very cute kid. The ads had a very simple message that was communicated through the dog with the backdrop of a beautiful song "You and I in this beautiful world...". The Hutch network was personified as the dog and the Hutch brand automatically drew the brand personality of being adorable and cute. The dog was named Hutch dog and became very popular in India. The dog became the brand ambassador and a great brand asset to Hutch. Hutch leveraged this popularity of the dog and used the dog in its websites and in all its communications.

In 2007, Vodafone acquired 67% stake in Hutchisson and re-branded Hutch telecom into Vodafone. Vodafone very well understood that Hutch dog represents the network and communicated the change to Vodafone beautifully without losing the charm present in earlier Hutch ads. Later, Vodafone continued to use the Hutch dog in their "Happy to Help" campaign. Vodafone differentiates itself from other telecom operators through its value added services (VAS) and it wanted to educate the customers about it. Unfortunately, the Hutch dog had its limitations and was fired from the commercials and Vodafone brought in the 'Zoozoos'. The **Zoozoos** were used to launch Vodafone's VAS (Value Added Services) during the Indian Premier League (IPL) matches. Every ad featured a

humorous situation where the need for a particular Vodafone service was brought to the forefront. The Zoozoos stuck in the public's memory, and made sure that this particular ad campaign would not be forgotten easily.

While **Chester Cheetah** did the tricks for Cheetos; **Tony, the tiger**, made Kellogg's taste success through its magnetism. The **Kingfisher bird** – representing energy, youthfulness, enthusiasm, freedom with a touch of formality and discipline – did it for the Kingfisher group, and a middle-class mascot, *Chintamani*, did it for ICICI Prudential.

Mascots that took birth on foreign lands have become synonymous to their brands across the globe. One such character is the inimitable Ronald, the smiling child-friendly brand mascot of McDonald's, who continues to rule the imagination of kids the world over. Used by the company to convey its brand meaning through brand personalisation, Ronald was successful in establishing an instant connect with its target group i.e. kids and their mums, when he first debuted globally in 1963.

Even in India, where McDonald's set up business in 1996, Ronald was pivotal in changing the consumer perceptions from 'foreign', 'American', to 'fun', 'values, families and culture', 'comfortable and easy'. The brand communication and Ronald's own personality have dynamically evolved with McDonald's changing sales and marketing strategy.

And the instantly identifiable Colonel Harland David Sanders is not only the inventor of the KFC brand, but also the person behind the secret recipe of 'finger licking good' food. According to Unnat Varma, KFC Marketing Director India, "Our brand mascot – The Colonel – epitomises an expert, someone with a strong heritage; and yet is contemporary and is known as a mark of product quality and excellence."

WHY TO USE MASCOTS

The following points explain the advantages of using mascots in advertising.

1. *Economical:* In this age of expensive brand ambassadors, mascots provide a creative, sustainable, low-cost model for communicating a brand's values and personifying the company's desired image. Mascots are not as expensive as celebrities. The cost of creating these characters is as low as development of a normal commercial.

2. *Communication Channel between the Consumer and the Brand:* Mascots serve as communication channels telling the consumers about the product and its various features. The Zoozoo campaign was launched specifically to communicate to the consumers about the Value Added Services of Vodafone.
3. *Not Subject to Vagaries of Time:* The other advantage is that as mascots are created and owned by the companies, switching loyalties, which is a frequent incidence with celebrity endorsers, can be ruled out. For example, Aamir Khan starred in the first Pepsi commercial aired in India, but today he is a brand ambassador for Coke. However, one cannot think of the Amul Girl or Vodafone's Zoozoos swapping places.
4. *Brand Association:* Mascots are able to create for the public an association with the brand. Thus, mere visibility of a mascot in an ad, billboard, sponsorship of an event etc. will remind the consumer about the brand. Some mascots represent the essence and soul of the product promise. Thus, the muscleman of MRF tyres depicts what the brand stands for - Strength.
5. *Likability:* Vodafone's Zoozoos are a perfect example to explain how much a mascot can be liked by the public. Soon after they were aired on television, the Zoozoos and the ads became really popular. The Zoozoo concept immediately connected with the audiences and created an emotional connect with them. In April 2009, as the TVCs started being aired on television, they created the necessary buzz both in traditional as well as in social networking sites like Facebook, and Twitter and video sharing website, YouTube. For the week ended April 25, 2009, one ad on fashion tips was viewed 13,000 times on YouTube. In Oct, 2010, there were 1 million Zoozoo fans on facebook.
6. *Scope for Creative Flexibility:* If the mascots are animated characters, they give more scope for creative-flexibility. For instance, Fido Dido of 7-up has been used in a number of ways to show him going gaga over the 7-up bottle.
7. *Adds Value to Business:* Whether advertising at a global or local level, finding the right public face is critical for a company to add value to its business. Most mascots provide a fun, light-hearted way to get an organisation or company noticed in festivals, parades, sporting events, schools, store openings, civic events and even the media. Kids love mascots, and consumers easily remember them.

Moreover, a mascot brings instant identity in a charming, gracious, identifiable feel-good manner. "Mascots represent the true soul and identity of the brand personality and give it form and shape that is embedded in popular imagination for times to come. The success, however, depends on how well the fit is in terms of product, promise and imaginative creation of the mascot persona," opines Alyque Padamsee, advertising guru.

ISSUES TO BE CONSIDERED IN USING MASCOTS

A company needs to consider the following issues when it decides to use a mascot.

1. *Is the Mascot Relevant to the Brand:* The first thing is to check whether the category for which the mascot is being conceived is relevant or not. If it is a highly industrial category or a highly technical category, it may be prudent to look at other branding means rather than use brand mascots. This is because the target audience is serious and there is high probability that they may consider mascots frivolous and casual, thereby destroying the rational product story, the technical competence as well as the product efficacy image. While on the other hand, in categories like services, FMCGs or other consumer products, a brand mascot may work out to be relevant and effective.
2. *Is the Mascot Causing Distraction from the Brand:* If the mascot is able to attract consumers towards the brand, not only in terms of awareness, but also in terms of trials, purchase, consumption and repeat purchases, then the brand mascot is working. However, sometimes the mascot distracts the consumer from the brand and its products and service usage. For instance, many years ago 7-up lost its product usage because Fido Dido actually distracted consumers from the product. Consumers bought the concept of Fido-Dido - the 'Brand Mascot' (lunch boxes, schoolbags, water bottles and many other kid items designed using the mascot) and did not buy 7-Up, the brand itself. There is a very thin line between attraction and distraction and this must be worked on very carefully.
3. *Focus:* This means a consistent usage of the mascot in a company's advertisements. Over a period of time there has been a focus on the Amul Girl. Its consistent usage has definitely helped the business and created a special identity for Amul in the minds of the consumers. With its clever use of topical events, Amul's utterly butterly campaign has the distinction of entering the Guinness World Records as the longest running outdoor campaign and has won the brand several accolades. Even the advertising agency hasn't changed, and DaCunha and FCB Ulka, have played a pivotal role in the growth of Amul.
4. *Is the Brand Getting Sidelined:* Everything that a brand mascot stands for should keep the brand in the mainline and mainstream to bring out its core values and benefits. It should not let either the brand or its benefits getting sidelined. There was a feeling that *Gattu*, the mascot of Asian paints, had outlived its utility and the brand was brought back in the mainline with Gattu being removed so that the mother brand does not get sidelined. If a choice has to be made between the brand and the brand mascot, it is better that the brand mascot be sidelined because ultimately the brand is the hero, whereas the mascot is only a support.
5. *Intellectual Property Rights to Use the Mascot:* One issue that organisations that plan to use a mascot must be aware of pertains to intellectual property

rights. It is advisable for companies to enter into legal contracts for licensing and purchasing of mascots created by them to prevent copyright violations. This is because the value of a brand goes up when the mascot becomes a part of the brand, and any wrong use of the mascot may tarnish the brand image. There is also a possibility of people making unscrupulous use of the brand mascot for their own interests.

6. *Overuse of a Mascot:* Mascots provide a personal touch to marketing campaigns and this goes a long way in ensuring public acceptance of a brand. However, overuse of a mascot may result in an inability to communicate the core identity of what a brand stands for. It may be ineffective in driving customers to the brand and do little in terms of increasing sales.

CELEBRITY VERSUS MASCOT

The use of celebrity in advertising has become a trend and a perceived winning formula of corporate image building and product marketing. Associating a brand with a top-notch celebrity can do more than perk up brand recall. It is believed that the celebrities transfer their success, personality, status and power to the brand. They help the company in creating brand awareness, stimulate and revive the brands, establish product associations and ensure a higher recall. However, the advertising world has also realized that many brand ambassadors do not practice what they preach and sometimes controversies and unpleasant incidents connected with the celebrity may cause damage to the brand image. It is also observed that over exposure and multiple endorsements too can damage the image of product.

The Indian market which is saturated with celebrity endorsements has also seen the use of popular mascots. The Amul girl was born in 1967 and is still a popular mascot. The *Maharaja* of Air India, *Gattu* of Asian Paints and Onida's Devil will always have a special place in the history of Indian advertising. Amongst the new age mascots the popularity that Hutch's pug and Vodafone's zoozoos has received is tremendous.

The new age mascots are attractive and trendy. The advertisers have become more creative with the use of animation. The new age mascots have a lasting appeal and create a whole new persona for the product. They manage the product as efficiently as a celebrity. Moreover, in the current marketing scenario when the celebrity charisma is diminishing away, the world of advertising is turning back to mascots.

Celebrities get associated with too many products and therefore it is difficult to relate them with one particular brand, which is not the case with the mascots. For example, Shahrukh Khan endorses brands such as Pepsi, Airtel, Santro, Emami, and many more but Zoozoos are just associated with Vodafone. The strength of a mascot lies in its uniqueness, and its power of effectively communicating the ethos of the brand. For example, *Chintamani* (ICICI Prudential) solves all our worries related to tax savings and good returns paving a new way for 'no *chinta*'.

Moreover the mascots are not as expensive as celebrities. The cost of creating these characters is as low as development of a normal commercial.

Mascots are dynamic and they adapt with changing times. We should acknowledge how the Amul girl in polka dots has changed overtime, and Fido Dido has had makeovers with the changing time.

The Amul girl was born in 1967 is still a popular mascot. She has entered into the Guinness Book of World Records as the oldest outdoor campaign to survive in the market. All this goes on to prove that the mascots are more appropriate brand ambassadors. However, the impact and success of a mascot depends on how effectively it conveys the brand values and the ideas that consumers will associate with.

CONCLUDING NOTE

Mascots create a whole new persona for the product. A mascot is something which can stand out and break through the clutter. Moreover, unlike an ambassador, it is something very unique to a company, and is not subject to the vagaries of time. It can be moulded very easily, and establish itself in the minds of the public. While using mascots in advertising, care should be taken to ensure that everything a brand stands for should go well with the mascot being used. The mascot should be aimed at bringing out the core values and benefits which the brand stands for. It should not let either the brand or its benefits getting sidelined.

QUESTIONS FOR DISCUSSION

1. What do you mean by the term 'mascot'? Name some popular mascots (along with the brand names/companies) used by the Indian advertisers.
2. What are the advantages of using mascots in advertising?
3. What issues should be considered in using mascots in advertising?
4. Which do you think is more effective - using celebrities or mascots in advertising? Give reasons in support of your answer.

Case Study

THE 'AMUL' GIRL

One of the longest running mascots in Indian history is the Amul Girl, the chubby butter girl who warmed her way into the nation's heart in 1967. It all began in 1966 when Sylvester daCunha, then the managing director of the advertising agency, ASP (Advertising and Sales Promotion), clinched the account for Amul butter. The butter, which had been launched in 1945, had a dull, boring image, primarily because the earlier advertising agency which was in charge of the account preferred to stick to routine, corporate ads. Sylvester daCunha and Eustace Fernandez, Art Director at ASP, decided that they needed a girl who could coax her way into the Indian housewife's heart. Thus, the famous girl with her rolling eyes came into existence, signifying the innocence and joy of anyone who has not forgotten his childhood. The Amul girl's cute looks, innovativeness and witty comments on every current issue, week after week, has created a space in every Indian's heart.

For the first one year, the ads made statements of some kind or the other. In 1967, Sylvester decided that giving the ads a solid concept would give them extra mileage. It was a decision that would stand the daCunhas in good stead in the years to come. In 1969, when Bombay first saw the beginning of the *Hare Rama Hare Krishna* movement, Sylvester daCunha, Mohammad Khan and Usha Bandarkar, then the creative team working on the Amul account, came up with a clincher – 'Hurry Amul, Hurry Hurry'. Bombay reacted to the ad with an enthusiasm that was almost as devout as the Iskon fever.

That was the first of the many contemporary ads that were in the offering. From then on Amul began playing the **role of a social observer**. Over the years the campaign acquired that all important Amul touch.

India looked forward to Amul's **suggestive humour**. If the Naxalite movement was the happening thing in Calcutta, Amul would be up there on the hoardings saying, 'Bread without Amul Butter, *cholbe na cholbe na'* (won't do, won't do). If there was an Indian Airlines strike Amul would be there again saying, 'Indian Airlines Won't Fly Without Amul'.

There were other instances too. 'Heroine Addiction', Amul's little joke on Hussain had the artist ringing the daCunhas up to request them for a blow up of the ad. He said that he had seen the hoarding while passing through a small district in UP. He said he had asked his assistant to take a photograph of himself with the ad because he had found it so funny.

Whether they were by the roadside, near your office building, over by the bus stop, you could find them anywhere, and they took the nation by the storm. One of the wonderful things about the campaign was that the hoardings always stayed fresh in the minds of the consumer, with an ever evolving suggestive message which reflected the latest events in Indian society.

For all these years, the 'Utterly Butterly Girl' has had an unmatched fan following. The Amul Girl has been one of the longest running mascots in history, and has made its way into the Guiness Book of World Records as the longest running outdoor advertising campaign.

What's the mantra behind such a high level of integration between the mascot and the Amul brand? "Ever since Sylvester daCunha gave birth to the Amul Girl, and she began playing the role of a social observer, she has evoked an overwhelmingly positive response. Over the years, the ad campaign acquired a cult status. India looked forward to the evocative humour. No other brand ambassador could have given Amul brand the mileage which this little girl has given", said Amul's GM Sodhi.

Ever since its birth, the Amul Girl mascot has adorned posters, hoardings and the butter wrappers. Initially, the campaigns used to be hand painted (as was the case in those days). But with technology and high quality image building tools taking over the past few years, the moppet has transformed into a much more crisp and colourful image. And it is the same advertising agency, later named to DaCunha Communications, that has been associated with the campaign ever since.

The Amul ads has soaked so much into the psychic of the Indians that when anyone talks of butter in India - the Amul Butter Girl is immediately imagined.

Whether it was the Kargil War of 1999 or Bhajji-Symond's *'tamasha'* in Australia, Amul has always been at its creative best – associating its brand value with the happenings in these events. Sanju baba's "*Lagate Raho Maskabhai*" to Himesh's "*Aap ka Ammuuul*" - Amul has always presented it *maska marke*.

Even the topics concerning matters related to Indian society have not been able to give this butter a slip. It is exemplified by the "*Kuch Kuch Quota hai*" and "Bread Analyser test" campaigns.

But what's kept the brand going all these years? "We have changed the packaging, our technology and our approach to marketing based on the changing taste buds of our consumers. However, the only thing that has helped us sail smoothly is that we have not changed our core values—give the best quality product to the consumer, and the best possible price. It holds true in any era," said B.M. Vyas, Managing Director, GCMMF (Gujarat Co-operative Milk Marketing Federation).

In fact, it is not just the core values at Amul that have remained the same; the core team associated with the brand is still the same. Even the advertising agency hasn't changed, and Da Cunha and FCB Ulka, have played a pivotal role in the growth of Amul. This has helped Amul maintain consistency in its communication.

SOME AMUL AD PICS

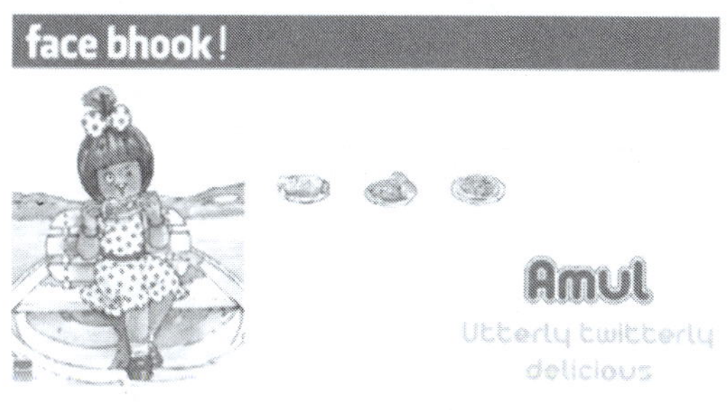

When we see the pun intended in all these Amul ads, we can imagine how simple thoughts can be. But to be able to see this simplicity in random thoughts requires a lot of creativity. Amul ads have been with us for more than 40 years now, letting us know how the world around us has changed, for the better or for the worse. This is an advertising campaign that has stood the tests of time, politics, national affairs, and private affairs. And that has been done by maintaining an Indian connection in all its campaigns. Truly, Amul is the "Taste of India".

Reference : http://www.amul.com/

Case Study

VODAFONE 'ZOOZOOS'

Background

Vodafone entered India in December 2005 by acquiring a 10 percent stake in Bharti Ventures Limited (Bharti) which later became Bharti Airtel Limited. However, as Bharti later ruled out further dilution of its stake, Vodafone started considering other options to increase its market share in India. In 2007, Vodafone took over Hutchison Essar for a price of around 19 billion dollars and became Vodafone Essar Limited (Vodafone Essar), a subsidiary of mobile network operator Vodafone Group Plc. (Vodafone) based in the UK.

Vodafone Essar's Advertising Campaigns

After successfully rebranding 'Hutch' as 'Vodafone', Vodafone Essar started expanding its presence in India. The company used almost all media channels to advertise its services. It not only advertised on television, but also in newspapers, the radio, and on hoardings across the country. When Vodafone took over Hutch, its advertisements did a good job in creating awareness that "Hutch is now Vodafone". The story was told by Hutch's brand ambassador-pug, the cute little dog. The ad opened with the famous "Hutch" pug resting in a pink kennel (Pink was the colour of brand "Hutch"). He leaves for a stroll. He comes back and finds a bigger red kennel instead of his pink one and the message that pops up is, "Change is good."

In 2008, Vodafone unveiled the 'Happy to Help' series during the first season of the Indian Premier League (IPL). The campaign highlighted Vodafone's array of customer care services like mobile stores, self service kiosks and mini-stores.

With the launch of the second season of IPL, Vodafone gave birth to the 'Zoozoos'.

The 'Zoozoos' Campaign

In November 2008, Vodafone Essar decided to launch an advertising campaign to communicate the VAS (Value Added Services) offered by the company. The company planned to air the ads during IPL Season 2. It was decided that Ogilvy and Mather (O&M) India, the advertising agency creating campaigns for Vodafone

Essar, would create separate ads for each service. During IPL Season 2, a different ad was shown each day, to attract the viewers' interest.

Vodafone was trying hard to capture the VAS Space because it is a potential cash cow for cellular companies. Vodafone also wanted to make the most of the IPL Season 2. Although IPL is a crowd puller, it is also a marketer's nightmare because of the clutter. IPL attracts all the deep pocket advertisers and to standout, one needs to think out of the box.

Ogilvy experimented with several characters and finally took its love for the term 'egghead' one step too far, creating characters that don the colour white (with black dots for eyes and a mouth), have heads resembling eggs, and disproportionately thin bodies. The idea was to tell the VAS stories in a world akin to, yet different, from humans. The creatures were then given a characterisation: they are to lead simple lives, speak a language of their own (something that sounds like gibberish), move in a certain way, and even emote like human beings, with big frowns or big grins to do the trick.

Thus, the Zoozoo was born. Zoozoo is a semi alien semi-human character living in an earth-like place. These are very very simple beings who are very expressive. They laugh aloud, cry loud and have a child like simplicity around them.

The Making of 'Zoozoos'

Zoozoos are not animated characters. They are human beings who were made to wear body suits.

Prakash Varma, ad filmmaker, Nirvana Films, who directed the commercials revealed that the Zoozoos were a big challenge to create. The practical aspects of how they will move, talk, gesticulate and emote were very important. Essentially, costume design and artwork were crucial elements.

"It took me three weeks of pre-production to understand how it will work," says Varma. There were two fabrics that were considered for the body suits, and one was rejected for it had too many wrinkles and was shiny. The wrinkles would have shown when the characters moved, thereby shattering the illusion of animation. "So we chose the more practical, thicker fabric", Varma explains.

The production team divided the outfit into two parts: the body and the head. The body part of the outfit was stuffed with foam in some places, while the head was attached separately. To make it look bigger than a human head, a harder material called Perspex was used, which in turn was stuffed with foam (with scope for ventilation).

If one wishes to understand the size of this head, here's a fact: a human head would typically reach up to the mouth level of this giant Zoozoo head. "We kept the hands and legs thin, which is why we cast women – and occasionally children – wearing the costumes," says Varma. The thin limbs, contrasted with big bellies and a bulbous head, all add to the illusion that these creatures are 'smaller' than humans. Sets were created to suit the size of the Zoozoos.

Cinematically, this size was a trick: the creatures look smaller than they actually are on screen, to portray a different world of sorts. For this, the speed of shooting was altered: Nirvana Films shot it in a high-speed format to make them look the size that they do.

Furthermore, simple sets and backdrops were created and spray painted with neutral greys – a colour of choice so that attention isn't diverted from the main characters. For a supposedly 'outdoor' shot, even the shadow of a Zoozoo was kept 'live' and not done in post production: it was painted in a darker shade of grey on the ground. An even lighting was maintained throughout.

There was virtually no post production work done.

The films were shot by Nirvana Films in Cape Town, South Africa, with the help of a local production house there, called Platypus.

THE LAUNCH OF THE CAMPAIGN

On 20 April 2009, Vodafone Essar launched the Zoozoos advertising campaign. During the IPL Season 2, a total of 30 different TVCs including Cricket Alerts, Beauty Alerts, Phone Backup, *Chhota* Credit, Vodafone Maps, Vodafone Call Filter, Live Games, Musical Greetings, etc. were aired.

The Zoozoo Ads

The Response

Soon after they were aired on television, the Zoozoos and the ads became really popular. Commenting on their popularity, Rajiv Rao (Rao), Executive Creative Director, South Asia, Ogilvy and Mather India (O&M India), the advertising agency which created the ads, said "What makes them (Zoozoos) so endearing is that they are innocent people living in a simple world unlike ours, who laugh loud when they laugh. And who seem to be in an in-between world of animation and reality."

According to Prasoon Joshi, Executive Chairman of McCann Erickson India (May 2009), "Zoozoos have given something interesting to the Indian ad industry which has been seeing the same ideas dished out time and again. The 'zoozoo' concept has immediately connected with the audiences and any creative that can create an emotional connect with an audience has hit the right spot."

In April 2009, as the TVCs started being aired on television, they created the necessary buzz both in traditional as well as in social networking sites like Facebook, and Twitter and video sharing website, YouTube. All the TVCs were available both on YouTube and Twitter. For the week ended April 25, 2009, one ad on fashion tips was viewed 13,000 times on YouTube. On Google.co.in, the word 'Zoozoo' became the third highest search word on May 04, 2009. In Oct, 2010, there were 1 million Zoozoo fans on facebook.

Despite the high brand recall that this advertising campaign ensured for Vodafone Essar, not everyone was impressed by the company's ad strategy. Some analysts were doubtful about whether the ads would attract people living in the semi-urban and rural areas of India. They also wondered whether the popularity of the 'Zoozoos' advertising campaign would actually help the company increase its revenues.

Factors that Made the Campaign Successful

The success of Zoozoo is the success of minimalism and simplicity. Although the production process of Zoozoo ads is not simple, there is simplicity of the concept and the execution. Zoozoo also highlights the power of storytelling. Each ad tells a very simple story. Afterall brands are made through story telling.

Another factor that aided the success of Zoozoo is the scale of the campaign. Every day one new zoozoo ad was aired during the IPL season. This unprecedented scale kept the curiosity high among the viewers.

Vodafone has taken Zoozoo beyond advertising. The fan club in the facebook page of Zoozoo has already touched 1,00,000 and counting. The brand came out with an interactive quiz that showed the type of Zoozoo you are. There are also mobile downloads of wallpaper, screensaver etc. All these have transformed into a great viral movement. There are already a plethora of mail forwards and blogposts celebrating Zoozoos.

Concluding Note

ZooZoo is a great marketing story. Vodafone has benefitted immensely by this campaign. It caught the attention and fancy of the consumers, aroused curiosity, told stories and made people retell the story. 'ZooZoo' is a classic example of being remarkable.

CHAPTER 13

MEDIA DECISIONS

CONTENTS

The term media is plural for medium. In advertising terms, medium is a channel of communication, such as newspapers, magazines, radio and television. A medium is a vehicle for carrying the message of an advertiser to the prospects. It is indeed a vehicle by which advertisers convey their messages to a large group of prospects and thereby, aid in closing the gap between the producer at one end and the consumer at the other end.

Advertising has been instrumental in the phenomenal growth of the media. In the nineteenth century, publishers of newspapers and magazines were faced with the stagnant circulation of their publications, with the result that profits were limited. This was due to the fact that the entire cost of writing and production was covered by subscriptions and news-stand revenue only. If the circulation was to be increased, it was possible only when prices were reduced. With lower prices, the circulation went up, resulting in a widespread reach of advertisers for their selling messages that, in turn, earned more money for the media. Both the media and the advertisers seem to have been benefited in the process. The publishers increased their audiences, and profit; at the same time, advertisers could reach effectively to their prospective customers, making mass marketing possible for them. Today, every medium, be it a newspaper or a magazine, the radio or television, has a department with the responsibility of selling advertising space and time. The media themselves do advertise and promote the sale of their advertising space and time, for this is one of the important activities of the media.

With the existing traditional media like television and newspapers, and continuing proliferation of new media options like the internet, the advertiser's task of selecting the right medium/media to advertise has become very important. In addition to this, finding out how many people will be reached by the selected media, whether it is cost-efficient to select a particular medium, what is the right time to advertise in the selected medium and what geographic areas should be covered by the medium are some very important media decisions which a media planner has to take care of. This chapter deals with these main issues involved in media planning.

MEDIA PLANNING

Media Planning refers to the process of selecting media time and space to disseminate advertising messages in order to accomplish advertising and marketing objectives of an organisation. The basic goal of a media plan is to find out that combination of media which enables the advertiser to communicate the message in the most effective manner at lowest cost.

According to *George E. Belch*, "Media planning is the series of decisions involved in delivering the promotional message in the most cost-effective manner to the largest number of potential customers at lowest cost."

According to *Wells Burnett,* "Media planning is a decision process regarding use of advertising time and space to assist in achievement of advertising objectives."

According to *S.W.Dunn,* "Media planning is the process of determining how to use time and space of media to achieve advertising objectives."

Media planning involves taking the following decisions (also called, media decisions).

1. Deciding on the desired reach, frequency and impact
2. Choosing among the major media types (Media Mix)
3. Selecting specific media vehicles
4. Deciding on media timing (Media Scheduling), and
5. Deciding on geographical media allocation

STEP I: DECIDING ON DESIRED REACH, FREQUENCY AND IMPACT

The goal of a media plan is to reach as many people as possible in the target audience as often as the budget allows. Attaining this goal would require the media planner to work carefully with the concepts of reach, frequency, impact, exposures and GRPs and TRPs.

Reach (R) is the percentage of media audience exposed at least once to the advertiser's message during a specific time frame. Reach can be calculated with the help of the following formula:

$$\text{Reach} = \frac{\text{Number of househo的 truned in}}{\text{Number of houshousehold in the area}} \times 100$$

Thus, if a media plan reaches 50,000 households out of 2,50,000 households in a given area, during a specific time frame, then, reach = 50,000/2,50,000 × 100 = 20%.

Reach is one of the most important terms in media planning and has the following characteristics.

1. When reach is stated, media planners are aware of the size of the target audience. For example if a media plan targets roughly 8o lakh of women who are 20-25 years old, then a reach of 50% means that 40 lakh of the target audience will be exposed to some of the media vehicles in the media plan.
2. Reach measures the accumulation of audience over time. Because reach is always defined for a certain period of time, the number of audience members exposed to the media vehicles in a media plan increases over time. For example, reach may grow from 20% in the first week to 60% in the fourth week. The pattern of audience accumulation varies depending on the media vehicles in the media plan.
3. Reach does not double count people exposed multiple times if the media plan involves repeated ads in multiple media categories. Thus, if for example, an individual is exposed to an ad of Fiama Di Wiills Shampoo four times during one month, which is the specific time frame of a given media plan, he/she will be counted only once while calculating the reach. This is because reach represents the total number of people exposed to the marketing communication.

Frequency (F) refers to the average number of times different households or individuals are reached by a medium in a given period of time. The frequency of advertisement exposure of the target market depends upon the amount of reinforcement of the image required or the amount of reminding required having sustaining patronage from the target customers. The greater the frequency, the greater the probability of the advertisement message making a deep and lasting impression.

Let us assume that a particular media plan for a product A is designed to reach the target audience by advertising on the television channel Ten Sports during the Twenty-Twenty Series which will last for about a month. Now, a frequency of 3 would mean that, on an average, audience members of the Twenty-Twenty series had three opportunities to see the ad of product A.

Thus, from the above explanation we see that reach indicates the media dispersion while frequency shows the media repetition.

Impact (I) refers to the qualitative value of an exposure through a given medium. Thus, an ad for Revlon lipstick would have a higher impact in the magazine *Femina* than in *India Today*.

The relationship between reach, frequency and impact is captured in the following concepts.

- **Total Number of Exposures** (E): This is Reach times the average Frequency. Thus, E=R x F. This measure is also referred to as **Gross Rating Points** (GRP). If a given media schedule reaches 70 percent of the homes with an average exposure frequency of 3, the media schedule is said to have a GRP of 210 (70 x 3).
- A related measure to GRP is TRP i.e. **Television Rating Point**. A Television Rating Point is a measure of the purchased television rating points representing an estimate of the component of the target audience within the gross audience. In the case of a TV advertisement that is aired 5 times reaching 50% of the gross audience with only 60% in the target audience, it would have a GRP of 250 (5 x 50) . TRP in is this case should be 60% of GRP = 60% of 250 i.e. TRP= 150. This is the rating point in the target, 60% of the gross rating.
- **Weighted Number of Exposures** (WE): This is Reach times average Frequency times average Impact. Thus, WE= R x F x I.

The above terms are interrelated and inter-dependant and a different mix of these elements would yield different patterns of message delivery. Media planning, particularly under a given budget, must take into consideration the elements of reach, frequency, continuity and size. Reach is most important while launching new products, extension of well-known brands or infrequently purchased brands, or going after an undefined target market. Frequency is most important when there are strong competitors, high consumer resistance, a complicated story to tell, or a frequent purchase cycle.

Unfortunately, there is no single combination of these elements that is ideally suited to all kinds of advertising. Each time the advertiser has to make the most suitable pattern to get the most out of the advertising rupees he spends. However, the advertising budget would continue to be a limiting factor in the final adoption of a specific pattern.

Many advertisers also believe that a target audience needs a large number of exposures for advertising to work. They believe that too few repetitions can be a waste, because they will hardly be noticed. According to Krugman, there must be three exposures to an advertisement i.e. a person should see an ad three times if the ad has to work. Another factor arguing for repetition is that of forgetting. The job of repetition is to put the message back into memory. The higher the forgetting rate associated with the brand, product category, or message, the higher the warranted level of repetition.

Frequency Distribution, Effective Frequency and Effective Reach

Media planners also consider frequency distribution in order to fully understand how many exposures different people experience, that is, how many people will see an ad once, twice, three times, etc. This lets the media planner estimate the effective reach of the plan at the level of effective frequency needed by the campaign.

Effective Frequency refers to the minimum number of media exposures for a communication goal to be achieved, while **effective reach** refers to the reach (% of households) at the effective frequency level. Media planners choose an effective frequency based on the communication goals. Communication goals may vary from building awareness, preference, attitude change to trial, purchase, and repurchase. To change brand attitude requires more exposures (higher effective frequency) than does creating brand awareness. If the effective frequency is set for a given communication goal, the reach at that effective frequency level will be the effective reach.

Let us go back to the Twenty-Twenty example discussed earlier in the chapter. Let us also assume that the ad for product A is shown once in the first half of a game and once in the second half of the game. A total of 25% of households see the ad twice by watching the entirety of the game. During the first half, 14% of households see the ad once but then don't watch the second half. Another 14% join the game in progress and see the ad once during the second half. Thus, 14+14 = 28% see the ad just once. This leaves 47% of households (100% - 25% - 28%) who never see the ad. In summary, the frequency distribution is: reach of 25 at the frequency of 2; reach of 28 at the frequency of 1; and reach of 47 at the frequency of 0 (also called non-reach). If the advertiser believes that its ads are only effective if they are seen at least twice, then the effective reach is 25.

Now, if the ad for product A is also shown once during the highlights of the match and 23% of the households see the ad during the highlights as a result of which the frequency distribution has changed, media planners need to work with the new frequency distribution. Let us assume that the new frequency distribution is represented in Table13.1 given below.

Table 13.1: Frequency Distribution of the Media Plan

Frequency	Reach (%)
0	30
1	19
2	28
3	23

If the advertiser believes that its ads are only effective if they are seen at least twice, then the advertiser will want to know what percentage of households saw the ad two or more times. In this example, the effective reach is 51 because that is the sum of the reaches for frequencies 2 and 3 combined.

STEP II: MEDIA MIX (CHOOSING AMONG MAJOR MEDIA TYPES)

Media Mix decision involves two decisions to be made by the media planners:

1. Choosing between media concentration and media dispersion
2. Choosing among the various media categories

Media Concentration vs. Media Dispersion

A media planner's first media mix decision is to choose between a media concentration approach and a media dispersion approach. The media concentration approach uses fewer media categories and greater spending per category. This lets the media planner create higher frequency and repetition within that one media category. Media planners will choose a concentration approach if they are worried that their brand's ads will share space with competing brands, leading to confusion among consumers and failure of the media objectives.

Concentrated media strategy lets advertisers spend a higher percentage of their budget on frequency and reach because only one set of creative materials will need to be prepared. But a concentrated strategy is also an "all-eggs-in-one-basket" strategy. If the particular ad is not well received or the particular media category only reaches a fraction of the intended target audience, then it will perform poorly.

In contrast, media planners choose a media dispersion approach when they use multiple media categories, such as a combination of television, radio, newspapers and the internet. Media planners will use dispersion if they know that no single media outlet will reach a sufficient percentage of the target audience. For example, a concentrated approach using only ads on the internet might reach only 30% of the target consumers because some consumers don't use the internet. Similarly, a concentrated approach using a particular magazine might reach only 30% of the target audience, because not every target customer reads this magazine. But a dispersed approach that advertises in print magazine as well as on websites might reach 50% of the target audience. Media planners also like the dispersion approach because they feel that consumers who see multiple ads in multiple media for a given brand may be more likely to buy.

Media Category Selection

Whether media planners select media concentration or media dispersion, they still must pick the media category for the media plan. Different media categories suit different media objectives.

The different media available to advertisers for advertising their products are as follows.

1. Print Media - Newspapers and Magazines.
2. Electronic Media - TV and Radio (also referred to as broadcast media), Cinema Advertising

3. Direct-mail advertising - mail advertising directly to prospective customers via a postal service
4. Outdoor advertising - Billboards
5. Digital Interactive Media – Internet
6. Other Media – Yellow Pages, Product Placements, Infomercials, Speciality Advertising

The creative requirements of a media category affect the media planners' decision of which media to choose for advertising. Each media category has unique characteristics. For example, television offers visual impact that interweaves sight and sound, often within a narrative storyline. Magazines offer high reproduction quality but must grab the consumer with a single static image. Rich media ads on the internet can combine the best of TV-style ads with interactive response via a click to the brand's own Web site. Media planners need to consider which media categories provide the most impact for their particular brand. The costs of developing creative materials specific to each media category can also limit the media planners' use of the media dispersion approach.

Chapter 14 of the book discusses the major media types along with their advantages and limitations.

STEP III: SELECTING SPECIFIC MEDIA VEHICLES

Media vehicle refers to a specific newspaper, magazine, radio station, television program, outdoor advertising location, edition of Yellow Pages, etc., that can be employed to carry advertisements or commercials. For example, India Today magazine is a media vehicle in the magazine category of advertising media, Zee TV is a media vehicle in the television category of advertising media.

Thus, in the second step, while choosing the media category if an advertiser has selected television to advertise his brand of washing powder, in the third step of media vehicle selection, he might choose Star Plus channel to advertise his product, since he expects that most women and housewives (target audience) will watch this channel.

Similarly, a manufacturer of cosmetics like lipsticks and nail polish, in the second step, may choose magazines to advertise his products. In the third step of media vehicle selection, he can then choose Femina magazine to advertise his products as he feels that it would reach a large percentage of the target audience.

However, the selection of media vehicle is not so easy a decision. With reach and frequency considerations in mind, media buyers will compare media vehicles in terms of various quantitative and qualitative criteria.

Quantitative criteria consist of factors such as vehicle ratings, audience duplication with other vehicles, geographic coverage and costs. Media buyers will choose vehicles with high ratings and less cross-vehicle audience duplication when they need high levels of reach. Media buyers also evaluate the geographic coverage of media vehicles when implementing spot advertising such as heavy advertising in certain geographic regions. Finally, media buyers pay attention to the costs of each media vehicle. When two media vehicles are similar in major aspects, media buyers choose the less expensive media vehicle.

As per the media vehicle cost, media planners calculate the ***cost per thousand persons*** reached by a vehicle. This cost is represented by **CPM** which means cost per thousand (M is the Latin abbreviation for 1000). Let us now see how this cost is calculated.

$$\text{CPM} = \frac{\text{Cost of Advertising in the vehicle}}{\text{Circultion of media vehicle}} \times 1{,}000$$

If a full-page four-colour ad in Femina magazine costs Rs.69,000 and the estimated readership of Femina is 30 lakh people, then the cost of exposing the ad to 1,000 persons is calculated as follows.

$$\text{CPM} = \frac{₹\ 69{,}000}{30{,}00{,}000} \times 1{,}000 = ₹\ 23$$

On the other hand, the same ad in some other magazine may cost Rs.45,000 but may reach only 10 lakh persons. The CPM for this media vehicle will be Rs.45 as shown below.

$$\text{CPM} = \frac{₹\ 45{,}000}{10{,}00{,}000} \times 1{,}000 = ₹\ 45$$

The media planner in this case will rank the two magazines by cost per thousand and favour the magazine with the lowest cost per thousand for reaching target consumers. A media planner must also remember that several adjustments have to be applied to the cost per thousand (CPM) measure.

- First, the measure should be adjusted for audience quality. For instance, for a baby soap ad, a magazine read by 10 lakh young mothers will have an exposure value of 10 lakh, but if read by 10 lakh old men, will have almost a zero exposure value. Thus, if the cost of advertising in a magazine is, say, Rs. 84,000, and the circulation of the magazine is 84 lakh people, out of which only 30 lakh is your target audience then, CPM will be Rs. 28 (Rs.84,000/30lakh X 1,000) and not Rs. 10 (Rs.84,000/30lakh X 1,000).
- Second, the exposure value should be adjusted for the audience-attention probability. For instance, the readers of India Today magazine may pay more attention to the news and other articles than to advertisements in the magazine.

In contrast to these quantitative criteria, **qualitative criteria** in the choice of media vehicle are those that are primarily judgmental, such as vehicle reputation, editorial environment, reproduction quality, and added values. For example, media vehicles vary in reputation; newspapers such as The Times of India and The Hindustan Times generally enjoy high reputation. Furthermore, the editorial environment can be more or less favorable for advertisers. The impact of food ads, for instance, can be enhanced when they appear around articles about health or nutrition. Likewise, some magazines are better in reproduction quality than others, which enhance the impact of the ads. Finally, some media vehicles offer added values. Added values take various forms, and they benefit advertisers without additional cost. For example, a newspaper may publish a special page whose editorial context fits an advertiser's products. Media buyers can work with the media to invent creative forms of added values for advertisers.

STEP IV: MEDIA SCHEDULING (DECIDING ON MEDIA TIMING)

Media scheduling decision involves media planners deciding when to advertise. Here, the advertiser faces a macro-scheduling problem and a micro-scheduling problem.

The *macro-scheduling problem* involves decision regarding the pattern in which advertising should be timed for a given year. Given a fixed annual budget, should all months receive equal amounts of money or should some months receive more of the budget while other months receive less or nothing? Media planners can choose among four methods of scheduling: continuity, concentration, flighting, and pulsing.

1. *Continuity scheduling* spreads media spending evenly across months. For example, with an annual budget of Rs.12,00,000 a year, continuity scheduling would allocate exactly Rs.100,000 per month. This method is used in case of frequently purchased items like soaps and toothpastes, and ensures steady brand exposure over each purchase cycle for individual consumers. It also takes advantage of volume discounts in media buying. However, because continuity scheduling usually requires a large budget, it may not be practical for small advertisers.

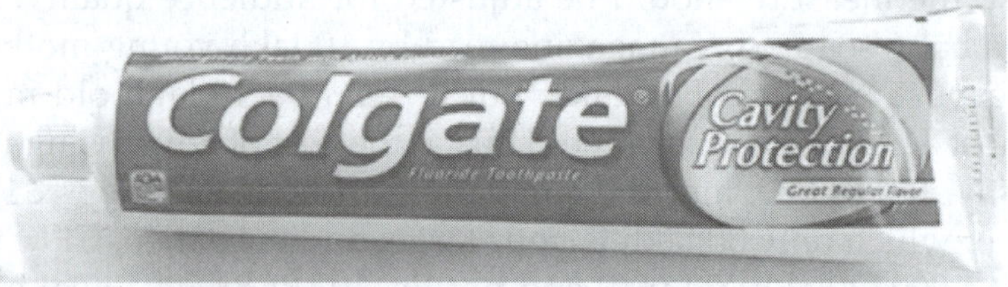

Advantages:
- Works as a reminder
- Covers the entire purchase cycle
- Cost efficiencies in the form of large media discounts

2. *Concentration scheduling pattern* calls for spending the entire amount available for advertising in a single period. Such a scheduling pattern makes

sense for those products which are seasonal. Let us suppose that 80 percent of a product's sales occur between April and September. The firm can follow here concentration scheduling pattern where the advertising for its product will be concentrated in the period from April to September. Concentration strategy can be followed by marketers of products like refrigerators.

Advantages:

- Maximization of the impact of the commercials by airing them at key strategic times.
- Products are not advertised during the off-season. This results in little waste since advertising is concentrated during the best purchasing cycle period.

3. ***Flighting scheduling pattern*** (also called 'bursting') alternates advertising across months, with heavy advertising in certain months and no advertising at all in other months. Any period of time during which the messages are appearing is called a flight, and a period of advertising inactivity is usually called a hiatus. For example, with a given budget of Rs.12,00,000 a year a brand could spend Rs.200,000 per month during each of following months – January, March, May, July, September and November ; and spend nothing during the other months, in hopes that the impact of advertising in the previous month can last into the following month. To take an example, advertising for the gift packs of chocolates sold by Cadburys is mostly done during the festive seasons *of Rakshabandhan, Diwali, Bhai Dooj,* Christmas and New Year, when it is known that many people buy gifts for the festivals. The Cadbury's commercial shown here was telecast during the *Rakshabandhan* festival in 2010 and 2011.

Advantages:

- The advantage of the flighting technique is that it allows an advertiser who does not have funds for running spots continuously to conserve money
- Maximization of the impact of the commercials by airing them at key strategic times.
- Little waste since advertising is concentrated during the best purchasing cycle period.

4. ***Pulsing scheduling pattern*** combines the continuity and flighting scheduling methods, so that the brand maintains a low level of advertising across all months but spends more in selected months. For example, an airline like Kingfisher Airlines might use a low level of continuous advertising to maintain brand awareness among business travelers. Kingfisher Airlines might also have seasonal pulses to entice summer-weary consumers to fly to various places. In budget allocation terms, a consumer goods brand may, with a budget of Rs.12,00,000 a year, spend Rs.50,000 in each of the twelve months to maintain the brand awareness and spend an additional Rs.1,00,000 in January, March, May, July, September and November to attract brand switchers from competing brands. The pulse scheduling method takes advantage of both the continuity and flight scheduling methods and mitigates their weaknesses.

Advantages:

- All the advantages of continuity and flighting are possible

Figure 13.1 shows the various scheduling patterns discussed above.

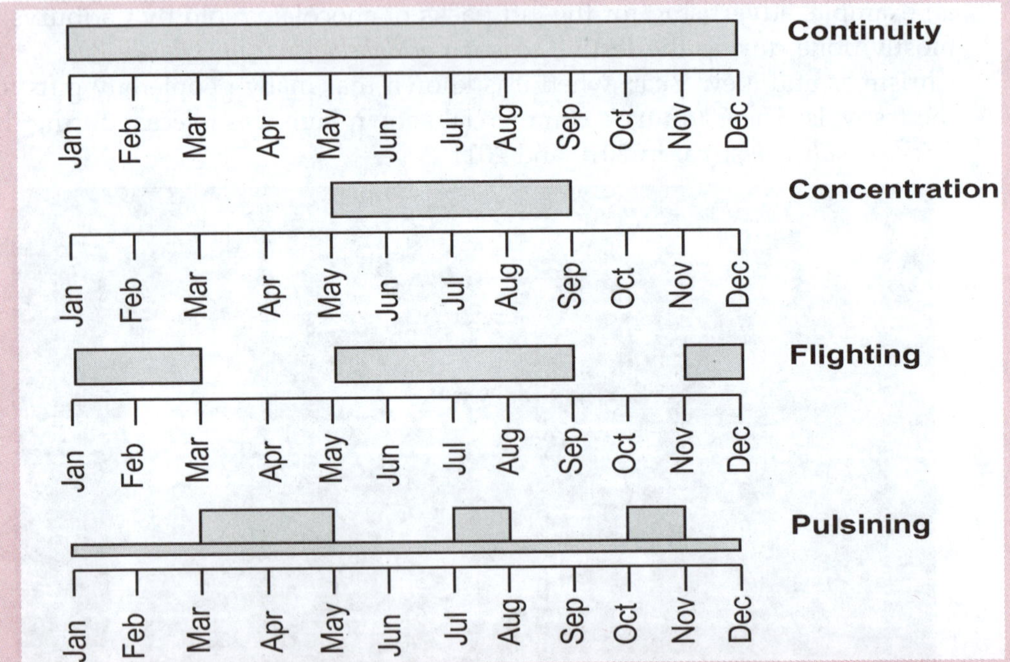

Figure 13.1: *Spread of Advertising Expenditure under various methods of Media Scheduling*

Factors Affecting Media Scheduling Decisions

Which scheduling method is the most appropriate for a given campaign depends on several important factors which are discussed below.

1. *Seasonality:* The first, and most important, factor is sales seasonality. Companies don't advertise leather coats in summer and suntan lotions in winter. Likewise, some products sell faster around specific holidays, such as flowers on Valentine's Day, Chocolate Gift Packs on *Rakshabandhan* and *Diwali*, and ornaments around *Diwali* and the wedding season. Companies with seasonal products are more likely to choose flight scheduling to concentrate their advertising for the peak sales season. Other goods, however, such as everyday products like milk and toothpaste, may lack a seasonal pattern. Everyday goods may be better advertised following the continuity approach. Media planners can use a breakdown of sales by month to identify if their brand has seasonal fluctuations, which can serve as a guide for the allocation. They can allocate more money to high-sales months and less to low-sales months.
2. *Product Purchase Cycle:* The second factor that affects advertising scheduling is the product purchase cycle, that is, the interval between two purchases. Fast-moving consumer goods such as bread, soft drinks and soaps require continuous weekly advertising in a competitive market to constantly reinforce brand awareness and influence frequently-made purchase decisions. In contrast, less-frequently purchased products such as a vacuum cleaner may only need advertising a few times a year.
3. *Interval between Decision Making and Consumption:* The third factor that affects media scheduling is the time interval between when the purchase decision is made and when a product or service is actually bought and consumed. For example, many families who take summer vacations may plan their trips months before the actual trips. That is, they make purchase decision in advance. Thus, travel industry advertisers will schedule their ads months before the summer. Advertising has to be in sync with the time of decision making, instead of the actual consumption time.
4. *Buyer Turnover:* Buyer turnover expresses the rate at which new buyers enter the market. The higher this rate, the more continuous the advertising should be.
5. *Forgetting Rate:* The forgetting rate is the rate at which the buyer forgets the brand. The higher the forgetting rate, the more continuous the advertising should be.

Media Scheduling decision also involves a *micro-scheduling problem*. The micro-scheduling problem calls for allocating advertising expenditures within a short period to obtain maximum impact. Suppose a firm decides to buy 30 radio spots in the month of June. Advertising messages for the month can be concentrated between the 15th to the 20th day of the month, or dispersed continuously throughout the month, or dispersed intermittently during the month following the concentration, continuity, flighting and pulsing scheduling methods as discussed above.

STEP V: DECIDING ON GEOGRAPHICAL MEDIA ALLOCATION

In addition to allocating advertising by media category, media planners must allocate advertising by geography. In general, a company that sells nationally can take one of three approaches to geographic spending allocation:

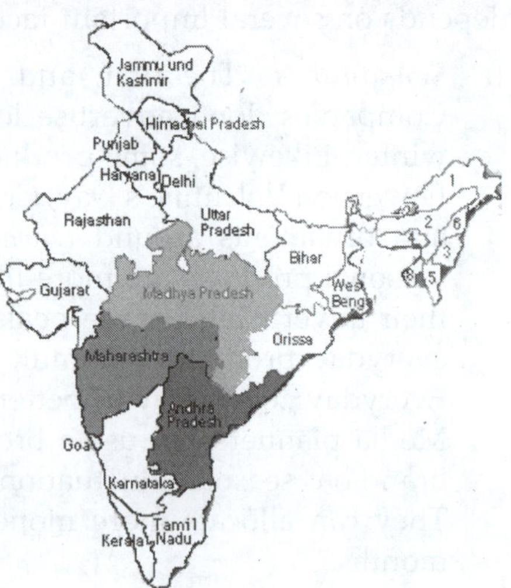

(*i*) a national approach (advertise in all markets),
(*ii*) a spot approach (advertise only in selected markets), or
(*iii*) a combined national plus spot approach (advertise in all markets with additional spending in selected markets)

For instance, a company makes "national buys" (i.e. chooses a national approach) when it places ads in nationally circulated magazines. It makes "spot buys" (i.e. uses the spot approach) when it buys space in regional editions of magazines.

Media planners will choose a national approach if sales are relatively uniform across the country, such as for Surf Excel detergent powder or Maruti Alto car. A national approach will reach a national customer base with a national advertising program. For many other products, however, a company's customers are concentrated in a limited subset of geographic areas, which makes a spot approach more efficient. For example, the sale of tractors is much higher in the agricultural states of India like Punjab, Haryana, etc. A spot approach will target these states and not the other states.

CONCLUDING NOTE

Media planners are playing an increasingly important role in today's advertising industry because of the continuing proliferation of new media options and the increased complexity of media decisions. A careful consideration of the various dimensions of a media plan - be it deciding on the desired reach, frequency and impact, choosing a particular media category to advertise in, selecting a specific media vehicle, deciding when to advertise or selecting the geographical areas to be covered by advertising - can produce a plan which can help in achieving advertising objectives.

QUESTIONS FOR DISCUSSION

1. What do you mean by the term 'Media Planning'? What are the various decisions to be taken while drawing the media plan of an organisation?

2. Write short notes on:
   (a) Reach (b) Frequency (c) Impact
   (d) TRP (e) CPM
3. What are the implications of using a media concentration approach and a media dispersion approach?
4. Discuss the various quantitative and qualitative criteria in choosing between different media vehicles.
5. What is the meaning of media scheduling? What are the various scheduling methods that an advertiser may choose from for advertising his product?
6. Write short notes on:
   (a) Continuity Scheduling Pattern
   (b) Concentration Scheduling Pattern
   (c) Flighting Scheduling Pattern
   (d) Pulsing Scheduling Pattern
7. Discuss the various factors affecting media scheduling decisions.
8. Name three products each which use the
   (a) Continuity Scheduling Pattern
   (b) Concentration Scheduling Pattern
   (c) Flighting Scheduling Pattern
   (d) Pulsing Scheduling Pattern

CHAPTER 14

TYPES OF MEDIA

CONTENTS

An advertising medium is a channel of communication like newspapers, radio, television, etc. through which an advertisement is transmitted to the target group of customers. It is a vehicle by which advertisers convey their messages to a large group of prospects and thereby aid in closing the gap between producer on one end and the consumer on the other end. Advertising can become effective only when suitable media of advertising are used. A major portion of advertising budget is spent on buying media time and space. Therefore, choice of advertising media is a critical decision in the area of advertising.

The different media available to advertisers for advertising their products are as follows.

1. Print Media – Newspapers, Magazines and Journals
2. Electronic Media - Radio and TV (also referred to as broadcast media), Cinema Advertising
3. Direct-mail advertising - mail advertising directly to prospective customers via a postal service
4. Outdoor advertising – Billboards
5. Point of Purchase advertising
6. Digital Interactive Media – Internet
7. Other Media – Yellow Pages, Product Placements, Infomercials

Let us now consider each of these advertising media one by one.

NEWSPAPERS

Newspapers reach all places and are read by all types of people. Therefore, newspaper advertising has a general and wide appeal. Newspapers can be classified on the basis of frequency of publication (daily, weekly, etc.), on the basis of language (English, Hindi, etc.), on the basis of time (morning, evening and day editions) and on the basis of geographic area covered (national or regional). The choice of a particular newspaper for advertising depends upon several factors such as circulation of the paper, the people who read it, the geographical area it covers, the cost of space and the general reputation of the paper.

Advantages

1. Newspapers reach every nook and corner. Thus, their coverage is high.
2. Due to wide circulation of newspapers, the cost of advertising per reader is low.
3. High frequency enables speedy preparation and publication of advertisement.
4. They offer a lot of flexibility. According to the convenience and necessity of the advertiser, the shape and size of advertisement can be changed.
5. Visual appeals can be created.
6. Advertisement can be repeated daily to remind customers about the product/ service and to create a lasting impression.
7. Newspapers also offer the advantage of geographic selectivity. People in a particular geographical area can be reached through regional or local newspapers.

Limitations

1. People read newspapers for reading the news and may not pay much attention to the newspaper advertisements.
2. A newspaper has a very short life due to which the advertisements may have a temporary effect.
3. This medium of advertising fails to carry message to illiterate people.
4. The quality of reproduction of newspapers is poor due to poor quality of paper and limited use of colour and visuals.
5. Most newspapers are cluttered with advertisements. Thus, a particular ad may escape the attention of the reader. The ads may also fail to draw the reader's attention, particularly when they are small in size or print.

MAGAZINES AND JOURNALS

Magazines and journals may be weekly, fortnightly, monthly or quarterly publications. Trade and technical journals are published for the professional use of auditors, company secretaries, doctors, bankers, teachers, lawyers etc. Special magazines for women and children are also published. Magazines like "India

Today", "Business India", "Business World", "Readers Digest" etc., are some of the popular magazines in India.

Advantages

1. Advertisements placed in magazines have a long life. A magazine is preserved for a week, fortnight or month and is read time and again.
2. High quality paper, printing and colour are used in magazines. Thus, reproduction of advertisements is better in magazines than in newspapers.
3. The ability of magazines to reach specialized audiences is a primary advantage of magazine. For instance, magazines like Femina and *Sarita* can very effectively reach the women audience.
4. A magazine is read more carefully and at leisure. Thus, there is a little chance of the advertisement escaping the reader's attention.
5. A magazine with high credibility lends prestige to the advertised product also.
6. Advertisers can distribute various sales promotion devices, such as product samples, coupons etc. through magazines.

Disadvantages

1. Magazine advertising lacks flexibility as changes in the copy of magazine cannot be made quickly.
2. Preparation of cost of magazine is higher and hence, advertising cost also would be higher.
3. Magazines have a limited circulation and cannot provide wide coverage.
4. Some readers look at an issue of a magazine after a long time. So the advertisement may take a long time to have an effect on the reader.
5. It takes time to print, bind and distribute the magazines. Thus, magazine advertising does not offer the benefit of timeliness to the advertiser.

RADIO ADVERTISING

Radio advertisements are broadcast from the transmitting stations of the commercial service of All India Radio and FM Radio. Whether used concurrently with other media, or used as a stand-alone advertising method, radio has proven time and again to be a cost-effective, powerful choice. It is effective both for increasing brand awareness and driving direct sales, and can be targeted to both national and local audience. Radio has especially gained more popularity after the launch of various FM radio stations and an increase in the popularity of radio advertising has also been noticed since then.

Advantages

1. Radio advertising has the advantage of wider coverage. The message also reaches the illiterates who can not read and write.
2 Radio is a low cost means of advertising. The advertising cost per person is very less as radio enjoys a very wide coverage.
3. The advertisement can be repeated daily and several times during the day. The advertisements can reach the people when they are traveling or relaxing or even working.
4. High degree of audience selectivity is possible in terms of specific radio programmes and geographical coverage (by selecting the national or local radio channels).
5. Radio advertising commands high attention. People are more receptive to the message as spoken words have a greater impact than written words.

Disadvantages

1. Radio advertising has a very short life. If the listener is inattentive, he will miss it.
2. Faulty transmission may make the advertisement inaudible.
3. Radio advertisements can appeal to the ear but not to the eye as no picture of the product is visible. Product demonstration is not possible.
4. Detailed messages can not be given due to the cost factor.
5. Radio advertisements need frequent repetition otherwise, people will forget the message. At the same time, frequent repetition of advertisements may cause boredom.
6. These days, there is a lot of clutter in radio advertising, and so, the listener may lose interest in the commercials being broadcast.
7. There is a tendency among the listeners to surf the channels during commercial breaks.

TELEVISION ADVERTISING

Television has become the fastest growing medium of advertising due to rapid expansion of cable networks. Both short commercials and sponsored programmes are used in the television advertising. It makes appeal through both the eye and the ear.

Tables 14.1 and 14.2 list the top advertisers on Indian television in 2008 (categories and brands, respectively) on the basis of ad volumes.

Table 14.1: The top advertisers on Indian Television (2008) – Categories

Rank	Categories	Ad Duration
1	Cellular Phone Service	27483
2	Social Advertisements	19345
3	Toilet Soaps	14605
4	Corporate/Brand Image	12864
5	Shampoos	12861
6	Aerated Soft Drinks	11617
7	Cellular Phones	11094
8	DTH Service Providers	9034
9	Life Insurance	8807

Note: *All figures are in thousands and are based on ad volumes in seconds*
Source: ***AdEx India-A Division of TAM Media Research***

Table 14.2: The top advertisers on Indian Television (2008) - Brands

Rank	Categories	Ad Duration
1	Airtel Cellular Phone Service	4859
2	Reliance Mobile	4550
3	Vodafone Cellular Phone Service	2929
4	Idea Cellular	2452
5	Tata Sky	2446
6	Colgate Dental Cream	2104
7	Virgin Mobile	1936
8	Pepsi	1870
9	Lux Strawberry Cream	1869
10	Sprite	1791

Note: All figures are in thousands and are based on ad volumes in seconds
Source: ***AdEx India-A Division of TAM Media Research***

Advantages

1. TV appeals to both the senses of sound and sight. As a result, it combines the two to produce a high impact on communication.
2. It has a very wide coverage as majority population watches television.
3. It reaches even those people who are illiterate. It thus, reaches all kinds of people.

4. The advertisement can be directed at a particular target group by broadcasting the ad during a particular programme and in a particular channel.
5. Through this medium, products can be shown and demonstration can be made and the product features explained.
6. It provides colour visibility making the message all the more attractive and impressive.

Disadvantages

1. Television advertising is very costly. Television commercial slots are sold at very high rates and the cost of production of a television commercial is also very high.
2. There is so much clutter of advertisements on television that many advertisements escape the attention of the viewer.
3. In case of television advertising, the message has to be repeated again and again to have a lasting impression else, it is easily forgotten.
4. People have a tendency to surf the channels during commercial breaks. Thus, there are many ads which the viewer may not view at all.
5. Television advertisements are sometimes disliked by the viewers due to exaggeration, offensive statements, deception and misleading claims.

CINEMA ADVERTISING

Films are a popular medium of advertising. Business firms get short films or cinema slides prepared and distribute them to selected cinema houses for display. These are shown before the start of regular shows and during intermission. The film contains, apart from pictures, a running commentary on the features, uses and superiority of the product.

Advantages

1. It has a mass appeal and covers all classes of people - poor, middle and rich.
2. Cinema advertising is very effective due to combination of voice, visuals and entertainment.
3. Audience selectivity is possible to some extent. Advertisers can advertise in local cinema theatres to reach local population.
4. It also helps to explain and demonstrate the use of a product.

Disadvantages

1. Cinema advertising is very expensive. The cost of production of advertising films to be distributed to cinema houses is very high.
2. It involves a lot of waste as before the show and during intervals, many people are not present in the theatre (as they are busy buying popcorns, soft drinks etc.) and very few who are present in the theatres are busy talking.
3. For screening of advertising films, the co-operation of the theatre owners is essential.
4. The audience may get irritated when more advertising films are shown.

DIRECT MAIL ADVERTISING

Direct mail refers to advertisements that are sent directly at the addresses of a target group of customers. A mailing list of potential customers to whom the message is to be sent is prepared. The advertisement is sent in the form of sales letters, folders, pamphlets, price lists, catalogues, etc.

Advantages

1. The message is directly addressed to the customers.
2. The message can be altered to suit different conditions.
3. Advertisements can be timed according to the wishes of the advertiser.
4. Detailed information about the product can be given.
5. If the right list of prospects is made, there is little wastage.
6. The great attraction of this method is its capacity to create and maintain personal contact.
7. The effectiveness of the advertisement can be measured easily. Feedback can be obtained through reply envelops.
8. The sales campaign is hidden from the competitors.

Limitations

1. It is not cheap, especially when printing and postage charges are high.
2. The preparation of proper mailing list is not an easy job.
3. The list prepared becomes obsolete in a short span of time.
4. The rejections and returns in posts are too many.
5. It is more applicable to industrial products, where the customers are limited.
6. Direct mail advertising is not suitable for illiterate people.
7. It has a "junk mail" image.

OUTDOOR ADVERTISING

This is the medium where posters, bill boards, electrical displays, etc are used to advertise the products and services. Posters are pasted on walls at important public places. Bill boards or large sized hoardings are fixed at busy street crossings. Sign boards are displayed on buses, railway coaches and other public vehicles. Colourful electric signs or neon signs are

put up at railway stations, bus stops and other public places and on high rise buildings. Billboards have been transformed over the years, and now advertisers use colourful, digitally produced graphics, backlighting, sounds, movement, and even three-dimensional-images on the billboards.

Advantages

1. Outdoor advertising is capable of gaining more attention.
2. It offers great selectivity. It could be used locally, regionally or even nationally.
3. Once the board is exhibited, it could be kept there for quite a long time.
4. It is a very good medium to stress the brand names and package identity.
5. Coverage is greater.
6. Cost is low.

Disadvantages

1. It has to be brief. Therefore, detailed explanation is not possible.
2. The exact effect created on prospects is difficult to measure.
3. It could be used only as a supplement to the other kinds of advertising. For example, it cannot be used for introducing a new product but it is an effective way to remind about an existing product.

POINT-OF-PURCHASE ADVERTISING

Banners, posters and stickers put inside the retail shops, chemist shops and shopping malls help to influence the last minute buying decision of the customer. These dealer displays serve as silent salesmen.

Advantages

1. Point-of-purchase advertising reminds the buyers about the product/brand and encourages them to buy products on impulse. For instance, a transparent box at the payment counter where the retailer stocks his chocolates, might urge a customer to buy a chocolate, as an impulse purchase.
2. It also secures dealers' cooperation and inspires them to stock the product/brand.

Disadvantages

1. Problem of creativity in the development of point-of-purchase material.
2. Improper placement of the material fails to secure the desired response from the customers.

INTERNET

With the increase in the use of internet all around the globe, the internet has become the most important medium of not only trade and commerce but also of advertising and promotions. Online advertising has changed the world of advertising. Internet advertising has been very useful in generating traffic to websites and in turn helps them do more business. When the correct banners and advertisements of the product or service are placed on many websites on the internet, there are chances that many people go through those websites and visit the website. One major advantage is that it is much cheaper considering the coverage it can provide to the advertiser.

With the growing popularity and usage of internet, the significance of advertising on websites remains unchallenged. With the power and reach of internet, the firm will have a huge target market. Advertising online is very effective. A combination of online advertising methods can be used to get the desired result. For instance, the firm can place all the online advertisements on a website that has the maximum visitors a day. This is crucial because more visitors will ensure that the firm gets good numbers of visitors to the website and business through online advertising. For instance, the ad of Idea 3G and Swift on espncricinfo.com shown here was given on a day when India was playing a cricket match against England.

The firm can create an advertisement that is attractive and interesting and delivers the message clearly. The most common form is the banner ads for online advertising. Chapter 15 of the book talks in detail about online advertising.

Advantages

1. Advertisements can reach a very large number of potential buyers globally.
2. Web advertisements are accessed on demand for all the 24 hours a day, 365 days a year and costs are the same regardless of audience location.
3. One-to-one direct marketing is possible.
4. Web advertisements can be interactive and targeted to specific interest groups and individuals.

5. Contents can be updated, supplemented or changed at any time at a minimum cost.
6. Multimedia will create more attractive advertisements.
7. Internet ads can efficiently use the convergence of text, audio, graphics and animation.
8. Internet advertising can be used to introduce new products or alternatives to existing products.

Disadvantages

1. Internet advertising is still in its infancy and has a limited market.
2. Some audience might only see the advertisement or visit the site, without acting on the message.
3. Cost is high in many circumstances.

YELLOW PAGES

It is a printed directory of local business names & products organized by type of product. You can find a full page ad, back page ad (inner/outer cover) & other small ads in yellow pages. It allows you to place your business listing or ad in selected classifications within the book, with the theory being that when people need your product or service, they look up the classification and contact you. Yellow Pages advertising is an important medium to consider in fast-paced, information-hungry society.

Advantages

1. One ad works all year long.
2. It gives your prospect a method of easily locating and contacting your business, even if they didn't initially know your name.

Disadvantages

1. Commitment for the entire year of advertising.
2. You are immediately placed with a group of your competitors, making it easy for the prospect to do comparison shopping.
3. Some classifications are so cluttered with advertising that the advertisement gets buried and thus, becomes ineffective.
4. It is only effective when a prospect looks you up in the correct classification.

PRODUCT PLACEMENTS

Product Placements refer to the promotion of a product/brand in a movie in such a way so as to enter the subconscious mind of the consumers. Such a placement of products/brands in movies is done by the advertiser in addition to using other conventional advertising media. People do not know that unknowingly they are putting these brands at the back of their minds because of the silent advertisement by the marketer in the movies, especially when the brands are projected to be used in the day-to-day activities of their favourite stars in the movies.

In "*Baghban*", Amitabh Bachchan is ICICI bank manager. The companies like Tata tea, Archies, Zip Telecom, & Ford also have been contextually fit to give the movie a real touch. In "*Main Hoon Na*", Shahrukh Khan is seen wearing Levis apparel, Reebok shoes, eats at Pizza Hut, sips coffee from Cafe Coffee Day, rescues Sushmita Sen from abductors who carry her in Santro, seen munching Ruffles Lays and sipping Pepsi. In Hrithik Roshan starrer "*Koi Mil Gaya*" Cadbury's India brand team started working with its director Rakesh Roshan for the milk additive brand 'Bournvita' right at the story stage and if one happens to watch this movie it can be seen that the product placement is a contextual fit. Bournvita brand is very subtly entering the subconscious mind of the consumers though the company is engaged with the other conventional advertising & marketing strategies also.

INFOMERCIALS

Infomercials are television commercials that run as long as a typical television program (can be as long as 30 minutes). Infomercials (also known as teleshopping) are normally shown at a time other than peak hours, such as late at night or early in the morning. Infomercials are often made to closely resemble actual television programming, usually talk shows, with minimal acknowledgement that the program is actually an advertisement. Infomercial advertisers may make use of flashy catchphrases or employ celebrities as guests or hosts in their ad.

Advantages

1. It saves time as the consumer can get a lot of information about the product simply by sitting at home.
2. Infomercials have a high impact as the demonstration of the product can be given in detail.

Limitations

1. Boredom in watching a 30-minute ad.
2. It is expensive to create ad films.
3. People quickly change the channel when they see such infomercials.

FACTORS AFFECTING CHOICE OF MEDIA

The choice of a suitable advertising medium by a firm requires a careful consideration of the following factors.

1. *Nature of the product:* The product to be advertised is a very important determinant of the advertising medium used. Consumer products such as soaps, toothpastes, soft drinks etc. are meant for the masses and thus, should be advertised using radios, television, cinema and newspapers and magazines which have a wide appeal. On the other hand, industrial products like tools,

machinery and equipment can be advertised in trade, technical and professional journals.

2. *Nature and size of the market:* The geographical area to be covered is another important factor in the choice of advertising medium. Advertising in local markets can be done more profitably through local newspapers, local radio stations, outdoor displays and local cinema theatres. On the other hand, when the entire national market is to be covered, the advertiser should use national newspapers and television while internet would be a wise choice in case international market is to be covered.
3. *Objectives of advertising:* The objective of the advertising campaign is another important factor in selecting the right advertising medium. For instance, when the objective is to introduce a new product in the market, a combination of various media may be used. Direct mail advertising is useful if the objective is to prepare ground for the visit of a salesman.
4. *Type of audience:* The audience to whom the message is addressed is an important consideration in choosing the appropriate medium of advertising. Illiterate and poor people can better be approached through radio and television. Newspapers, magazines, direct mail and internet can be used to convey message to the educated and well-to-do customers.
5. *Type of message:* The length and life of the advertising copy also determines the advertising medium to be chosen. Small advertisements can be given economically in radios, televisions and outdoor displays like billboards but for a large advertising copy, newspapers and magazines are more appropriate. In case a lasting impression is to be created, magazines and billboards may be used as they have a sufficiently long life. Newspapers, radio and television advertisements have a short life unless repeated regularly.
6. *Circulation of media:* Newspapers, television and other media having wide circulation are useful when the message is to be conveyed to a large number of people. Magazines, direct mail and other media having limited circulation are useful when the message is to be carried to a limited number of people.
7. *Cost of media:* The amount of funds available for advertising and the cost of the medium per prospect are important considerations in the choice of the media. The cost of an advertising medium per prospect can be calculated by dividing the total advertising cost incurred on a particular medium by the number of prospects covered by that medium.
8. *Media used by the competitors:* The media used by competitors also influence the choice of the medium of advertisement. The advertiser can determine the media pattern preferred by the competitors by analyzing the expenditure pattern of competitors in different media. It is advisable to follow the industry pattern unless there are valid reasons for selecting other media.
9. *Advertising budget:* the amount of funds available for advertising is an important factor in choice of advertising medium. A company having sufficient amount of funds for advertising can choose any advertising medium including the costly mediums like television. On the other hand, a company

having limited funds has a limited choice as far the advertising medium to be used is concerned.

CONCLUDING NOTE

An advertising medium is a channel of communication through which advertisement is transmitted to the target group. Advertising can become effective only when suitable media is used. A major proportion of advertising budget is spent on buying space and time on various media. Therefore, choice of advertising media is a critical decision. Before the choice is made, it is necessary to compare and evaluate the different media. Advertisers may use a mix of two or more media to get their message across to the target customers.

QUESTIONS FOR DISCUSSION

1. What are the different advertising media available to an advertiser for advertising his products?
2. Evaluate newspapers and magazines as a medium of advertising used by an advertiser.
3. Discuss the advantages and disadvantages of advertising on radio.
4. "Television advertising appeals through both eyes and ears." What are the other advantages that this medium offers to the advertisers? Does it also suffer from some drawbacks?
5. "Internet has emerged as a very popular medium of advertising in the recent past." Do you agree? What are the advantages and disadvantages of using this advertising medium?
6. What do you understand by product placements? Give examples of some product placements that the advertisers have used in the recent past.
7. Explain the various factors that should be kept in mind while deciding about the advertising media to be used.
8. Write short notes on:
   (a) Cinema Advertising (b) Direct Mail Advertising
   (c) Outdoor Advertising (d) Point-of-Purchase Advertising
   (e) Infomercials
9. Which advertising media and media vehicles would you suggest for advertising the following products? Give reasons.
   (a) Women Cosmetics (b) Books
   (c) Sports shoes (d) Children DVDs
   (e) Mobile Phones

CHAPTER 15

ONLINE ADVERTISING

CONTENTS

The number of internet users is on a rapid rise worldwide. Internet is used by people of all ages and types. Internet has become a major medium for communication and entertainment and is equally important when compared with the traditional entertainment and informative media such as television, radio, newspaper, magazines etc. The huge successes of Microsoft, Yahoo, Google, Amazon, etc. have proved that online advertising is here to stay and flourish. Sensing enormous potential in online advertising, the marketing departments of most large companies have set up e-advertising groups.

MEANING OF ONLINE ADVERTISING

Online advertising is a form of promotion that uses the Internet and the World Wide Web for the purpose of delivering marketing messages to attract customers. Examples of online advertising (also known as internet advertising) include contextual ads on search engines' result pages, banner ads, pop-ups, social network advertising, interstitial ads, e-mail marketing, etc.

TYPES OF ONLINE ADVERTISING

1. *Banner Ads* - A web banner or banner ad is a form of advertising on the World Wide Web. This form of online advertising involves embedding an advertisement into a web page. A banner can highlight the product/service/offer of the advertiser and by clicking on it the user will be taken to the advertiser's website, where he can create a suitable landing page to provide the user further information. Figure 15.1 shows a banner ad by HP on rediff.com.

   Cost: Usually paid by each thousand displays (CPM).

   Advantage: Good for branding and getting the message in front of customers' eyes.

   Disadvantage: Does not usually convert directly to sales - sales occur at a later stage based on customer recall.

Figure 15.1: *HP's Banner ad on rediff.com*

2. *Leader boards :* A leader board is a popular type of banner advertisement. At standard dimensions of 780 x 90 pixels, a leader board is the width of the page and typically lies between the title area at the top of a Web page and the content. Leader boards are thought to offer advertisers a great deal of space in a prominent position without intruding on content. Figure 15.2 shows a leader board ad for HP just under the title area of yahoo.com. The webpage also carries a banner ad of the same product lower down along with the contents of the webpage.

   Cost: Usually paid by each thousand displays (CPM).

   Advantage: A large flashy ad that customers will find hard to ignore.

   Disadvantage: May not convert directly to sales well. Customers will soon learn to ignore this ad type.

Figure 15.2: Leader board Ad for HP on yahoo.com

3. ***Skyscrapers :*** The extra-long, skinny ads running down the right or left side of a website are called skyscrapers. Figure 15.3 shows a skyscraper ad for Samsung Phones on yahoo.co.in

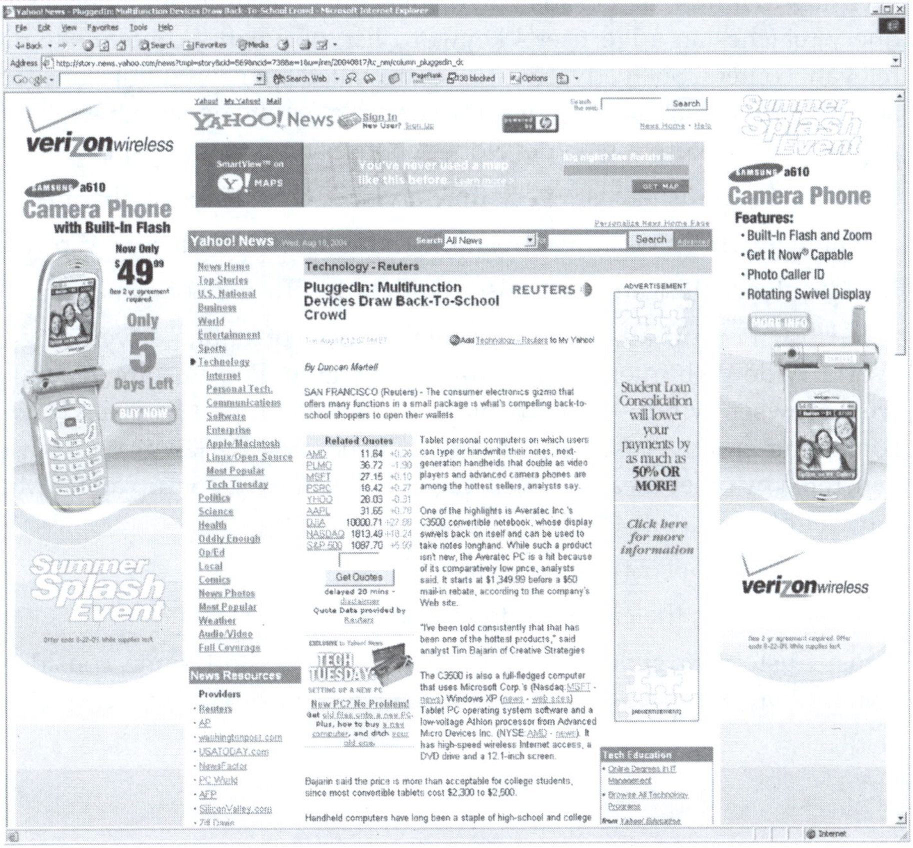

Figure 15.3: A Skyscraper Ad for Samsung on yahoo.co.in

Cost: Usually paid by each thousand displays (CPM).

Advantage: A large flashy ad that customers will find hard to ignore.

Disadvantage: May not convert directly to sales well. Customers will soon learn to ignore this ad type.

4. ***Floating Ads :*** These ads appear when you first go to a webpage, and they "float" over the page for five to 30 seconds. While they are on the screen, they obscure your view of the page you are trying to read, and they often block mouse input as well. These ads appear each time that page is refreshed.

   Advantage: They grab the viewer's attention and cannot be ignored. They can take up the entire screen, therefore from a branding point of view, they are much more powerful than a banner ad or a sidebar ad.

   Disadvantage: Many users get highly irritated because of these ads.

5. ***PPC - Pay Per Click Advertising :*** Pay per click (PPC) is an internet advertising model used to direct traffic to websites, where advertisers pay the hosting service when the ad is clicked. Cost per click (CPC) is the sum paid by an advertiser to search engines and other Internet publishers for a single click on their advertisement, which directs one visitor to the advertiser's website.

   Websites that utilize PPC ads will display an advertisement when a keyword query matches an advertiser's keyword list, or when a content site displays relevant content. Such advertisements are called sponsored links or sponsored ads, and appear adjacent to or above organic results on search engine results pages, or anywhere a web developer chooses on a content site.

   Cost: As it sounds, a cost every time a visitor that clicks on the link.

   Advantage: This method can result in extremely cost effective direct sales.

   Disadvantage: This can be expensive with little return if not managed carefully.

6. ***Pop-Ups :*** Pop-up ads or pop-ups are a form of online advertising on the World Wide Web intended to attract web traffic. Pop-ups are generally new web browser windows to display advertisements. The pop-up window containing an advertisement is usually generated by JavaScript, but can be generated by other means as well. Figure 15.4 shows a pop-up ad for Microsoft Silverlight.

   Cost: Generally a cost per thousand.

   Pros: Harder for the customer to ignore.

   Cons: Customers generally find them irritating, and some consider them spam. Many surfers use software that blocks pop-ups.

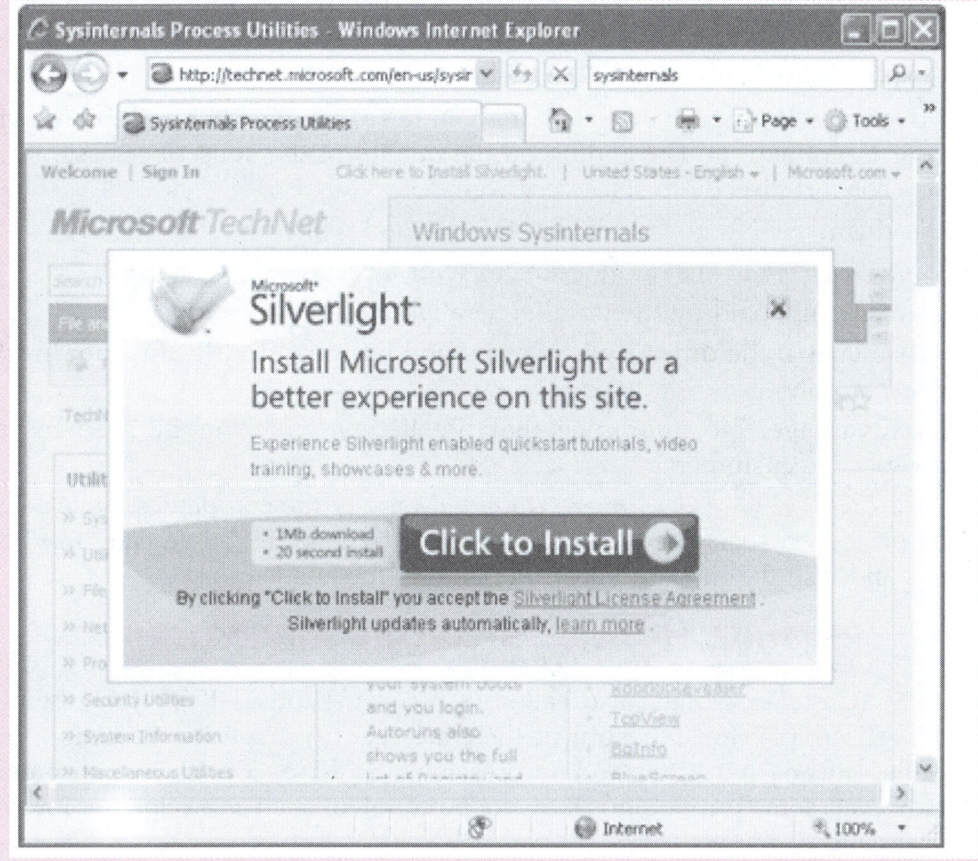

Figure 15.4: A Pop-Up Ad for Microsoft Silverlight

A variation on the pop-up window is the ***pop-under advertisement***, which opens a new browser window hidden under the active window. Pop-under ads do not interrupt the user immediately and are not seen until the covering window is closed, making it more difficult to determine which web site opened them.

7. *Interstitial Ads :* Interstitial pages are a form of advertisement on the web that appear between the web pages that the user requests. Because interstitials load in the background, they are a preferred way of delivering ads that contain large graphics, streaming media, or applets.

   Cost: Generally a cost per thousand.

   Advantage: Visitor is much more likely to look at the ad, and to look at it for longer than a banner ad.

   Disadvantage: Some visitors may find this annoying.

8. *Page Sponsorship :* A "Brought to You By" mention on a page.

   Cost: Usually paid by the period.

   Advantage: If correctly targeted, this can help convince the hard-to-convert customers. This may present excellent branding opportunities.

   Disadvantage: No guarantee that this method will convert to clicks.

9. *Newsletter Sponsorship :* A "Brought to You By" mention in a newsletter sent to subscribers.

   Cost: Usually a cost per mailing.

   Advantage: If properly targeted, this can raise awareness of your brand with your target market. Depending on the quality of the subscriber base, it can also convert directly to sales very well.

   Disadvantage: No guarantee that this method will convert to clicks.

10. *Paid Listings :* Inclusion in a directory for a cost.

    Cost: Usually paid by the term (generally by the year)

    Advantage: If the directory is relevant and has good traffic, this can directly result in sales.

    Disadvantage: No guarantee that the listing will ever be seen by the prospective customers.

11. *Social Networking site advertisement* : Many of the companies make ads to be posted on social networking sites (like facebook). People can "like" the ads and visit the links to know more about the ads.

REVENUE MODELS IN ONLINE ADVERTISING

- **CPM** (Cost Per Mille), also called "Cost Per Thousand" (CPT), is where advertisers pay for exposure of their message to a specific audience. "Per mille" means per thousand impressions, or loads of an advertisement. However, some impressions may not be counted, such as a reload or internal user action.
- **CPV** (Cost Per Visitor) is where advertisers pay for the delivery of a targeted visitor to the advertisers' website.
- **CPV** (Cost Per View) is when an advertiser pays for each unique user view of an advertisement or website (usually used with pop-ups, pop-under ads and interstitial ads).
- **CPC** (Cost Per Click) is also known as Pay per click (PPC). Advertisers pay each time a user clicks on their listing and is redirected to their website. They do not actually pay for the listing, but only when the listing is clicked on. This system allows advertising specialists to refine searches and gain information about their market. Under the pay per click (PPC) pricing system, advertisers pay for the right to be listed under a series of target words that direct relevant traffic to their website, and pay only when someone clicks on their listing which links directly to their website. CPC differs from CPV in that each click is paid for regardless of whether the user makes it to the target site.
- **CPA** (Cost Per Action) or (Cost Per Acquisition) advertising is performance based and is common in the affiliate marketing sector of the business. In this payment scheme, the publisher takes all the risk of running the ad, and the advertiser pays only for the amount of users who complete a transaction,

such as a purchase or sign-up. This model ignores any inefficiency in the sellers web site conversion funnel.

- **CPL** (Cost Per Lead) advertising is identical to CPA advertising and is based on the user completing a form, registering for a newsletter or some other action that the merchant feels will lead to a sale.
- **CPO** (Cost Per Order) advertising is based on each time an order is transacted.
- **CPE** (Cost Per Engagement) is a form of Cost Per Action pricing. Differing from cost-per-impression or cost-per-click models, a CPE model means advertising impressions are free and advertisers pay only when a user engages with their specific ad unit. Engagement is defined as a user interacting with an ad in any number of ways.

ADVANTAGES OF ONLINE ADVERTISING

The internet has opened up new communication options for personalized messages to be delivered to targeted customers. Reading habits are changing fast. More prospective customers are going online everyday and they are spending more quality time online than on traditional media. This explains why online advertising is being increasingly used by advertisers.

The following points explain the advantages of advertising online.

1. *Wider Coverage:* The online advertising gives the ads a wider coverage and this globally wider coverage helps in making the advertisements reach more audiences, which may ultimately help the advertiser in getting better results through his online advertising campaign.
2. *Use of Multimedia Tools:* The medium of online advertising offers unparalleled multimedia tools that can make ads very powerful and effective. Marketers can present their information with pictures, animation, sound and text.
3. *Creative:* In addition to large marketing potential, the medium offers unlimited opportunities for creativity.
4. *Targeted Audience:* The medium has the advantage of targeting precise customer groups.
5. *Easy to Track and Measure Conversion:* Measurability and easiness to track the conversion makes online advertising miles ahead on the traditional advertising methods. With the help of impressions, clicks, and conversions, advertisers can easily judge the effectiveness of the messages in their ads. A lot of effective analytics tools are available to measure online advertising campaigns which help in more improvisation of the ads.
6. *Cheaper Conversion Rates:* Because of the benefits of targeted marketing and effectiveness tracking, conversion rates in online advertising are cheaper than in traditional advertising.
7. *Informative:* In online advertising, the advertiser is able to convey more details about the product to the audience and that too at relatively low cost. Most of the online advertising campaigns are composed of a clickable link to

a specific landing page, where users get more information about the product mentioned in the ad.

8. *Brand Recall:* Online advertising, in combination with traditional media ads, can increase brand recall.
9. *Direct Response from Customers:* The biggest strength of online advertising is the direct response that it offers to both customers and advertisers. Audiences are just one click away from the advertisers, creating a unique opportunity for advertisers to engage in two-way communication with buyers.
10. *Lower Cost:* In comparison to traditional forms of advertising, online advertising is cheaper. Often, advertisers are charged only when visitors click on their ads.
11. *Flexible Payment:* Payment flexibility is another added advantage of online advertising and marketing. In offline advertising the advertiser needs to pay the full amount to the advertising agency irrespective of the results. But in online advertising there is the flexibility of paying for only qualified leads, clicks or impressions.
12. *Better ROI:* Since online advertising is mainly focused on performance based payment, the ROI is sure to be far better when compared with traditional advertising.

DISADVANTAGES OF ONLINE ADVERTISING

Despite all the benefits of online advertising, there are some disadvantages, which include the following.

1. *Scope:* Internet advertising is still in its infancy and has a limited market. Although increasing number of people are becoming tech-savvy and availing the web for their benefit, the average customers are still seen to vote for the traditional forms of advertising.
2. *Technical Obstacles:* The nature of a lot of display advertising is intrusive, so pop-up blockers (any software or application that disables pop-ups on a Web browser) can often prevent ads from being served as they were intended by the advertisers. Most browsers now block pop-ups. There are also extensions available for the Firefox browser, such as Adblock Plus, that will block advertising on Web pages. Technologically savvy consumers are increasingly using these methods to limit the advertising that they see.
3. *Connection Speed:* Bandwidth can also be an issue, although this is a shrinking problem.
4. *Advertising Overload:* Consumers are suffering from advertising fatigue because of advertising overload. Every advertiser wants to grab the attention of every consumer, but with so much information on the platter at a time, it is impossible to digest so much and the consumer, in turn, ignores most of the advertisements, resulting in low rates of return. Thus, while new technologies can provide great results, as soon as the market moves mainstream, it can get saturated.

5. *Additional Costs:* Usually the company advertising online hires a professional, be it a freelancer or some company to design his site and to strategically advertise the concerned product or service. This adds to the additional cost. Although it can be beneficial in the long run if your internet advertisement is successful and the product sells, one can suffer huge loss if it is not so.

INTERNET ADVERTISING IS MEASURABLE

Unlike any other form of advertising, online advertising is highly measurable. There are several ways through which you can measure ad success such as click-through rate, page impressions, cost per sale, etc.

Online advertising helps in tracking site visitors. While Pay-per-Click and some other forms allow advertisers to target ideal markets while keeping costs low, they also put crucial information about those ads and customers at the advertisers' fingertips.

Perhaps a certain ad has a high rate of clicks; tracking programs allow the advertiser to track ad's bounce rates, or the percentages of people who came to the site and then promptly left. Metrics can be deceiving: a high click rate may sound good, but a high bounce rate is an indicator that a website's visitors are not finding the content for which they are looking.

By looking at the metrics on impressions, click-through rates, bounce rates, and other numbers, an advertiser has the opportunity to improve their landing pages, as well as their ads and keywords.

PPC (Pay per Click) allows an advertiser to discover information about the people who are clicking on ads. A tracking program can pinpoint the geographical location of visitors and what keywords they used to find you, as well as how long they remained on the site and which pages they visited.

CONCLUDING NOTE

Online advertising, over time, has matured, and today internet advertisers use multiple forms of online advertising tools, including banner ads, pop-up ads and many others. The continuing progress of technology and innovative ideas have made significant contributions to making online advertising exciting, interactive, and affordable to organisations.

QUESTIONS FOR DISCUSSION

1. What is the meaning of online advertising?
2. Discuss the various types of online advertisements used by an advertiser.
3. Discuss the various revenue models in online advertising.
4. Discuss the advantages of online advertising.
5. What are the various problems faced by advertisers who advertise online?
6. Write short notes on:
   (a) Banner ads (b) Leader Boards (c) Pop-ups

Case Study

MOTOROLA'S MOTORAZR2 CAMPAIGN

Objective: To launch the latest mobile from Motorola's bouquet of world famous mobile phones in the Indian Market.

Interactive Medium used: Internet

The launch of Motorola's Motorazr mobile handset was divided in two phases – first phase created interest among users through interactive medium and the second phase showcased the mobile phone to the Indian audience through innovative creatives.

First Phase

Challenge: The first phase focused on creating curiosity towards the product launch. The product being launched was an upgrade of the previous version on Motorazr mobile handset. The new mobile model had sharper features than its predecessor.

Since the objective was to create curiosity amongst a fairly affluent, gizmo friendly, upwardly young audience, 'teaser creatives' were chosen to execute this campaign. Campaign was launched on the web, and on-ground to synchronize the teaser activity.

Campaign Planning

Keeping in the mind the single point focus of launching an upgraded version of a model which was already a very popular one within the audience, objective was to make the user switch to the new model instantly on its launch. The teaser banners were developed on the concept 'Sharper than ever'.

To extend the media reach of the campaign, the teaser banners were launched on four *most famous web portals in India* (msn, indiatimes, *zapak* and yahoo) on one single day. The banners were highly innovative and engaging to bring the proposition to life.

Media Highlights: *Synchronized outbreak on all the major portals*

The Internet campaign was launched on 24th August 2007 on the home pages of the four web portals. The launch campaign used creatives which themselves were one of the first of their kinds used for a product launch. The objective was to make the product appear as the sharpest object and so the creative version was in sync with it. The animation started with a copy reading 'Dangerously Desirable' & 'Sharper than ever'. Thereafter, a sharp razor like image animation 'Z' appeared from behind the content on the home page, cutting the page in between and leaving a message 'are you ready for Razr2 experience'. The sound effects in the background enhanced the experience of the animation. A click on the banner took the user to a landing page which was specially designed to spread the launch date with a message 'launching on 27th August'. The same animated effect was displayed in the landing page also.

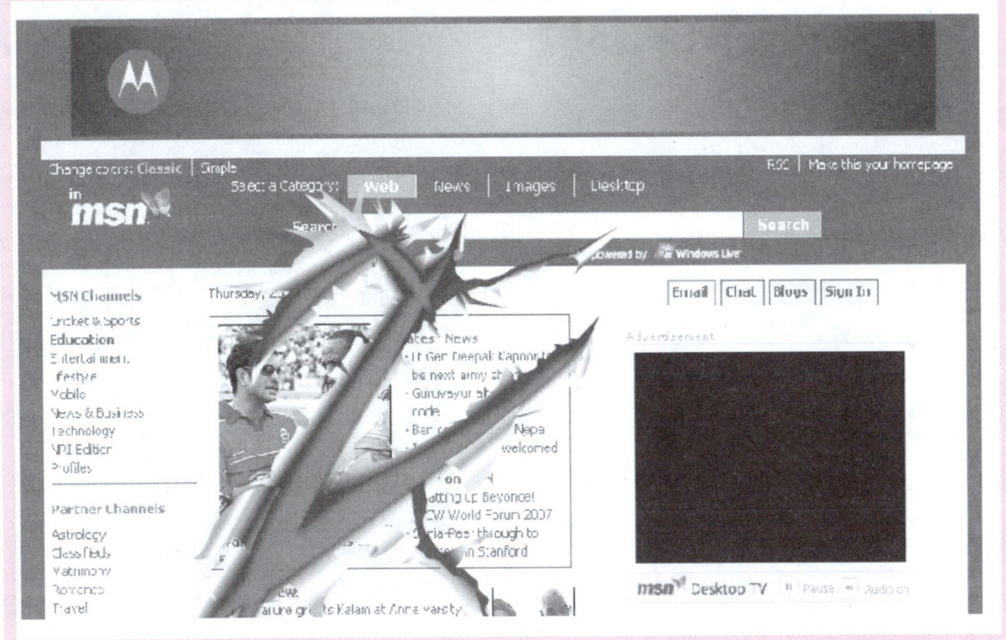

Figure 1: *Over the page banners with content cutting effect on msn.co.in*

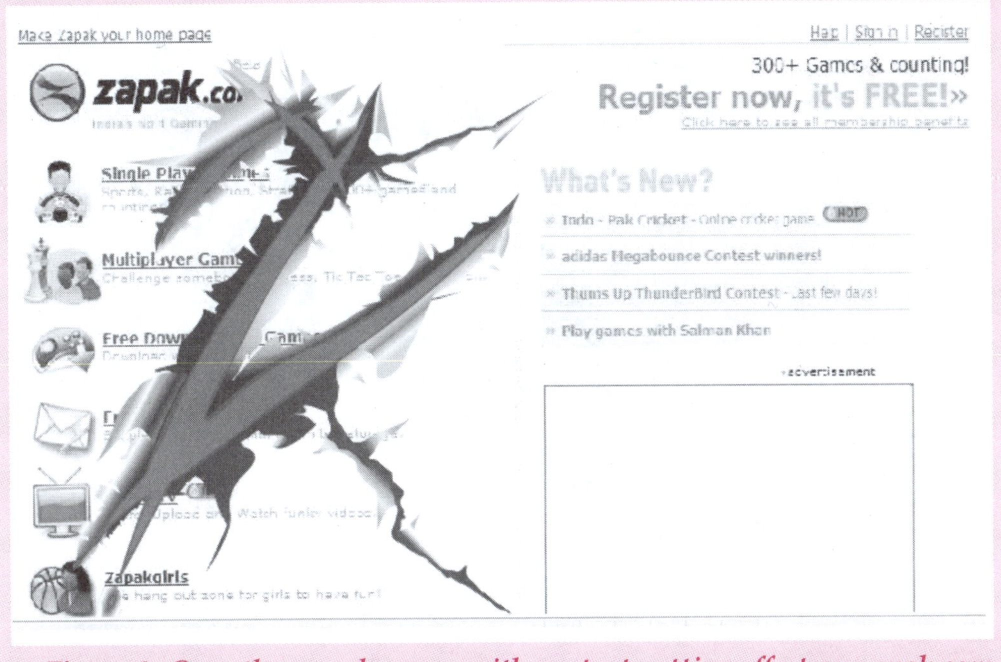

Figure 2: *Over the page banners with content cutting effect on zapak.com*

Figure 3: *Banner ad on zapak.com*

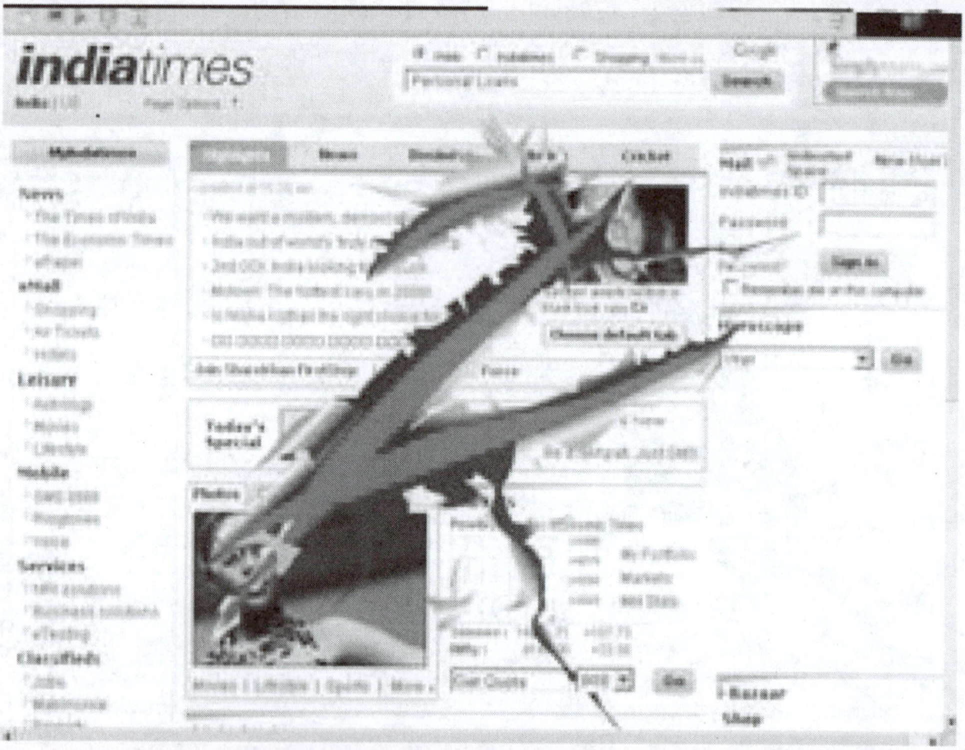

Figure 4: *A sharp 'Z' cutting the indiatimes.com page in between*

Figure 5: *Creatives on yahoo.co.in*

The impact through size and visibility of these properties across the main portals made the MotoRazr2 campaign an instant hit and a talking point in media circles. The response on day one itself was very promising with over 75,000 users clicking on the teaser banners.

First Phase Campaign Results

- Exposures: Around 3 Million Exposures in one day alone
- Interactions: Over 75,000 interactions (Initial Response)
- Media Used: msn.co.in, indiatimes.com, zapak.com, Yahoo.co.in

Second Phase

Objective: The second phase clearly chalked out the objective of introducing the product to the audience through brand building across media properties and maximizing interactions.

Media Highlights: The launch phase saw a multimedia campaign across the internet, TV and outdoor hoardings. The launch banners were also created keeping in mind the message 'sharper than ever'. A second time page cutting banner on

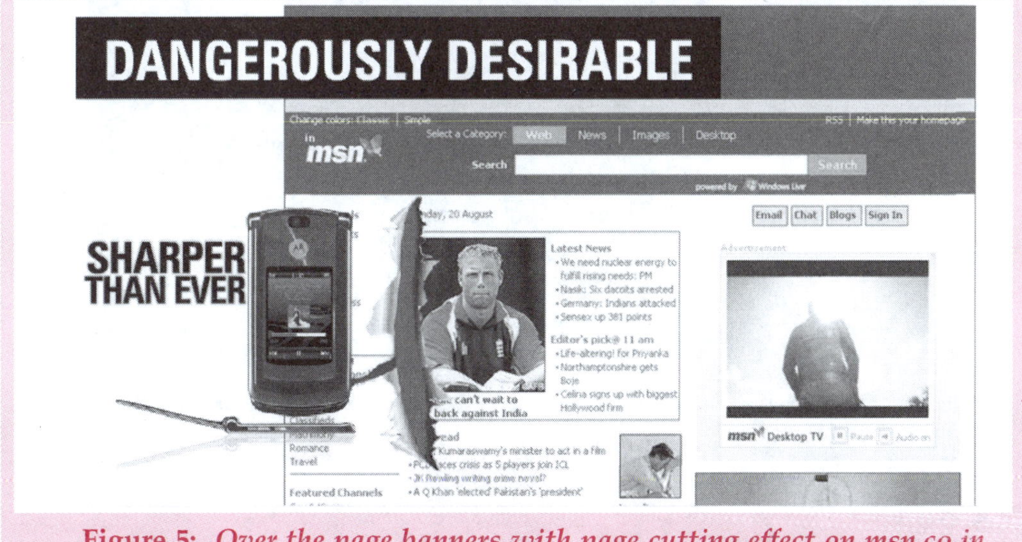

Figure 5: *Over the page banners with page cutting effect on msn.co.in*

msn, the other banner copy started with a mobile phone cutting the banner from the centre and then revealing the new phone from behind. Apart from expandable banners & video ads, messenger text links were also served specially targeting to desired audience on chat messenger.

Figure 6: *Banner Ads on zapak.com and indiatimes.com*

Figure 7: Page Tear Ad on yahoo.co.in

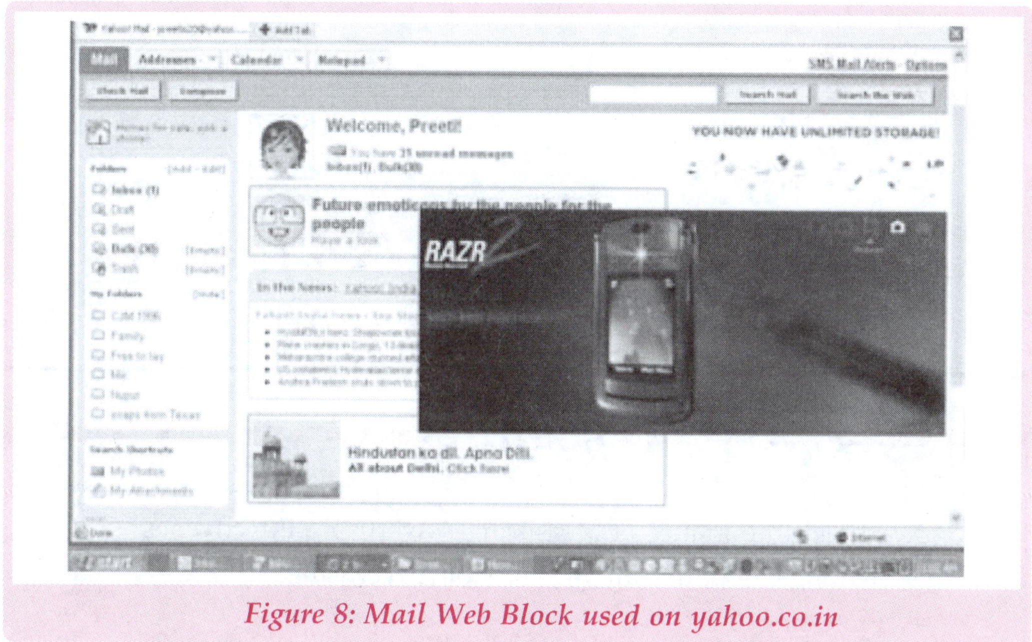

Figure 8: Mail Web Block used on yahoo.co.in

The campaign yielded results that were almost 100 % more than the expected, because of quality of good creatives & a combination of video ads with other activities.

Second Phase Campaign Results

- Exposures: Around 40 Million Impressions
- Interactions: 300 thousand interactions (Initial Response)
- Media Used: msn.co.in, Yahoo.co.in, Indiatimes.com & zapak.com (Instead of going too thin on media, the strategy was to concentrate on 4 Mass Portals and reach maximum users. These portals cover almost 80 % of mass Indian internet audience).
- High Point: Over the page banners & video banners did exceptionally well for the campaign.

Source: http://quasar.co.in/
Reproduced with permission

CHAPTER 16

MEASURING ADVERTISING EFFECTIVENESS

CONTENTS

Every year companies spend huge sums of money on advertising. Advertisers would want to measure the effectiveness of advertising to justify spending large sums of money on advertising. John Wanamaker's famous quote, "I know that half of my advertising money is wasted... I just don't know which half", calls upon the advertisers to evaluate their advertising campaigns to avoid any costly mistakes in advertising. In other words, it is important to determine how well the advertising campaign is working and to measure its performance against predetermined advertising objectives.

MEANING

Measuring advertising effectiveness refers to evaluation of advertising results against the predetermined standards of performance or objectives. Advertising effectiveness can be measured either before launching the advertisement (pre-testing) or after launching the advertisement (post-testing). Measuring advertising effectiveness is supposed to be one of the most difficult tasks in advertising.

Advertising objectives can be sales or communication objectives. In the evaluation process, it is estimated to what extent the advertising campaign has been able to achieve its sales or communication objectives. Thus, *the evaluation of an advertising campaign should focus on two key areas:*

- *Evaluating the Communication Effects of advertising* – is the intended message being communicated effectively to the intended audience?
- *Evaluating the Sales Effect of advertising* – has the campaign generated the intended sales growth?

If advertising fails to achieve the desired results, the money spent on advertising will go waste. Box 16.1 lists down some important points regarding measurement of advertising objectives.

Box 16.1: Measuring Advertising Effectiveness

- Determining whether an advertising campaign accomplishes its advertising objectives.
- Difficult to determine the effectiveness of advertising because -
  - ads may have several objectives,
  - ads work over extended time periods, and
  - results may not be observable
- Thus, one of the most difficult tasks in advertising
- Effectiveness can be measured either before launching the advertisement (pre-testing) or after launching the advertisement (post-testing).
- Evaluation of advertising effectiveness may aim at evaluating the communication effect and/or sales effect of advertising.

NEED AND IMPORTANCE OF MEASURING ADVERTISING EFFECTIVENESS

The need and importance of measuring advertising effectives arises due to the following reasons.

1. *To justify the cost of advertising:* Advertising is a costly affair. Evaluation of advertising effectiveness helps the advertising manager to justify the amount spent on advertising. Thus, the advertising manager carries out a cost-benefit analysis of advertising in which costs of advertising is compared with the benefits of advertising. If benefits of advertising are more than the costs, the advertising manager can justify the amount spent on advertising to the top management.
2. *To exercise control on advertising campaign:* Evaluation of advertising effectiveness helps to exercise control over advertising campaign. Through evaluation, the advertising manager comes to know whether advertising results are in accordance with advertising objectives. In case advertising results are not in accordance with advertising objectives, timely corrective action can be taken by making necessary adjustments in ad campaigns.
3. *For evaluation of advertising copy:* Measuring advertising effectiveness helps to evaluate the advertising copy and the messages given in the ad. Sometimes,

advertisements may be well-remembered and liked by the audience, but if the audience is not able to remember the brand name, or understand the message or the appeal used in the ad then such advertising cannot bring desired results to the organisation. By evaluating ad effectiveness, the advertiser can find out the weaknesses in the message content, appeals, etc. so that in future more effective ad copy can be designed.

4. *For effective media planning and media scheduling:* Evaluation of advertising effectiveness helps to know the impact of advertising in different media on the target audience. Consequently, the advertiser can take better decisions regarding media selection and media scheduling like selecting suitable media vehicles, time of issuing the ad, their frequency, appropriate television channels, television programmes, size of a print ad (full page or half page), etc.

5. *To reduce wastage in the amount spent on advertising:* By evaluating advertising effectiveness, the advertiser can come to know which ad is not effective in increasing sales or in communicating the message to the target audience. Such ads can then be discontinued. Thus, wasteful advertising expenditures can be reduced.

EVALUATING COMMUNICATION EFFECTS OF ADVERTISING

The communication effects of advertising can be evaluated by carrying out communication-effect research. One main objective of advertising is to communicate the desired message to the target audience. The effectiveness of advertising depends on the effectiveness of communication. *Communication-effect research seeks to determine whether an ad is communicating effectively.*

The communication effect can be measured in terms of effect of an ad on memory, knowledge or attitude of consumers. According to the communication-effect approach, if an ad is able to communicate the message to the target audience effectively, then the ad is evaluated as effective. If more viewers and readers are able to recall/recognize/identify the ad message, then it indicates that the ad is able to communicate the message effectively. Also called copy testing, communication-effect research can be done before an ad is put into media or after it is printed or broadcast.

Pre-testing

Pre-testing of advertisements is done before an ad is put into media. The following are the major methods of pre-testing the ads.

1. *Portfolio Tests:* Portfolio tests ask consumers to view or listen to a portfolio of advertisements. Consumers are then asked to recall all the ads and their contents. The recall level of an ad indicates its ability to stand out and have its message understood and remembered. (Recall tests are explained under the heading post-testing in this chapter.)

2. *Consumer Feedback Method:* The consumer feedback method asks consumers for their reactions to a proposed ad. They respond to questions such as-
   - What is the main message you get from this ad?
   - How does the ad make you feel?
   - What happened in the commercial?
   - What thoughts came to your mind?
   - Is there anything in the ad you don't understand?
   - What do you like or dislike in the ad?
   - What do you remember seeing in the ad?
   - What brand is being advertised in this ad?
   - Do you intend to try it or buy it?
3. *Laboratory Tests:* Laboratory tests use equipments to measure physiological reactions (like heartbeat, pupil dilation, perspiration, blood pressure, etc.) to an ad. These tests attempt to capture changes in the nervous system or emotional arousal during exposure to an ad. Several kinds of physiological instruments and methods are used to observe reactions to advertisements. These are explained below.
   - **Eye camera** – This is an instrument that photographs eye movements, either by photographing a small spot of light reflected from the eye or by taking a motion picture of eye movement. The device can be used to record the point on a print advertisement where the eye focuses a lot of times. Analysis can determine what the reader saw, what part of the ad he or she returned to and what point was fixed upon.
   - **Pupillometrics** – Pupillometrics deals with eye dilation. Eyes widen when something interesting or pleasant is seen, and contract when confronted with unpleasant, distasteful, or uninteresting things. An interesting application is the use of pupillometrics in evaluating television ads.
   - **Brain Waves** – Some companies test ads by means of the amount, nature, and distribution of the brain waves evoked. Consumers are placed into seats and have electrodes placed on different parts of their scalps. As the ad is shown to them, the brain wave activity in various regions of their brains is recorded. These measures cover various frequency ranges and are averaged over time and normalized for each individual being tested. Analysis of the frequency and the amplitude of this activity can be interpreted to check the attention-getting power of different parts of the commercial, as well as of the ad as a whole.

Post-testing

These types of tests are conducted after the ad has been run to determine whether the ad met its objectives. The following are the different types of post-tests used to measure advertising effectiveness.

1. ***Memory Tests:*** Memory tests are based on the assumption that an advertisement leaves a mental residue with the person who has been exposed to it. Thus, one way of measuring advertising effectiveness is to contact consumers who saw the ad and find out what they remember. Memory tests fall into two major categories: recognition tests and recall tests.

   One way to measure advertising effectiveness is to show the advertisement to people and ask them whether they remember having seen it before. This kind of test is called ***recognition test***.

   In a ***recall test,*** respondents who have read the magazine or newspaper are asked to report what advertisements or brands they remember seeing. The interviewer may go through a deck of cards containing brand names. If a respondent says that he remembers seeing an advertisement for a brand, the interviewer asks him to describe everything he can remember about the ad. Similarly, when a television commercial is run on a television channel during a particular time slot, the interviewer may try to ask from people who had seen the television programme a series of questions such as-

   - Do you remember seeing a commercial for any brand of soup?
   - (If no) Do you remember seeing a commercial for Knorr Soup?
   - (If yes to either of the above questions) What did the commercial show? What did the commercial say about the product?

   The first type of question is called ***unaided recall*** because the particular brand is not mentioned. The second question, in which the specific brand name is mentioned, is an example of ***aided recall***. The answers to the third set of questions are noted. The test requires that the respondents link a specific brand name, or at least a particular product category, to a specific commercial. If the commercial fails to establish a tight connection between the brand name and the selling message, the commercial will not get a high recall score.

2. ***Persuasion Tests:*** In persuasion tests, the consumers are asked how likely they are to buy a specific brand. Next they are exposed to an advertisement of that brand, along with the advertisements of other products and brands. After exposure, researchers again ask the respondents what they intend to purchase. The researcher analyses the results to determine whether intention to buy has increased as a result of exposure to the advertisement.

3. ***Inquiry Tests:*** Inquiry tests measure the number of responses to an advertisement. The response can be a call to a toll-free number, an e-mail, a website visit, a coupon return, a visit to a dealer, an entry in a contest, a call to a salesperson, or an actual transaction.

   Inquiry tests are used to evaluate the effectiveness of alternative advertisements using a ***split-run technique*** in magazines, where there are two versions of the magazine printed, one with ad A and the other with ad B.

The ad that pulls the most responses or the most number of inquiries is deemed to be more effective.

EVALUATING THE SALES EFFECTS OF ADVERTISING

The sales effects of advertising can be evaluated by carrying out sales-effect research. Sales-effect research seeks to determine whether the advertising campaign has generated the intended sales growth. Advertising's sales effect is generally more difficult to measure as compared to its communication effect. This is because sales are influenced not only by advertising but by many other factors like the product's features, price, packaging, competitor's actions, etc. Moreover, the effect of advertising on sales may be realized in the long run. In the short run, advertising may not generate immediate sales.

Researchers try to measure the sales impact through analyzing either historical or experimental data. The ***historical method*** involves comparing past sales with past advertising expenditures. Researchers may also use ***experiments*** to measure advertising's sales impact. For example, to test the effects of different advertising spending levels, a company could vary the amount it spends on advertising in different markets and measure the differences in the resulting sales levels. It could spend some fixed amount in one market area, half the amount in another area, and twice the amount in a third area. If the three market areas are similar, and if all other marketing efforts in the areas are the same, then differences in sales in the three areas could be related to advertising level. More complex experiments could be designed to include other variables, such as differences in the ads or media used.

Companies are generally interested in finding out whether they are underspending or overspending on advertising. One approach to answer this question is explained below.

A company's share of advertising expenditures produces a share of voice (that is, proportion of company's advertising of that product to all advertising of that product) that earns a share of consumer's minds and hearts and ultimately a share of market.

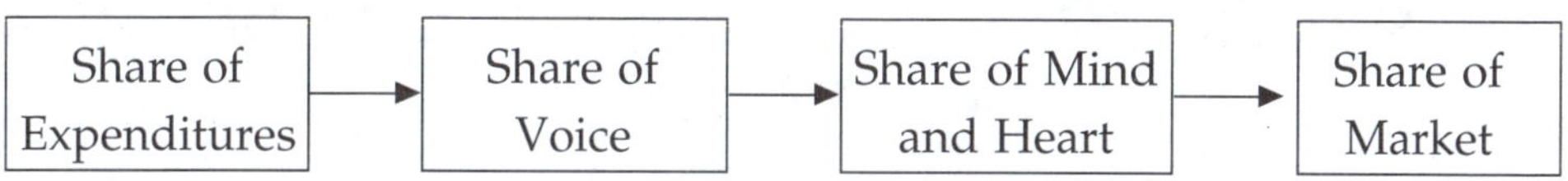

Let us assume the following data for three well-established firms-X, Y and Z, selling an almost identical product at an identical price.

Table 16.1: *Calculation of Share of Voice and Advertising Effectiveness*

Firms (1)	Advertising Expenditure (Rs.) (2)	Share of Voice (%) (3) = (2)/Total ad expenditure	Share of Market (%) (4)	Advertising Effectiveness (5)= (4)/(3) X 100
X	50,00,000	50	40	80
Y	30,00,000	30	30	100
Z	20,00,000	20	30	150
Total	1,00,00,000	100	100	

Note: An advertising effectiveness rating of 100 means an effective level of advertising expenditure. A rating below 100 means a relatively ineffective advertising level, and a level above 100 indicates a very effective advertising level.

Adapted from: Kotler, Philip "Marketing Management", 10th edition, Prentice Hall of India Pvt. Ltd, (1999), p.596

From Table 16.1, it can be seen that firm X spends Rs.50 lakh out of the industry's total advertising expenditures of Rs.1 crore. Thus, firm X's share of voice is 50% (50 lakh/1 crore). However, its share of market is only 40%. By dividing firm X's share of market by its share of voice, we get an advertising effectiveness ratio of 80, suggesting that the firm is either overspending or underspending on advertising. Similarly, firm Y is spending 30% of total advertising expenditures (i.e., its share of voice is 30%) and has a market share of 30%. Advertising effectiveness ratio of 100 means that firm Y is spending its money efficiently. Firm Z is spending only 20% of the total advertising expenditures (i.e., its share of voice is 20%) and has a market share of 30%. Advertising Effectiveness ratio of 150 means that firm Z is spending its money on advertising very efficiently.

ADVERTISING RESEARCH TECHNIQUES USED IN CASE OF PRINT ADS

The advertising research technique used by Starch, a leading print pre-testing service, is discussed below.

Test ads are placed in magazines which are then circulated to consumers. These consumers are contacted later and interviewed. Recall and recognition tests are used to determine advertising effectiveness. Starch prepares three readership scores.

1. *Noted:* Percentage of readers of an issue of magazine who remembered seeing the ad in the issue.

2. *Associated:* Percentage of readers who saw part of the ad that clearly indicates the brand or advertiser.
3. *Read Most:* Percentage of readers who read 50% or more of the written material in the ad.

   Scores in each area are then compared which can provide valuable insights into an ad's performance.

ADVERTISING RESEARCH TECHNIQUES USED IN CASE OF BROADCAST ADS

The following tests have been suggested for testing the effectiveness of broadcast ads.

1. *On-air tests:* In this test, the respondents are recruited to watch a programme on a television channel during the test commercial or are selected based on they having viewed the programme. They are then asked questions about commercial recall.
2. *In-home tests:* A videotape of commercials is taken to the homes of target consumers who then view the commercials. They are then questioned about the commercial.
3. *Theatre tests:* Consumers are invited to a theatre to view a potential new television programme or a movie along with some commercials. Before the show begins, the consumers indicate their preferred brands in different categories. After viewing the show, consumers are again asked to choose their preferred brands in different categories. Preference changes are assumed to measure the commercial's persuasive power.
4. *Trailer tests:* In this test, the shoppers in a shopping centre are shown a series of commercial and are given coupons to be used in the shopping center in a simulated shopping situation. By evaluating redemption, advertisers can estimate the commercial's influence on purchase behaviour.

ADVERTISING RESEARCH TECHNIQUES USED IN CASE OF RADIO ADS

One way to simulate the exposure to radio ads is to recruit respondents to a central location. A radio plays in the background, which contains the test ad. The consumer is then asked about the recall of the radio ads, followed by a re-exposure and diagnostic questionnaire. Also, a variation of the test is to allow the changing of the radio stations, providing a measure of the radio ad's likeability.

ADVERTISING RESEARCH TECHNIQUES USED IN CASE OF ONLINE ADS

Evaluation of the effectiveness of online ads makes use of the measurement of the following:

1. Hits – User requests for a file
2. Impressions – The number of times a viewer sees an ad
3. Click-throughs – When a user clicks on an ad to get new information

Table 16.2 gives examples of some advertising objectives and how to measure success in the accomplishment of these objectives.

Table 16.2: Measurement of Success in Achieving Advertising Objectives

Advertising Objectives	How to Measure Success
Stimulate an increase in sales	Number of enquiries for advertisement, number of enquiries converted into sales
Remind customers about existence of a product	Test customer awareness both before and after the advertising campaign, Number of enquiries
Inform Customers	Test customer awareness, Number of requests for further information
Build a brand image	Test customer awareness of brand recognition and perceived values
Sales	Level of repeat purchase
Build customer loyalty and relationship	Levels of customer retention
Change customer attitudes	Measure demographic profile of purchases, measure type of goods ordered by new purchasers, compare with previous data

Table 16.3 lists down the key factors of effectiveness of an ad and also suggests the types of research questions that advertisers can use to determine effectiveness.

Table 16.3: Effectiveness Research Questions

Effect	Research Questions
Perception	
Awareness / Noticed	What ads do you remember seeing? What ads were noted?
Attention / Interest	What ads did you find interesting? Did you read/watch most of them?
Brand Linkage	What brand is being advertised in this ad?
Recognition (Aided) Relevance	Have you seen this ad?How important is the product message to you?
Cognition	
Clarity	What thoughts came to your mind? What happened in the commercial?
Comprehension	Are the product features/benefits understood?
Confusion	What is the main message? Is there anything in the ad that you don't understand?
Recall (Unaided) and Brand Recall	What do you remember seeing in the ad? What brands were advertised?

Table 16.3: Effectiveness Research Questions

Effect	Research Questions
Emotion	
Liking	How did the ad make you feel? What feelings did the ad stimulate? What did you like or dislike in this ad?
Persuasion	
Attitude Change	In the product category (e.g. soap, toothpaste etc.), which brand did you choose?
Preference	What brand do you prefer?
Intention	Did you intend to try it or buy it?
Argument	What are the customers' reasons to buy it?
Believability	Do you believe the claims made?
Association	What is the personality of the brand?When you think of this brand, what products/ qualities/ features/ lifestyle do you think of?
Action	How many people responded (called/ used the coupon/ visited website/ visited dealer)?

Adapted From: Wells, Moriarty and Burnett, "Advertising: Principles and Practice", 7th edition, Pearson Education (2007), p.535

PROBLEMS IN MEASURING ADVERTISING EFFECTIVENESS

A company may face the following problems in measurement of advertising effectiveness.

1. *Cost:* The most common reason that companies provide for not measuring their advertising effectiveness is the cost of conducting a measurement program. Often companies believe that the money used for measuring their advertising effectiveness can better be spent on creating more advertisements or improving their product.

   Although this might possibly be true, let us consider the flip side of it. If the company does not measure the effectiveness of its current advertising program, they will not know if this program reaches their desired audience, sends the desired message or meets its intended goals. Being able to increase the advertising budget or improve the product will not help the company if the message is sent to the wrong audience or if the message that is comprehended by the consumers is different from the message that the company intended to send. As a result even the slightest evaluation effort can go a long way in ensuring that the desired message is sent to the appropriate audience and hence saving the company a lot of money.

2. *Research Problems:* The evaluation process of an advertising campaign can be very complicated, time consuming and expensive for a company that is trying to start such an effort. In addition, it can be very difficult to isolate and evaluate the effects of only one of the company's marketing efforts. For example, it might be very difficult to isolate the contribution of the company's television commercial from their overall marketing effort as a consumer does not make a purchase decision on the basis of what they see in a television commercial but consider a variety of factors (brand image, previous experience with the company, price of the product, etc.) when making a purchase decision. Thus, to measure effectiveness of one of these factors with the help of sales accomplished is very difficult.
3. *Disagreements on what, when and where to measure:* There are a variety of methods used while determining what, when and where to measure the effectiveness of an advertising programme. Choosing the appropriate measurement method depends largely on the industry the firm is in, the objectives of the programme, the media used and the person who will be analyzing the results. For example, sales manager may want to measure the contribution of the advertising programme on sales, whereas top executives may be interested in the effects of the programme on the company's image. These differences often lead to a great deal of confusion between the managers and might lead them to abandon the evaluation programme altogether.

CONCLUDING NOTE

Measuring advertising effectiveness helps the advertising manager to know how well the ad campaign is working and what worth the company is getting after spending a huge amount of money on advertising. Measuring advertising effectiveness helps to avoid costly mistakes, helps in selecting best advertising copy, in justifying the costs of advertising, in exercising control over the advertising campaign and helps in reducing wastage in advertising expenses. Thus, measuring advertising effectiveness is always in the interest of the organisation.

QUESTIONS FOR DISCUSSION

1. Discuss the need and importance of measuring advertising effectiveness.
2. How can communication effect of advertising be evaluated?
3. What are the various ways of evaluating sales effect of advertising?
4. What are the common methods for measuring advertising effectiveness?
5. Discuss some of the pre-testing and post-testing techniques used to measure advertising effectiveness.
6. Discuss some advertising research techniques used in case of:
   (a) Print ads (b) Broadcast ads
7. Write a short note on recall tests used for measuring advertising effectiveness.
8. What are the problems faced in measuring advertising effectiveness?

CHAPTER 17

ADVERTISING AGENCIES

CONTENTS

An advertising agency (or ad agency) is a service provider that works for clients to create an effective and goal oriented advertising campaign aimed at representing the company positively in the eyes of its target customers. Businesses hire advertising agencies to connect with their target customers. In the face of stiff competition, every company wants to break through the advertising clutter and create a favourable space for itself. Ad agencies help clients to do just this by creating persuasive and unique ad campaigns that make the brand stand out in the minds of customers.

Advertising agencies involve people with specialized knowledge and skills who are well-informed in all aspects of marketing, advertising and consumer behaviour. They have detailed knowledge of media and markets. They include skilled writers, artists, market analysts, media experts, etc. These specialists combine their talent to create effective advertisement for clients of the agency. Thus, an advertising agency is a specialized organisation which helps its clients to use advertising for marketing their goods and services in an effective manner.

MEANING OF AN ADVERTISING AGENCY

An advertising agency is an independent business organisation which undertakes the work of planning, preparing and executing advertising campaigns for its clients.

The *planning* aspect involves the study of the client's product or service, to understand its position in relation to the competitor's product or service, understanding the target market, their changing needs as well as the other trends in the marketing environment and, accordingly, formulating the advertising campaign. The *preparing* aspect involves writing, designing and production of an ad copy. The *execution* phase involves contacting the right kind of media for time and space, delivering the ads to media, checking and verifying the release of advertisement in media, making payment to the media and billing the clients.

Advertising agencies charge remuneration for the services that they render. Their remuneration comes from commission given by media, fees charged from the clients and percentage service charges on purchase of advertising material for its clients. Agencies sometimes provide many non-advertising services for which it charges extra fee on agreement basis.

Some of the top advertising agencies in India are:

- Mudra
- Lowe Lintas
- Ogilvy & Mather (O&M)
- JWT
- Leo Burnett
- FCB Ulka
- McCann Erickson
- Hindustan Thompson Associates
- Rediffusion-DY&R
- Saatchi & Saatchi

DEFINITIONS

According to *American Association of Advertising Agencies*, an advertising agency is -

i. an independent business organisation

ii. composed of creative and business people

iii. who develop, prepare and place advertisements in advertising media

iv. for sellers seeking to find customers for their goods and services.

This definition offers clues as to why so many advertisers hire ad agencies:

- Agencies are independent organisations (not owned by the advertiser, the media or the suppliers), so they bring an outside, objective viewpoint to the advertiser's business.
- Agencies employ a combination of business people and creative people.
- The agency provides yet another service by researching, negotiating, arranging, and contracting for commercial space and time with the various print and electronic media. Because of its media expertise, the agency saves the client time and money.

According to *Philip Kotler*, "Advertising Agency is a marketing service firm that assists its clients in planning, preparing, implementing and evaluating various activities of advertising campaign."

According to *Rozer and Borton*, "Advertising agency is a group of persons who have a specialization in advertising. It includes ad copywriters, ad designers, media selectors and advisors for various advertising issues.

FEATURES OF AN ADVERTISING AGENCY

From the foregoing analysis, it can be said that an advertising agency has the following features:

1. It is an *independent business* organisation, owned independently, and not by the advertiser or the media.
2. It *works for advertisers/clients* seeking to find customers for their goods and services.
3. It is *composed of creative people* like writers, artists, market analysts, researchers, media experts, etc. They combine their talent to create effective advertisement for the client.
4. An ad agency *serves its client by providing various services* like planning, preparing and implementing various activities of an ad campaign, media research, consumer research, follow up of ad, measuring the advertising effectiveness etc.
5. It *charges fee and service charges* from its clients. It also takes commission from media in which it issues advertisements.

FUNCTIONS OF AN ADVERTISING AGENCY

The various functions performed by advertising agencies for their clients include the following:

1. Account Management
2. Creative Function
3. Media Planning and Placement
4. Research

Let us now discuss these functions briefly.

Account Management

An account in advertising language is nothing but the client whose products and services are advertised and to whom the services are rendered. The client's satisfaction is of paramount importance for any agency and thus, a good rapport and communication with the client are absolutely essential.

While managing the account of the client, an advertising agency functions with an Account Manager or Account Executive. Within an advertising agency the account manager or account executive is tasked with handling all major decisions related to a specific client. This Account Executive performs the marketing and sales function. He presents the agency's point of view to the client. He also represents the client by representing the advertiser's point of view to the other members/departments of the agency working on the account. This requires good communication skills which should be used with a lot of tact and diplomacy. The Account Executive also performs sales promotion for the agency. He has to maintain old accounts as well as develop new accounts. He is responsible for obtaining the client's acceptance and approval of the advertising campaign prepared and the individual advertisements and the media plan. He is supposed to be fully familiar with the marketing and advertising problems of the advertiser and should effectively participate in offering acceptable solutions to those problems.

For very large clients, such as large consumer products companies, an advertising agency may assign an account manager to work full-time with only one client and, possibly, with only one of the client's product lines. For smaller accounts an account manager may simultaneously manage several different, though non-competing, accounts.

Creative Function

The creative department is responsible for creating and producing the advertisements. The advertising copy is written, the layout is prepared, illustrations are drawn, photography is finalized and a correct mechanical form for running it in the selected media is produced.

An agency's creative team consists of specialists in graphic design, film and audio production, copywriting, computer programming, and much more. The Account Executive discusses the client's problem on all aspects with the creative team. The creative team then works on the problem until it comes up with a workable solution of the problem in terms of a print or electronic advertising campaign.

Researchers

Research is a key function in an advertising campaign. The decisions on media selection, campaign design, creativity etc. are taken on the basis of findings of the research that buys advertising agency. Research makes every decision systematic and logical as it is based on facts and figures.

The research department is responsible for gathering the necessary information related to the client's problem. Collecting data and market intelligence is important for the agency to access a client's market situation, including understanding customers and competitors, and also are used to test creative ideas. For instance, in the early stages of an advertising campaign researchers may run focus group sessions with selected members of the client's target market in order to get their reaction to several advertising concepts. Researchers are also used following the completion of an advertising campaign to measure whether the campaign reached its objectives.

Media Planners

Once an advertisement is created, it must be placed through an appropriate advertising media. Each advertising media has its own unique methods for accepting advertisements, such as different advertising cost structures (i.e., what it costs marketers to place an ad), different requirements for accepting ad designs (e.g., size of the ad), and different time schedules (i.e., when the ad will be run).

Understanding the nuances of different media is the role of a Media Planner, who looks for the best media match for a client and also negotiates the best deals. The media planner has to allocate the advertising budget amongst media. He has to select the appropriate media. He decides about the frequency, size and position of an advertisement. He decides about its publication date. He receives the tear-off copies from the media when the ad is published. He is guided by the media research which he undertakes, or by research undertaken by an outside agency. It is ensured that the media plan is carried out properly so as to achieve the campaign's communication objective.

TYPES OF ADVERTISING AGENCIES

On the basis of services offered, advertising agencies can be of the following types.

(a) Full Service Agencies which offer all the services

(b) Specialized Agencies or Limited Service Agencies which offer only selected or specialized services.

Full Service Agencies

These are large or medium sized agencies capable of conducting a complete advertising campaign. They may have subsidiary companies or an association with other companies dealing with marketing research, public relations, media buying, film production, advertising, sales promotion, etc. Thus, these agencies are able to handle all the tasks involved in an advertising campaign be it designing of the campaign, buying media space, conducting marketing research, undertaking sales promotion, building public relations, etc. This means that a full service agency performs all the functions of an advertising agency – account planning, creative function, media planning and research. These agencies handle the advertising campaigns for the top most advertisers.

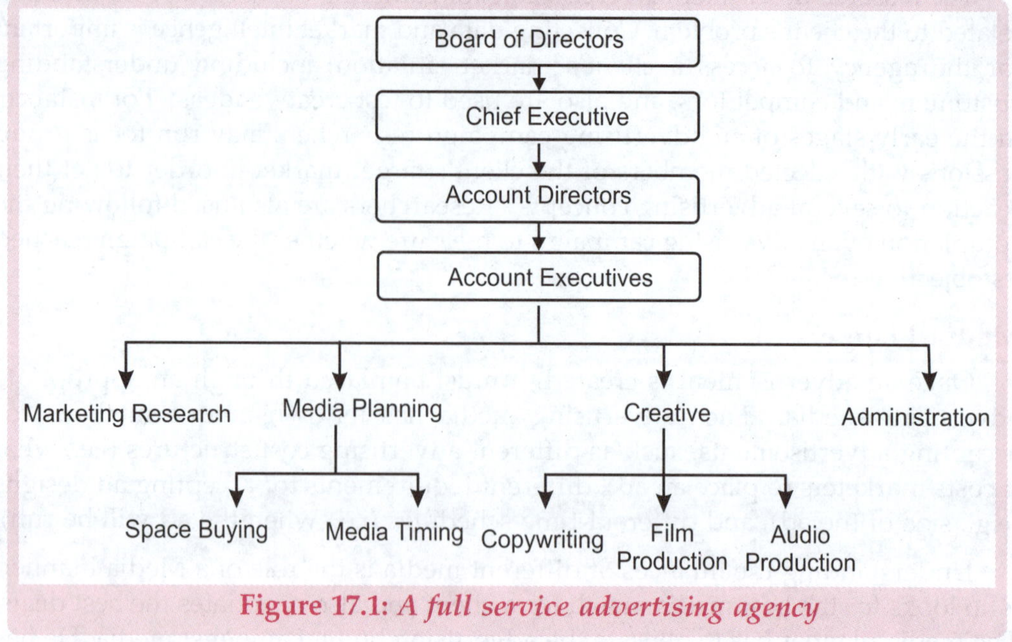

Figure 17.1: ***A full service advertising agency***

Figure 17.1 shows the departments and functions of a full service advertising agency.

Specialized Agencies

These agencies do not provide the entire range of advertising services. Rather, they provide specialized services in a particular area like media buying, copywriting, etc. Firms which do not want to avail of complete range of advertising services may opt for those specialized agencies which meet their specific requirements. Creative Boutiques and Media Buying Agencies are some examples of specialized agencies.

(a) Creative Boutiques

A Creative Boutique is a kind of a specialized agency that provides only creative services. It is usually small in size, with a few members who concentrate only on the creative execution of the client's marketing communications. A creative boutique will have writers and artists as its staff. There is no staff for media, research or strategic planning.

The client may seek outside creative talent for two reasons:

- Because he wants an extra creative effort
- May be because its own employees of the in-house agency or the agency that he has appointed do not have sufficient skills in this regard.

The full-service agencies also sub-contract work to creative boutiques when they are very busy or want to avoid adding full time employees to their pay roll. These boutiques generally perform creative function on a fee basis.

(b) Media Buying Agencies

A media buying agency is a specialized agency which buys media time and space in bulk from various media and sells them to different advertisers according to their needs.

The task of purchasing advertising media has grown more complex as specialized media proliferate, so media buying services have found a niche by specializing in the analysis and purchase of the advertising time and space. Agencies and clients generally develop their own media plans and then hire the buying services to execute them.

Some media buying agencies do help advertisers in planning their media strategies. Because media buying agencies purchase such large amounts of time and space, they receive large discounts and can save the small agency's or client's money on media buying. Media buying agencies are paid a fee or commission for their work.

IN-HOUSE ADVERTISING AGENCIES

An in-house agency is an ad agency set up, owned and operated by the advertiser. Many companies use in-house agencies exclusively, others combine in-house efforts with those of outside agencies.

A major reason for using in-house agency is to reduce advertising and promotional costs. Companies with very large advertising budgets pay a substantial amount to outside agencies in the form of media commissions. With an internal structure, these commissions go to the in-house ad agency. An in-house ad agency can also provide related work such as sales presentations and sales force material, package design, and public relations at a lower cost than the outside agencies.

Saving money is not the only reason explaining why the companies use in-house ad agencies. Time savings, bad experience with outside agencies, and the increased knowledge and understanding of the market that come from working on the advertising and promotion for the product or service day by day are also reasons. Companies can also maintain a tighter control over the process and more easily coordinate promotions with the firm's overall marketing programmes.

Critics of the in-house agencies say that they can give the advertiser neither the experience nor the objectivity of the outside agency and nor the range of services. They argue that the outside agencies have a more specialized staff and attract the best creative staff. Also flexibility is higher since if the company is not satisfied with the agency it can be dismissed, whereas changes in an in-house agency could be slower and more disruptive.

Advantages:

1. An in-house agency decreases the advertising cost by saving the commission which would otherwise go to the outside agency.

2. It allows greater control over advertising activities.
3. It also allows increased coordination between the advertiser and the agency personnel.

Disadvantages:

1. In-house agency faces the problem of dearth of talent as it cannot attract the best talents considering its narrow range of work.
2. There is too much management control to give free reign to creativity.
3. It lacks the experience that an outside agency gains by handling a lot of clients.

It is due to these disadvantages that more and more organisations now believe in outsourcing their advertising work to the outside agencies. They may use either full-service agencies or specialized agencies depending on their advertising requirements. These organisations believe that the outside agencies have more talented people, experience and knowledge to understand and solve each client's unique advertising problem and can help them to achieve their advertising objectives.

In-house agencies may later evolve into multi-client full-fledged agencies. For example, Lintas and Mudra evolved beyond the founding client Unilever and Reliance, respectively.

AGENCY COMPENSATION

Advertising agencies get paid for their services in the following ways:

1. Commission
2. Fee
3. Percentage Charges
4. Incentive Based System

1. *Commission*

The commission system of compensating the advertising agencies for the services rendered by them is the most traditional method. The agency is paid a fixed commission, which is usually 15%, from the media, on any advertising space or time purchased for the advertiser/client.

For instance, the agency places an order to purchase a full page ad in a national newspaper costing Rs.50,000. The newspaper (i.e. the media) will bill the agency for Rs.50,000 less 15% (i.e. less Rs.7,500) commission. The media also offers a 2% (Rs. 1,000) cash discount for early cash payment, which the agency passes over to the client. Thus, agency will bill the client for Rs.50,000 less 2% cash discount. Thus, the client will pay Rs.49,000 and 15% commission of Rs.7,500 is kept by the agency.

2. *Fee*

Agency executives might feel that 15% commission is inadequate for the services rendered to the client. Thus, in addition to the commission, the agency charges a fixed fee based on the work done. For instance, the agency may charge a fixed fee for a television commercial created by it which will be used over a long period of time.

Sometimes, the agency is paid through a combination of fees and commission method. The media commissions received by the agency are adjusted against the agreed fee. If the received commissions are less than the negotiated figure, the client has to make up for the difference.

Another variant of this method is the cost-plus method under which the client agrees to pay a fee based on the costs of the work the agency performs, plus some mutually agreed margin of profit for the agency. Thus, under this method, the agency is required to keep detailed records of the costs incurred in performing the desired services for the client.

3. *Percentage Charges*

Sometimes an agency buys some services like market research, artwork, printing, etc., from outside for the client. While billing the client, it adds some percentage of these charges as a markup. These charges are known as percentage charges.

For instance, if an agency pays Rs.1,00,000 for research conducted for its client, it may add 17.65% of these charges i.e. Rs.17,650 and bill the client for Rs.1,17,650. (Note that with these percentage charges, the agency will also earn a commission of 15% as 17.65% of Rs,1,00,000 = 15% of Rs.1,17,650).

4. *Incentive Based System*

Some companies use incentive based system to compensate agencies for their performance. The basic idea is to compensate the agency on the basis of how well the agency has been able to achieve the predetermined goals identified jointly by the client and the agency. Performance criteria may relate to market share, sales, or the quality of agency's creative work. The Incentive Based System is a good way to work in theory but in practice, it is very difficult to implement. The results achieved by the client are not only dependent on the agency's creative work but also on competitive advertising over which the client and the agency has no control. In such a situation, holding the agency responsible for the results is not fair.

FACTORS TO BE CONSIDERED WHILE SELECTING AN ADVERTISING AGENCY

The advertisers should keep in mind the following factors while selecting an advertising agency:

1. **The range of services offered:** Advertising agencies may be full service agencies or limited service agencies. A full service agency starts with an advertising brief given by the client, which is taken through the stages of development of detailed plans, creating campaigns, giving them the final

form after processing them through various stages involving art work, photography, etc., and arranging for placement in various media according to the agreed schedule. On the other hand, limited service agencies provide a few services and are generally specialized in those services. The advertiser should keep in mind his requirements at the time of selection. Generally speaking, the greater the range of services offered by the agency, more fully it can serve the client's needs.

2. **Assistance in preparing or reformulating marketing plans:** This may be of value to those clients who are new in a product category or are faced with a new type of a problem or are not aware about modern management approaches.
3. **Marketing and advertising research:** These are research companies specialized in marketing research, advertising research, or both. Some advertising agencies may have a full fledged research department which can undertake specified studies, the cost of which will normally be borne by the advertiser. Some agencies may not have a research department. They may, however, have a research team which may undertake limited research as requested by the agency teams working on different accounts.
4. **Agency team:** The agency team includes management specialists, market researchers, copywriters, media experts, production managers and art directors. The attitude, thinking, experience and personalities of the team members go a long way in the selection of an agency.
5. **Accounts handled:** The advertisers may look at the accounts that the agency handles and the accounts it has gained and lost. The work that the agency has done for the other clients matters a lot in the selection process.
6. **Compatibility:** Compatibility here refers to the personal equation of the advertiser with the client. The focus is on developing a strong client-agency relationship so that successful campaigns can be produced.
7. **Creativity:** Creativity is the main element in advertising. If the advertising agency is capable of great creative efforts, it is selected. Style, clarity, impact, memorability, and action are taken into account while evaluating creativity. Creativity can also be evaluated by considering the jingles, advertising story woven around the product, creative use of celebrity etc., which the agency has handled with previous accounts.
8. **Agency stability:** An agency which has been long in existence generally performs efficiently and effectively. Thus, one of the basic requirements is that the advertising agency must be known and should have some stability. Most of the clients do not prefer unknown agencies or agencies which have not been in existence for long.

In addition to the above, the process of agency evaluation involves regular assessment of two aspects of performance area – financial and qualitative.

The *financial assessment* focuses on how the agency conducts its business to verify costs and expenses, the number of personnel hours charged to an account and what payments are made to media and other outside service suppliers.

Qualitative assessment explores the agency's efforts devoted in planning, developing and implementing the client company's advertising campaign and an assessment of the achievements. For a qualitative assessment even the small things matter; such as a quick turnaround time, creativity because this is what the agency is in the business of, value added in terms of giving the clients a creative edge by giving them a creative leap etc. One can also evaluate agencies by their track record of losing clients or acquiring new clients and retaining them.

The parameters on which an ad agency's creative services dept is evaluated are as follows:

- Agency regularly produces fresh ideas and original approaches?
- Creative executions are consistently on strategy?
- Research is effectively used in strategic development and in pre-post testing of advertising?
- Creative group is knowledgeable about the company's products, markets and strategies?
- Creative group is concerned with good and consistent advertising communications and develops campaigns/ads that exhibit this concern?
- Creative group produces on time and submits for review in time to permit orderly revisions?
- Creative group performs well under pressure?
- Agency presentations are well organized with sufficient examples of proposed executions?
- Creative group participates in major campaign presentations?
- Agency presents ideas and executions not requested but which they feel are good opportunities?
- Creative group takes constructive criticism and redirection?
- Creative group effectively controls costs?
- Overall evaluation of creative services

CLIENT-AGENCY RELATIONSHIP

The client-agency relationship is very important to the success of the campaign. Agencies do their best to keep their clients well informed and share information, and it only makes sense for the client to do the same in order to maximize campaign potential.

Clients and their advertising agencies are constantly striving to improve their client-agency relationship. Clients should work closely with their respective agencies and give their input on decisions made. The fact remains that the industry is so young that there are thousands of opportunities available and time to consider only a select few. By sharing data and other information with each other, the client and the agency increase the likelihood of making better decisions in the future and eliminating repeated mistakes.

Following are the key areas on which the client organisation should focus in order to do their part in nurturing and strengthening the client-agency relationship.

1. Giving the agency the necessary time and resources to do its best work.
2. Ensuring that all relevant information is made available to the agency.
3. Working with the agency in a collaborative manner that puts a premium on mutual respect.
4. Identifying and articulating the outcomes that the agency's work is expected to produce.
5. Providing clear and complete direction to the agency.
6. Providing constructive and timely feedback to the agency.

The role of an advertising agency in strengthening its relationship with its clients requires the following:

1. The agency personnel must listen to and empathetically understand the client's needs.
2. The agency should be open-minded in its approach to appreciate anyone that can be a source of good creative ideas, including the client.
3. Agencies should understand that their clients' data are highly confidential.
4. The agency's creative work should be most suited to the client's marketing objectives, rather than focusing on awards.
5. The agency must not treat the client's money wastefully and stay within the budget limits.
6. The agency must respect and meet the agreed upon deadlines.

The bottom line is that the work an agency produces is as strong as the relationship between the client and the agency. Thus, both the client and the agency must work to develop a strong relationship between them and to produce successful ad campaigns.

CONCLUDING NOTE

Advertising is a complex job. It requires specialized knowledge and skills. A business firm might not have the requisite knowledge and skills to do the complete job of advertising itself. Thus, business firms engage advertising agencies for creation and production of advertisements. An advertising agency also helps a business firm in selecting a theme for advertising, writing the copy, deciding the layout, deciding the media, buying media time and space and carrying out advertising research. Advertising agencies need to be remunerated for the services that they provide to their clients. The right choice of an ad agency and the client-agency relationship are critical factors in determining the success of an ad campaign.

QUESTIONS FOR DISCUSSION

1. Give the definition of an advertising agency. Give some examples of Indian advertising agencies.
2. Discuss the various functions performed by an advertising agency.
3. What is the difference between a full service agency and a limited service agency?
4. What are the pros and cons of using an in-house advertising agency?
5. What are the various ways of fixing remuneration of advertising agencies for the services provided by them?
6. What factors should be kept in mind while selecting an advertising agency?
7. Write short notes on:
   (a) Creative Boutiques
   (b) Media Buying Agencies
   (c) Client-Agency Relationship

Appendix 17.1

STANDARDS OF PRACTICE FOR ADVERTISING AGENCIES

(As approved by the Advertising Agencies Association of India)

Every member of the Association shall carry on his profession and business in such a manner as to uphold the dignity and interests of the Association.

Obligations to Clients

1. Member Agencies must continue to render full Agency Service in reasonable conformity to the Association Agency Service Standards.
2. Member shall retain either commission granted by media owners or charge the clients a service fee which shall never be less than 15% of the Client's gross expenditure. Nor shall they supply material for advertising on any basis that can be considered as direct or indirect or secret, rebating. Where no commission is allowed by the Media Owner, the member will charge his clients minimum of 15% on the gross cost.
3. Member will not accept discount or commission, other than the regular agency commission allowed by the publishers without the client's knowledge and consent.
4. Member shall at all time use their best efforts to obtain for their clients the lowest rates to which such clients are entitled.

Obligation to Suppliers

Member shall take all steps to assure themselves as to the financial soundness of their clients.

Obligations to Fellow Agencies

1. Members are required to use fair methods of competition; not to offer the services enumerated above or services in addition to them without adequate remuneration or extension of credit facilities or banking services.
2. Members shall neither prepare nor place any advertisement in any medium, which
   - is knowingly a copy or a plagiarism of any other advertisement of any king whatsoever;
   - makes attacks of a personal character, or makes uncalled for reflections on competitors or competitive goods;
   - is indecent, vulgar, suggestive, repulsive or offensive either in theme or treatment;
   - is objectionable medical advertising and an offer of free medical treatment, advertising that makes remedial or curative claims, either directly or by interference not justified by the facts of common experience;

- concerns a product known to the member to contain habit forming or danger drugs; or any advertisement which may cause money loss to the reader, or injury in health or morals or loss of confidence in reputable advertising and honorable business or which is regarded by the Executive Committee of the Advertising Agencies Association of India , as unworthy.

3. In the event of a member providing to the satisfaction of the Executive Committee that a client has withdrawn his Account on the grounds of the member's refusal to undertake unethical Advertising no other member shall accept any business whatever from the said clients.

Source: www.asci.org

Case Study

THE SUCCESS STORY OF THE MUDRA GROUP

The Mudra Group is one of India's leading advertising agencies. It delivers innovative brand solutions to its clients through its four agency networks - Mudra India (Branding & Communication), DDB Mudra (Influence & Behavioural Change), Mudra Max (Integrated Engagement & Experience) and Ignite Mudra (Partnerships for Entrepreneurs).

Mudra's Clients

Some of Mudra's clients are Aircel, Amrutanjan, Amway, Bank of Baroda, Castrol, Dabur, Disney, Electrolux, Femina, Future Group, Godrej, HBO, HP, Hindustan Unilever, ITC, Jet Airways, Johnson & Johnson, Jyoti Laboratories, Larsen & Toubro, LIC, Max New York Life, Novartis, Panasonic India, Pepsico, Philips, Paras Pharmaceuticals, Reliance ADAG, Samsung India, Shell Foundation, The Economic Times, UNICEF, Uninor, Union Bank of India, Virgin India, and Volkswagen, amongst others.

The Success Story of Mudra

1980 - 25th March - A G Krishnamurthy founded Mudra

Mudra Ahmedabad was born with 15 employees, 500 sq.ft space, Rs 40,000 and Vimal as its first client.

Launch of Vimal ('Only Vimal')

This is the brand that launched Mudra and took it on its road to destiny. What began with sarees, moved towards suitings, shirtings and dress materials. The advertising used India's best known photographers and models and pioneered double spread colour ads. Cricketers such as Ravi Shastri and Allan Border endorsed the brands, leading to the genesis of cricketers endorsing brands.

1983 - Launch of Rasna ('I love you Rasna' campaign)

Rasna launched a soft drink concentrate with a range of nine flavours on a platform that offered both taste and economy. In 1986, Rasna became India's largest selling soft drink concentrate.

1985 - Mudra launched Godrej Powder Hair Dye

Godrej Powder Hair Dye was launched as a safe and natural dye. In 2008, it was relaunched as a hair colourant and called Godrej Expert Powder Hair Dye. Mudra also handles other brands in the Godrej portfolio such as Godrej No.1 soaps and Godrej Ezee. In a span of just 10 years, Godrej No. 1 became the 3rd largest in the soaps category.

1987 - The 1987 Cricket World Cup, won the Paras account

Mudra handled the Reliance Cup, which was the 1987 Cricket World Cup. Mudra's relationship with Paras Pharmaceuticals began this year, going on to build brands like Moov, Itchguard, Dermicool, Livon and Recova.

1989-90 - Nationwide growth, collaboration with DDB Needham World-wide

Mudra spread its wings - Delhi, Bangalore, Chennai and Hyderabad operations commenced. In 1990, Nestle walked in as the first MNC client and Mudra signed a collaboration agreement with DDB Needham Worldwide.

1991 - Birth of Mudra Institute of Communications, Ahmedabad

MICA is the first residential academic institution in the Asia-Pacific region, dedicated to meet the needs of the Integrated Marketing Communications industry. MICA produces many professionals in the field of advertising, communications & marketing.

1992 - Launch of Dhara Sunflower Oil

('*Dhara Dhara Shudh Dhara*' and 'My Daddy Strongest')

Dhara Sunflower oil was under the umbrella brand Dhara in 1992. Positioned on the platform of absolute purity, the campaigns remain one of the most loved in the history of Indian advertising.

1995 - Nestle Polo launched, Relationship with Samsung and Dabur began

The 'Mint with Hole' campaign was recognized as 'The Brand Launch of the Year'. This campaign was highly awarded across ad forums and categories like film, press and outdoor. It won the 'Campaign of the Year' award and was instrumental in Mudra winning the A&M 'Agency of the year' award. Mudra's Relationship with Samsung and Dabur also began this year.

1996 – McDonald's entered the India market

(McDonald's *mein hai kuch baat*)

From being perceived as a westernized place for the rich to now being known as a family restaurant that makes you smile, McDonald's has taken a big leap in the consumer's mind. The change of perception was made possible through a carefully executed communication plan that also complemented the strategic changes in pricing and menu, leading to an almost perfect example of a successfully executed campaign.

1997 - Positioning of Peter England as 'The Honest Shirt'

The 'honest shirt' campaign helped Madura Garments attain sales of 2 million shirts in the year 1998. It achieved that figure within just four years and it is the first brand in the mid-segment category to cross Rs. 100 crores in India.

2002 - Launch of Reliance Infocomm

(Reliance India-Mobile - *Kar lo duniya muthi mein*)

"Make a phone call cheaper than a postcard and you will usher in a revolutionary transformation in the lives of millions of Indians." - Dhirubhai Ambani

2003 - Madhukar Kamath came on Board

Madhukar Kamath returned to take charge at Mudra.

2004 - Mudra won the Big Bazaar account

(*Is se sasta aur accha kahin nahin!)*

Mudra won the account for Future Group's hypermarket chain - Big Bazaar. The biggest retail brand of India is also the fastest growing retailer of the world. Big Bazaar, a brand that celebrates Indianness in its own unique way, has revolutionized the way Indian consumers shop for daily needs. Over the last few years, Mudra has contributed to the brand's growth tremendously. During this journey, Mudra created successful campaigns such as the 'Great Indian Shopping Festival' - which generated business worth $ 130 million and attracted over 20 million walk-ins.

2007 - Madhukar Kamath elected as AAAI President

Madhukar Kamath succeeded Srinivasan K Swamy, CEO, RK Swamy BBDO, as the President of the Advertising Agencies Association of India (AAAI) and **in 2008, he assumed chairmanship of ASCI.**

2008 - Lauch of BIG TV (*Ho toh BIG ho*), Pratap Bose comes on board

Reliance ADAG made a big splash with the launch of its DTH offering - BIG TV. The creative concept is based on 'Life isn't for living small'. Within 50 days of its campaign launch, BIG TV received an unprecedented 500,000 installation requests. This is the fastest half million in the history of the DTH industry globally.

The same year, Mudra was instrumental in the rebranding of the Union Bank of India ('Your dreams are not yours alone'). This involved fundamental changes such as the logo, as well the structure and processes of the organisation. Mudra re-branded Union Bank of India by positioning it as a partner in fulfilling their consumer's dreams. 2008 was also an important year in attracting senior talent in the form of Pratap Bose, the former CEO of O&M India who joined the Mudra group as its chief operating officer (COO). He also serves on the Group's executive board.

2009 - Launch of Ignite Mudra, Volkswagen's brand campaign

Mudra Group launched a specialist agency in Ahmedabad called Ignite Mudra, to cater to the brand building needs of entrepreneurs nationally and internationally. The same year, DDB Mudra also unveiled Volkswagen's first brand campaign. To kick-off VW's brand campaign, DDB Mudra created a never done before print roadblock. On November 11th, 2009, 68.6 lakhs readers were introduced to Volkswagen. The Times of India, India's largest selling English news daily, was blocked nationally by a single ad.

2010 - First Time Ever 'A Talking Newspaper'

Mudra created a history in 2010 when in association with The Times of India and The Hindu, it came up with a 'Talking Newspaper' for the launch campaign of Volkswagen Vento.

Awards (as on 20th July, 2011)

- **International Awards** won 236 (Cannes , D&AD, Clio, One Show , Ad Fest, Communication Arts, New York Festival & others)
- **National Awards** won 931 (Abby, CAG, Emvies, Ad Club , PMAA, AAAI, OAC Awards, Showcase of India & others)

- Mudra's founder AG Krishnamurthy, has been honored multiple times Some of the recent awards won by the group are given below:
- **Brand Equity Ad Agency Reckoner - 2010**

  Mudra India ranked No.5, DDB Mudra ranked No.7, Mudra Max ranked No.11, Tribal DDB India ranked No.5
- Mudra Max won **Campaign Asia Pacific - Agency of The Year, India** and **Subcontinent Specialist Agency 2010**
- DDB Mudra's campaign for **Volkswagen Vento** won **'Most Innovative Campaign' of the Year** by NDTV Profit **2011**
- Tribal DDB India bags Gold at **Yahoo's Big Idea Chair Awards 2011**

(Compiled from www.mudra.com)

Unit–III
Legal and Ethical Aspects of Advertising in India

CHAPTER 18

Legal Aspects of Advertising in India

CONTENTS

Advertising is an important tool for a marketer to generate buyers' interest in his products and services. It is also immensely useful to consumers as it helps them in choosing the right products and services. However, with growing competition and in an attempt to increase their sales and market share, manufacturers and service-providers may be tempted to engage in deceptive and misleading advertising. This impairs public confidence in advertising. Thus, there is a need to put a check on unscrupulous advertisements to protect consumers against deceptive and misleading advertising and, at the same time, ensuring that advertisements are in the public interest. To achieve this objective, a number of laws have been enacted by the government.

STATUTORY PROVISIONS GOVERNING ADVERTISING

The major enactments which contain measures for the regulation of advertising in India are given in Box 18.1. The major provisions of these laws are briefly discussed below.

Box 18.1: Major Laws Regulating Advertising in India

1. The Consumer Protection Act, 1986
2. The Competition Act, 2002
3. The Drugs and Magic Remedies (Objectionable Advertisements) Act, 1954
4. The Trade Marks Act, 1999
5. The Cable Television Networks (Regulation) Act, 1995
6. The Cigarettes and Other Tobacco Products (Prohibition of Advertisement and Regulation of Trade and Commerce, Production, Supply and Distribution) Act, 2003
7. The Indecent Representation of Women (Prohibition) Act, 1986
8. The Indian Penal Code, 1860
9. SEBI (Disclosure and Investor Protection) Guidelines, 2000

REGULATION OF ADVERTISING UNDER THE CONSUMER PROTECTION ACT

The Consumer Protection Act, 1986 (CPA), is basically intended to protect and promote the interest of consumers. It provides effective safeguards to consumers against supply of defective goods, provision of deficient services, and other forms of their exploitation. The Act provides for the setting up of a three-tier machinery, consisting of District Forums, State Commissions and the National Commission. It also provides for the formation of consumer protection councils in every district and state, and at the apex level.

Under the Consumer Protection Act, an unfair trade practice, insofar as it relates to advertising, refers to any unfair method or deceptive practice adopted for promoting the sale, use or supply of any goods, or the provision of any service.

Misleading and Unfair Advertising

As provided under the Act, the following statements, whether made orally or in writing or by visible representation (i.e. advertisements in radio, newspapers, magazines, television etc.), would amount to an unfair trade practice.

1. If it falsely represents that the goods or services are of a particular standard, quality, quantity, grade, composition, style or model,

2. If it falsely represents any re-built, second-hand, renovated, reconditioned or old goods as new goods,
3. If it falsely represents that the goods or services have sponsorship, approval, performance, characteristics, accessories, uses or benefits,
4. If it gives to the public any warranty or guarantee of the performance, efficacy or length of life of a product or of any service that is not based on an adequate or proper test thereof,
5. If it makes to the public a false promise to replace, maintain or repair an article or to repeat or continue a service until it has achieved a specified result,
6. If it materially misleads the public about the price of any product or service.

In a case filed with the National Consumer Dispute Redressal Commission, (***Ramesh vs. Prakash Moped House and Hero Honda Ltd.***), Mr. Ramesh, a resident of Karnataka, purchased a Hero Honda motorcycle model CD 100 on 26-2-1993 from Prakash Moped House. Ramesh purchased this bike based on the claims made in the advertisements by the Hero Honda company in the daily newspapers and magazines before the date of his purchase. In each of these advertisements, it was claimed that the vehicle will give mileage of 80 kms per liter of petrol under standard conditions. On the numerical figure of 80 there was an asterisk (*) mark and an endorsement in small print at the foot of the advertisement said, "At speed of 40 km per hour/130 kms". The advertiser also gave the name of various authorized dealers and M/S Prakash Moped House was one of these authorized dealers from whom Ramesh purchased his motorbike. The complainant, Mr. Ramesh, also filed four advertisements to support his claim, three of which were in newspapaers of March 1992, May 1992, December 1992 and one was in the magazine of January 1993. Mr. Ramesh made the allegation that he was misled by the advertisement and the motorcycle was giving not more than 55 kms in one liter of petrol, that is, 25 kms less than what was promised and hence he should be refunded his money. The National Commission held that such a practice amounts to an unfair trade practice as it falsely suggests about the performance characteristics of the product which it did not have under normal conditions and the advertisement was without any clear warning of the circumstances under which such claim can be made.

In ***Aakash vs. M/S Durga Electronics*** (2002), M/S Durga Electronics released advertisements announcing a scheme whereby anyone purchasing an Akai CTV (Colour Television) model 2167 of 21 inches or CTV model 2107 of 21 inches was promised an Akai 14 inches CTV free. Mr. Aakash bought Akai CTV after seeing this ad but M/S Durga Electronics went back on its promise. The National Commission directed that having made an offer to the consumers, Durga Electronics is bound to honour the same. Thus, if one makes an offer to the public at large through advertisements for promotion of his goods, there is no room for going back on the offer.

Consequences of Misleading and Unfair Advertising: An advertiser who violates the legal requirements of the CPA regarding advertising shall face one or more of the following consequences.

1. Temporary injunction against the advertising campaign.
2. Cease-and-desist order against the advertising campaign.
3. Direction for issuing of corrective advertising
4. Payment of compensation to the aggrieved person for any loss or injury caused to him.
5. Payment of cost of litigation to be made to the aggrieved person by the advertiser.
6. Imposition of imprisonment, or fine, or both on the erring party in case of non-compliance of the direction given by the consumer court.

Moreover, since the cases decided by consumer courts are often reported in newspapers and law magazines, the company concerned gets adverse media reporting, which eventually lowers corporate image.

ADVERTISING AND THE COMPETITION ACT

Earlier, under the Monopolies and Restrictive Trade Practices (MRTP) Act, 1969, if any advertisement was considered prejudicial to the public interest, then the Monopolies and Restrictive Trade Commission was empowered to pass a cease-and-desist order, in addition to awarding compensation for any loss or injury caused to any person. Now, the Competition Act, 2002, has repealed and replaced the MRTP Act, 1969. The Competition Act came into force on the 31st March, 2003.

The Competition Act, 2002, is intended to prevent practices having adverse effect on competition, to promote and sustain competition in markets, to protect the interests of consumers, and to ensure freedom of trade carried on by other firms in the market, in India. Under the Act, any excessive expenditure made by a firm on advertising may amount to an anti-competitive practice. The Act also prohibits the abuse of dominant position by an enterprise. Thus, an enterprise should not take advantage of its dominant position, so as to create entry barriers for small companies, through its large-scale and heavy advertising expenditure.

In case the advertisements of a firm encourage an anti-competitive practice or take undue advantage of its dominant position, so as to create entry barriers for small companies, the Competition Commission of India (CCI) can conduct an inquiry and can pass appropriate order. Thus, any anti-competitive practice can have severe consequences, including the imposition of a fine, or imprisonment, or both.

India has a rich body of decided cases under the Monopolies and Restrictive Trade Practices Act, 1969. The MRTP Act lays down that any statement, oral or written or by visible representation, which gives false or misleading facts about goods or services or disparaging the goods, services or trade of another person shall amount to unfair trade practice.

There are many cases of **Disparaging Advertising** which have been decided under the MRTP Act, 1969.

Disparagement as per The New International Websters' Comprehensive Dictionary means, to speak of slightingly, undervalue, to bring discredit or dishonor upon, the act of depreciating, derogation, a condition of low estimation or valuation, a reproach, disgrace, an unjust classing or comparison with that which is of less worth, and degradation." According to the Concise Oxford Dictionary, disparage means "to bring dis-credit on, slightingly of and depreciate." Thus, if a company, in its advertisements, brings some sort of a disgrace or passes a derogatory remark or undermines the value of a competitor's product, it would be a case of disparaging advertising.

Dabur India Ltd vs. Colgate Palmolive India Ltd

Dabur India Ltd filed a suit against Colgate Palmolive India Ltd for their advertisement that showed a celebrity telling them the ill-effects of toothpowder in a red container which resembled Dabur Lal Dant Manjan Powder. It was argued that the impugned advertisement represented Dabur Lal Dant Manjan Powder as severely detrimental to dental health and in particular damaging tooth enamel. Delhi High Court granted an interim injunction on the ground that the advertisement was disparaging.

Colgate Palmolive India Ltd vs. Hindustan Lever Ltd

HLL in its television advertisement for New Pepsodent showed samples of saliva being taken from two children, hours after brushing. According to the advertisement, one of them had brushed his teeth with New Pepsodent and the other with 'a leading brand of toothpaste'. Also, while taking their samples, they were asked the name of the toothpaste that they had brushed their teeth with in the morning. One of them replied Pepsodent and the other boy's response was muted. However, the lip movement of the boy indicated that he said Colgate. Moreover, at the time of muting, the sound of the jingle used in Colgate's advertisement was used. The advertisement then showed that the saliva of the 'leading brand of toothpaste' contained more germs. Held, it was a case of disparaging advertisement.

Similarly, in ***Pepsi Co. Inc. and Ors. vs. Hindustan Coca Cola Ltd. And Anr.***, it was argued that by calling the cola drink of the appellants "Wrong Choice Baby" and by indicating that their drink is sweet in taste and is for kids disparaged the appellant's product. It was held that **tradesman can say that his goods are best or better. However, by comparison, the tradesman cannot slander nor say that the competitor's product is bad or inferior.**

Regal vs. Ujala Case

A television advertisement promoting Ujala liquid blue showed that 2-3 drops were adequate to bring striking whiteness of clothes while several spoons of other brands were required. A lady holding a bottle of Ujala was looking down on another bottle and saying '*chhi, chhi, chhi!*' in disgust. The manufacturers of Regal, a competing brand, approached the MRTP Commission saying that the advertisement was disparaging its goods. The Commission said that the bottle did not have any label. The commission elaborated that in order to establish a case of disparaging advertising under the MRTP Act, it must be established that the disparagement is of the goods, services or trade of another, and that the goods of another person must be identifiable in the advertisement. The Commission held that since the bottle in the advertisement did not carry any label and also it had no similarity with the bottle of any other brand, so it could not be a case of disparagement of goods. Thus, **superiority in the quality of one's product is not sufficient to establish a case of disparaging advertising.**

In *Smithkline Beecham Pharmaceutical (I) Ltd. vs. Paras Pharmaceuticals Limited* (2002), Paras who is engaged in manufacture of back pain medicine under the name "MOOV", in its ad campaigns represented that bottled products are ineffective. Smithkline is also engaged in the manufacture of back pain medicine under the name "IODEX" which is packed in bottles. The MRTPC held that the advertisements of Paras has an element of misleading the buyer by using tricky language and visual image against the product "IODEX" of Smithkline, and therefore is an unfair trade practice. Thus, while one is allowed to puff its product and claim to be one of the best in the market, it cannot belittle the other by a mere statement which is bound to have effect on the gullible customers watching the television, which has become more or less a household gadget.

In *Kouni Travels India Limited vs. Thomas Cook India Limited* (2002), Thomas Cook published an advertisement in one of the leading newspapers containing false statement and misrepresentation regarding the price at which Kouni Travels offered tour packages to Europe and USA. Thomas Cook also made false claims in respect of its own tour prices thereby showing that Kouni Travels charges much more than what Thomas Cook charges, thus disparaging the tours and services of Kouni Travels. The MRTP Commission passed an order stopping Thomas Cook from carrying out such advertisements.

ADVERTISING OF DRUGS AND MAGIC REMEDIES

In recent years, there has been a great increase in the number of objectionable advertisements published in newspapers and magazines, promoting the sale of drugs and remedies which claim to cure various incurable diseases. These advertisements cause the ignorant and the unwary to resort to self-medication with harmful drugs and appliances or to resort to quacks who indulge in such advertisements for treatment which is harmful.

In order to curb such unscrupulous practices, the Drugs and Magic Remedies (Objectionable Advertisements) Act (DMR Act) was passed in the year 1954. The Act seeks to control advertisements of drugs in certain cases and to prohibit the advertisement of remedies claiming magical effect.

The Act defines "drugs" as medicines for the internal or external use of human beings or animals, or any substance intended to be used for or in the diagnosis, cure, mitigation, treatment or prevention of disease in human beings or animals. Under the Act, the term "magic remedy" includes a talisman, *mantra, kavacha*, and any other charm of any kind, which is alleged to possess miraculous powers for or in diagnosis, cure, mitigation, treatment or prevention of any disease in human beings or animals, or for affecting or influencing in any way the structure or any organic function of the body of human beings or animals.

The DMR Act prohibits the advertisement of drugs for the treatment of certain diseases and disorders, including the following.

1. the procurement of miscarriage in women or prevention of conception in women;
2. the maintenance or improvements of the capacity of human beings for sexual pleasure;
3. the correction of menstrual disorder in women; and
4. the diagnosis, cure, mitigation, treatment or prevention of any disease, disorder or condition specified in the Act, which includes blindness, cancer, cataract, deafness, diabetes, fits, goiter, heart diseases, hysteria, insanity, leprosy, obesity, paralysis, plague, sexual impotence and tuberculosis.

Moreover, the publication of any advertisement referring to any magic remedy which claims to be efficacious for any of the purposes specified above is also prohibited by the Act.

In an advertisement of *Sanjeevan Retinopathy Clinic (Diabetic Eye Problem)*, the ad claimed - "Our researched treatment not only cures the symptoms (blindness, blurred vision, black spots or floaters in the vision) but also cures it root cause successfully". The ASCI suo motu registered a complaint in February, 2008 saying that the ad appears to claim treatment for 'blindness', a disease which is mentioned in Schedule of The Drugs & Magic Remedies (Objectionable Advertisements) Act, 1954. Thus, the ad appears to be misleading and is in contravention of the provisions of the said Act.

ADVERTISING OF TRADE MARKS

Advertising of trademarks is regulated by the Trade Marks Act, 1999, which has repealed and replaced the Trade and Merchandise Marks Act, 1958. The Act defines a "trade mark" as a mark capable of being represented graphically and which is capable of distinguishing the goods or services of one person from those of others.

The Act seeks to provide for the registration and better protection of trade marks and to prevent the use of fraudulent marks on products and services. Thus, any method of advertising designed to create confusion in the minds of the public, as between the products and services of one firm and another, shall not be permitted. Any person who falsely applies a trade mark shall be punishable with imprisonment, or fine, or both.

Aquafina Case

PepsiCo, owner of the trademark 'Aquafina', was granted a permanent injunction by the Delhi High Court, restraining a Delhi based company, Rashmi Sales Corporation, from using the trademark 'Aquafina' for their water purifiers.

S.M.Dyechem vs. Cadbury India Limited Case

In S.M.Dyechem Vs. Cadbury India Limited (Trademark infringement - Piknik Vs. Picnic), S.M.Dyecham filed a trademark infringement suit against Cadbury India alleging that there has been infringement of its trademark PIKNIK by Cadbury's use of similar sounding PICNIC trademark in advertisements, both identifying chocolate products. Though the High Court initially granted an injunction in favour of S.M.Dyechem the same was vacated subsequently. S.M.Dyechem appealed to Supreme Court arguing that the misspelling in its PIKNIK trademark was an essential feature and Cadbury's PICNIC trademark was phonetically and visually similar and adoption of even one essential feature by Cadbury would infringe its rights. The Supreme Court dismissed S.M.Dyechem's appeal holding that in trademark cases, attention must be paid to the "comparable strength" of the contesting parties apart from balance of convenience and the relative strength of the case was in favour of Cadbury.

ADVERTISING ON CABLE TELEVISION

There has been a mushrooming growth of cable television networks over the recent years as a result of the availability of signals of foreign television networks via satellites. In order to regulate unscrupulous and undesirable cable television programmes and advertisements, the Cable Television Networks (Regulation) Act was passed in 1995. It was subsequently revised in 2000 and 2002.

Under the Act, a comprehensive Advertising Code has been prescribed by the Central Government under Rule 7 of the Cable Television Networks Rules. The Code provides that advertisements carried in the cable service must be so designed as to conform to the laws of the country and should not offend morality, decency, and religious susceptibilities of the viewers. As per the amendment made in 2000, the Code bans advertisements which directly or indirectly promote the production, sale or consumption of

(a) cigarettes, tobacco products, wine, alcohol, liquor, or any other intoxicant; and

(b) infant milk substitutes, feeding bottles, or infant foods.

The Programme and Advertising Codes prescribed under the Cable Television Network Rules, 1994 (Rule 6 and 7) are given in detail in Annexure 18.3 at the end of the chapter.

ADVERTISING OF TOBACCO PRODUCTS

The Cigarettes and Other Tobacco Products (Prohibition of Advertisement and Regulation of Trade and Commerce, Production, Supply and Distribution) Act, 2003, briefly referred to as the 'Tobacco Act', is an important enactment to prohibit the advertising and sales promotion of tobacco products. Under the Act, tobacco products include cigarettes, cigars, cheroots, *beedis*, cigarette tobacco, pipe tobacco, *hookah* tobacco, chewing tobacco, snuff, *pan masala* or any chewing material having tobacco as one of its ingredients (by whatever name called), *gutka*, and toothpowder containing tobacco.

The Act prohibits advertising of cigarettes and other tobacco products. Moreover, no person, for any direct or indirect pecuniary benefit, is allowed to engage in any of the following activities.

1. displaying, or permitting the display of any advertisement of cigarettes or any other tobacco product;
2. selling, or permitting the sale of a film or video tape containing advertisement of cigarettes or any other tobacco product;
3. distributing, or permitting the distribution of any leaflet, hand-bill or document which contains an advertisement of cigarettes or any other tobacco product.

However, the above restrictions do not apply to an advertisement of tobacco products on a package containing such products, or the display of the advertisement at the entrance or inside a warehouse or a shop where such products are offered for distribution or sale. Anyone who contravenes the provisions regarding advertisements of tobacco products as provided under the Tobacco Act shall be punishable with imprisonment, or fine, or both.

A separate chapter on 'Surrogate Advertising in India' talks about various laws banning tobacco and liquor advertising in India and how the advertisers are using the lacuna therein to advertise the brand names of their liquor and tobacco products.

INDECENT REPRESENTATION OF WOMEN IN ADS

The Indecent Representation of Women (Prohibition) Act, 1986, seeks to prohibit indecent portrayal of women through advertisements, or in publications, writings, paintings, figures, or in any other manner.

The Act defines "indecent representation of women" as "the depiction in any manner of the figure of a woman; her form or body, or any part thereof in such way as to have the effect of being indecent, or derogatory to, or denigrating women, or is likely to deprave, corrupt or injure the public morality or morals".

The Act prohibits the publication or exhibition of any advertisement which contains indecent representation of women.

However, such a publication shall not be prohibited if such a representation has been made in any ancient monument within the meaning of the Ancient Monuments and Archaeological Sites and Remains Act, 1958; or if such a representation is proved to be justified as being for public good on the ground that it is in the interest of science, literature, art, learning or other objects of general concern.

REGULATION UNDER THE INDIAN PENAL CODE

The Indian Penal Code (IPC), 1860, makes it a punishable offence to advertise any obscene publication or its distribution, sale, hire or circulation. It is also an offence under the IPC to publish advertisements relating to any lottery which is not a state lottery or which is not authorized by the State Government. The IPC prohibits the sale, distribution, public exhibition or circulation of any obscene book, pamphlet, paper, drawing, painting, representation, figure or any other obscene object. The following advertisements would be considered as offensive and may attract punishment of imprisonment and/or fine under the IPC. Advertisements which:

- Promote by words, spoken or written, or by signs or by visible representations, disharmony or feelings or enmity, hatred or ill-will between different religious, racial, language or religious groups or castes or communities, on grounds of religion, race, place of birth, residence, language, caste or community.
- Make or publish any assertion that any class of persons cannot, by reason of their being members of any religious, racial, language or regional group or caste or community, bear true faith and loyalty to the sovereignty and integrity of India.
- Assert, counsel, advise, propagate or publish that any class of persons, by reason of their being members of any religious, racial, language or regional group or caste or community, be denied or deprived of their rights as citizens of India or is likely to cause disharmony or feelings of enmity or hatred or ill-will between such members and other persons.
- Insult by words, either spoken or written, by signs or by visible representations, the religion or the religious beliefs or a place of worship of a class of citizens with deliberate and malicious intention of outraging the religious beliefs of that class.

ADVERTISING OF SHARE ISSUES

The Securities and Exchange Board of India (SEBI) has issued comprehensive guidelines on advertisements to ensure investor protection from unscrupulous practices of companies offering shares and debentures to the public. These guidelines on issue advertisements are contained in Chapter IX of SEBI (Disclosure and Investor Protection) Guidelines, 2000. Under the SEBI Guidelines, the term 'advertisement' has been assigned a very broad meaning. As defined under the Guidelines, advertisement includes notices, brochures, pamphlets, circulars, show cards, catalogues, hoardings, placards, posters, insertions in newspapers, pictures, films, cover pages of offer documents as well as radio, television, etc. The major guidelines on issue advertisements are the following.

1. The advertisement should be truthful and should not contain any untrue or misleading statement.
2. If the advertisement contains statements about the performance or activities of the company, in the absence of any qualifying statements, in a way which gives an exaggerated picture of the performance or activities of the company, it shall be considered to be misleading.
3. If the advertisement contains an inaccurate portrayal of past performance of the company or its portrayal in a manner, which implies that past gains or income will be repeated in future, it shall be considered to be misleading.
4. Any statement promising or guaranteeing rapid increase in profits should not be contained in the advertisement.
5. The language used in the advertisement should be clear and understandable, avoiding extensive use of technical and legal terminology.
6. Celebrities, models, fictional characters, landmarks or caricatures should not form part of the advertisement.

ASCI'S CODE OF ADVERTISING

In addition to the various regulations discussed above, the code of advertising laid down by the **Advertising Standards Council of India (ASCI)** also regulates advertising. The code of ASCI is similar to the Advertising Standards Authority (ASA) Code of the UK and seeks to achieve the acceptance of fair advertising practices in the best interests of the consumer.

The ASCI is concerned with safeguarding the interests of the consumers while monitoring and guiding the commercial communications. The Council's code for self-regulation in advertising specifies that all advertising shall be truthful, honest, decent, legal, and safe for consumers, particularly minors, and fair to the competitors.

With a view to achieving "the acceptance of fair advertising practices in the best interest of the ultimate consumer", the Council prescribes the following basic guidelines.

1. To ensure the truthfulness and honesty of representations and claims made by advertisements and to safeguard against misleading advertisements.
2. To ensure that advertisements are not offensive to generally accepted standards of public decency.

3. To safeguard against the indiscriminate use of advertising for the promotion of products which are regarded as hazardous to society or to individuals to a degree or of a type, this is unacceptable to society at large.
4. To ensure that advertisements observe fairness in competition so that the consumer's need to be informed on choices in the market-place and the canons of generally accepted competitive behaviour in business are both served.

This Code for Self-Regulation has been drawn up by people in professions and industries in or connected with advertising, in consultation with representatives of people affected by advertising.

Some Cases decided by the ASCI

ASCI's complaint cell, Consumer Complaints Council (CCC), has, in the recent past, identified the following advertisements objectionable.

- ***Sunsilk Fuitamin Shampoo***: HLL could not substantiate the implied claim that the fruit vitamins in the shampoo contributes to hair growth. The advertisement was discontinued.
- ***Rotomac Pens***: The use of the words *"Sab kuch dikhta hai"* in the advertisement was found to be vulgar and the advertisement had to be withdrawn.
- ***Lifebuoy Gold***: The advertisement claimed that the product was certified by the Medical Technologists Association. The claim could not be substantiated and ASCI ordered for the modification of the advertisement.
- ***Gaspoint Marketing India Pvt Ltd***: The advertisement showed a torn Rs500 note, a crack on Mahatma Gandhi's forehead and a torn Ashok Stambh. It was held that the advertisement had a derogatory effect on the national emblem, national currency and a national leader. The ASCI thus ordered for the advertisement to be withdrawn.
- ***Colgate***: The claim in the advertisement 'no germs no cavities' was considered as an exaggerated and misleading claim and the advertisement had to be withdrawn.
- ***Snax Biscuits (Britannia Industries Ltd)***: The mention of words *"Mona Ko"* in the ad was considered derogatory to the rival brand Monaco. The campaign was discontinued.
- ***Lifebuoy Plus (HLL)***: The advertisement claimed that the product was certified by the Family Physicians Association of India. The claim could not be substantiated and the ad was modified.
- ***Alfa Water Purifiers***: The statement "Boiling water destroys vital salts and minerals" was found to be misleading. ASCI ordered for the modification of the advertisement.
- ***Horlicks:*** GlaxoSmithKline's (GSK) Consumer Healthcare also came under ASCI's scrutiny when the GSK's Horlicks' ad, *"Exam ka bhoot bhagao"* suggested that Horlicks was essential for health during exams, required to

be substantiated. The council felt the claims made by the advertiser for Horlicks were misleading, on account of the exaggeration, forcing GSK to discontinue the campaign.

The role of ASCI in regulating advertising has been acclaimed by various agencies including the Government. However, it lacked the force of legal recognition. The Government of India has at last, taken note of this and by one stroke on 2nd August 2006 vide a notification in The Gazette of India: Extraordinary {Part II –sec. 3(i)}, made sure that at least as far as TV Commercials go, they abide by the ASCI code. The amendment made in Cable Television Networks (Amendment) Rules, 2006 now states:

"(9) No advertisement which violates the Code for Self-Regulation in Advertising, as adopted by the Advertising Standards Council of India (ASCI), Mumbai for public exhibition in India, from time to time, shall be carried in the cable service."

Thus, the Ministry of Information and Broadcasting has adopted the ASCI's self-regulatory code for television ads. Before this, it was a voluntary decision of the organisation whether to comply with ASCI's code but now ASCI's code has received a legal recognition.

A separate chapter on ASCI talks in detail about the ASCI's Code and the decisions made with respect to it.

GENERAL RULES OF CONDUCT IN ADVERTISING

In addition to working within the legal framework, an advertiser should also follow the general rules of conduct in advertising. The general rules of conduct in advertising are given below.

1. Advertising shall be designed as to confirm to the laws of the country and should not offend against morality, decency and religious susceptibilities of the people.
2. No advertisement shall be permitted which-
   a. derides any race, caste, colour, creed and nationality
   b. is against any of the directive principles, or any other provision of the Constitution of India
   c. tends to incite people to crime, cause disorder or violence or obscenity in any way
   d. presents criminality as desirable
   e. adversely affects friendly relations with other States
   f. exploits the national emblem, or any part of the Constitution or the person or personality a national leader or State Dignitary
   g. relates to or promotes cigarettes and tobacco products, liquor, wines and other intoxicants.

CONCLUDING NOTE

The statutory provisions relating to advertising discussed above have important implications both for the marketers and the consumers. An understanding of these provisions would make the Indian consumers more enlightened as regards their rights and the protection available to them under various laws. For the marketer, these provisions spell out the areas where a check is required to be maintained for protecting their own interests, of the consumers and the general public. These measures envisage that the marketers take due care in designing their advertisements and in ensuring that their advertisements are truthful, honest, decent and fair. A failure to do so on their part can lead to severe consequences ranging from adverse publicity to diminished corporate reputation, to consumer boycotts, payment of compensation and punitive damages, and other legal sanctions. Conversely, a truthful advertisement can contribute to a good corporate reputation and, thus, increase repeat business.

QUESTIONS FOR DISCUSSION

1. Discuss the various laws regulating advertising in India.
2. Discuss the regulation of advertising in India under the Consumer Protection Act with the help of some decided cases.
3. What do you mean by disparaging advertising? Discuss some cases of disparaging advertising in India.
4. Discuss the role of ASCI in regulating advertising in India. (Also refer Chapter 20)

Appendix 18.1

CODE FOR COMMERCIAL ADVERTISING OVER ALL INDIA RADIO

The following standards of conduct are laid down in order to develop and promote healthy advertising practices in All India Radio. Responsibility for the observance of these rules rests equally upon the Advertiser and the Advertising Agency.

General Rules of Conduct in Advertising:

1. Advertising shall be designed as to confirm to the laws of the country and should not offend against morality, decency and religious susceptibilities of the people.
2. No advertisement shall be permitted which:-
   - derides any race, caste, color, creed and nationality;
   - is against any of the directive principles, or any other provision of the Constitution of India;
   - tends to incite people to crime, cause disorder or violence, or breach of law or glorifies violence or obscenity in any way;
   - presents criminality as desirable;
   - adversely affects friendly relations with foreign States;
   - exploits the national emblem, or any part of the constitution or the person or personality of a national leader or State Dignitary;
   - relates to or promotes cigarettes and tobacco products, liquor, wines and other intoxicants;
3. No advertisements message shall in any way be presented as News.
4. No advertisements shall be permitted the objects whereof are wholly or mainly of a religious or political natures; advertisement must not be directed towards any religious or political end or have relation to any industrial dispute.

Proviso: "But advertisements in the form of spots and jingles on payment of prescribed fees, from Political parties / Candidates / any other person shall be accepted only in respect of General Elections to Lok Sabha / General Elections to the State Assemblies / General Elections to Local bodies during the period when the model Code of Conduct is in force. Such advertisements shall be subject to pre-broadcast scrutiny by the Election Commission of India / authorities under the Election Commission of India in respect of elections to Lok Sabha and the State Assemblies and State Election Commissions in the case of Local bodies. "

(As per DG: AIR's I.D.No. 15/3/2008-PIV dated November 20, 2008).

5. Advertisements for services concerned with the following shall not be accepted:-

   Money lenders;

   - Chit funds;
   - Saving schemes and lotteries other than those conducted by Centeral and State Government organisations, nationalised or recgonised banks and public sector undertakings;
   - Matrimonial agencies;
   - Unlicenced employment services;
   - Fortune tellers or sooth-sayers etc. and those with claims of hypnotism;
   - Foreign goods and foreign banks.
   - Betting tips and guide books etc. relating to horse-racing or the other games of chance.

6. The items advertised shall not suffer from any defect or deficiency as mentioned in Consumer Protection Act 1986.
7. No advertisement shall contain references which are likely to lead the public to infer that the product advertised or any advertised or any of its ingredients has some special or miraculous or super-natural property or quality, which is difficult of being proved, e.g. cure for baldness, skin whitener, etc.
8. No advertisement shall contain the words 'Guarantee' or 'Guaranteed' etc., unless the full terms of the guarantee are available for inspection by the Directorate General, All India Radio, are clearly set out in the advertisement and are made available to the purchaser in the writing at the point of sale or with the goods; in all cases, terms must include details of the remedial action available to the purchaser. No advertisement shall contain a direct or implied reference reference to any guarantee which purports to take away or diminish the legal rights of the purchaser.
9. Advertisers or the agents must be prepared to produce evidence to substantiate any claims or illustrations. The Director General reserves the right to ask for such proofs and get them examined to his full satisfation. In case of goods covered by mandatory quality control orders, the advertiser shall produce quality certificate from the institutions recognised by the Government for this purpose.
10. Advertisements shall not contain disparaging or derogatory references to another product or service.
11. Testimonials must be genuine and used in a manner not to mislead the listeners. Advertisers or Advertising Agencies must be prepared to produce evidence in support of their claims.
12. No advertisement of any kind of jewellery (except artificial jewellery) or precious stones shall be accepted.
13. Information to consumers on matters of weight, quality or prices of products where given shall be accurate.

14. Advertisements indicating price comparisons or reductions must comply with relevant laws.
15. No advertisement shall be accepted which violates AIR Broadcast Code which is reproduced below:-
    - Criticism of friendly countries.
    - Attack of religious or communities.
    - Anything obscene or defamatory;
    - Incitement to violence or anything against maintenance of law and order;
    - Anything amounting to contempt of court;
    - Aspersions against the integrity of the President and Judiciary;

Note: Advertisements concerning jewellery, foreign goods and foreign banks, besides those related to Indian Equity / Debenture issued for NRIs will, however, be accepted as far as the external services of All India Radio are concerned.

- anything affecting the integrity of the Nation and criticism by name of any person.

16. Any such effects which might startle the listening public must not be incorporated in advertisements. For example, and without limiting the scope, the use of the following sound effects will not be permitted:
    - Rapid gunfire or rifle shots;
    - Sirens;
    - Bombardments;
    - Screams;
    - Raucous laughter and the like.
17. Any pretence in advertising copy must be avoided and such copy shall not be accepted by All India Radio. The 'simulation' of voices of a personality in connection with advertisements for commercial products is also prohibited unless bonafide evidence is available that such personality has given permission for the simulation and it is clearly understood that station broadcasting such announcements are indemnified by the advertiser or advertising agency against any possible legal action.

Advertising and Children

18. No advertising for a product or service shall be accepted if it suggests in any way that unless the children themselves buy or encourage other people to buy the products or services, they will be failing in their duty or lacking in loyalty to any person or organisation.
19. No advertisement shall be accepted which leads children to believe that if they do not own or use the product advertised they will be inferior in some way to other children or that they are liable to the condemned or ridiculed for not owning or using it.
20. No advertisement likely to bring advertising into contempt or disrepute shall be permitted. Advertising shall not take advantage of the superstition or

ignorance of the general public.

21. No advertising of talismans, charms and character-reading from photographs or such other matter as well as those which trade on superstition of general public shall be permitted.

22. Advertising shall be truthful, avoid distorting facts and misleading the public by means of implications by false statements, as to :
    - the character of the merchandise, i.e. its utility, materials, ingredients, origin etc.
    - the price of the merchandise, its value, its suitability or terms of purchase.
    - the services accompanying purchase, including delivery, exchange, return, repair, upkeep etc.
    - personal recommendations of the article or service.
    - the quality or the value of competing goods or trustworthiness of statement made by others.

23. Testimonials of any kind from experts etc. other than Government recognized standarisation agencies shall not be permitted.

24. No advertisement shall be permitted to contain any claim so exaggerated as to lead inevitably to disappointment in the minds of the public.

25. Methods of advertising designated to create confusion in the mind of the consumer as between goods by one maker and another maker are unfair and shall not be used. Such methods may consist in:
    - the imitation of the trademark of the name of competition or packaging or labeling of goods; or
    - the imitation of advertising devices, copy, layout or slogans.

26. Indecent, vulgar, suggestive, repulsive or offensive themes or treatment shall be avoided in all advertisements. This also supplies to such advertisements which themselves are not objectionable as defined above, but which advertise objectionable books, photographs or other matter and thereby lead to their sale and circulation.

27. No advertisement in respect of medicines and treatments shall be accepted which is in contravention of the code relating to standards of advertising medicines and treatments.

Note I : In all other respect, the Director General will be guided for purposes of commercial broadcasting in All India Radio by Code of Ethics for Advertising in India as modified from time to time (relevant excerpts appended at Annexure-I).

Note II: Notwithstanding anything contained herein, this code is subject to such modification/ directions as may be made / issued by the Director General from time to time.

Note III: All advertising agencies shall adhere to the standards of practice as prescribed by Advertising Agencies Association of India, Bombay, as given in Annexure III.

Procedure for Enforcement of the Code:

Complaints or reports on contraventions of the code, received by All India Radio may in the first instant be referred by Director General to Advertiser's Association concerned with request for suitable action. If complaints under the Code cannot be satisfactorily resolved at Association's level, they shall be reported to Director General who will than consider suitable action. For any Complaints under the Code received by All India Radio concerning a party outside the preview of various member Association(s), the Director General will draw attention of such party to the complaint and where necessary, take suitable action on his own.

Appendix 18.2

PROGRAMME AND ADVERTISING CODES OF THE CABLE TELEVISION NETWORK RULES, 1994

The programme and Advertising codes prescribed under Rules 6 and 7 of the Cable Television Network Rules, 1994, are given below.

Rule- 6: Programme Code

1. No programme should be carried in the cable service which:-
   (a) Offends against good taste or decency;
   (b) Contains criticism of friendly countries;
   (c) Contains attack on religions or communities or visuals or words contemptuous of religious groups or which promote communal attitudes;
   (d) Contains anything obscene, defamatory, deliberate, false and suggestive innuendos and half truths;
   (e) is likely to encourage or incite violence or contains anything against maintenance of law and order or which promote anti-national attitudes;
   (f) Contains anything amounting to contempt of court;
   (g) Contains aspersions against the integrity of the President and Judiciary;
   (h) Contains anything affecting the integrity of the Nation;
   (i) Criticises, maligns or slanders any individual in person or certain groups, segments of social, public and moral life of the country ;
   (j) Encourages superstition or blind belief;
   (k) Denigrates women through the depiction in any manner of the figure of a women, her form or body or any part thereof in such a way as to have the effect of being indecent, or derogatory to women, or is likely to deprave, corrupt or injure the public morality or morals;
   (l) Denigrates children;
   (m) Contains visuals or words which reflect a slandering, ironical and snobbish attitude in the portrayal of certain ethnic, linguistic and regional groups;
   (n) Contravenes the provisions of the Cinematograph Act, 1952.
   (o) is not suitable for unrestricted public exhibition.

"Provided that no film or film song or film promo or film trailer or music video or music albums or their promos, whether produced in India or abroad, shall be carried through cable service unless it has been certified by the Central Board of Film Certification (CBFC) as suitable for unrestricted public exhibition in India".

Explanation : For the purpose of this clause, the expression "unrestricted public exhibition" shall have the same meaning as assigned to it in the Cinematograph Act, 1952 (37 of 1952);

2. The cable operator should strive to carry programmes in his cable service which project women in a positive, leadership role of sobriety, moral and character building qualities.
3. No cable operator shall carry or include in his cable service any programme in respect of which copyright subsists under the Copyright Act, 1957 (14 of 1957) unless he has been granted a licence by owners of copyright under the Act in respect of such programme.
4. Care should be taken to ensure that programmes meant for children do not contain any bad language or explicit scenes of violence.
5. Programmes unsuitable for children must not be carried in the cable service at times when the largest numbers of children are viewing.
6. No cable operator shall carry or include in his cable service any television broadcast or channel, which has not been registered by the Central Government for being viewed within the territory of India".

"Provided that a cable operator may continue to carry or include in his cable service any Television broadcast or channel, whose application for registration to the Central Government was made on or before 11th May, 2006 and is under consideration, for a period of three months from the date of this notification, or till such registration has been granted or refused, whichever is earlier."

"Provided further that channels uplinking from India, in accordance with permission for uplinking granted before 2nd December, 2005, shall be treated as "registered" television channels and can be carried or included in the cable service."

Rule-7: Advertising Code

1. Advertising carried in the cable service shall be so designed as to conform to the laws of the country and should not offend morality, decency and religious susceptibilities of the subscribers.
2. No advertisement shall be permitted which-
   - i. derides any race, caste, colour, creed and nationality;
   - ii. is against any provision of the Constitution of India.
   - iii. tends to incite people to crime, cause disorder or violence, or breach of law or glorifies violence or obscenity in any way ;
   - iv. presents criminality as desirable;
   - v. exploits the national emblem, or any part of the Constitution or the person or personality of a national leader or a State dignitary;
   - vi. in its depiction of women violates the constitutional guarantees to all citizens. In particular, no advertisement shall be permitted which projects a derogatory image of women. Women must not be portrayed in a manner that emphasizes passive, submissive qualities and encourages them to play a subordinate, secondary role in the family and society. The cable operator shall ensure that the portrayal of the female form, in the

programmes carried in his cable service, is tasteful and aesthetic, and is within the well established norms of good taste and decency;

vii. exploits social evils like dowry, child marriage.

viii. promotes directly or indirectly production, sale or consumption of-

A. cigarettes, tobacco products, wine, alcohol, liquor or other intoxicants;

B. infant milk substitutes, feeding bottle or infant food.

3. No advertisement shall be permitted, the objects whereof, are wholly or mainly of a religious or political nature; advertisements must not be directed towards any religious or political end.

A. No advertisement shall contain references which hurt religious sentiments.

4. The goods or services advertised shall not suffer from any defect or deficiency as mentioned in Consumer Protection Act, 1986.

5. No advertisement shall contain references which are likely to lead the public to infer that the product advertised or any of its ingredients has some special or miraculous or super-natural property or quality, which is difficult of being proved.

6. The picture and the audible matter of the advertisement shall not be excessively 'loud;

7. No advertisement which endangers the safety of children or creates in them any interest in unhealthy practices or shows them begging or in an undignified or indecent manner shall not be carried in the cable service.

8. Indecent, vulgar, suggestive, repulsive or offensive themes or treatment shall be avoided in all advertisements.

9. No advertisement which violates the standards of practice for advertising agencies as approved by the Advertising Agencies Association of India, Bombay, from time to time shall be carried in the cable service.

10. All advertisement should be clearly distinguishable from the programme and should not in any manner interfere with the programme viz., use of lower part of screen to carry captions, static or moving alongside the programme.

Appendix 18.3

CODE OF STANDARDS FOR ADVERTISING OF MEDICINES AND TREATMENT

The programme and Advertising codes prescri

This code has been drafted for the guidance of advertisers, manufactures, distributors, advertising agents, publishers and suppliers or various advertising media. The harm to the individual that may result from exaggerated, misleading or unguaranteed claims justified the adoption of a very high standard and the inclusion of considerable detail in a Code to guide those who are concerned with this form of advertising.

Newspaper and other advertising media are urged not to accept advertisements in respect of any other product or treatment from any advertiser or advertising or publicity relating to that product or treatment. The provisions of this Code do not apply to an advertisement published by or under the authority of a Government, Ministry or Department, nor to an advertisement published in journals circulated to Registered Medical Practitioners, Registered Dentists, Registered Pharmacists or Registered Nurses.

General Principles:

1. *Cure:* No advertisement should contain a claim to cure any ailment or symptoms of ill-health, nor should any advertisement contain a word or expression used in such a form or context as to mean in the positive sense the extirpation of any ailment, illness or disease.
2. *Illness etc., properly requiring medical attention:* No advertisement should contain any matter which can be regarded as offer of medicine or product for, or advise relating to, treatment of serious diseases, complaints, conditions, indications or symptoms which should rightly receive the attention of a Registered medical practitioner (see Sec.2).
3. *Misleading or Exaggerated Claim:* No advertisement should contain any matter which directly or by implication misleads or departs from the truth as to the composition, character or action of the medicine or treatment advertised or as to its suitability for the purpose for which it is recommended.
4. *Appeals to fear:* No advertisement should be calculated to induce fear on the part of the reader that he is suffering, or may without treatment suffer from an ailment, illness or disease.
5. *Diagnosis or treatment by correspondence:* No advertisement should offer to diagnose by correspondence diseases, conditions or any symptoms of ill-health in a human being or request from any person or a statement of his or any other person's symptoms of ill-health with a view to advertising as to or

providing for treatment of such conditions of ill-health by correspondence. Nor should any advertisement offer to treat by correspondence any ailment, illness, disease or symptoms thereof in a human being.

6. *Disparaging references:* No advertisement should directly or by implication disparage the products, medicines or treatments of another advertiser or manufacturer or registered medical practitioner or the medical profession.
7. *College, clinic, institute, laboratory*: No advertisement should contain these or similar terms unless an establishment corresponding with the description used does in fact exist.
8. *Doctors, hospitals etc.:* No advertisement should contain any reference to doctors or hospitals, whether Indian or foreign, unless such reference can be sustained by independent evidence and can properly be used in the manner proposed.
9. *Products offered particularly to women:* No advertisement of products, medicines or treatments of disorders or irregularities peculiar to women should contain expression which may imply that the product, medicine or treatment advertised can be effective in inducing miscarriage.
10. *Family Planning:* Advertisements for measures or apparatus concerning family planning would be permissible in so far as they conform to the generally accepted national policy in this behalf.
11. *Illustrations:* No advertisement should contain any illustration which by itself or in combination with words used in connection therewith is likely to convey a misleading impression, or if the reasonable reference to be drawn from such advertisement infringes any of the provisions of the Code.
12. *Exaggerated copy:* No advertisement should contain copy which is exaggerated by reason of improper use of words, phrases or methods of presentation e.g., the use of word's magic, magical, miracle, miraculous.
13. *Natural remedies:* No advertisement should claim or suggest contrary to the fact that the article advertised is in the form in which it occurs in nature or that its value lies in its being a natural product.
14. *Special claim:* No advertisement should contain any reference which is calculated to lead the public to assume that the article, product, medicine or treatment advertised has some special property or quality which is in fact unknown or unrecognized.
15. *Sexual weakness, premature aging, loss or virility:* No advertisement should claim that the product, medicine or treatment advertised will promote sexual virility or be effective in treating sexual weakness or habits associated with sexual excess or indulgence or any ailment, illness or disease associated with those habits. In particular such terms as 'Premature aging', 'loss of virility' will be regarded as conditions for which medicines, products, appliances or treatment may not be advertised.

16. **Slimming, weight reduction or limitation or figure control:** No advertisement should offer any medical product for the purpose of slimming, weight reduction or limitation or figure control. Medical products intended to reduce appetite will usually be regarded as being for slimming purposes.
17. *Tonics:* The use of this expression in advertisements should not imply that the product or medicine can be used in the treatment of sexual weakness.
18. *Hypnosis:* No advertisement should contain any offer to diagnose or treat complaints or conditions by hypnosis.
19. *Materials to students:* Materials meant for distribution in educational institutions must not carry advertisement of anything other than those of value to students.

CHAPTER 19

Ethical Issues in Advertising

CONTENTS

In today's challenging market economy, advertising has become an important element of the society. Moreover, advertisements play a powerful constructive role in the economic growth of a country. On the contrary, they can often play a negative role in hurting the sentiments of an individual or the society. Hence, it is important that advertising professionals observe high ethical standards in regard to truthfulness, human dignity and social responsibilities.

Ethics is a set of moral principles that guide actions and create a sense of responsible behaviour. It is about being able to analyze ethical questions and dilemmas in professional decision making in terms of right and wrong and to determine one's obligations and responsibility to do the right thing. Many laws and regulations are put into force that determine what is permissible in advertising.

However, not every issue is controlled by rules. Advertisers are often faced with decisions regarding appropriateness of their actions which are based on ethical considerations rather than what is within the law. Certain actions may be within the law but still unethical. Advertising law and regulations can only go so far in ensuring ethical practices in advertising. Ultimately, professionals in the industry have to be guided by their own ethical principles.

This chapter discusses a variety of ethical issues, listed below, that challenge the standards of advertising professionals.

1. Misleading Claims
2. Reinforcing Stereotypes
3. Use of sex appeal and nudity in advertisements
4. Concealment of Facts
5. Manipulative Advertising
6. Portraying a particular Body Image
7. Advertisements directed at children
8. Advertisements showing dangerous/hazardous actions
9. Surrogate Advertising
10. Subliminal Advertising
11. Puffery
12. Weasel Claim

MISLEADING CLAIMS

Advertising claims are considered to be unethical if they are misleading. At present, there are numerous regulations monitoring the display of obscene and misleading advertisements in India. However, it is not uncommon to see various advertisements which are patently false and misleading promoting dubious products and making unsubstantiated claims.

To ensure the truthfulness and honesty of representations and claims made by advertisements and to safeguard against misleading advertisements, the Advertising Standards Council of India (ASCI) Code lays down that advertisements must be truthful. All descriptions, claims and comparisons which relate to matters of objectively ascertainable fact should be capable of substantiation. Advertisers and advertising agencies are required to produce such substantiation as and when called upon to do so by the Advertising Standards Council of India. Also, the code states that advertisements shall neither distort facts nor mislead the consumer by means of implications or omissions. Advertisements shall not contain statements or visual presentation which directly, or by implication, or by omission, or by ambiguity, or by exaggeration, are likely to mislead the consumer about the product advertised or the advertiser or about any other product or advertiser.

In an advertisement of Gillette Victor Plus Blade (Gillette India Ltd.), 2008, the Voice Over (VO) in the ad said, "blade lasts for three weeks", and the fine print read, "on the basis of one shave every three days". A complaint was received against the ad saying that the consumer is led to believe that the blade lasts for 21 shaves whereas it lasts for only 7 shaves. Fine print appears on the screen for a short time that one cannot read it fully. The ASCI held that the ad was misleading and the television commercial had to be withdrawn.

Similarly, in another advertisement of 'Tall You Cosmetic' (2008), the ad stated "It makes you proud to have good height. Apply 'Tall You' once a day on sole for 3-6 months". A complaint against the ad was received saying that bones attain their final heights after 20 years of age. Height cannot be increased by any medicines, exercise or by any cosmetics. Thus, the ad is totally misguiding the public. Further, the claim needs to be substantiated with proof, additional supporting information with details of tests/trials conducted. The ASCI held that the claim implies that 'Tall You' can increase height, which appears to be false and was not substantiated. Thus, the ad was misleading by ambiguity.

In 2009, in an advertisement of Surya tube light, the ad claimed "Surya Tubelight lasts 3 times longer than others". In response to a complaint received against the ad, the ASCI held that the claim, Surya Tubelight "lasts 3 times longer than others", was not substantiated with comparative data of other brands. Thus, the ASCI ordered for the modification of the TVC.

REINFORCING STEREOTYPES

A stereotype is a representation of a group that emphasizes a trait or group of traits that may or may not communicate an accurate representation of the group. Sometimes the stereotype is useful (e.g. athletes are fit) and aids communication by using easily understood symbolic meanings, but sometimes the stereotype relies on a characteristic that is negative or exaggerated (e.g. women shown as sex objects) and, in doing so, reduces the group to a caricature.

Gender Roles: Historically, advertising has portrayed gender in distinct and predictable stereotypes. Men are usually shown as strong, independent, and achievement-oriented; women are shown as nurturing and empathetic, but softer and more dependent, and they are told that the products being advertised will make their lives less stressful and manageable.

Harmful female stereotypes take a number of forms. Women are portrayed as indecisive, childlike, frivolous, obsessed with their own physical appearance, submissive to men, sexual objects or simple housewives doing the routine household chores. An ad of ING Vysya Life Insurance which showed a girl child as a burden on parents by saying "*Dikhne mein toh pyaari hain, yeh khushiyaan thodi bhaari hain*", received a lot of criticism. However, some advertisers are recognizing the diversity of women's role in today's life. There are advertisements which show the right portrayal of the modern day, independent woman. Advertisements by TVS Scooty, for instance, portray a modern day independent girl who makes her own choices. Also, an insurance ad by HDFC where a father feels proud of his daughter getting him a big car and says, "*Beti badi ho gayi, aur car bhi*" gives a portrayal of a girl child in a very positive way. Exhibit 19.1 shows how the ad of Hero Honda Pleasure portrays a modern, independent girl.

Senior Citizens: Another group that is often subject to stereotyping is that of senor citizens. Critics often object to the use of older people in roles that portray them negatively.

However, we also have advertisements which give a positive portrayal of older people. For instance, "*Na sar jhuka hai khabhi, aur na jhukaenge khabhi*", the jingle used in advertisement for HDFC Pension Plans gives the right portrayal of elderly people. Consider Exhibit 19.2 which shows the right portrayal of a girl child and aged people in the advertisements of HDFC Standard Life.

Exhibit 19.1: *Hero Honda Pleasure "Why should boys have all the fun?" portrays a present day modern, independent girl*

Hero Honda made a foray into the scooty segment, with Hero Honda Pleasure, targeted at the female riders. Hero Honda in its earlier advertisements also had focused on freedom and empowerment to women. This time it thought of taking it forward to small towns, with a small town girl taking a guy for a ride. The pleasant ride starts when Priyanka Chopra gives a lift to a guy on her scooty after knowing that he is visiting a certain Mr. Singh to meet his daughter Manjeet, whom the guy calls 'silly village girl'. Out of curiosity he asks Priyanka whether she is acquainted with Manjeet, to which Priyanka snaps back stating that Manjeet resembles a buffalo and drops the guy back to the very same railway station, slyly disclosing that she is the Manjeet he had come to meet. As the boy hits his head in anguish, Priyanka says, "Why should boys have all the fun?"

FCB Ulka, the advertising agency, got an awesome response for the ad. Not only did it entertain the audience, it also presented the fairer sex as one that is smart, intelligent and makes its own choices.

Exhibit 19.2 Portrayal of a Girl Child and Aged People in HDFC Standard Life Insurance Ads

Girl Child: HDFC Standard Life received *Laadli* Media Award 2007 for its 'Big car' TV commercial. (The award is given to professionals in print and electronic media and ad makers for gender sensitive news reports, articles, print, TV ads, and films). It showed how a daughter wants to be more responsible towards her family and asks her dad to upgrade to a bigger car by offering him the extra money required to buy the car.

The TVC opens in the compound of a house. Father is checking something inside the bonnet of an old small car. His daughter, around 27-28 years old, is working on a lap top next to him. Daughter: "Dad". Father: "*Bolo*". Daughter: "*Nayi car lene mein hee bhalaai hai.*" Dad nods in agreement without looking up. Daughter continues affirmatively as she signs on a cheque. Daughter: "*Aur woh bhi badi wali.*" Dad looks at her and asks, "*Huh, Badi kyon*?" Daughter, walks towards him with swinging hand in air and says, "*Kyonki Toolika Sharma chahti hai uske dad style se travel kare.*" Dad goes back to checking the engine and says in a light hearted tone, "*Aur extra paise dad dega kya?*" Daughter replies firmly: "*Nahi. Mere dad ki beti.*" and hands him the cheque. Dad looks at the cheque and questions, "*Itne paise aaye kahaan se*?" Daughter says, "Relax dad, *plan kiya.*" Dad doesn't know what to say as he looks at the cheque. Daughter pleads: "Please...dad". Mother enters with tea. She senses something serious and questions them, "*Aree Kya hua*?" Father looks at her and says emotionally, "*Car badi ho gayi, aur beti bhi.*" The daughter smiles with pride.

HDFC Standard Life received this award for two years consecutively. In 2006, it won for the 'Papa' TV commercial, which challenged the stereotype parents saving only for their son's education or daughter's wedding. The company took a bold step by showing parents saving for their daughter's education abroad, demonstrating progressive thinking.

Aged People: A boy insists his grandfather to buy him a bicycle as a birthday present. The boy's father takes notice of this and the next day goes to the grandfather and says, "*Babuji, Binku ne kal jo cycle dekhi thi na, toh maine socha...*" and gives him a cheque so that he can buy his grandchild's desired bicycle and adds, "*warna usey bura lagega.*" At this the grandfather calls Binku who comes riding his favourite bicycle. As the father sees this, he expresses his astonishment to the grandfather. The grandfather in turn returns him the cheque and comments, "*rakh lo, warna mujhe bura lagega.*" Voice Over: "Pension plans from HDFC Standard Life. *Retirement ke liye aaj hi plan kare. Taaki yeh haath jab bhi badey, dene ke liye badey.*"

HDFC Standard Life was one of the first private insurers to break the ice using the idea of self respect ("*Sar Utha Ke Jiyo*") instead of 'death' to convey its brand proposition. This was later followed by other players in the industry.

USE OF SEX APPEAL AND NUDITY

The portrayal of women as sex objects seems to be an increasingly popular trend in the ad world these days. Portraying women as objects of desire and displaying their bodies to sell products is probably an example of the most sexually exploitative advertisements. Take for instance, the television commercial of Axe deodorant which shows women in beach wear running after a man who has used Axe deodorant. The idea is to use svelte attractive figures of women to grab attention and stimulate desire, which advertisers expect to be transferred to the product. By portraying women as objects of desire, advertisements create an atmosphere that devalues women as people and encourage sexual harassment.

Advertising that portrays women as sex objects is considered demeaning, particularly if sex is not relevant to the product. Ads for lingerie, condoms etc. fall into a gray area because sex appeals for these products are usually relevant. But for other products, advertisers ought to make more thoughtful arguments on behalf of their products rather than resorting to such cheap tactics.

Advertisers are also using the element of nudity in the advertisements to promote their products. One of the Levis commercial ads showed a bare-chested young man with his jeans unbuttoned revealing partly his innerwear, and said "My girlfriend's sister turns me on". The ad stated that, "Bare what's inside, live unbuttoned". The statement itself cannot be termed as decent and culture-sensitive. These types of advertisements can cause severe offence.

Exhibit 19.3 talks about some Indian ads which have made use of sex appeal and nudity.

Exhibit 19.3: Use of Sex Appeal and Nudity in Indian Ads

Let us take a look back at the ads that used sex appeal to sell various products, were deemed unfit for public consumption and were ultimately banned.

One of the ads that still remains embedded in the consciousness of the ad-aware Indian is that of a nude Milind Soman and Madhu Sapre posing naked along with a python for 'Tuffs' shoes. The ad was considered obscene and led to a lot of public protest.

In the 1990s, Pooja Bedi had a steamy shower with Marc Robinson to sell the condoms branded 'Kamasutra'. The October 1991 issue of 'Debonair' magazine sold out in a matter of days, the reason being that the issue carried ads, featuring Pooja Bedi and Marc Robinson, for the Kamasutra Condoms. The ad created a lot of public outrage, questions were asked in the Parliament, and complaints were sent to the Advertising Standards Council of India (ASCI). Ultimately, the ad was banned.

In a directive to the television channels issued by the Ministry of Information and Broadcasting (MIB) in 2008, the Ministry prohibited the "transmission or re-transmission" of the Lux Cozy advertisement. The scantily clad man in the ad of Lux Cozy had the tagline "*Apna Luck Pehen Ke Chalo*" as the scantily clad man got a peck on the cheek by a grateful female for finding her lost dog. Lux Cozy was also in the news in July 2007 when the MIB had issued orders banning the ad along with Amul Macho's

"*Yeh to bada twaing hain*" ad. The ad showed a young woman washing her husband's underwear with very suggestive actions.

The surrogate advertisement for AC Black Whisky (the advertised product was AC Black Apple Juice) had stirred up a bit of controversy recently. In the ad a man took a sip of his drink and looked at an attractive woman on the other side of the room, and her neckline got lower and lower with every sip. As he sipped for the kill, he found his shirt open. The woman also was playing the same game. The tagline said, "*Kuch Bhi Ho Sakta Hai*" (Anything is possible). The TVC was subsequently taken off the air.

CONCEALMENT OF FACTS

Concealment of facts is yet another ethical ground on which advertisements are criticized. When advertisers conceal facts, they suppress information that is unflattering, that is, they present only the brighter side of the story. They neglect to mention those facts which would make their products less desirable. For instance, advertises of products like hair colours do not mention that the product contains harmful chemicals which may harm the hair. Similarly, advertisers of detergent powder do not mention that the detergent contains harmful chemicals which can damage the skin. Concealing facts or information raises a severe ethical concern because when consumers are deprived of comprehensive knowledge about a product, their choices would be distorted.

MANIPULATIVE ADVERTISING

Many advertisements are designed to create demand and touch the emotions of people. Advertisements may use different kinds of emotions to arouse feelings in people which might push towards purchase of the product. For instance, using patriotic feeling in advertisements- Tata Salt-"*Desh Ka Namak*" and Hero Honda-"*Desh Ki Dhadkan*". Similarly, advertisements of products like baby oils, baby shampoos, diapers, etc. use the emotions of mothers in an attempt to sell their products.

PORTRAYING A PARTICULAR BODY IMAGE

Advertising has been criticized for glorifying glamorous looks in both men and women. The ideal image of beauty that the advertisements portray creates insecurities in both men and women about the way they look.

Playing on consumers' insecurities about their appearance presents advertisers with a classic ethical dilemma because self-image advertising can also be seen as contributing to self-improvement, as far as one's looks are concerned. Sometimes, however, such strategies are questionable because they lead to dangerous practices. Some critics point out that women place their health at risk in order to cultivate an unrealistic or even unhealthy physical appearance. The perfect body type image portrayed by most ads is difficult for most women to attain and may therefore, harm their self-image.

Here again the problem of stereotyping based on physical appearance exists for men and women. Female models in advertisements are shown as excessively thin and having the perfect beauty whereas, males are portrayed as having ideal V-shaped body with a well developed chest and arm muscles and wide shoulders tapering down to a narrow waist.

These days, the idea of perfect fairness is not only restricted to women with a plethora of fairness products like fairness creams and fairness soaps in the markets. Advertising has started spreading this idea of perfect fairness amongst males also. Celebrities like Shahrukh Khan and Shahid Kapoor are endorsing some brands of fairness creams made especially for men. The advertisement of Emami Fair and Handsome cream shows Shahrukh Khan giving a fairness cream to a young guy to get a new look. Thereafter, this guy gets a new improved complexion and wins over a girl.

The standard of attractiveness is a socio-cultural phenomenon that advertising mirrors, as well as shapes. Responsible advertisers must, therefore, use models of more normal size and weight as a way to reduce the insecurities among people about the way they look, especially the young people who seem to be most open to messages about cultural standards of beauty and physical attractiveness.

ADVERTISEMENTS DIRECTED AT CHILDREN

Use of children in advertising is also arguable. Advertisers use children not only to promote products meant especially for children but apart from this, there are many commercial ads where marketers are using children to promote the products, which are not meant for children. Intelligent advertisers know that children of modern era have a strong influencing power on their parents. Children are the most vulnerable segment of the target market. Some advertisements try to convince children towards the purchase/use of the advertiser's product, for instance, trying to attract children by offering free gifts and toys on purchase of products. Such a practice of advertisers is unethical.

For instance, McDonald's targets children as their main clientele in India. Children are an enormously powerful medium for marketing consumer goods in India. They not only influence markets in terms of the parental decision-making to buy certain kinds of products, they are also future consumers. After all, brand impressions, once formed, can stay for a lifetime. Thus, McDonald's has done everything possible to attract children. It's "Happy Meals" and the accompanying toys are a great attraction for children. During their visits, kids are showered with knickknacks like balloons. McDonald's also promotes birthday parties complete with cake, candles, and toys in television advertising aimed directly at kids.

Promoting Unhealthy Products: Another area of concern is that advertisements which promote unhealthy foods, like soft drinks, have a derogatory effect on children. Soft drinks companies focus their attention and advertising budgets on the children's market, through sponsorship of music events and link-ups with the most attractive and popular movie stars, pop singers and sports celebrities. In India, glamorous Bollywood stars like Amitabh Bachchan, Shahrukh Khan, Aamir Khan, Hrithik Roshan, Kareena Kapoor, Ranbir Kapoor etc. promote soft drinks. The websites of these soft drink companies apart from offering a host of promotional campaigns also offer computer and mobile phone downloads like wallpapers, screensavers, ringtones, videos etc. Today's youth icons from the cricket world, like Sachin Tendulkar, Virender Sehwag and Dhoni, endorse Pepsi. The sponsorship of a sport like cricket, in particular, may cultivate positive attitudes by associating the product with characteristics which young people admire. In the wake of the recent controversies shrouding Coke and Pepsi, regarding allegations of containing pesticides, these stars not only endorsed these soft drinks but also went so far as to claim that they were safe.

Aerated soft drinks, apart from promoting the wrong kind of images, have long been suspected of leading to lower calcium levels and higher phosphate levels in the blood. When phosphate levels are high and calcium levels are low, the situation that ultimately leads to poor bone mineralization, which explains the greater risk of broken bones in children who consume soft drinks. Exhibit 19.4 shows the guidelines on advertising of foods and beverages directed at children under 13 years of age as per the ASCI code.

Exhibit 19.4: ASCI's Self - Regulation Guidelines on Advertising of Foods & Beverages directed at Children under 13 years of age

1. Advertisements should not mislead consumers to believe that consumption of product advertised will result directly in personal changes in intelligence, physical ability or exceptional recognition. Such claims if made in advertisements should be supported with adequate scientific substantiation. All nutritional and health benefit claims in foods & beverage advertisements are required to be substantiated scientifically.
2. Unless a food product has been nutritionally designed as a meal replacement, it should not be portrayed as such.
3. Messages in advertising to children will portray accurately the products, in a way that is in keeping with their ability to understand.
4. Advertisements should not show over consumption of Foods & Beverages. It should reflect moderation in consumption and portion sizes appropriate to occasion or situation. Advertising of promotional offers on Food & Beverage products should also not show excessive consumption.
5. Advertisements should not undermine the role of parental care and guidance in ensuring proper food choices are made by children.
6. Visual presentation of foods and beverages in advertisement should not mislead the consumers of the material characteristics of the products advertised.

(Source: http://www.ascionline.org/)

ADS WITH DANGEROUS/HAZARDOUS ACTIONS

Advertisements have a significant influence on people's behaviour. As such, advertisers must be careful not to depict unsafe or dangerous practices in their advertisements, which, if emulated by people, can cause harm or injury. Thus, advertisers are encouraged to depict advertisements, in a manner which promotes safe practices, like wearing of helmets and fastening of seatbelts, not using mobiles/cell phones when driving, etc.

In an advertisement of Anchor Weather Proof Switches, the visual in the TVC showed people throwing and splashing water on their electric sockets to show that it is waterproof. A complaint received against the ad stated that children may try the same actions on non-water proof sockets in their homes and get killed due to shock. The ASCI held that the visual depiction of, "touching the Switchbox after it has been sprayed with water", accidentally, in a sequel featuring young children, was a hazardous act, likely to be emulated by minors, in a manner which could cause injury. Thus, the ASCI directed for the modification of the TVC.

In an advertisement of Coca Cola during Diwali time (2008), the TVC showed a minor boy playing with a fire cracker (*fuljhadi*) in a dangerous way. A complaint received stated that by watching this TVC, children may get provoked/tempted to perform the similar act which is against the safety standard of using fire crackers and harmful in nature for the children. The ASCI held that the visual showing "use of sparklers in a dangerous manner", manifests a disregard for safety and is likely to encourage negligence. Thus, it ordered that the TVC should be withdrawn.

The guidelines on self regulation on advertisements for automotive vehicles states that advertisements should not:

(a) portray violation of the Traffic Rules,

(b) show speed maneuverability in a manner which encourages unsafe or reckless driving, which could harm the driver, passengers and/or general public,

(c) show stunts or actions, which require professional driving skills, in normal traffic conditions which in any case should carry a readable cautionary message drawing viewer attention to the depiction of stunts.

In an advertisement published in The Telegraph, Calcutta (2008), four people were shown sitting on a motorbike and the ad headline stated, "Ready to buy a car?" In a complaint received against the ad it was stated that the ad is hazardous and harmful. It also appears to be in violation of the Motor Vehicles Act, 1988. The ASCI concluded that the ad shows a dangerous practice and manifests a disregard for safety without justifiable reason. Also, the ad is considered to be in breach of the law, and portrays violation of the Traffic Rules. Thus, it ordered that the ad should be discontinued.

In an advertisement of Timex watches (2008), the TVC showed "a boy and a girl are driving their respective cars. They are talking to each other whilst driving. At a given time, the girl drives with the same speed in reverse. The ASCI 'suo motu' registered a complaint stating that this is in gross violation of safety norms and will encourage reckless driving which could harm the driver and the passenger. It also said that the cautionary message shown in the TVC is not of a readable font size.

SURROGATE ADVERTISING

When the laws of a country do not permit advertising of a certain product category, the advertisers take the shelter of a brand extension. The term 'surrogate' means substitute. The term 'surrogate advertising' means using the brand image of one product extensively to promote another product of the same brand.

Considering the harmful effects of advertising in promotion of unhealthy products, the Government of India banned the advertising of liquor and tobacco products. As a reaction to this, liquor and tobacco companies started seeking other ways of endorsing their products. They found an alternative way of advertising through which they could keep reminding the consumers about their liquor and tobacco brands. They introduced various other products in the market with the same brand name. When these products are advertised, it keeps reminding the customers about the liquor and tobacco products with the same brand name, the advertisement of which is banned.

The liquor industry is a prominent player in this game. Few surrogate advertisements in the liquor industry are Haywards' soda, Kingfisher mineral water, Bagpiper soda and cassettes and CDs, Smirnoff cassettes and CDs, Teacher's Achievement Awards, etc. These products bear exactly the same brand name and logo, which we had seen earlier in their liquor advertisements. It was surprising to know that liquor giants like McDowell's and Seagram's have entered into new segments lie cassettes and CDs, mineral water etc. Later it was found that the basic aim of these surrogate advertisements was to promote their liquor products like beer, wine, vodka etc. Their brand extensions were just an act of bypassing the advertisement ban.

A similar trend is followed by companies making tobacco products like cigarettes, pan masalas etc. Some examples of surrogate advertisements in this category are Red and White Bravery Awards, Wills Lifestyle, Manikchand Filmfare Awards etc.

A detailed discussion on surrogate advertising is done in chapter 21 of this book.

SUBLIMINAL ADVERTISING

The term 'subliminal' means below the threshold of consciousness. The idea is that certain things are heard, seen or felt that never reach our conscious thought process, but may still be recorded somewhere in our subconscious mind and have an impact on our behaviour.

For the past many years the advertisements of Fair & Lovely beauty cream (a product of Hindustan Unilever Ltd.) have been portraying fame and fortune related to fair and beautiful women. In their advertisements a tube of fairness cream will bring them immense success and fame. According to them the key to fame is simply and miraculously a tube of fairness cream. That, apparently, is all that really stands between us and fame and fortune: a 14 day experiment with a tube of cream, which is supposed to do a miracle for you.

The TVC of Fair and Lovely shows that only fair complexion gives you the path to success. When top models appear in these ads that imply that talent, individuality and intellect are only secondary and useless without a fair complexion; a potentially hazardous message is conveyed to the audience especially young girls.

By looking at the print advertisement of Fair and Lovely you see that fair complexion is the main factor being highlighted once you are fair only then you are glamorous and successful. It shows the difference in your complexion after using the cream.

Also, most of the advertisements of Fair & Lovely beauty cream suggest that a "fairer girl gets the boy". In some other TVCs, they have portrayed the young woman who, after using Fair & Lovely becomes attractive and therefore gets a good job. This implies that the main qualification for a woman to get a job is the way she looks. The ads also suggest that girls have to define themselves in terms of the men they attract. Somewhere, in the subconscious mind, an Indian consumer who is seeing such an ad time and again is led to believe that that dark skin, especially on women, is somehow inferior. As a reaction to such advertisements, there are many consumers, especially girls, who start buying such products in a hope to look beautiful and thus, become successful in life, because their subconscious mind has got a message that dark skinned people cannot be successful either in their professional or in their personal lives. However, many critics are of the opinion that Hindustan Unilever Limited (HUL) had violated Indian advertisement ethics by openly insulting a majority of dark skinned Indian women.

PUFFERY

Puffery is defined as "advertising or other sales representations, which praise the item to be sold with subjective opinions, superlatives, or exaggerations, vaguely and generally, stating no specific facts". Campbell Soup, for instance, has used the slogan "America's Favourite Food", which is vague and exaggerated and cannot really be proven. Similarly, Eveready's claim "nothing outlasts an Eveready battery" is an example of puffery.

The response of people to the use of puffery in advertisements is mixed. Some research suggests that the public might expect advertisers to be able to prove the truth of superlative claims, and other researches indicate that reasonable people do not believe such claims.

In an advertisement of Star Global Education (IELTS), the ad claimed, "India's Finest IELTS Training Academy". The ASCI held that there was no comparative analysis vis-à-vis other educational institutes in India to make the claim. In another advertisement of Amaron Batteries, the ad stated, "India's most powerful battery", whereas the advertiser did not provide any comparative data in support of the claim.

WEASEL CLAIM

A weasel word is a modifier that practically negates the claim that follows. Weasels are those words or claims that appear substantial in the first look but disintegrate into hollow meaninglessness on analysis. Commonly used weasel words include helps, like, virtual or virtually, acts or works, can be, as much as, refreshes, comforts, tackles, fights, the feel of, the look of, looks like etc. For instance, 'Helps control dandruff symptoms with regular use'. The weasels include 'helps control', and possibly even 'symptoms' and 'regular use'. The claim is not 'stops dandruff'.

Examples of Weasel Claim:

1. "Listerine fights bad breath". The claim is 'fights', not 'stops'.
2. Protex Happydent Sugar Free Gum claims, "Helps reduce risk of tooth decay".
3. Pepsodent Complete Germicheck claims, "Helps prevent gum problems caused by germs", "Fights tooth decay".
4. Orbit Chewing Gum claims, "Helps keep teeth white", "Helps prevent tooth decay".

DETERMINING WHAT IS ETHICAL

An important job of the advertiser is to evaluate advertising on ethical grounds. There are laws and regulations governing the practice of advertising, but there are also codes of conduct, as well as personal and professional decision-making guidelines for the advertisers. The chapter has explained various such codes and guidelines as has been defined by the ASCI. Another way of determining the ethicality of advertising is to review it on the basis of the following three criteria.

1. Social ethics
2. Professional ethics
3. Personal ethics

Social Ethics: Applying ethical values and principles to advertising is necessary if it is to be socially responsible. Social Responsibility, a corporate philosophy based on ethical values, motivates a person to perform a useful function within society and to make its impact on society positive rather than negative. It also urges to consider what is acceptable to a society and what is not. This is true in case of its advertising also. Thus, certain ads from Idea Cellular, especially the one which tries and create a society where there will be no caste discrimination, have received a lot of appreciation from people both from the advertising field as well as the general public. On the other hand, many ads which use sex appeal and nudity invite a lot of criticism as they are against the values, customs and traditions of the Indian society.

Professional Ethics: Professional ethics are often expressed in a code of standards that identifies how professionals in the industry should respond when faced with ethical questions. Exhibit 19.5 reproduces a part of the code given by the American Association of Advertising Agencies in this respect.

Exhibit 19.5: A part of the Code of American Association of Advertising Agencies

We, the members of American Association of Advertising Agencies, in addition to supporting and obeying the laws and legal regulations pertaining to advertising, undertake to extend and broaden the application of high ethical standards. Specifically, we will not knowingly create advertising that contains

- False or misleading statements or exaggerations, visual or verbal
- Testimonials that do not reflect the real opinion of the individual(s) involved
- Price claims that are misleading
- Claims insufficiently supported or that distort the true meaning of practical application of statements made by professional or scientific authority
- Statements, suggestions or pictures offensive to public decency or minority segments of the population

We recognize that there are areas that are subject to honestly different interpretations and judgment. Nevertheless, we agree not to recommend to an advertiser, and to discourage the use of, advertising that is in poor or questionable taste or that is deliberately irritating through oral or visual content or presentation.

Comparative advertising shall be governed by the same standards of truthfulness, claim substantiation, tastefulness, etc. as apply to other types of advertising.

In India, the Advertising Standards Council of India (ASCI) has adopted a Code for Self-Regulation in Advertising. It is a commitment to honest advertising and to fair competition in the market-place and is expected to be followed by all concerned with advertising - advertisers, media, advertising agencies and others who help in the creation or placement of advertisements. ASCI seeks to ensure that advertisements conform to its Code for Self-Regulation which requires advertisements to be truthful and fair to consumers and competitors, within the bounds of generally accepted standards of public decency and propriety, and not used indiscriminately for the promotion of products, hazardous or harmful to society or to individuals particularly minors, to a degree unacceptable to society at large.

Personal Ethics: Decisions about ethics are made based on laws and regulations and professional codes, but more importantly, on an internal moral compass that senses when something is right or wrong. This moral compass tells you when an advertising idea is misleading, insensitive, or too manipulative. It is then the responsibility of the advertising professional to use this personal judgment and moral reasoning in rejecting such an idea.

AN ETHICAL CHECKLIST FOR ADVERTISERS

According to Gene R. Laczniak and Patrick E. Murphy, the following ethical checklist can help advertisers come up with ads which are not questionable on ethical grounds.

1. In terms of its social impact, does advertising

- reinforce negative stereotypes?
- damage people's self-concept and create insecurities?
- market dangerous products?
- contribute to cultural pollution?
- violate public standards of good taste?

2. In terms of its strategic decisions, does an advertisement

- target vulnerable groups?
- harm children?
- make unsubstantiated claims?
- appeal to base motivations such as envy and greed?
- drive demand for unnecessary purchases?

3. In terms of tactics, does an advertisement...

- use inappropriate stereotypes?
- use ideas, words or images that are offensive or insensitive?
- manipulate people's emotions unnecessarily?
- make false, deceptive, or misleading claims?
- use puffery?

The use of this ethical checklist can help advertisers come up with advertisements which pass the test of ethics and are in a good public taste.

CONCLUDING NOTE

Advertising is a highly visible business activity and any lapse in the ethical standards can lead to severe consequences for the company. An advertisement which is questionable on ethical grounds invites criticism. It may also lead to some action taken against the advertisers by public interest groups, consumer protection councils and bodies like the ASCI. Thus, professionals in the advertising industry need to have strong ethical standards while designing their ad campaigns. They should always try to eliminate the socially harmful aspects of advertising and observe high ethical standards with regard to truthfulness, human dignity and social responsibility. In this way, they will make an exceptional and important contribution to human progress and to the common good.

As Leo Burnett, says, "***Let's gear our advertising to sell goods, but let's recognize also that advertising has a broad social responsibility***".

QUESTIONS FOR DISCUSSION

1. Discuss the various ethical issues in advertising.
2. How does advertising reinforce stereotypes? Discuss in context of the gender roles and portrayal of aged people in advertisements.
3. What do you mean by subliminal advertising?
4. What is the meaning of puffery? Give some examples of use of puffery in advertisements?
5. "Advertising should be socially, ethically as well as legally responsible." Comment.
6. Write short notes on:
   (a) Weasel Claim
   (b) Advertisements Directed at Children
   (c) Misleading Advertisement
7. Think of an advertisement that you found to be unethical. What was unethical about it? How do you think it can be regulated?

CHAPTER 20

Advertising Standards Council of India

CONTENTS

The Advertising Standards Council of India (ASCI) is a self-regulatory voluntary organisation of the advertising industry established in 1985. The role and function of ASCI & its Consumer Complaints Council (CCC) is to deal with complaints received from consumers and industry, against advertisements which are considered as false, misleading, indecent, illegal, leading to unsafe practices, or unfair to competition, and consequently in contravention of the ASCI Code for Self-Regulation in Advertising.

In recent years the quantity of false, misleading and offensive advertising has resulted in consumers having an increasing disbelief in advertising, and a growing resentment of it. Misleading and false advertising also constitutes unfair competition. It could lead to market-place disaster or even litigation. If this kind of advertising continues, it won't be long before statutory regulations and procedures are imposed which make even fair, truthful, decent advertising cumbersome. This certainly will affect the ability to compete and grow.

The Advertising Standards Council of India has adopted a Code for Self-Regulation in Advertising. It is a commitment to honest advertising and to fair competition in the market-place. It stands for the protection of the legitimate interests of consumers and all concerned with advertising - advertisers, media, advertising agencies and others who help in the creation or placement of advertisements.

GOAL OF ASCI

The goal of ASCI is to maintain and enhance the public's confidence in advertising. ASCI seeks to ensure that advertisements conform to its Code for Self-Regulation which requires advertisements to be:

- Truthful and fair to consumers and competitors.
- Within the bounds of generally accepted standards of public decency and propriety.
- Not used indiscriminately for the promotion of products, hazardous or harmful to society or to individuals particularly minors, to a degree unacceptable to society at large.

ASCI propagates its code and a sense of responsibility for its observance amongst advertisers, advertising agencies and others connected with the creation of advertisements, and the media.

ASCI encourages the public to complain against advertisements with which they may be unhappy for any reason and ensures that each complaint receives a prompt and objective consideration by an impartial committee Consumer Complaints Council (CCC) which takes into account the view point of the advertiser, and an appropriate decision is communicated to all concerned. ASCI endeavours to achieve compliance with its decisions through reasoned persuasion and the power of public opinion.

ASCI'S CODE FOR SELF REGULATION

The Code for Self Regulation given by ASCI has been drawn up by people in professions and industries in or connected with advertising, in consultation with representatives of people affected by advertising and has been accepted by individuals, corporate bodies and associations engaged in or otherwise concerned with the practice of advertising with the following as basic guidelines with a view to achieve the acceptance of fair advertising practices in the best interests of the ultimate consumer.

- Chapter I of the Code seeks to ensure the truthfulness and honesty of representations and claims made by advertisements and to safeguard against misleading advertisements.
- Chapter II of the Code seeks to ensure that advertisements are not offensive to generally accepted standards of public decency. Advertisements should contain nothing indecent, vulgar or repulsive which is likely, in the light of generally prevailing standards of decency and propriety, to cause grave or widespread offence.

- Chapter III of the Code seeks to safeguard against the indiscriminate use of advertising in situations or of the promotion of products which are regarded as hazardous or harmful to society or to individuals, particularly minors, to a degree or of a type which is unacceptable to society at large.
- Chapter IV of the Code seeks to ensure that advertisements observe fairness in competition so that the consumer's need to be informed on choices in the market-place and the norms of generally accepted competitive behaviour in business are met.

  Chapters I, II, III and IV of the code are explained in Annexure 20.1 given at the end of this chapter.

Both the general public and an advertiser's competitors have an equal right to expect the content of advertisements to be presented fairly, intelligibly and responsibly. The Code applies to advertisers, advertising agencies and media.

OBSERVANCE OF THE CODE

The responsibility for the observance of this Code for Self-Regulation in Advertising lies with all who commission, create, place or publish any advertisement or assist in the creation or publishing of any advertisement. All advertisers, advertising agencies and media are expected not to commission, create, place or publish any advertisement which is in contravention of this Code. This is a self-imposed discipline required under this Code for Self-Regulation in Advertising from all involved in the commissioning, creation, placement or publishing of advertisements.

This Code applies to advertisements read, heard or viewed in India even if they originate or are published abroad so long as they are directed to consumers in India or are exposed to significant number of consumers in India.

ORGANISATION OF ASCI

The Board of Governors (16 members) of ASCI ensures equitable representation of Advertisers, Agencies, Media and other Advertising Services, the individual member firms being leaders in their respective industries or services. The Consumer Complaints Council CCC (21 members as in 2010) has 12 non-advertising professionals representing civil society, who are eminent and recognised opinion leaders in their respective disciplines such as medical, legal, industrial design, engineering, chemical technology, human resources and consumer interest groups; 9 are advertising practitioners from the member firms.

CONSUMER COMPLAINTS COUNCIL

The Board of Governors appoint the Consumer Complaints Council (CCC), on receiving a complaint against an advertisement. The Consumer Complaints Council examines and investigates the complaints received from the consumers and the general public, including the members of the company, regarding any breach of the Code of Conduct and/or advertising ethics and recommends the action to be taken in that regard.

COMPLAINTS DECIDED BY THE CCC

The Consumer Complaint Council has played a fair and supportive role in ensuring that the complaints received against advertisements are dealt with promptly and are treated with the confidence which they deserve. The Council has been instrumental in mediation with advertisers and agencies concerned, thus avoiding time-consuming and costly litigation in many instances.

Quarterly Compilation Reports of CCC decisions to members on consumer and industry complaints against advertisements provide valuable case/reference material for proactive observance of the Code for Self-Regulation. This reference material provides material on various cases where the complaints against advertisements were upheld and not upheld by CCC.

Some of the **cases where the complaints received against advertisements were upheld** (i.e. actions were taken on the complaints) by CCC are discussed below.

1. Coca Cola India Pvt. Ltd. (Thumbs Up)

Ad Description: The ad showed actor Akshay Kumar with a lady occupant driving a car in a very rash and negligent manner for a 'Thumbs Up bottle'. He then meets with an accident and is shown in the hospital with a fractured leg, and sipping a bottle of Thumbs Up.

Complaint received: Any individual inspired by this ad, if attempts to perform such daredevil acts, there is a big likelihood that he will lose his life/limb, and therefore, this ad should be prohibited.

CCC's decision: CCC held that the actions portrayed in the visuals depicted in the TVC show dangerous practices and manifest a disregard for safety without justifiable reason. The ad portrays violation of the Traffic Rules, and shows speed in a manner which encourages unsafe or reckless driving, which could harm the driver, passengers and/or general public. CCC ordered for the TVC to be modified.

2. Hindustan Unilever Ltd. (Axe Deodorant – Dark Temptation)

Ad description: TVC shows a boy spraying Axe deodorant on himself and he gets converted into a boy made of chocolate, as the fragrance of the deodorant is of chocolate. As he walks on the street, the girls start licking him, two girls lick and bite his ears on both sides, in the bus a girl bites his butts, enjoys the taste and licks her lips. The boy is shown enjoying it all.

Complaint received: The ad is in bad taste and is vulgar as it shows the girls kicking and biting the boy. The scene of the girl biting his butts is highly objectionable. Two similar complaints were also received by ASCI.

CCC's decision: Visuals of the girls licking the chocolate boy and girl biting his rear was indecent and likely to cause grave or widespread offence. CCC ordered for the modification of TVC.

3. Kent RO systems Ltd. (Kent RO Water Purifier)

Ad claim: "Only Kent Mineral RO Water Purifier retains all essential minerals and gets you and your family 100% pure water".

Complaint received: Advertiser should provide proof, supporting technical information with details of reports of tests/trials conducted from an independent recognised testing institution.

CCC's decision: The claim was false since there are other products in the same category providing this service (and thus, Kent is not the only water purifier which provides 100% pure water). The advertiser assured that the claim will be modified.

4. HDFC Standard Life Insurance Co. Ltd. (Life Insurance Plans)

Ad description: The TVC shows a child at home searching for his remote controlled car which is lost. A male guest present in his home tells the child that he would get him a new car in place of the one that is lost, to which the child replies that his father would get one for him. Then the guest says what if your father gets lost. On hearing this, the child becomes sad. Luckily the father returns and tells the child that even if his father gets lost, he will ensure that his son can buy his own car.

Complaint received: This is a very scary ad for kids of impressionable age and even scary for fathers.

CCC's decision: The ad is likely to frighten children of impressionable age and thus, the TVC should be modified.

5. Diageo India Pvt. Ltd. (Smirnoff)-Print Ad published by India Today

Ad states: "What is celebration without a little flavour in it?"

Complaint received: The ad is compelling the customer to consume alcohol on festive occasions. The ad does not mention that Smirnoff is an alcohol drink and also that alcohol is injurious to health. The ad does not carry the message "not for minors".

CCC's decision: The ad is a surrogate ad for a liquor product – Smirnoff. India Today assured that the said ad will not appear again in future.

6. Heinz India Pvt. Ltd. (Complan)

Ad claim: 'Children taking Complan are found to grow taller by 3 cms, as compared to non Complan drinkers".

Complaint received: Claim is totally false and not supported by any scientific research and thus, the advertisement is misleading.

CCC's decision: CCC held that the claim was not substantiated. Also, the advertisement was in breach of law as it was in contravention of the Drugs and Cosmetic Rules, 1945. Subsequently, the advertiser provided the results of the study conducted by an independent scientific research in substantiation of the claim. Also, the advertiser confirmed that they are not covered under the Drugs and Cosmetic Act. They are governed by the Prevention of Food Adulteration Act.

7. Idea Cellular Ltd. (Idea – Walk and Talk)

Ad description: TVC shows people from different professions on various locations and situations walking and talking on mobile, two men carrying a huge hoarding climbing staircase, walking on the pavement and talking on mobile."

Complaint received: TVC encourages an unsafe act of walking while talking on the mobile phone which could cause injury to a person or others or both. Seven similar complaints were received against the same TVC.

CCC's decision: Some action sequences as depicted in the TVC shows dangerous practices and manifest a disregard for safety without a justifiable reason. The advertiser assured appropriate modification of the TVC.

8. ING Vysya Life Insurance Company Ltd.

Ad description: First scene - a teenage girl happily showing her father her admission to MBA. Her father is initially happy until he sees the financial cost involved. At that time, the ground breaks beneath him and he falls a few feet through the ground. Second scene - a nurse handing over a new born baby girl to the father. The father is initially happy, until he thinks of the financial cost in bringing up the child. At that time, the ground breaks under his feet and he also falls. Advertisement says, "*Dikhne mein toh pyaari hai, yeh khushiyan thodi bhaari hai*".

Complaint received: Advertisement is anti-girl child and deeply offensive to all females, giving the message that they are nothing more than burdens.

CCC's decisions: Advertisement when viewed as a whole portrays avoidable 'gender insensitivity' and the advertisement is likely to cause offence. The ad campaign had to be ended.

9. Cadbury India Ltd. (Cadbury Fruity Gems)

Ad description: The ad shows a child eating fruits and another child eating Gems of the same flavour. In the end, the child eating fruits is shown eating Cadbury Fruity Gems instead of fruits.

Complaint received: The ad has influenced the complainant's six year old daughter so much that she did not want to eat fruits and wanted to eat only Cadbury Fruity Gems.

CCC's decision: CCC held that the ad exploits the vulnerability of minors. The advertiser assured appropriate modification of the TVC.

10. Go Airlines (India) Pvt. Ltd. (Free Flight Offer)

Ad offer: The ad on the website offered 1 free ticket for every 5 flights taken on Go Air flights, all flights to be taken before March 31, 2009.

Complaint received: This offer was not made good to the complainant.

CCC's decision: CCC held that the claim/offer made on the advertiser's website was misleading. Subsequently, the advertiser assured that they have made good the offer to the complainant.

In addition to the above cases, there have also been **cases where the complaints were not upheld by CCC** (i.e. the decision was given in favour of the advertiser). Let us now read about few such cases.

1. Info Edge (India) Pvt. Ltd. (Naukri.com)

Ad description: The ad shows an employee distorting his boss name "*Hari Sadu*" by spelling it as H for Hitler, A for Arrogant, R for Rascal, I for Idiot.

Complaint received: 'Hari' is one of the sacred and pious names of Lord Vishnu. The ad is highly disrespectful in that sense and should be withdrawn.

CCC's decision: Portrayal of a fictitious character in the TVC in a humorous situation was not likely to give rise to grave or widespread offence.

2. Cadbury India Ltd. (Cadbury's Chocolates)

Ad description: A sister is annoyed because her brother has come to her on the *Rakhi* day without any gift. The sister ties the *Rakhi* tightly on her brother's wrist in rage. Then the brother gives Cadbury's Chocolates as gift to his sister which makes her happy.

Complaint Received: Visual depiction of a sister tying a *Rakhi* while she is full of rage militates against the basic root of this very sacred *Raksha Bandhan Parva*. The commercial makes a mockery of this festival by conveying the message that sisters only look out for gifts on this day.

CCC's decision: CCC held that the TVC depicted a humorous situation which was not offensive.

3. Idea Cellular Ltd. (Idea)

Ad description: The TVC shows as there is no adequate school facility in rural area, the education is done on mobile.

Complaint received: The ad creates a wrong picture of education system in rural Maharashtra.

CCC's decision: The ad does not denigrate the education system in Maharashtra.

CONCLUDING NOTE

As a result of prompt and effective follow ups, there have been positive responses received from advertisers and agencies in respect of CCC recommendations on complaints which were upheld. There has been a number of instances wherein advertisers/agencies have withdrawn or modified their advertisements appropriately, merely on their being approached by ASCI for comments in respect of complaints received. The acceptance of ASCI's role in judging complaints against advertisements is in the interest of all practitioners in advertising and consumers who are the targets of such advertisements.

QUESTIONS FOR DISCUSSION

1. Discuss the role of ASCI in regulating advertising in India.
2. Briefly discuss ASCI's code for Self Regulation in advertising.
3. Discuss how the Consumer Complaints Council (CCC) of ASCI has played an important role in dealing with some of the objectionable advertisements in the recent past.

Appendix 20.1

ASCI'S CODE FOR SELF REGULATION IN ADVERTISING

CHAPTER I

To ensure the truthfulness and honesty of representations and claims made by advertisements and to safeguard against misleading advertisements

1. Advertisements must be truthful. All descriptions, claims and comparisons which relate to matters of objectively ascertainable fact should be capable of substantiation. Advertisers and advertising agencies are required to produce such substantiation as and when called upon to do so by the Advertising Standards Council of India.

2. Where advertising claims are expressly stated to be based on or supported by independent research or assessment, the source and date of this should be indicated in the advertisement.

3. Advertisements shall not, without permission from the person, firm or institution under reference, contain any reference to such person, firm or institution which confers an unjustified advantage on the product advertised or tends to bring the person, firm or institution into ridicule or disrepute. If and when required to do so by the Advertising Standards Council of India, the advertiser and the advertising agency shall produce explicit permission from the person, firm or institution to which reference is made in the advertisement.

4. Advertisements shall neither distort facts nor mislead the consumer by means of implications or omissions. Advertisements shall not contain statements or visual presentation which directly or by implication or by omission or by ambiguity or by exaggeration are likely to mislead the consumer about the product advertised or the advertiser or about any other product or advertiser.

5. Advertisements shall not be so framed as to abuse the trust of consumers or exploit their lack of experience or knowledge. No advertisement shall be permitted to contain any claim so exaggerated as to lead to grave or widespread disappointment in the minds of consumers.

   For example:

   (a) Products shall not be described as 'free' where there is any direct cost to the consumer other than the actual cost of any delivery, freight, or postage. Where such costs are payable by the consumer, a clear statement that this is the case shall be made in the advertisement.

   (b) Where a claim is made that if one product is purchased another product will be provided 'free', the advertiser is required to show, as and when called upon by The Advertising Standards Council of India, that the price paid by the consumer for the product which is offered for purchase with the advertised incentive is no more than the prevalent price of the product without the advertised incentive.

(c) Claims which use expressions such as "Upto five years' guarantee" or "Prices from as low as Rs. Y" are not acceptable if there is a likelihood of the consumer being misled either as to the extent of the availability or as to the applicability of the benefits offered.

(d) Special care and restraint has to be exercised in advertisements addressed to those suffering from weakness, any real or perceived inadequacy of any physical attributes such as height or bust development, obesity, illness, impotence, infertility, baldness and the like, to ensure that claims or representations directly or by implication, do not exceed what is considered prudent by generally accepted standards of medical practice and the actual efficacy of the product.

(e) Advertisements inviting the public to invest money shall not contain statements which may mislead the consumer in respect of the security offered, rates of return or terms of amortisation; where any of the foregoing elements are contingent upon the continuance of or change in existing conditions, or any other assumptions, such conditions or assumptions must be clearly indicated in the advertisement.

(f) Advertisements inviting the public to take part in lotteries or prize competitions permitted under law or which hold out the prospect of gifts shall state clearly all material conditions as to enable the consumer to obtain a true and fair view of their prospects in such activities. Further, such advertisers shall make adequate provisions for the judging of such competitions, announcement of the results and the fair distribution of prizes or gifts according to the advertised terms and conditions within a reasonable period of time. With regard to the announcement of results, it is clarified that the advertiser's responsibility under this section of the Code is discharged adequately if the advertiser publicizes the main results in the media used to announce the competition as far as is practicable, and advises the individual winners by post.

6. Obvious untruths or exaggerations intended to amuse or to catch the eye of the consumer are permissible provided that they are clearly to be seen as humorous or hyperbolic and not likely to be understood as making literal or misleading claims for the advertised product.

7. In mass manufacturing and distribution of goods and services it is possible that there may be an occasional, unintentional lapse in the fulfilment of an advertised promise or claim. Such occasional, unintentional lapses may not invalidate the advertisement in terms of this Code.

In judging such issues, due regard shall be given to the following:

(a) Whether the claim or promise is capable of fulfillment by a typical specimen of the product advertised.

(b) Whether the proportion of product failures is within generally acceptable limits.

(c) Whether the advertiser has taken prompt action to make good the deficiency to the consumer.

CHAPTER II

To ensure that advertisements are not offensive to generally accepted standards of public decency.

Advertisements should contain nothing indecent, vulgar or repulsive which is likely, in the light of generally prevailing standards of decency and propriety, to cause grave or widespread offence.

CHAPTER III

To safeguard against the indiscriminate use of advertising in situations or of the promotion of products which are regarded as hazardous or harmful to society or to individuals, particularly minors, to a degree or of a type which is unacceptable to society at large.

1. No advertisement shall be permitted which:

   (a) Tends to incite people to crime or to promote disorder and violence or intolerance.

   (b) Derides any race, caste, colour, creed or nationality.

   (c) Presents criminality as desirable or directly or indirectly encourages people - particularly minors - to emulate it or conveys the modus operandi of any crime.

   (d) Adversely affects friendly relations with a foreign State.

2. Advertisements addressed to minors shall not contain anything, whether in illustration or otherwise, which might result in their physical, mental or moral harm or which exploits their vulnerability. For example, Advertisements:

   (a) Should not encourage minors to enter strange places or to converse with strangers in an effort to collect coupons, wrappers, labels or the like.

   (b) Should not feature dangerous or hazardous acts which are likely to encourage minors to emulate such acts in a manner which could cause harm or injury.

   (c) Should not show minors using or playing with matches or any inflammable or explosive substance; or playing with or using sharp knives, guns or mechanical or electrical appliances, the careless use of which could lead to their suffering cuts, burns, shocks or other injury.

   (d) Should not feature minors for tobacco or alcohol-based products.

(e) Should not feature personalities from the field of sports, music and cinema for products which, by law, either require a health warning in their advertising or cannot be purchased by minors.

3. Advertisements shall not, without justifiable reason, show or refer to dangerous practices or manifest a disregard for safety or encourage negligence.

4. Advertisements should contain nothing which is in breach of the law nor omit anything which the law requires.

5. Advertisements shall not propagate products, the use of which is banned under the law.

6. Advertisements for products whose advertising is prohibited or restricted by law or by this code must not circumvent such restrictions by purporting to be advertisements for other products the advertising of which is not prohibited or restricted by law or by this code. In judging whether or not any particular advertisement is an indirect advertisement for product whose advertising is restricted or prohibited, due attention shall be paid to the following:

(a) Visual content of the advertisement must depict only the product being advertised and not the prohibited or restricted product in any form or manner

(b) The advertisement must not make any direct or indirect reference to the prohibited or restricted products

(c) The advertisement must not create any nuances or phrases promoting prohibited products

(d) The advertisement must not use particular colours and layout or presentations associated with prohibited or restricted products

(e) The advertisement must not use situations typical for promotion of prohibited or restricted products when advertising the other products

CHAPTER IV

To ensure that advertisements observe fairness in competition such that the consumer's need to be informed on choice in the market-place and the canons of generally accepted competitive behaviour in business are served.

1. Advertisements containing comparisons with other manufacturers or suppliers or with other products including those where a competitor is named, are permissible in the interests of vigorous competition and public enlightenment, provided:

(a) It is clear what aspects of the advertiser's product are being compared with what aspects of the competitor's product.

(b) The subject matter of comparison is not chosen in such a way as to confer an artificial advantage upon the advertiser or so as to suggest that a better bargain is offered than is truly the case.

(c) The comparisons are factual, accurate and capable of substantiation.

(d) There is no likelihood of the consumer being misled as a result of the comparison, whether about the product advertised or that with which it is compared.

(e) The advertisement does not unfairly denigrate, attack or discredit other products, advertisers or advertisements directly or by implication.

2. Advertisements shall not make unjustifiable use of the name or initials of any other firm, company or institution, nor take unfair advantage of the goodwill attached to the trade mark or symbol of another firm or its product or the goodwill acquired by its advertising campaign.

3. Advertisements shall not be similar to any other advertiser's earlier run advertisements in general layout, copy, slogans, visual presentations, music or sound effects, so as to suggest plagiarism.

4 As regards matters covered by sections 2 and 3 above, complaints of plagiarism of advertisements released earlier abroad will lie outside the scope of this Code except in the under-mentioned circumstances:

(a) The complaint is lodged within 12 months of the first general circulation of the advertisements/campaign complained against.

(b) The complainant provides substantiation regarding the claim of prior invention/usage abroad.

Source : http://www.asci.org/

Chapter 21

SURROGATE ADVERTISING IN INDIA

Contents

Advertising has often been criticized for promoting such products to people which undermine their health and for causing economic harm. Considering the harmful effects of some products, the Government of India banned the advertising of liquor and tobacco products by introducing certain laws and regulations. As a reaction to this, liquor and tobacco manufacturers started seeking other ways of endorsing their products. They found an alternative way of advertising through which they can keep on reminding the consumers about their liquor and tobacco brands. They have introduced various other products in the market with the same or similar brand name. When these products are advertised, it keeps reminding the customers about the liquor and tobacco products with that brand name, the advertisement of which is banned. This phenomenon, known as "surrogate advertising", has become a common practice in Indian advertising.

MEANING OF SURROGATE ADVERTISING

When the laws of a country do not permit advertising of certain products, the advertisers devise new means of advertising. Such situation was witnessed when the Government of India banned the advertising of tobacco and liquor products in the country. The manufacturers of tobacco and liquor products introduced various other products, such as sodas, fruit juices, cassettes and CDs in the market with the same brand name and also sponsored various events and festivals. When such substitute products (surrogates) are advertised, it keeps reminding the customers about the liquor and tobacco products with the same brand name, the advertisement of which is banned. This phenomenon, known as 'surrogate advertising', can be defined as duplicating the brand image of one product extensively to promote another product of the same brand.

Surrogate advertising can also be defined as **the strategy used by manufacturers and advertisers to promote a product in the guise of another, when the advertisement of the former is banned by the law of the land.** The practice of surrogate advertising has ethical and legal dimensions.

GENESIS OF SURROGATE ADVERTISING

Surrogate advertisements took off, not long ago, in the UK, where the British housewives protested strongly against liquor advertisements "luring" away their husbands. The liquor industry found a way around the ban: Surrogate advertisements for cocktail mixers, fruit juices and soda water using the brand names of the popular liquors.

In India, surrogate advertisements gathered momentum with the amendment to the Cable Television Networks Regulation Rules, 1994 in the year 2000, which prohibits tobacco and liquor advertisements on TV channels.

The Advertising Code, given in Rule 7 (2) (viii) of the Cable Television Networks Rules, 1994, as amended in the year 2000, provides that

No advertisement shall be permitted which promotes directly or indirectly the production, sale or consumption of-

(a) cigarettes, tobacco products, wine, alcohol, liquor or other intoxicants;

(b) infant milk substitutes, feeding bottle or infant food.

It was this ban on advertising of liquor and tobacco products that led to the ingenuity of the advertisers who came up with 'surrogate advertising' as a solution to the ban imposed on advertising of liquor and tobacco products.

PREVALENCE BEFORE THE BAN

Direct advertising of liquor and tobacco products was rampant before the enforcement of the Cable Television Networks Regulation Rules as amended in the year 2000. Billboard advertising of international and domestic brands of cigarettes and chewable forms of tobacco was a common sight. Surrogate advertising was a very common practice. Many of us may still recall the famous ads of '*Pan Parag*' with the jingle '*Pan Parag pan masala Pan Parag*', and Bagpiper's "*Khub jamega rang jab mil baithenge teen yaar- aap, main, aur Bagpiper*".

Sponsorship of sports events and cultural events by tobacco companies were common methods of promoting tobacco brand names. e.g. 'Wills' (brand of Indian Tobacco Company - ITC) used to sponsor Indian cricket team/matches. Tennis tournaments were sponsored by 'Gold Flake' cigarette (brand of Godfrey Phillips India Ltd. - GPI, a subsidiary of Phillip Morris). Boat racing was sponsored by 'Four Square' cigarettes (brand of GPI). Polo events and golf were sponsored by 'Classic' (cigarette brand of ITC). 'Charms', a cigarette brand sponsored the 'Spirit of freedom concert', a musical event. 'Manikchand', manufacturers of *gutkha* (chewing tobacco), patronized the Filmfare awards ceremony.

In March 1997, ITC paid US$ 16 million to put its logo on the Indian cricket teams' uniforms. In December 1999, the Four Square brand of GPI ran the 'Gold in Gold' contest, offering gold gift options, which required that entrants to the contest, besides being tobacco users, collect 4 inserts from Four Square Gold cigarette packs. These contests and offers were advertised to entice existing customers and recruit new ones to use their harmful product.

In the absence of any legislative measures to ban advertising and promotion of liquor and tobacco products, it was not easy to control the advertising and promotional activities of companies manufacturing liquor and tobacco products. For instance, the Wills "Made for Each Other" contest became one of the most popular contests sponsored by a cigarette manufacturer in the 1980s. With lucrative offers, including a holiday abroad for the winning couple, it attracted much controversy over glamorising and minimising the dangers of smoking filter cigarettes. One of the requirements for entry to the contest was that either of the couple should be a smoker. A Delhi-based consumer group, Voluntary Organisation in the Interest of Consumer Education (VOICE), protested against the said contest by filing public interest litigation before the Monopolies and Restrictive Trade Practices Commission (MRTPC), terming it unethical. The case was eventually lost by VOICE. Subsequently, VOICE appealed to the Supreme Court against MRTPC's judgment, but lost the case in the Supreme Court as well.

With the Indian government banning the advertising of tobacco and liquor products in the country, it became possible to hold any manufacturer responsible for promoting any such product. However, the ban led to another problem, which the liquor and tobacco industry has witnessed in the last few years, the problem of surrogate advertising.

SURROGATE ADVERTISEMENTS BY LIQUOR COMPANIES

The liquor industry is a prominent player in the area of surrogate advertising. Surrogate advertisements used by liquor companies include 'Bagpiper' soda, cassettes and CDs, 'Hayward's' soda, 'Royal Challenge' golf accessories and mineral water, 'Kingfisher' mineral water, 'White Mischief' holidays, 'Smirnoff' cassettes and CDs, 'Imperial Blue' cassettes and CDs, and 'Teacher's' achievement awards. These products bear exactly the same brand name and logo, which they used earlier in their liquor advertisements. It was surprising to know that liquor giants, like McDowell's and Seagram's, had entered into new segments, like cassettes and CDs, and mineral water. Later, it was found that the basic aim of such surrogate advertisements was to promote their liquor products, like beer, wine and vodka. Their brand extensions were just an eyewash to bypass the advertisement ban.

Understanding the gravity of the situation, the Indian Broadcasting Foundation (IBF) decided that the liquor manufacturing units must get production of the advertisement approved both at the storyboard stage and after the production of the commercial. It also ruled that that if liquor companies promote any juice, mineral water or soda, these should be shown in a proper manner and not as trimmings to liquor advertisement. These constitute a welcome step, but the key point lies in its enforcement.

One recent example of surrogate advertising is IPL, which gets sponsorship from certain liquor brands. In 2008, the Health Minister challenged the name of the Bangalore Indian Premier League (IPL) cricket team, 'Royal Challengers' as the authorities felt that it was an obvious and blatant form of surrogate advertising for the liquor brand "Royal Challenge". However, the Supreme Court of India observed that the team was not named 'Royal Challenge', the liquor brand, but 'Royal Challengers'. 'Only those who drink can be attracted by these things', the bench observed in a lighter vein, alluding to the fact that a name would not have any effect on non-drinkers.

SURROGATE ADVERTISEMENTS BY TOBACCO COMPANIES

The tobacco industry is no far behind in exhibiting its ingenuity to ward off the ban on advertising tobacco products. One can see a trènd of surrogate advertisements by companies making tobacco products like cigarettes and *pan masalas*. Examples of surrogate advertisements in this category include 'Red and White' Bravery Awards, '*Manikchand*' Filmfare Awards, and Four Square' white water rafting.

Tobacco companies in India are increasingly investing in non-tobacco products by the same brand name, as the tobacco product and are aggressively advertising these products through all available media. *Gutka* brands, such as '*Rajnigandha*', 'Goa 1000' and '*Pan Parag*', skirt the ban on tobacco advertising on television channels by resorting to surrogate advertising for *paan masala* bearing the same brand name. A plethora of advertisements on *paan masala* and *supari* have mushroomed on media channels. Companies advertise *paan masala*, bearing the same brand name as other tobacco products and highlighting that *paan masala* is a non-tobacco product.

Manikchand launched an attractive scheme for its retailers and distributors in May 2001. The company offered a scratch coupon on purchase of a box of this *gutka*, which gave the purchaser 2, 3, 5 or 10 pouches of *gutka* absolutely free. This strategy was planned with the intent to coax the retailer to buy bulk stock for sale and encourage a personal user to buy in bulk, indirectly making him more addicted to the product.

With the broadcasters continuing to telecast advertisements of brands that are also used for cigarettes, tobacco, wine, alcohol and liquor amongst other products, the Ministry of Information and Broadcasting (MIB) recently directed the broadcasting channels to "withdraw all such advertisements else broadcast license will be suspended or cancelled". This move is likely to impact the advertising of brands including those of 'Kingfisher', '*Pan Bahar*', '*Pan Vilas*', '*Chaini Khaini*' and '*Rajnigandha*'. In a recent directive issued to all channels, including the news and current affairs channels recently, the ministry said that it has observed violations of cable laws pertaining to the telecast of such advertisements. The ministry has also directed the companies to withdraw all such advertisements or else face stringent action, including suspension or prohibition of broadcast.

LEGISLATIVE MEASURES

Surrogate advertisements are not only misleading, but also false and dishonest in many cases. With surrogate advertising so widespread, let us see how various legislative measures in India are intended to control it.

1. The Cable Television Networks Regulation Rules,1994 {amended in 2000 and 2003, framed under the Cable Television Networks (Regulation) Act, 1995}

In India, surrogate advertisements gathered momentum with the amendment to the Cable Television Networks Regulation Rules in 2000, which prohibited tobacco and liquor advertisements on television.

The Advertising Code specified under Rule 7 (2) (viii) of Cable Television Networks Regulation Rules as amended in 2000 prohibits advertisements which promote, directly or indirectly production, sale or consumption of -

(a) cigarettes, tobacco products, wine, alcohol, liquor or other intoxicants;

(b) infant milk substitutes, feeding bottle or infant food.

2. The Cigarettes and Other Tobacco Products (Prohibition of Advertisement and Regulation of Trade and Commerce, Production, Supply and Distribution) Act, 2003.

This Act seeks to ensure that effective protection is provided to non-smokers from involuntary exposure to tobacco smoke and to protect children and young people from being addicted to the use of tobacco.

Section 3(a) of the Act defines 'advertisement' as 'any visible representation by way of notice, circular, label, wrapper or other document, and includes any announcement made orally or by any means of producing or transmitting light, sound, smoke, or gas'.

Thus, surrogate advertisements clearly fall within the definition, as it involves making the tobacco labels clearly visible to people through other products by the same name. Moreover the public is always reminded orally of the tobacco's brand name through the advertisements of such other products. So such advertisements are liable to be a subject matter of this Act and, therefore, subject to its regulatory measures.

According to Section 5(1) of the Act, no person engaged in, or purported to be engaged in the production, supply or distribution of cigarettes or any other tobacco products shall advertise, and no person having control over a medium shall cause to advertise cigarettes or any other tobacco products through that medium, and no person shall take part in any advertisement which directly or indirectly suggests or promotes the use or consumption of cigarettes or any other tobacco products.

Further, as provided under Section 5(3) of the Act, no person, shall, under a contract or otherwise, promote or agree to promote the use or consumption of—

(a) cigarettes or any other tobacco product; or

(b) any trade mark or brand name of cigarettes or any other tobacco product in exchange for a sponsorship, gift, prize or scholarship given or agreed to be given by another person.

Certain amendments were made in the above Act in 2005, clarifying that the word 'indirect advertisement' mentioned in Section 5(1), would mean:

1. The use of a name or brand of tobacco products for marketing, promotion or advertising other goods, services and events;
2. The marketing of tobacco products with the aid of a brand name or trademark which is known as, or in use as, a name or brand for other goods and service;
3. The use of particular colours and layout and/or presentation which are associated with particular tobacco products; and
4. The use of tobacco products and smoking situations when advertising other goods and services.

Thus, this section not only restricts advertisement and promotion of tobacco products for direct/ indirect pecuniary benefit, but also covers promoting tobacco through brand extensions and sponsorships.

3. Advertising Standard Council of India (ASCI) Code

The ASCI is a voluntary self-regulation council, registered as a not-for-profit company, under section 25 of the Companies Act, 1956. It is formed to safeguard against the indiscriminate use of advertising for the promotion of products which are regarded as hazardous to society or to individuals to a degree or of a type which is unacceptable to society at large. The responsibility for the observance of this Code for Self-Regulation in Advertising lies with all who commission, create, place or publish any advertisement or assist in the creation or publishing of any advertisement. All advertisers, advertising agencies and media are expected not to commission, create, place or publish any advertisement which is in contravention of this Code.

Chapter III.6 of the ASCI Code provides that advertisements for products whose advertising is prohibited or restricted by law or by this Code must not circumvent such restrictions by purporting to be advertisements for other products the advertising of which is not prohibited or restricted by law or by this code. In judging whether or not any particular advertisement is an indirect advertisement for product whose advertising is restricted or prohibited, due attention shall be paid to the following:

(a) Visual content of the advertisement must depict only the product being advertised and not the prohibited or restricted product in any form or manner.

(b) The advertisement must not make any direct or indirect reference to the prohibited or restricted products.

(c) The advertisement must not create any nuances or phrases promoting prohibited products.

d) The advertisement must not use particular colours and layout or presentations associated with prohibited or restricted products.

(e) The advertisement must not use situations typical for promotion of prohibited or restricted products when advertising the other products.

Thus, the ASCI's Code on advertising specifically prohibits surrogate advertising.

The ASCI's role in regulating advertising in India has been appreciated by various agencies, including the Government. However, it lacked the force of legal recognition. The Government of India, at last, took note of this and by one stroke, on 2nd August 2006, vide a notification in the Gazette of India Extraordinary {Part II –sec. 3(i)}, made sure that at least as far as TV commercials are concerned, they abide by the ASCI Code. The amendment made in the Cable Television Networks (Amendment) Rules, 2006, now provides:

"(9) No advertisement which violates the Code for Self-Regulation in Advertising, as adopted by the Advertising Standards Council of India (ASCI), Mumbai, for public exhibition in India, from time to time, shall be carried in the cable service".

4. Framework Convention on Tobacco Control (FCTC)

FCTC is a convention developed by the World Health Organisation (WHO) as a model code of conduct to be adopted by any country desirous of enforcing strict anti-tobacco rules.

Article 13 of the convention deals with tobacco advertising, promotion and sponsorship. It provides that even if the constitution doesn't permit a comprehensive ban on tobacco advertising, it can resort to other ways too, which include:

1. Prohibiting advertisements which create an erroneous impression on consumers,
2. Restrict use of direct/indirect incentives encouraging public use of tobacco,
3. Restrict media advertising in a period, and
4. Restrict tobacco sponsorships of public events.

India can follow the detailed guidelines for surrogate advertising given in this convention.

CASES OF SURROGATE ADVERTISING IN INDIA

ASCI's complaint cell, Consumer Complaints Council (CCC), has played a fair and supportive role in ensuring that the complaints received against surrogate advertisements are dealt with promptly. Some of the cases (2006-2009), where the complaints received against surrogate advertisements were upheld by CCC, are discussed below.

1. The Johnnie Walker Blue Label Whisky Case

This ad was published in Business India (November 2008 issue). It showed a whisky glass inscribed with the words "Johnnie Walker Blue Label Blended Scotch Whisky". The ad read: "Whiskies so rare that some of the distilleries no longer exist. The master blender at Johnnie Walker & Sons can detect a single part of flavour in a billion, a skill and craft that is exceptionally rare", "Only about one in ten thousand are considered to possess the exceptional flavours and properties sought for Johnnie Walker Blue Label", "These last precious drops can truly never be replaced". The complaint was received in January 2009 stating that the ad appeared to be a surrogate ad for a liquor brand- 'Johnnie Walker Blue Label Whisky'. The CCC decided in February 2009 that the ad amounted to a surrogate advertisement. Business India gave an undertaking not to publish the said promotion again.

2. The Seagram's Blender's Pride Case

This ad was published in Business India (November 2008 issue). It read: "Taste blend", "Taste that speaks for itself". The visual depiction of brand name, logo, brand symbol, suggested a well-known brand of liquor. A complaint received against the ad in January 2009 was that the ad appeared to be a surrogate ad for a liquor brand, 'Seagram's Blenders Pride'. The CCC decided in February 2009 that the ad was a surrogate ad for a liquor product, 'Seagram's Blenders Pride'. The advertiser assured that an appropriate modification of the ad would be made.

3. The Smirnoff Case

This ad was published in India Today (November 2008 issue). It read: "What is celebration without a little flavour in it?" The complaint against the ad (March 2009) argued that the ad compelled the consumer to consume alcohol at home on festive occasions (the ad was published in November which is Diwali time in India). Moreover, the ad did not mention that 'Smirnoff' was an alcohol drink, and that alcohol was injurious to health. The ad also did not carry the warning "Not for minors". The CCC held in March 2009 that the ad was a surrogate ad for a liquor product, 'Smirnoff'. The media, India Today, undertook not to publish the ad in future.

4. The Kingfisher Premium Packaged Drinking Water Case

This ad was published in The Week on 31st Dec, 2006. The headline of the ad read: "Where the Night Rocks". "Packaged Drinking Water" was written in fine print. The visual depicted "a dancing couple". The ad also had visual depiction of a liquor brand name, 'Kingfisher Premium'. According to the complaint, in the absence of specific information, the advertisement appeared to be a surrogate advertisement for a liquor brand, 'Kingfisher Premium'. The CCC observed in April 2007 that the visual and the headline of the ad did not bear any relevance to the product advertised, Kingfisher Premium, the packaged drinking water and it appeared to be a surrogate advertisement for 'Kingfisher Premium'. The ad was withdrawn.

5. The Mc Dowell & Company- RomanoV Case

The ad published in Bombay Times (March 2006) read: "VonamoR spanking new RonamoV". The visual of the ad depicted 'admiration for a young man'. The ad stated in fine print 'CD Rack'. There was also the visual of a tall tumbler bearing the brand name- 'RomanoV'. The complaint against the ad in March 2006 stated that 'RomanoV' appeared to be a liquor brand name. 'VonamoR' spelt in reverse, was apparently suggestive of the same brand name. The ad was misleading by ambiguity (when shows admiration for a young man, CD rack, and tumbler) and was suggestive of a liquor brand. The CCC held that there was no supporting data to establish the sustainability of the promotion in the absence of comments from the advertiser. It was held that the ad was misleading by ambiguity and was a surrogate ad for a liquor product which was considered to be in breach of the law. Consequently, the ad campaign was suspended.

6. The White Mischief Holidays Case

The ad published in Bombay Times (May 2006) read: "I'm in the mood for Mischief". The visuals showed X-Ray Vision Sunglasses, a man wearing sunglasses and admiring two scantily clad women on a beach. According to the complaint, the ad copy read in conjunction with the visual depicted, appeared to be indecent. The ad was misleading and suggestive of a liquor brand, 'White Mischief'. It was not apparent as to what product or service was being promoted-' X-Ray Vision Sunglasses' or 'White Mischief Holidays'. The CCC found no supporting data to establish the sustainability of the promotion provided by the advertiser and observed that it appeared to be a surrogate ad for a liquor brand, 'White Mischief'. The ad was withdrawn.

7. The Royal Mist Case

The ad published in the Times of India (Feb 2007) read: "Royal Mist- 100% Premium Grain", "Enchantingly Smooth", "Misty Nights" (in fine print). It was complained that the ad could mislead consumers regarding the product advertised for sale. Visual depiction of brand name was suggestive of a well-known brand of liquor product, 'Royal Mist'. In the absence of specific information, the ad appeared to be a surrogate ad for the liquor brand. The CCC observed that the visuals depicted and the copy mentioned did not refer specifically to a product or service being promoted. The slogan "Cast a Spell", and the bylines, "100% premium grain", and "Enchantingly Smooth", refer to features generally associated with a liquor brand. The ad appeared to be a surrogate ad for a liquor brand, 'Royal Mist'. The ad was withdrawn. The advertisers modified the ad and the modified version of Royal Mist ad was published again in the Times of India, in June 2007, against which again a complaint was received.

The ad headline stated "100% premium grain means 100% smoothness". The copy mentioned "World over, premium, wholesome grains stand for quality of the highest order. In the same tradition, Royal Mist has been uniquely crafted and made from 100% pure, premium grains-Perfected for you to derive maximum satisfaction out of every moment". The visual had shown grains in a tumbler. In the second complaint, visual depiction of brand name was suggestive of a well-known brand of liquor product, 'Royal Mist'. The advertisement was claimed to be a surrogate advertisement for the liquor. The CCC found the advertisement to be a surrogate advertisement for the liquor.

The advertiser assured the CCC to make appropriate modification in the ad before any future release. The case, however, points out how the advertisers are able to remind the customers about their liquor brands time and again by simply withdrawing one ad and coming up with another, defeating the whole purpose of the ban on liquor and tobacco products.

It appeared that the ASCI very promptly solved the cases of surrogate advertising. However, by the time the unethical or improper advertisement appeared and a complaint was filed against it, there was a lapse of time. By the time the CCC received the complaint, processed it and wrote to the advertiser, the advertising agency, and the media further time was lost. Moreover, by the time the advertiser agreed to withdraw or modify the ad, the damage was already done. The advertiser was already able to remind the customers about his liquor and tobacco brands. Thus, there is a need to frame stricter laws and impose heavy penalty on companies and advertising agencies involved in the practice of surrogate advertising.

Self Regulation by ITC

During March 2001, ITC announced a self-imposed ban on tobacco promotion. It withdrew from sponsorship of sports events. This included withdrawing its support to the Indian cricket team, which was sponsored by Wills. ITC had realized that continued sponsorship of sports events in India had begun to yield limited mileage. It was time for them to switch to other forms of advertising, especially brand stretching. Apart from freeing resources by discontinuing sports sponsorship, they wanted to project that they were practising responsible corporate behaviour. Furthermore, sports sponsorship had no appeal for women. Therefore, alternate products of interest to both women and men were linked to the Wills logo: Wills Sports Wear and Wills Club Life range of evening wear were introduced and are available at Wills Lifestyle outlets all over the country and also accessible via the internet. ITC also launched the John Players range of men's wear in 2003. This transition from sports to fashion wear thus extended the constituency to both men and women. ITC recently announced its decision to dissociate the Wills brand name from its cigarette business so that the Wills apparel outlets do not face the charges of surrogate advertisement under the Indian Tobacco Control Act.

MEASURES FOR CURBING SURROGATE ADVERTISING

1. All direct and indirect forms of tobacco advertising, promotion and sponsorship should be expressly prohibited.
2. The law should clearly define the terms 'advertising', 'sponsorship' and 'promotion'.
3. Strict laws should be enacted to penalise the companies making use of surrogate advertisements for promotion of banned products. Substantial penalties should be imposed on those who circumvent the ban.
4. Action should be provided against the advertising agencies concerned with surrogate advertisements.
5. Consumer awareness should be created to help people understand the negative impact of surrogate advertisements. They should be encouraged to file complaints with the ASCI against surrogate advertisements of liquor and tobacco products.
6. Commercial display of tobacco products should be banned to discourage and prevent point-of-sale advertising.
7. Brand name and logos of liquor and tobacco products should not be visible to people when such brands support sports and other popular events.
8. The prohibition of surrogate advertisement should also include the print and outdoor media, and the new electronic media, such as the Internet.

CONCLUDING NOTE

In India, the Cable Television Networks Rules, the Cigarettes and Other Tobacco Products Act and the ASCI's Code of advertising prohibit surrogate advertising by manufacturers of liquor and tobacco products. The decisions given by ASCI and the directions issued by the Ministry of Information and Broadcasting, and the Indian Broadcasting Foundation have also aimed to put a check on the practice of surrogate advertising. However, advertising law and regulations have been violated time and again by liquor and tobacco manufacturers to advertise their brand names to consumers. The relevant laws should be more stringent and provide heavy penalty on the manufacturers of liquor and tobacco products who use surrogate advertisements for promoting their liquor and tobacco brands. Moreover, the advertising agencies designing surrogate ads should be dealt with strictly. Without stricter laws and imposition of penalty, the very purpose of regulatory measures banning liquor and tobacco advertising would not achieve their objectives.

QUESTIONS FOR DISCUSSION

1. Discuss the meaning of surrogate advertising. How is the use of surrogate advertising a problem of ethical and legal concern?
2. How has surrogate advertising been used by Indian liquor and tobacco companies?
3. What are the various legislative measures in India that aim to control the practice of surrogate advertising?
4. Discuss some of the cases of surrogate advertising that the Indian advertising industry has witnessed in the recent past.
5. Suggest some measures for controlling the practice of surrogate advertising in India.

Chapter **22**

COMPARATIVE ADVERTISING IN INDIA

CONTENTS

Comparative advertising is a widely used form of commercial advertising in many countries. Comparative advertising basically involves making comparison between two products or services, by one of the competitors with the sole intention of showing his product as superior to the other. This type of advertising intends to influence consumer behaviour by comparing the features of the advertiser's product with that of the competitor's product.

MEANING OF COMPARATIVE ADVERTISING

Comparative advertising is advertising where one party advertises his goods or services by comparing them with the goods or services of another party. Such other party is usually his competitor or the market leader of that good or service. The comparison is made with a view towards increasing the sales of the advertiser, either by suggesting that the advertiser's product is of the same or a better quality to that of the compared product or by denigrating the quality of the compared product. It often involves the use of identical logos and trademarks, a play on words, clash of celebrities, research claims, etc.

Trade rivalries have been an old phenomenon in the advertising world and the customers have witnessed innumerable product wars on their television sets.

In India, the concept of comparative advertising emerged in the nineties. The nineties era witnessed the Pepsi-Coke war which was followed by Complan-Horlicks tug of war and the latest one is the Rin-Tide war. All these advertisements disparaged (denigrated) the competitor's product to showcase the superiority of their product in the market.

Exhibit 22.1 discusses some prominent Ad Wars that the Indian Advertising Industry has witnessed in the recent past.

Exhibit 22.1: Prominent Ad Wars witnessed by the Indian advertising industry in the recent past

Pepsi- Coke

The Pepsi-Coke ad war is one of the oldest examples of comparative advertising. It started in the 1980s when Pepsi launched its ad showing consumers preferring Pepsi over Coca Cola in a blind taste test. The next one came in 1996, when Pepsi introduced its punch line "Nothing Official about It", after Coca Cola was declared as the official sponsor of the Cricket World Cup that year.

This war continued through subsequent take-offs on Mountain Dew, Sprite and Thumps Up – by both brands. The virtual war had been very prominent since 2003 after the aggressive ads of Mountain Dew and Thumps Up. Very recently, PepsiCo launched a TV ad featuring Ranbir Kapoor, Deepika Padukone and Shah Rukh Khan enacting a comic scene around an alien. Coca Cola launched its parody on Pepsi through Sprite's "*Seedhi Baat, No Bakwaas*" punch line, featuring the look-alikes of the three actors seen in the Pepsi advertisement.

Horlicks – Complan

The brand war between the two popular health drinks, Horlicks and Complan, is not a new one in India. In September 2008, Heinz, the parent company of Complan, filed a court case against GSK's Horlicks for showing Horlicks as a better and cheaper option than Complan, in terms of nutritional value and market price. The war between these two brands has evolved into aggressive advertising through print and electronic media, showing comparisons in attributes such as protein content, growth, ingredients, flavours and cost.

Nestle – Cadbury

Cadbury always makes commercials with which people in general would like to be associated with. Its recent line of ads for Dairy Milk, with the tag line – "*meetha hai khana aaj pehli tareekh hai*" – urges people to consume Cadbury chocolate on the first of every month as people gets their salaries on that day. It successfully captured people's attention.

But Cadbury's competitor Nestle, soon launched a spoof on the Cadbury ad advising people to consume Nestle Munch everyday and not just on the first of the month. Its tag line, "*Khao bina tareeq dekhe*" directly challenges Cadbury by saying "Enjoy Munch without looking at the calendar." The "*Aaj Pehli Tarikh Hai*" v/s "*Sirf Pehli Tarikh Ko Nahin, Kabhi Bi Kha Sakte Hai*" ad war is an example of ridicule through comparative advertising.

Proctor & Gamble – Hindustan Unilever:

Procter & Gamble (P&G) and Hindustan Unilever (HUL), the two major producers of consumer goods, have been involved in comparative advertising for a long time now. Though earlier, the comparison was subtle or in the form of market price comparisons, now they have come out in the open, taking the ad war to a different level.

It started on February 25 (2010), when HUL' s Rin, filed a court case against P&G's Tide Natural for claiming that it contained natural ingredients like sandalwood and lemon, though it was a synthetic detergent. Apart from the court case, HUL also launched a nation-wide ad campaign which blatantly claimed that Rin is better than Tide as it offers more whiteness ("*behtar safedi*").

Subsequently Tide took HUL to court and the ad was withdrawn. But this ad was so strategically launched on TV channels that it coincided with a long weekend, guaranteeing enough visibility among consumers. Even after the ad was withdrawn, the HUL spokesperson re-iterated that the advertisement was based on independent laboratory tests based on international protocols and proved that Rin offers superior whiteness.

Earlier a commercial for HUL's Clinic All Clear Shampoo had spoofed P&G's Head & Shoulders. HUL's ad showed Bollywood actress, Bipasha Basu, searching for a girl with zero dandruff. The girl with dandruff mentions the name of her shampoo, making a muted reference to Head & Shoulders.

STATUTORY FRAMEWORK FOR REGULATING COMPARATIVE ADVERTISING IN INDIA

The Monopolies and Restrictive Trade Practices, 1969 (MRTP Act) and the Trade Marks Act, 1999 work in tandem to provide the basic structure that govern Comparative Advertising in India.

The Monopolies and Restrictive Trade Practices, 1969 (now repealed and replaced by the Competition Act, 2002)

Earlier, under the Monopolies and Restrictive Trade Practices (MRTP) Act, 1969, if any advertisement was considered prejudicial to the public interest, then the Monopolies and Restrictive Trade Commission was empowered to pass a cease-and-desist order, in addition to awarding compensation for any loss or injury caused to any person. Now, the Competition Act, 2002, has repealed and replaced the MRTP Act, 1969. The Competition Act came into force on the 31st March, 2003.

The Competition Act, 2002, is intended to prevent practices having adverse effect on competition, to promote and sustain competition in markets, to protect the interests of consumers, and to ensure freedom of trade carried on by other firms in the market, in India. Under the Act, any excessive expenditure made by a firm on advertising may amount to an anti-competitive practice. The Act also prohibits the abuse of dominant position by an enterprise. Thus, an enterprise should not take advantage of its dominant position, so as to create entry barriers for small companies, through its large-scale and heavy advertising expenditure.

In case the advertisements of a firm encourage an anti-competitive practice or take undue advantage of its dominant position, so as to create entry barriers for small companies, the Competition Commission of India (CCI) can conduct an inquiry and can pass an appropriate order. Thus, any anti-competitive practice can have severe consequences, including the imposition of a fine, or imprisonment, or both.

India has a rich body of decided cases under the Monopolies and Restrictive Trade Practices Act, 1969, which has laid down the basic framework governing the practice of comparative advertising in India.

Section 36A of MRTP Act lists several actions to be an 'unfair trade practice'. The provision which pertains to comparative advertising is contained in ***Section 36A(1)(x) of the MRTP Act.***

Section 36A (1) (x) of the MRTP Act defines an unfair practice as a trade practice which, for the purpose of promoting the sale, use or supply of any goods or for the provisions of any services, adopts any unfair method or unfair or deceptive practice including any of the following practices, namely :-

the practice of making any statement, whether orally or in writing or by visible representation which gives false or misleading facts disparaging the goods, services or trade of another person.

Thus, Section 36 A of the MRTP Act purports that unfair trade practices are those which lead to disparagement of the goods, services or trade of another person.

Concept of Disparagement

The term 'disparagement' has not been defined in any statute, but judicial pronouncements have adopted its dictionary meaning.

'Disparagement' as per the New International Webster's Comprehensive Dictionary means, to speak of slightingly, undervalue, to bring discredit or dishonour upon, the act of depreciating, derogation, a condition of low estimation or valuation, a reproach, disgrace, an unjust classing or comparison with that which is of less worth, and degradation. According to the Concise Oxford Dictionary, disparage means "to bring discredit on, slightingly of and depreciate." Thus, if a company, in its advertisements, brings some sort of a disgrace or passes a derogatory remark or undermines the value of a competitor's product, it would be a case of disparaging advertising.

There are many cases of 'Disparaging Advertising' which have been decided under the MRTP Act, 1969.

Trade Marks Act, 1999

The Trade Marks Act, 1999 came into place after The Trade and Merchandise Act Marks Act, 1958 was repealed. The Act defines a "trade mark" as a mark capable of being represented graphically and which is capable of distinguishing the goods or services of one person from those of others.

The Act seeks to provide for the registration and better protection of trade marks and to prevent the use of fraudulent marks on products and services. Thus, any method of advertising designed to create confusion in the minds of the public, as between the products and services of one firm and another, shall not be permitted. Any person who falsely applies a trade mark shall be punishable with imprisonment, or fine, or both.

Section 29 (8) of the Trade Marks Act, 1999 provides certain limitations to comparative advertising, according to which advertising infringes on a trade mark when it:

(a) takes unfair advantage and is contrary to honest practices in industrial or commercial matters; or

(b) is detrimental to its distinctive character; or

(c) is against the reputation of the trade mark.

Section 30 (1) of the Act says: Nothing in Section 29 shall be preventing the use of registered trademarks by any person with the purposes of identifying goods or services as those of the proprietor provided the use:

(a) is in accordance with the honest practices in industrial or commercial matters, and

(b) is not such as to take unfair advantage of or to be detrimental to the distinctive character or repute of the trade mark.

CASES OF COMPARATIVE ADVERTISING IN INDIA

Comparative advertising in India was initially covered by the MRTP Act, 1969 as being a potentially unfair trade practice. It was only after the recent enactment of the Trade Marks Act, 1999 that some headway was made in the direction of comparative advertising vis-à-vis intellectual property jurisprudence. However, as the Competition Act was only made enforceable in 2003, comparative advertising case law in India is yet to truly develop. In the mean time, the MRTP Act, 1969 was also repealed and replaced by the Competition Act, 2002. However, there are a significant number of comparative advertising cases decided by the courts under the MRTP regime. While the focus of these cases was largely on the protection of the consumer rather than the use of infringed trademarks, they provided the groundwork for the present legal viewpoint towards comparative advertising in India.

The leading judgments in this respect were the two Reckitt & Colman cases. In the case of *Reckitt & Colman of India Ltd. vs. Kiwi,* the Delhi High Court held that statements made by manufacturers claiming their product to be the best will not give a cause of action for disparagement/denigration of competitor's product. However, any statements that portrays competitors' similar goods in bad light while simultaneously promoting the manufacturers own goods, is not permitted and will be equivalent to disparagement. In the given case, both parties were in the business of manufacturing shoe polish.

The defendants, whose brand name was 'Kiwi' marketed an advertisement comparing a bottle of their shoe polish with another bottle, marked as 'Product X'. The plaintiff claimed that 'Product X' bore a striking resemblance in design to their own product namely, 'Cherry Blossom' and that the advertisement disparaged its product. Based on the stated reasoning, the Delhi High Court granted an injunction against the defendants.

The Calcutta High Court took it a step further in the case of ***Reckitt & Colman of India Ltd. vs. MP Ramachandran & Anr.*** As per the facts of this case, the plaintiffs were engaged in the manufacturing of blue whitener under the name of 'Robin Blue' for which they had a design registration over the bottle. The defendants, who were in the same business, issued an advertisement comparing their product to others stating that not only was their product cheaper, but also more effective. In this depiction they compared their product to a bottle having the same shape and pricing as that of the plaintiff's product. While holding that the advertisement was made with the intent to disparage and derogate the plaintiff's product, the Calcutta High Court laid down five principles in aiding the grant of injunctions in such matters, stating that:

1. A tradesman is entitled to declare his goods to be best in the world, even though the declaration is untrue;
2. He can also say that my goods are better than his competitors', even though such statement is untrue;
3. For the purpose of saying that his goods are the best in the world or his goods are better than his competitors' he can even compare the advantages of his goods over the goods of others;
4. He, however, cannot while saying his goods are better than his competitors', say that his competitors' goods are bad. If he says so, he really slanders the goods of his competitors. In other words he defames his competitors and their goods, which is not permissible;
5. If there is no defamation to the goods or to the manufacturer of such goods no action lies, but if there is such defamation an action lies and if an action lies for recovery of damages for defamation, then the Court is also competent to grant an order of injunction restraining repetition of such defamation.

These principles were used in the much publicized case of ***Pepsi Co. Inc. vs. Hindustan Coca Cola Ltd.*** (2001). However, this case differed from the cases aforementioned in respect of the fact that herein the Delhi High Court also dealt with copyrights and trademark related issues.

The plaintiff in the instant case claimed disparagement of trademark and copyright in two advertisements of the defendants. Both advertisements allegedly desecrated the plaintiff's products with derogatory remarks. One of the advertisements depicted a thinly veiled substitute of Pepsi as a "*bachhon wali drink*" while mocking Pepsi's advertising slogan by saying "*Yeh Dil Mange No More*". The entire commercial conveyed to the viewers that kids should prefer 'Thums Up' over 'Pepsi' if they want to grow up.

There is another side to the coin as well, ***when the statement disparaging the plaintiff's product is true in comparative advertising, no relief can be given to the plaintiff.*** In ***Reckit Benckiser (India) Limited vs. Naga Limited and Ors.***, the plaintiff had filed a suit for permanent and mandatory injunction, being aggrieved by the defendant's television commercial. The issue was whether the defendant could be held to have disparaged the plaintiff's product even though no false statements have been made by the defendant. And it was held that if a competitor makes the consumer aware of his mistaken impression, the plaintiff cannot be heard to complain of such action. The judge commented, "I find it difficult, not impossible, to hold a party liable for defamation when all that has been stated by the competitor is the truth. Truth is always a complete defence against any assault or challenge regardless of whether any damage is sustained as a result of it."

REGULATION OF COMPARATIVE ADVERTISING BY ASCI

Advertisements in India are regulated by the Advertising Standards Council of India which is a self regulatory body and lays down a code to be followed by the advertising industry which is not in competition with the law. With respect to comparative advertising, the code lays down as follows:

To ensure that advertisements observe fairness in competition such that the consumers need to be informed on choice in the market-place and the canons of generally accepted competitive behaviour in business are both served;

1. Advertisements containing comparisons with other manufacturers or suppliers or with other products including those where a competitor is named, are permissible in the interests of vigorous competition and public enlightenment, provided:

    a. It is clear what aspects of the advertiser's product are being compared with what aspects of the competitor's product.

    b. The subject matter of comparison is not chosen in such a way as to confer an artificial advantage upon the advertiser or so as to suggest that a better bargain is offered than is truly the case.

    c. The comparisons are factual, accurate and capable of substantiation.

    d. There is no likelihood of the consumer being misled as a result of the comparison, whether about the product advertised or that with which it is compared.

e. The advertisement does not unfairly denigrate, attack or discredit other products, advertisers or advertisements directly or by implication.

2. Advertisements shall not make unjustifiable use of the name or initials of any other firm, company or institution, nor take unfair advantage of the goodwill attached to the trade mark or symbol of another firm or its product or the goodwill acquired by its advertising campaign.

3. Advertisements shall not be similar to any other advertiser's earlier run advertisements in general layout, copy, slogans, visual presentations, music or sound effects, so as to suggest plagiarism.

COMPARATIVE ADVERTISEMENTS: BENEFIT TO CONSUMERS AND MARKETERS

Benefits to the Consumers

The increase in competition has resulted in a greater use of comparative advertising by companies to tell consumers why their products should be bought. With a number of brands sold in the market, consumers are confused and lost. A consumer who plans to buy a high value, durable product, has some tough decisions to take. It is here that comparative advertising steps in.

1. Comparative advertising **can play the role of a salesman** who helps remove and clarify doubts about a brand. A person who has already gone through the various stages in the buying process like need recognition and information search may be stuck because he is not able to make comparative evaluation between the brands which he has shortlisted. It is at this stage that **comparative advertising helps the consumer to take a better decision**.
2. Comparative advertising can give very compulsive reasons to a potential consumer to buy a product, and the very fact that the challenger is confident, can create a positive impression.
3. Because of the interest evoking ability, comparative advertisements often succeed in increasing the extent to which consumers process the information.
4. Consumers, sometimes, gets to know about the weak points/shortcomings of the competing brand.

Thus, it is clear that comparative advertising has its own advantages. It helps in informing customers on the comparative features of two competitive brands. Comparative advertising truly gives an opportunity to help consumers decide on which product is better and what is best suited for him. Though, comparative advertising has created a lot of controversy, out of all this, the consumer may emerge awakened. The consumers may ultimately become more discerning with their evaluation skills sharpened.

Benefits to the Marketer

Comparative advertising also offers some benefits to the marketers.

1. Follower brands can compare with the leader brand. A follower who compares himself with the leader gains in terms of being perceived similarly, and positioning itself near the leader, by putting itself and the competitor on the same consideration set. Thus, comparative advertising is an effective positioning tool for the marketers.
2. If comparisons are genuine and can be substantiated, positive results can be attained.
3. A brand may also be able to reveal the weaknesses of the competing brand through competitive advertisements.

While comparative advertising may have its advantages, advertisers should tread on this path cautiously and avoid overdoing it. It is alright to offer logical reasons in order to drive home product superiority. However, there is no point in using comparison unless there is genuine superiority.

Box 22.1 shows some of the points that emerge from research done on comparative advertising.

Box 22.1: Research on Comparative Advertising

Research done is ambiguous on whether or not comparative advertising helps in improving the image of the challenging brand. While it may help in damaging the image of the challenged brand or denigrating it, it cannot be conclusively said whether it helps enhance the image of the challenging brand itself. However, the following points emerge from the research done on comparative advertising.

1. Comparisons offered to consumers who are more educated and have the cognitive ability to understand arguments might be more effective. On the other hand, in the case of consumers whose cognitive ability is less, comparative advertising may have little effect. The advertisers in such cases may have to resort to cheap gimmicks to denigrate the competitor's products which may not be in the interest of consumers and the industry as well.
2. Comparative ads are found to be more effective for categories where consumers tend to use their analytical mind. Comparative ads tend to fail where consumers use imagery while evaluating the brands. For example, products like automobiles use comparative ads extensively and with effectiveness.
3. When a comparison is made over something insignificant or trivial it is sure to boomerang. Consumers may soon find out the truth. The company unnecessarily takes the risk of exposing itself.
4. Comparative advertising that names competitors can lead to greater customer confusion about which brand is sponsoring the brand.

GUIDELINES TO BE FOLLOWED

We have seen from the discussion in this chapter that the court decisions on various cases of comparative advertising in India have tried to avoid the misuse of comparative advertising to disparage a competitor's product. The onus of ensuring healthy competition, however, does not merely lie with the courts. It is of equal importance that the marketers of products engage in comparative advertising engage in the activity within the permissible parameters of the law. Establishing a brand marketing policy within a company ought to be as important as watching for use and misuse of a brand by other competitors. It is important to keep the following guidelines in mind while engaging in the activity:

- A comparison should be made based on verifiable facts about the advertisers' and the competitors' products/services, which can be substantiated.
- Keep the primary goal of the advertisement limited to inform the consumer and not to unfairly attack, criticize, or discredit other products, advertisers or advertisements directly or by implication.
- The advertisement should not make unjustifiable use of any firm, company or institution and should not take unfair advantage of the goodwill of any trade name or symbol of another firm.
- If a comparison is based on clinical tests, results there should be sufficient proof that they were conducted by an independent/objective body. Partial results or differences should not be shown in the advertisements because consumers may draw improper conclusions from them.
- The product or services being compared should reflect their value and usefulness to the consumer. The comparative advertisement should be informative and convey positive merits of the product/service.

It is of utmost importance for both companies and the judiciary to work in tandem to restore the parity in comparative advertising whereby fair trade practices; trade mark protection and consumer interest can go hand in hand.

CONCLUDING NOTE

Comparative advertising aims to objectively and truthfully inform the consumer, and promotes market transparency, keeping down prices and improving products by stimulating competition. Healthy competition is necessary in a capitalist society, and hence comparative advertising is welcome. But the way it functions these days, comparative advertising has been reduced to a dirty game of mockery between brands and hardly affects the informed consumers' choices. Today, ad agencies, in order to project their clients as the most superior, often parody the commercials of their competitors, leading to virtual wars in the advertising industry. Therefore, it is important to protect the interests of such competitors by not allowing comparative advertising to cause confusion, mislead, or discredit a competitor.

QUESTIONS FOR DISCUSSION

1. What is the meaning of comparative advertising? Discuss some of the prominent advertising wars witnessed by the Indian advertising industry in the recent past.
2. Discuss the statutory framework for regulating comparative advertising in India.
3. How does ASCI regulate the use of comparative advertising by the advertisers?
4. Discuss the benefits of comparative advertisements to the consumers and the marketers.
5. What precautions should be taken by an advertiser who wants to make comparative claims in his ads?

Appendix 22.1

CODE FOR COMMERCIAL ADVERTISING OVER ALL INDIA RADIO

The following standards of conduct are laid do

United States

Comparative Advertising is permitted in the United States, but the ads must compare similar products. Also, companies can't claim that their prices are lower than the competition unless they can prove that the same products are sold at other places for higher prices. Under the Lanham Act, companies or plaintiffs are required to prove five elements to win a false advertising lawsuit about an ad containing a comparative claim. They must prove that:

1. False statements have been made about either product.
2. The ads actually deceived or had the tendency to deceive a substantial segment of the audience.
3. The deception was "material" or meaningful. In other words, the plaintiff must show that the false ad claim is likely to influence purchasing decisions.
4. Falsely advertised goods are sold in interstate commerce.
5. The suing company has been or likely will be injured as a result of the false statements, by either loss of sales or loss of goodwill.

In addition to the Lanham Act, consumers also may rely on state laws governing unfair competition and false ad claims if the consumer is a victim of a false comparative claim. In California, for example, the Business and Professional Code prohibits "unlawful, unfair, or fraudulent business practices" and "unfair, deceptive, untrue, or misleading" advertising.

The 1969 Federal Trade Commission (FTC) Policy Statement on Comparative Advertising encouraged the use of comparisons that name the competitor or the competitive product. However, the negative consequences of false and confusing comparative claims led the FTC to require "clarity, and, if necessary, disclosure to avoid deception of the consumer."

For example, in ***Tommy Hilfiger Licensing Inc. vs. Nature Labs*** {LLC (2002}) , Nature Labs, a shop selling pet perfumery, used "Timmy Holedigger" as its trademark as well as the slogan "If you like Tommy Hilfiger, your pet will love Timmy Holedigger". Tommy Hilfiger, one of the best recognized U.S. fashion labels, brought a lawsuit against Natural Labs for, among other things, trademark infringement, unfair competition, trademark dilution and commercial fraud. The court held that the use of a trademark similar to Tommy Hilfiger by the defendant is a fair parody, a type of "freedom of speech" protected under the First Amendment of the United States Constitution. Consumers were more likely to laugh at the humour in the parody than be confused about the origin of the products. Moreover, the comparison used by the respondent did not depreciate the claimant's products in any means. Therefore, the court dismissed all of the plaintiff's claims.

The American Association of Advertising Agencies has ten guidelines that advertisers should follow to ensure truthful comparative advertising. These are shown in Box 22.2.

Box 22.2: American Association of Advertising Agencies' Ten Guidelines for Comparative Advertising

1. The intent and connotation of the ad should be to inform and never to discredit or unfairly attack competitors, competing products or services.
2. When a competitive product is named, it should be one that exists in the marketplace as significant competition.
3. The competition should be fairly and properly identified but never in a manner or tone of voice that degrades the competitive product or service.
4. The advertising should compare related or similar properties or ingredients of the product, dimension to dimension, feature to feature.
5. The identification should be for honest comparison purposes and not simply to upgrade by association.
6. If a competitive test is conducted, it should be done by an objective testing service.
7. In all cases the test should be supportive of all claims made in the advertising that are based on the test.
8. The advertising should never use partial results or stress insignificant differences to cause the consumer to draw an improper conclusion.
9. The property being compared should be significant in terms of value or usefulness of the product to the consumer.
10. Comparisons delivered through the use of testimonials should not imply that the testimonial is more than one individual's, unless that individual represents a sample of the majority viewpoint.

Source: James B. Astrachan, "When to Name a Competitor", *Adweek* (May 23, 1988): 37.

Directives of the European Council

Until very recently comparative advertising was essentially not allowed in European countries. The European Union first addressed the issue of the comparative advertising in the late 1970's. According to current European Legislation, comparative advertisement is allowed only if it is not misleading, compares like with like, does not create confusion and discredit or take unfair advantage of a rivals trademark. The 1997 European Council Directive says that comparative advertisement shall, as far as the comparison is concerned, be permitted if the following conditions are met:

- it is not misleading;
- it compares goods or services meeting the same needs or intended for the same purpose;
- it objectively compares one or more material, relevant, verifiable and representative features of those goods and services, which may include price;
- it does not create confusion in the market place between the advertiser and a competitor or between the advertiser's trademarks, trade names, other distinguishing marks, goods or services and those of a competitor;
- it does not discredit or denigrate the trademarks, trade names, other distinguishing marks, goods, services, activities or circumstances of competitor;
- for products with designation of origin, it relates in each case to products with the same designation;
- it does not take unfair advantage of reputation of a trademark, trade name or other distinguishing marks of a competitors or of the designation of origin of competing products;
- it does not present goods or services as imitations or replicas of goods or services bearing a protected trademark or trade name.

China

It is interesting to note that the laws relating to comparative advertising in China are a total contrast to those of the US, UK and India.

Trade mark owners need to be careful with advertising in China. Aggressive campaigns which might work in other countries can be punished in China. The Advertising Law is primarily directed towards the protection of consumers' interests, as distinct from competitors' interests. In fact, Articles 7 and 12 of the Advertising Law effectively disallow comparative advertising, since the ultimate purpose of comparative advertising is to prove that the advertiser's products are better than its competitor's. Such comparison has the actual effect of disparaging other commodities or services. Moreover, according to the Criteria for Advertising Examination issued by the State Administration for Industry and Commerce (SAIC) in 1994, comparative advertising should not involve any direct comparison of specific products or services. Since these provisions tend to be either too vague or too strict, Chinese enterprises hesitate to engage in comparative advertising.

Case Study

RIN VS. TIDE

In 2010, Hindustan Unilever Limited, an Indian company targeted Procter and Gamble's detergent brand 'Tide' in the commercial for its detergent brand 'Rin'. This case study discusses in detail this case of comparative advertising in India.

The Background

There was a proxy war going on between Rin and Tide since December 2009. During December, P&G launched the low priced variant of Tide branded 'Tide Naturals'. Tide Naturals was priced significantly lower to Rin. Tide Naturals was launched at Rs 50 per kg , Rs 10 for 200 gms and Rs 20 for400 gms. Rin was priced at Rs 70 per Kg at that time. The reduced price of the Tide variant was an immediate threat to Rin. Since Tide already has an established brand equity, Rin was bound to face the heat. Although HUL had another low priced brand Wheel priced at Rs 32/Kg, Tide was not in the same category of Wheel.

Rin had to cut the price to resist the market share erosion. HUL was facing a steady erosion in the market share in most of the categories. In the detergent category itself, the brand faced a market share fall of 2.5% in December 2009. With P&G starting a price war, HUL had to react to it did by cutting the price of Rin by 30% and fixing it at Rs 50 per kg.

HUL also reacted to the Tide Natural's price war. It took P&G to the court regarding the Tide Natural's advertisement. The contention was that Tide Naturals was giving the impression to the consumers that it contained natural ingredients like *sandal.* The court had ordered P&G to modify the campaign and P&G had to admit that Tide Naturals did not contain any natural ingredients.

The Case

In 2010, Hindustan Unilever Limited targeted Procter and Gamble's detergent brand 'Tide' in the commercial for its detergent brand 'Rin'.

Facts - In the advertisement, one woman's basket had a packet of Rin detergent powder, while the other has a packet of Tide Naturals. The "Tide" lady boast confidently about its fragrance combined with whiteness, the theme on which the Tide Naturals campaign was based. The "Rin" lady did not show any reaction but had a beam on her face. Thereafter, the school bus stopped and dropped off two children.

The child of the woman carrying Tide was wearing a visibly dull shirt, while behind him a boy came out wearing a spotless white shirt, who ran towards his mother carrying the Rin packet.

Making the advertisement more aggressive, the boy asked his mother, "Why is *aunty* startled?" as the advertisement concludes with a voice-over that Rin is better than Tide when it comes to whiteness, and at a shocking price of Rs. 25. The advertisement also claimed that the claim of effectiveness was based on laboratory tests.

Decision - Justice Patheriya of Kolkata High Court ruled that the commercial amounts to a clear case of disparagement i.e. a manufacturer is not entitled to say that his competitor's goods are bad so as to puff and promote his goods and issued an injunction. The injunction was granted on the following grounds:

- The Hindustan Unilever Advertisement depicted "Tide Naturals" whereas the voice-over was for "Tide";
- The laboratory reports produced by Hindustan Unilever under cover of two affidavits in support of its claim of superior whiteness had inherent defects i.e. the advertisement drew comparison of samples of "Tide" and "Tide Naturals".

Concluding Remark

Although Indian marketing world have seen lot of comparative ads, the Rin vs. Tide is a rare case of direct comparative ad where the brand has taken the competitor brand's name and challenging it head on. This is the main reason why the commercial created a lot of news in the media.

Additional Case Studies

Case Study

PEPSI'S *'YOUNGISTAAN'* CAMPAIGN

About PepsiCo

PepsiCo is a world leader in convenience foods and beverages. Its world renowned brands are available in nearly 200 countries across the world. PepsiCo entered India in 1989 and in a short period of about 20 years has grown into the largest and one of the fastest growing food & beverage business in the country. Today, PepsiCo India's expansive portfolio includes refreshment beverages Pepsi, 7UP, Mirinda and Mountain Dew, in addition to low calorie options such as Diet Pepsi; Aquafina drinking water, Tropicana fruit juices, and juice-based drinks – Tropicana Nectars, Tropicana Twister and Slice.

Advertising Strategy of Pepsi

Pepsi has always been known for its interesting ads. There have been several campaigns over the years. Each campaign has had an objective and the ads were conceptualised based on the campaign objective. However, the core philosophy of refreshing the youth and giving them something new has never changed.

Over the years, various celebrities have been associated with brand Pepsi. India is a country with two big obsessions – Cricket and Bollywood. These two platforms have given India their youth icons, whom the youth has always looked up to for inspiration, trends, etc. Hence, talking the youth language through these celebrities has given the brand just the right connect with its target audience. Since its inception, Pepsi has been successfully associated with celebrities from these two fields, making it the number one cola amongst the youth. Over the years, Pepsi has had various celebs that have had a long standing relationship with the brand, and which has been mutually beneficial.

One quality that makes Pepsi ads endearing is that it talks the language of the youth, and changes this language as the youth changes with time. This has been one major reason for the Pepsi ads to make an impact. Also, giving the youth new phrases and language to express themselves, for example, Pepsi expressions ('*Yeh Dil Maange More*', '*Yeh Hai Youngistaan Meri Jaan*'), a new language (use of *Hinglish* was introduced by Pepsi), etc. adds to the popularity of its ads. In fact, the youth of India do not only consume Pepsi, but they have an appetite for Pepsi advertising. They eagerly wait for the next Pepsi ad to refresh their world. Some of the key points of Pepsi's advertising strategy are given below:

- Pepsi's target audience are mostly teenagers and young adults and their advertising reflects this in every possible way.
- Pepsi makes sure that the advertisements are made to suit the target audience's interests.

- The advertising strategy includes cool and trendy promos to attract more of the target audience.
- The advertising is mostly creative and has different elements like music and sports in addition to the use of Bollywood celebrities.
- Pepsi ads give the youth new phrases and language to express themselves, for example, '*Yeh Dil Maange More*', '*Yeh Hai Youngistaan Meri Jaan*'.
- Pepsi.com also plays an important role in advertising and attracts target audience by giving access to options like downloads, gaming, music mixing applications etc.

Pepsi's Advertisements Over the Years

Are you ready for the magic?

PepsiCo entered the Indian market in 1988 and its advertisements have been strongly directed at the youth, right from the beginning. Pepsi's first television commercial aired in 1989 had pop icon Remo Fernandez and Bollywood actress Juhi Chawla singing and dancing respectively, to the magic of Lehar Pepsi. The ad announced: "The magic has begun, Lehar Pepsi, The Choice of a New Generation." It was the first 90-second advertisement on Indian television.

"Hi I'm Sanjana, Got Another Pepsi?"

One of the earliest and most memorable television commercials from 1990 had Aamir Khan, Aishwarya Rai and Mahima Chaudhary playing typical youthful roles, and is much cherished and remembered for Aishwarya's words in the ad—"Hi I'm Sanjana, got another Pepsi?" It advertised 'Lehar Pepsi', which was how Pepsi Cola was known in India until 1991. The ad had the tagline, "*yeh hi hai right choice baby, aha*"

Yeh Dil Maange More

'*Yeh Dil Maange More*' was another significant advertising campaign launched by PepsiCo in India during the late 1990s. The campaign featured Amitabh Bachchan and Sachin Tendulkar. The advertisement had the essence of fun and excitement along with a very trendy slogan. The '*Hinglish*' slogan enjoyed tremendous recall among the youth and it is well-remembered by many even today.

Men in Blue

The 'Men in Blue' campaign that was launched by PepsiCo in conjunction with the 2003 World Cup in South Africa was another landmark advertisement campaign. It was the first instance where a marketer had attempted at branding a sports team. The 2003 World Cup team was composed predominantly of young players and thus their attitude and passion complemented the brand aura of Pepsi. Later, 'Men in Blue' became a common terminology that was used by cricket commentators and other media entities, when referring to the Indian cricket team.

Oye Bubbly

In 2005, the 'Oye Bubbly' campaign was launched by PepsiCo. Initially, the campaign featured Amitabh Bachchan and Priety Zinta (who is often referred as the bubbly girl). Later, in that year, PepsiCo launched an online commercial targeting the youth. The commercial, featuring Shahrukh Khan, was divided into three-parts. Within weeks of launching the online initiative, PepsiCo released a television commercial featuring Shahrukh Khan as a flirtatious snake charmer crazy about Pepsi. The commercial was basically a continuation of the 'Oye Bubbly' campaign launched earlier in 2005. The advertisement concluded with the '*Yeh pyaas hai badi*' tagline.

The Blue Billion

After branding the entire cricket team during the 2003 World Cup, PepsiCo was found to brand the entire nation as the 'Blue Billion' during the 2007 World Cup held in the West Indies. Branding experts opined that the tag was just perfect for a cricket-crazy nation like India. The campaign was supported by the slogan—"*Ooh aah India, Aaya India*". The '*Ooh aah*' chant was found to capture the imagination of the youth which enabled it to become the nation's new cricket anthem. A video triggering lots of patriotic sentiments was launched by the Cola major just before the commencement of the World Cup.

Pepsi 'My Can'

In 2007, PepsiCo introduced the slimmer and cheaper version of the 250 ml can and branded it as Pepsi 'My Can'. The product was priced at Rs. 15 only and it was promoted as a stylish and a sleek pack that reflected the style statement of today's youth. The television commercials for 'My Can' featured Shahrukh Khan along with John Abraham. Both represented the Indian youth and enjoyed tremendous popularity among the youth. Several sales promotion campaigns were also initiated along with the commercial, to involve the youth and make them more interested about Pepsi as a brand. Such campaigns were mainly conducted at colleges and at BPOs, two of the most happening places for the youth brigade.

Pepsi's Youngistan Campaign

Advertising Agency for the 'Youngistaan' Campaign: JWT (J. Walter Thompson) is the advertising agency behind Pepsi's *'Youngistaan'* Campaign.

Tagline: *'Yeh hai Youngistaan meri jaan'*

Target Market: Teenagers and young adults of metros and cities.

Celebrities Used: For this campaign, Pepsi used three very popular Bollywood celebrities- Shahrukh Khan, Ranbir Kapoor and Deepika Padukone.

The TVC:

A guy (Ranbir) asked his girlfriend (Deepika) if she would be having Pepsi in her room. The girl replied sarcastically that her elder brother would also be there and she left. Undeterred, he tried to climb up to her balcony only to come falling down with a dish antenna.

The girl's brother (Shahrukh) caught him and asked him where he is from. The boy looked at an electric board that read, *'Young Hindustaan Supermarket'* and he said in a robotic tone that he is from *'Youngistaan'* – another planet, adding that he planned to become his sister's bodyguard. The girl's brother allowed the boy in her room, where they enjoyed their Pepsi.

Time of Launch and Media Used

- The campaign was first launched on T.V during the tri-series matches in February, 2008
- The campaign was launched across radio, outdoor, Web and wireless platforms.
- Pepsi also launched a website for *Youngistaan* inside the Pepsi Cool Zone where the youngsters could visit and make comments on any topic.

- Pepsi also sponsored "Wassup *Youngistaan*" on MTV, a show where the youth voiced their thoughts.

Why the name 'Youngistaan'?

Regarding '*Youngistaan*' as a term, Soumitra Karnik (Karnik), vice-president and executive creative director at JWT, said, "As Pepsi is an irreverent, youth brand, we thought of coining a term that encapsulates its young target audience and brands this generation." Hari Krishnan, vice-president at JWT, opined, "*Youngistaan* is a feeling that is racing through every youthful nerve in the country today. Brand Pepsi will simply tap this energy and help the youth express this emotion." According to an official statement regarding the significance of the name '*Youngistaan*'—"As the name suggests, it represents a world of the youth, where the young generation likes to be in control. It brings forward their never-failing attitude, their desire to take on challenges and the power to turn things around."

Ranbir and Deepika were found to express their opinion on '*Youngistaan*' along with Shah Rukh Khan. Ranbir mentioned, "I am young, I believe in myself. I have dreams and I chase them. This is what *Youngistaan* means to me; it's a way of being, it's an attitude. In *Youngistaan*, I work really hard, but I party harder! Trust me, in *Youngistaan* somewhere something incredible is waiting to be known." Expressing her opinion on '*Youngistaan*', Deepika observed, "*Youngistaan* is about making choices and where life has endless possibilities. As a part of being a *Youngistaani*, it's not about where I am but about thinking fun, thinking big! It's about just being yourself and being confident." Shah Rukh Khan opined, "*Youngistaan* to me is a state of feeling young at heart. The first aspect of being a part of *Youngistaan* or having that state of heart is to believe that the best gift in life is life itself. I think you need to be successful, work hard, spread happiness and live life to the fullest. *Yeh hai Youngistan meri jaan*."

Commenting on the way the term '*Youngistaan*' is mentioned in the ad and its corresponding implications, Karnik observed, "We wanted Ranbir to discover the concept of *Youngistaan* accidentally. The idea was to show how the younger generation improvises really fast in the face of trouble." The '*Youngistaan*' commercial was found to be witty, humorous and in a way, it reflected the energy, excitement and irreverence of the young, confident India.

Online Advertising

Pepsi launched the Pepsi 'What's Your Way?' campaign where *Youngistaan* gave cool solutions to tricky day to day situations which often land them in a fix. *Youngistaanis* competed for the cool quotient online, by testing their cheek and wit to solve tricky situations presented to them. It gave the 4 coolest *Youngistaanis*, a chance to appear on the Pepsi 'My Can'. And everyday one youngster got the chance to become the '*Youngistaani* of the Day' entitling him/her to a month's supply of free Pepsi and Rs. 5,000 as SMS talk time.

Expressing his opinion regarding the *'Youngistaan'* concept, Hari Krishnan, Vice-President at JWT, said, "*Youngistaan* is a feeling that is racing through every youthful nerve in the country today. Brand Pepsi will simply tap this energy and help the youth express this emotion." Yahoo created a destination for *Youngistaanis*, where it hosted the same questions and users could come and give their wackiest answers. Not only did the site host the celeb situations but it also allowed the users to come and enter their own situations and let *Youngistaanis* answer them. The aim was for *Youngistaanis* to interact with the idea and even co-create their own situations, while having lots of fun.

Thus, it can be said that Pepsi through its '*Youngistaan*' campaign aimed at capturing its target audience in another cool, funky, attractive way. The insiders at PepsiCo referred to the campaign as yet another attempt at showcasing the 'GenNext' attitude.

Case Study

Online Advertising

LAUNCH OF MICROSOFT'S X-BOX

Product: Gaming Console (Microsoft's X-Box)

Objective: Bringing the World's favourite Gaming console to India by introducing the category in an organized set up for the first time.

Strategy: The launch was divided in two phases – First Phase to focus on generating a pre launch buzz and demand through the interactive medium, while the Second Phase saw the launch campaign of the console focusing on brand building advertising & viral marketing.

Interactive Mediums Used: Internet and Mobile (SMS + WAP)

This case study deals with only the digital advertising undertaken for the launch of the console.

First Phase of Online Advertising

Challenge: First Phase focused on generating demand for a category & brand which was getting introduced in India for the first time. Challenge was the time lag between user's intent of purchase and actual fulfilment. The campaign promised consumers a 10 % Discount + Amazing FIFA World Cup Freebies if they would pay upfront for the product which was going to be delivered to them after 3 months.

Interactive Solution: Since the objective was to reach out to a fairly affluent, gizmo friendly, upwardly mobile audience a combination of Internet and Mobile Media was chosen to execute this campaign. Viral Marketing was weaved in at every step of the campaign to maximize the media reach both on internet and mobile platforms. Campaign was seamlessly integrated on the web, mobile and on-ground to synchronize the lead generation activity from across the three platforms.

Campaign Planning & Viral Marketing:

- Keeping in the mind the single point focus of the campaign to generate qualified leads for X-Box, the campaign was planned to maximize the media reach through layers of multiple touch points. Once user submitted his intent to buy an X-BOX he was sent an immediate "Thank You" mail with an offer to induce buy-in and spread the word – Mail informing him about an offer on referring 3 friends for buying an X-BOX and if any one of the referred friend also buys an X-Box the referrer stood a chance to win an additional game.

- To extend the media reach of the campaign a parallel viral marketing promo was introduced whereby simply referring their friends to the offer users could win wireless mouse and keyboards.

Media Highlights

Synchronized outbreak on all the major portals: Internet campaign launch was synchronized with the first day of the FIFA World CUP i.e. 9th June 2006. All major properties on the home pages of mass portals (all combined reaching almost 80 % of the Indian audience logging on the internet on a particular day) were booked to break the campaign.

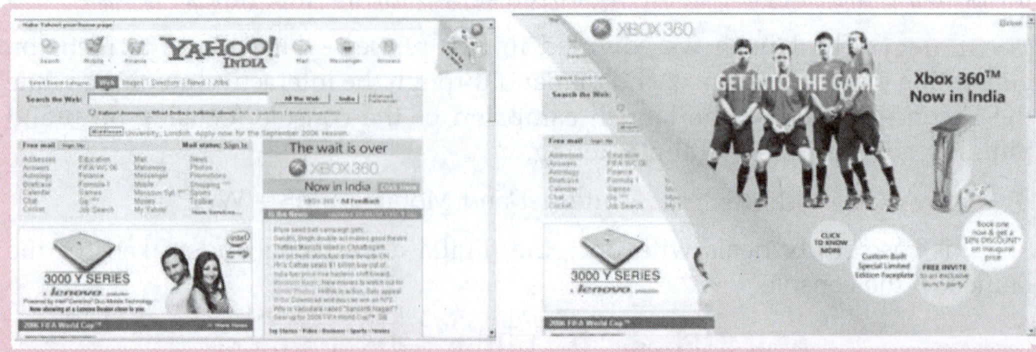

Advertisement on Yahoo.co.in – Page Tear

Advertisements of XBOX 360 on sify.com and rediff.com

Media Properties' used for the first time in any Microsoft Campaigns:

- Yahoo Page Tear
- Indiatimes Site Capture
- Hotmail Over the Page (OTP) Banner
- Yahoo Messenger Banner
- SMS Tag Lines

The impact through size and visibility of these properties across the main portals made the X-box campaign an instant hit and a talking point in media circles. The response on day one itself was very promising with almost 20,000 users visiting the website.

Association with FIFA World CUP: Association with FIFA World Cup got close to 21,000 users to the promo website. Online events see a spike in traffic and FIFA World cup seemed to be a perfect event to reach out to the target audience.

Second Phase of Online Advertising

Objective: The second phase clearly chalked out the objective of introducing the product to the audience through brand building media properties and maximizing interactions.

Media Highlights: The launch phase saw a multi media campaign across radio, TV, OOH and internet. Since the TVC was really clutter breaking and had a viral appeal it was used as a video banner with astounding results. Campaign delivered almost 100 % more than the expectation primarily because of high level of targeting, good creatives & interactive video ads.

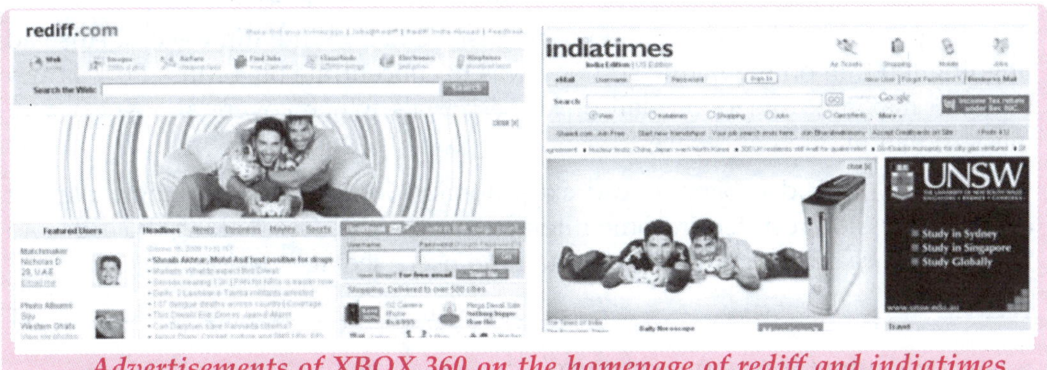

Advertisements of XBOX 360 on the homepage of rediff and indiatimes

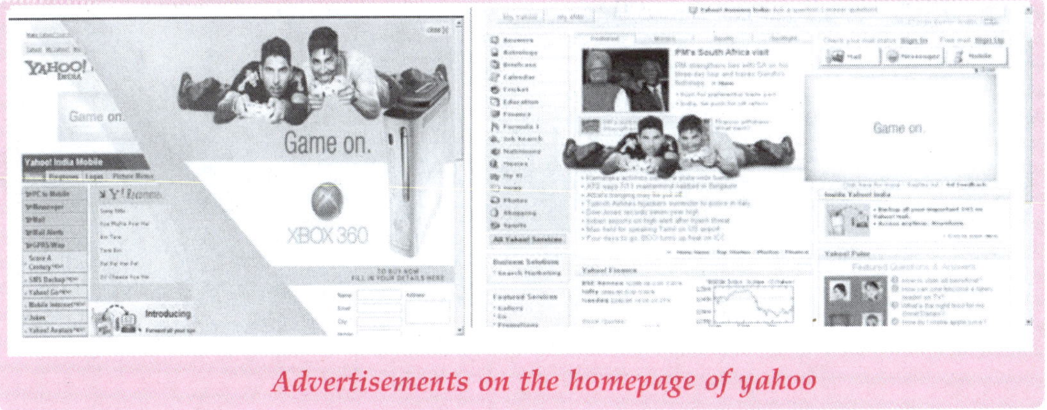

Advertisements on the homepage of yahoo

Video Banner

Second Phase Campaign Results:

Exposures: Around 10 Million Impressions

Interactions: 150 K interactions (Initial Response)

Cost per interaction: 0.33 USD (Maintaining the same cost per initial response for brand building campaign as for lead generation campaign)

Media Used: rediff.com, yahoo.co.in, msn.co.in and indiatimes.com. (Instead of going too thin on media the strategy was to concentrate on 4 Mass Portals and reach to maximum users of mail on these portals which covers almost 80 % of mass Indian internet audience).

High Point: Video Banners did exceptionally well for the campaign. Almost every impression resulted in some interaction from the user making the video ad i.e. the TVC reach to almost 7,00,000 unique users seeing it twice.

Source: http://www.quasar.co.in/

Reproduced with permission

Case Study

TATA DOCOMO "KEEP IT SIMPLE, SILLY"

Advertising Agency: DraftFCB Ulka

National creative director: KS Chakravarthy

Creative directors: Vasudha Misra and Ekta Verma

About Tata DOCOMO

Tata DOCOMO is Tata Teleservices Limited's telecom service on the GSM platform-arising out of the Tata Group's strategic alliance with Japanese telecom major NTT DOCOMO in November 2008.

Tata DOCOMO Scored with Simple Communication

Tata DOCOMO, the GSM brand of Tata Teleservices, has done miracles in a short span of time with its services. The best part of DOCOMO's ad campaigns was simple communication. Be it per second billing or pay per site (two key services that it was the first to launch in the market), the message was communicated to the target audience in a concise and clear manner. Besides, a new campaign was designed for every new scheme launched.

Tata DOCOMO's campaigns feature young and energetic people, who use the phone more as a tool for voice and business communication. Be it accessing Facebook, tweeting or chatting, these people tend to log on to their phone quite often. Tata DOCOMO has offered various exciting value added plans targeted to this generation. Tata DOCOMO has leveraged the power of simple communication and crisp messages. When Tata DOCOMO launched its services in India, it started with the punch line Hello India. It communicated the pay per site concept with the message, "Love just one thing? Pay per site." For the pay-per-second plan, which redefined how telecom operators bill their subscribers, the question posed was, "Why can't your operator count in seconds?"

This has not only built a high brand recall among target audiences, but also lured a massive number of subscribers to the network.

Tata DOCOMO's "Keep It Simple" Ad Campaign

Tata DOCOMO, the GSM brand of Tata Teleservices (TTSL), has run many successful ad campaigns since it started operations in 2008. Its previous campaign 'Do the New' was also very successful. In April, 2011, it launched yet another campaign titled 'Keep It Simple' with Bollywood actor Ranbir Kapoor, during the IPL season.

The brand's latest ad campaign titled 'Keep It Simple'; aims to propose 'simplicity in telecom' as the latest value proposition for the consumers. The campaign has been crafted by the brand's agency of record, DraftFCB Ulka.

Launched on April 8, 2011, the campaign titled 'Keep It Simple, Silly' was very visible all through the IPL (Indian Premier League) Season 4.

As the name suggests, the campaign is focussed on conveying how Tata Docomo simplifies the telecom experience for consumers by providing differentiated products and services.

The execution is in the form of a stand-up comedy show in which Ranbir Kapoor plays the stand-up comedian. Each individual advertisement starts by illustrating a particular complexity in the telecom category (such as automatic activation of unwanted services and billing errors, amongst others). Towards the end, the Tata Docomo product and/or service is then portrayed as a means of simplifying things.

The insight used is that our daily experiences with life and with our mobile phones are complicated, and we already have lots of things to worry about. Given this, the brand offers to keep the telecom part of people's lives simple by providing simple offerings related to bills, products, services and tariff options.

As per reports, the GSM service arm of Tata Teleservices Limited has invested close to Rs 50 crore (Rs 500 million) for the campaign featuring Bollywood actor Ranbir Kapoor.

Mr Gurinder Singh Sandhu, Head Corporate Marketing, Tata Teleservices, said: "Tata DOCOMO is an inspirational brand and so is the charm and personality of Ranbir Kapoor, India's young and fastest-rising Bollywood icon. He is youthful, dedicated, refreshingly different and a standout in a crowd—all of which qualities mesh so well with Tata DOCOMO's own brand persona. As a youth icon, Ranbir is a trend-setter and appeals to young audience—he is professional, dynamic and youthful. This is a perfect match with Tata DOCOMO, and we welcome him to the family and look forward to a long and meaningful association."

Commenting on the campaign, KS Chakravarthy (Chax), national creative director, Draftfcb Ulka, said, "There were many tricky challenges going into this campaign. First was the need to consolidate all our offerings under one simple, ownable brand idea – in our case, simplifying telecom. Second was to launch several very important, and in some cases, breakthrough products under this umbrella position. Third, leveraging Ranbir's youth icon status with our core younger audience while making him a meaningful property when we were speaking to an older, more mature audience that our new products were aimed at. And of course, doing all that in the two shooting days we had with him."

Arvind Wable, chief executive officer, Draftfcb Ulka, Delhi, added, "The idea behind this campaign is to bring out in a refreshingly different way the pain points that the mobile consumer suffers. It focuses on how Tata Docomo empathizes with the consumers and makes every effort to cut out the complexity and lack of transparency they have so far been subjected to by the service providers. And in effect, make life simple, so that the consumers can enjoy the Docomo mobility experience."

The new brand ambassador, Ranbir Kapoor had this to say "I have always believed in being different and doing things in a unique and new way—which is what made me jump at the chance to associate with Tata DOCOMO, which is such a close replica of my own persona. What really connects me to Tata DOCOMO is the youth appeal that they have. They keep it really simple, and that's what the whole format of this campaign is all about—Keep It Simple, Silly. We have too many things in our lives to worry about. Telecom is not something that we should have to worry about—all those bills, smart bills, products, services, tariff options... I love the simplicity of Tata DOCOMO and this new campaign—it will start with making people laugh, and make their lives oh so simple... We had a blast making this campaign and I hope people have a blast watching it too."

The company has introduced many service plans in sync with the messages it conveyed through the "Keep it Simple, Silly" Ad Campaign : a roam-free plan on post-paid, family plan, bill guarantee plan (the company pays the fine if one spots an error, no unwanted services and hassle-free talking to the customer care executives). Among its various variants, a few are listed below.

- Frog in the Pond – Roaming
- Family Plan
- Beauty Tips – Unwanted Services
- Complexity in Life – Invitation Card!
- Customer Executive
- Roaming – Uncle's House
- Spot an Error in the Bill and We Pay a Fine

Multiple executions of this ad were seen during the course of IPL season 4 matches. The creative team on this campaign included K S Chakravarthy (Chax), national creative director, and Vasudha Misra, creative director, DraftFCB Ulka.

Stand-up comedian Sanjay Rajoura provided inputs regarding the comic timing for the ads.

Besides television, the media mix included print campaigns, outdoor innovations and retail front displays.

Response to the Ad Campaign

According to Mr Gurinder Singh Sandhu, Head Corporate Marketing, Tata Teleservices, "On noticing the first few days' response to our campaign, we were thrilled to see that it had not only broken the IPL TVCs clutter within the category but across categories. This has been contributed by several factors like strong message, unique concept, highly relevant pinpoints of the category, great script, stylish treatment, refreshing tone and cheeky sense of humour. All of these have fallen beautifully in place to capture basic consumers' insights and concerns about a telecom service."

Concluding Note

The execution of the "Keep it Simple, Silly" ad campaign of Tata DOCOMO is such that it breaks the clutter. The stand-up comedy act used to deliver messages about the company's value added services is a very fresh concept and is very different from the usual telecom ads seen on television. Due to a different execution (stand-up comedy), by a popular brand ambassador (Ranbir Kapoor), and also because of the fantastic time of launching the campaign (IPL Season 4), the visibility of the ads has been very good and has definitely caught an eye of the viewer. However, it is still too early to say whether the value proposition of simplicity will get the desired results for the company.

Case Study

"ATITHI DEVO BHAVAH" CAMPAIGN

Background

The tourism industry is one of the most profitable industries in India and also contributes a substantial amount of foreign exchange. It is the largest service industry in India, with a contribution of more than 6% to the national GDP and more than 8% to the total employment in India. The tourism industry also helps growth in some other sectors such as horticulture, handicrafts, agriculture, construction and even poultry. Both directly and indirectly, increased tourism in India has and will create job opportunities in a variety of related sectors. According to the World Travel and Tourism Council, India will be the world's leading tourism hotspot, having the highest 10-year growth potential. However, according to the Ministry of Tourism (India), India is still not amongst the top 15 tourist destinations of the world. This is probably because of the following factors.

- Security and safety of international tourists
- Defacement of the national heritage monuments and tourist spots

And the prime reason for both these factors is the attitude of the Indian citizen at large - a low level of empathy for the tourists, and low or no sense of pride for our culture and heritage.

The challenge was to change this perspective and ensure that the tourism industry in India realises its true growth potential. Hence, the campaign "*atithi devo bhavah*".

What is "*Atithi Devo Bhavah*" ?

The campaign "*atithi devo bhavah*" is a pioneer initiative by Ministry of Tourism, Government of India. It is a nation-wide campaign that aims at sensitising key stakeholders towards tourists, through a process of training and orientation. The endeavour is to boost tourism in India, which in turn, would act as a catalyst for India's economic growth.

"*Atithi Devo Bhavah*" aims at creating awareness about the effects of tourism and sensitizing people about preservation of our rich heritage & culture, cleanliness and warm hospitality. It also re-instills a sense of responsibility towards tourists and re-enforces the confidence of foreign tourist towards India as a preferred holiday destination. The entire concept is designed to complement the 'Incredible India' Campaign.

"*Atithi Devo Bhavah*" is a social awareness campaign aimed at providing the inbound tourist a sense of being welcomed to the country. The campaign targets the general public as a whole, while focusing mainly on the stakeholders of the tourism industry.

Objectives

The key objective of the campaign was creating awareness leading to a behavioural shift - sensitising people to the need to behave responsibly towards tourists, national monuments and our rich heritage and culture.

Given the objective of awareness and behavioural change, it was imperative that the audience be involved. Simple broadcasting the message to the audience was not sufficient. "Guest is God" is a prominent part of the Indian culture. This was translated into the tag line of the brand campaign "*Atithi Devo Bhavah*" (Guest is God).

Brand Ambassador – Aamir Khan

Aamir Khan was roped in as the brand ambassador for the campaign. As a brand ambassador, Aamir Khan has taken up the task of promoting the rich cultural heritage of India and ways to preserve and enhance it. He also will try to instil the right attitude inside Indians and make them implement the true concept of 'guest is god'.

The famous Bollywood actor who is working without a remuneration, has a clear idea about the whole project. "Each social work is different. Through this, I want to remind people how great our country is and want to sensitize our people. I want to tell them what we are - we are warm and hospitable people. We have to protect those who are visiting our country. We must ensure that they have a good time and come back again."

Tourism Secretary, Sujit Banerjee, stated, "the Bollywood actor will sensitise people against spilling of garbage and scrawling of graffiti at tourist sites and promote amicable behaviour towards tourists." Along with Aamir, noted lyricist Prasoon Joshi and director Rakesh Om Prakash Mehra are also part of the project.

Some of the TVCs of the Campaign

In one of the TVCs, the local transport operators were shown harassing a few tourists. Then comes Aamir Khan and stops the rogues. He said that the tourists are our guests and in India guests are next to gods. He also said that if the tourists go disappointed from India they would never want to come back. He pointed out that it is because of these tourists that many of us earn our livelihood. All this makes it very important for us to adopt "*atithi devo bhavah*" in true spirit.

In another TVC of the campaign, Aamir Khan stepped forward and stopped a young guy from spoiling an old monument and urged the kids in the campaign and the audience, in general, that they should take a step forward and protect our national heritage.

Bringing the idea to life

After a detailed agency research, it was figured out that the key audience where there was a need to drive a behavioural change is the youth. This was because the incidence of graffiti on monuments, eve teasing, molestation etc. was highest in the age group of 18–30 years. Having zeroed down on this target group, the campaign then looked at the activities that this audience is involved in the digital space.

At the heart of the activity was launced a website (http://atithi.org.in) that hosted an interactive forum, especially developed to empower the audience to contribute their ideas on how to tackle graffiti and tourist molestation. The brand ambassador, Aamir Khan, was the spokesperson on the website as well.

To drive awareness about the campaign and traffic to this website, the agency conceptualised a Pan India campaign, comprising engaging interactive banners. The engaging banner ads asked viewers to write a love message for their beloved on India's magnificent monuments (The *Taj*, *Jantar Mantar*, *Qutub Minar*, and *Gateway of India*). When the user tried to do so with a mouse, the monument dodged the pencil—this was followed by a message from Aamir telling the user to protect the monument.

The campaign ran on over 2,600 youth-centric websites including Orkut, YouTube, MusicIndiaOnline and Gmail. These sites were shortlisted, keeping in mind the media consumption habits of the target group and were shortlisted on the basis of three key factors—reach of the website (measured in absolute numbers), audience skew (share of the target audience in the overall traffic on the website across audiences) and site stickiness (time spent by the audience on the website). Given the audience and their consumption of the internet medium, social media and search played a crucial role in the overall campaign.

Banner Ads

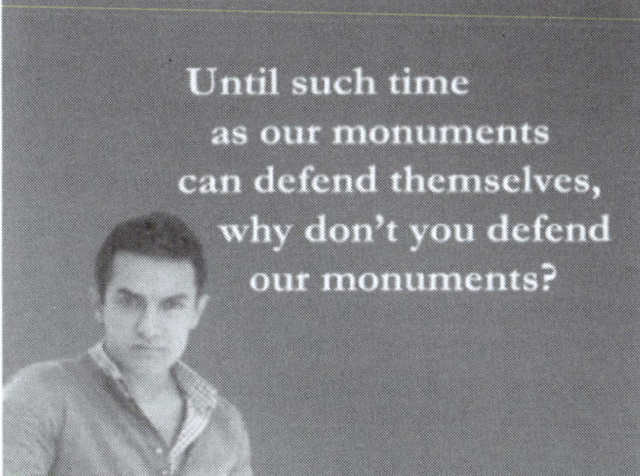

Results

The key objective of the campaign was creating awareness leading to a behavioural shift - sensitising people to the need to behave responsibly towards tourists, national monuments and our rich heritage and culture. As a long term objective, the campaign was to supplement the main campaign of the tourism ministry – 'Incredible India'.

In terms of the first objective, awareness, the campaign far exceeded the expectations. As highlighted earlier, at the heart of the Atithi Devo Bhavah activity was the microsite (http://atitihi.org.in). The campaign ran between February 2009 to May 2009 and the various activities that were done around the campaign (social media, banners, mailers, PR etc.) led to a huge boost in the traffic on the website. According to Google Analytics, the website witnessed close to 5 lakh visitors in the campaign period and 90.91% of these visits were new visits. This was much higher than the expected traffic of 3-3.5 lakh.

The media plan generated 181 million (1,81,921,968) views (Source: Agency Ad Serving Software). The social media activity also contributed to high reach and awareness of the campaign. The team got close to 8.5 lakh video views on You Tube alone.

The second objective of the campaign was to drive involvement so as to aid the behavioural shift. Close to 8.19 Lakh visitors clicked on the banners and mailers to visit the microsite and be part of the Atithi Devo Bhavah initiative. (Source: Agency Ad Serving Software).

The long term objective of this campaign was to supplement the main campaign - "Incredible India". The "*Atithi Devo Bhavah*" campaign ensured that through its social media activities, the Indian tourism website (www.incredibleindia.com) gained visibility through Google Search engine results as well. From a zero visibility, the website was now ranked amongst top ten searches on highly searched keywords.

References

http://www.incredibleindia.org/

http://www.afaqs.com/

Case Study

A New Dimesnsion to Ad Innovation

VOLKSWAGEN VENTO LAUNCH CAMPAIGN

About Volkswagen India

With its headquarters in Pune, Maharashtra (India), the Volkswagen Group is represented by three brands in India: Volkswagen, Audi and Skoda. Each brand has its own character and operates as an independent entity in the market.

Volkswagen Group India is a part of Volkswagen AG, which is globally represented by 9 brands- Audi, Bentley, Bugatti, Lamborghini, Scania, Seat, Skoda, Volkswagen Commercial Vehicles (Volkswagen Nutzfahrzeuge) and Volkswagen Passenger Cars. The product range extends from low-consumption small cars to luxury class vehicles and trucks. The Group operates 60 production plants around the world. In total more than 370,000 employees produce more than 26,600 vehicles or are involved in vehicle-related services each working day.

The highest volume brand of the Group is Volkswagen. Europe's most successful car brand has made successful inroads into the Indian market.

'Innovation' is the word for Volkswagen

Volkwagen India has always come up with very innovative ad campaigns. It has worked very closely with its advertising agency, Mudra (DDB), to come up with something new every time, as far its advertisements are concerned. Let us discuss some of these very innovative ad campaigns by Volkswagen India.

An innovative display of Touareg's power

Touareg is an SUV by Volkswagen that dominates the road. It can climb easily even a 45 degree hill. This was the perfect excuse to develop an innovative creative approach to demonstrate this innovative feature.

The agency created a dummy Touareg and attached it to the outside of a building, to give the impression that it was climbing vertically. The innovative approach fascinated passersby and attracted widespread press attention. Digitally, the agency took the idea of 45 degree climbing further, developing a rich media banner ad that unleashed an animated Touareg which would then descend (at a 45 degree angle) through the text of the page that the viewer was reading.

World's first cut out newspaper

Volkswagen's ad agency, Mudra, wanted to make sure that everyone knew that though Polo was a German car, it was made in and for India. The agency had a task of embedding the car in the Indian media. The agency took the idea literally and working with the Times of India, became the first brand in the world to cut a hole in a newspaper for marketing purposes. A Polo-shaped hole was punched in each copy of the morning newspaper. Inside the "newspaper with a hole" people could read about each of the innovative features of the Polo.

World's first 'handwritten' newspaper

Phaeton is Volkswagen's most luxurious model. In a world of mass produced vehicles, the Phaeton is exquisitely hand crafted. To bring this alive in an attention-grabbing and innovative way, the agency worked with the Hindustan Times on an innovative approach. For one day only, each page of the paper was printed in a different font, to make it look as if it had been written out by hand rather than printed by a printing press. According to the agency, this was never been done anywhere in the world before.

The commitment to innovation has continued for Volkswagen India with a constant stream of interesting and innovative activities.

In September, 2010, Volkswagen came up with yet another innovation in advertising - an advertisement which was considered a new dimension in advertising by people in the advertising fraternity and also by the general public. It came up with a 'talking newspaper' for the launch campaign of Volkswagen Vento.

A Talking Newspaper!!

The German automotive manufacturer launched its campaign for the New Vento with an innovation in September 21, 2010 edition of The Times of India and The Hindu. As readers opened the newspaper a light-sensitive chip attached to the page announced the arrival of a perfectly engineered car – the Vento.

This is the very first time the Indian audience has witnessed such communication, taking print advertising to another level altogether.

The newspaper read "Today's 36-page edition of Times of India (Delhi) is split into two sections: a 26-page news section, and a 10-page wraparound."

The opening page of the wraparound carried this announcement:

"The Times of India and Volkswagen have created four pages of content as part of a special media innovation. Don't miss reading and listening to this 'speaking newspaper'."

On the last page of the wraparound was a full-page Volkswagen ad for its new model Vento. As the page was opened, a light-sensitive speaker, weighing no more than a mere 10-15 grams and stuck on the extreme left panel in the advertisement read out the line in a loop:

"Best in class German engineering is here. The new Volkswagen Vento. Built with great care and highly innovative features. Perhaps that's why it breaks the hearts of our engineers to watch it drive away. (The ad showed a Volkswagen engineer crying looking at a finished Vento.) The new Volkswagen Vento. Crafted with so much passion, it's hard to let it go. Volkswagen. Das Auto."

Figure 1 shows the Volkswagen Vento print ad that the 'talking newspaper' carried.

Figure 1: Volkswagen Ad inserted in the Newspaper

www.volkswagen.co.in

Rear AC vent

Climatronic auto AC

Tiptronic 6-speed AT

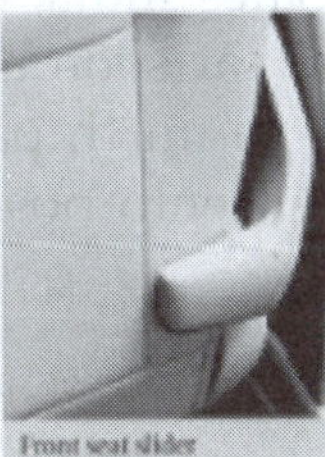
Front seat slider

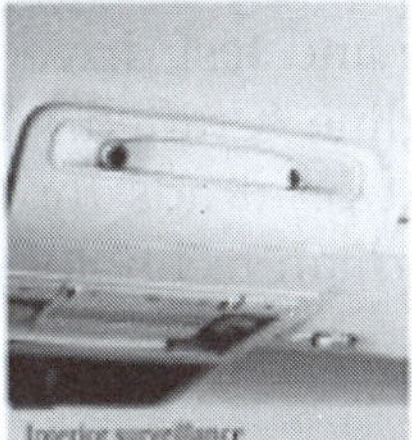
Interior surveillance

The New Volkswagen Vento.
Crafted with so much passion, it's hard to let it go.

The Volkswagen Vento is a car that's designed specially for India with great care and precision. Take for example the 1.6L powerful yet fuel-efficient engine that keeps the fuel station miles away. Or the 6-speed automatic gearbox with Tiptronic shifts. Or the innovative Front seat slider that offers extra legroom for passengers in the rear. Then there's the Climatronic auto AC, along with a Rear AC vent, which ensures a pleasant drive for every passenger, while the interior surveillance adds up to the passive safety. Even the rear axle is designed to take on difficult road conditions and make every ride, smooth. After all, the Vento is a car that's crafted out of pure passion. Perhaps, that's why our engineers find it so hard to let it go.

German engineering. Best in Class.

Volkswagen. Das Auto.

• Also available in 1.6L,105 PS Petrol (AT/MT) and Diesel (MT) engines • Terms and conditions apply • Accessories shown and features listed may not be part of standard equipment

The ad was carried in some 2.2 million copies. The same Volkswagen ad ran in other papers without the audio.

According to reports, this campaign would have caused Volkswagen a bomb. The Economic Times website reported that a similar device would cost about Rs 40. Try multiplying the figure with the print run of the newspapers and add to that other print and placement costs.

Volkswagen, no stranger to unconventional advertising, said the aim was to do something innovative to help raise awareness of the brand and drive traffic to showrooms.

Bhaskar Das, Executive President of The Times of India Group, described the advertisement as an innovation in co-creation that makes a statement for not just Times of India, but the entire print media.

Talking about the innovation, Bobby Pawar, Chief Creative Officer, Mudra Group, said, "The idea came from the fact that there is a lot of passion that goes into the making of Volkwagen Vento, hence the thought of parting with it becomes difficult for the engineers who make the machine. We thought of giving these engineers a voice.". He added, "The campaign has surely got everyone talking and created a buzz. I would call this as inventive thinking and one would see this campaign supported in 360 degree communications. We would also be looking at apertures in media to create more such surprises."

The Response

"With over 5,000 Ventos sold within the first three months, the response for this premium notch was excellent," said Lutz Kothe, Head - Marketing, Volkswagen Group Sales India, adding the fact that people actually wanted to see and test drive the car soon after the campaign was out. Launched with the tagline 'Crafted with so much passion, it's hard to let go', the follow-up TVCs and print ads for the Vento positioned the vehicle as a product with superior German technology.

References

http://www.volkswagen.co.in/

http://www.afaqs.com/

Case Study

LAUNCH CAMPAIGN OF TATA SKY+

Tata Sky, a leading Satellite Television provider, launched Tata Sky+, a new-age service that offers to the viewer the power to plan and control his TV viewing experience – allowing him to Pause, Record and Rewind Live TV.

Target Audience: A premium product, Tata Sky+ wanted to reach the premium metro audience, 25+, affluent families.

Communication Goal: To create awareness about various features of Tata Sky +

Campaign Launched in: August, 2008

Tagline: *Isko laga dala toh life aur bhi jhingalala*

Creative Agency: Ogilvy and Mather (O&M) India

Brand Ambassadors: Aamir Khan and Gul Panag

TVCs

Phase 1: In the first phase, which was a 14-second teaser ad, Aamir Khan was shown as a husband doing the household work and asking the viewers that why can't a man do the household work.

Phase 2: In the second phase, the TVC showed Aamir Khan and Gul Panag as husband and wife. The ad highlighted the "record" live TV as a feature of Tata Sky Plus. In the ad, the husband tries to help his wife in more than one way to please her so that he can watch the live telecast of a cricket match.The ad opens in the backdrop of an upper middle class apartment. The opening shot of the ad shows Aamir doing the household chores (making tea and breakfast for his wife, before she wakes up), greatly catching her by surprise, which is quite an interesting opening for an ad to get instant attention. Aamir leaves for office. The ad moves on. He returns in the evening, opens the door from outside, enters completely loaded with the laptop bag around his shoulder, hands stuffed with heavy bags containing vegetables, groceries etc. He looks tired and loaded, but cheerful. Gul Panag, the wife, is watching him from the sofa. The husband proceeds to make tea for both of them. Aamir comes across as somebody who's kind of managing the house almost single handedly. Gul's expressions all throughout are interesting. She seems perplexed, surprised, and inquisitive. Aamir doesn't seem usual to her.

Next shot, she manages to see the news paper, sports page headlines indicating that there is India- finals cricket match on TV that evening. Realization dawns on her face. Inquisitiveness on her face is replaced by a serene sense of control and understanding. She asks Aamir that whether he is doing all the work so that she allows him to watch the India finals match by sacrificing her serials for the evening. To which Aamir pretends ignorance of the match and its schedule.

Gul moves on to add that he actually need not take so much trouble, thanks to Tata Sky Plus. While he watches the match, her serial would keep getting recorded ("Record Live TV" – feature being highlighted) hence nobody actually misses anything! Aamir changes. Tea powder bottle still in hand, he confirms what Gul told him by talking charge of the Tata Sky remote.

Aamir hurls the tea powder bottle to Gul. In a sudden change in tone from the soft, accommodative one to a stern, authoritative one, he asks Gul to go and make some tea for him. This is followed by a pillow fight between them.

Phase 3: In the third phase, the ad focussed on the "pause" feature of Tata Sky Plus. The ad again featured the same Aamir-Gul couple. The ad opens with Aamir seated on the sofa watching a soccer match (through their Tata Sky Plus) and Gul seated some distance away. Suddenly they receive a phone call, which happens to be from Aamir's mother-in-law (*Mummyji*). Surprisingly enough Aamir is very much available to talking to *Mummyji* over the phone, that too while watching a soccer match (which he is shown to be very passionate about). He chats with his mother-in-law at length about day to day things in life, showing an air of involvement and sentimental attachment to his in-laws. His mother-in-law even gets into sounding a little apologetic about Aamir having to miss the match for talking to her. To which Aamir very cordially comforts her by indicating that the match wasn't really as important.

Gul is not surprised at all at Aamir's behaviour as she knows that Aamir has "paused the match" to talk to her mom, and is going to resume it from where he stopped, thereby not missing a single fraction of action in it. Again the utility of the feature – "Pause Live TV" has been very interestingly introduced in the context.

The ad ends nicely as well. Aamir finishes the call. Gul sarcastically asks him, what if her mother new the truth (implied...about Aamir's fictitious behaviour). Aamir in a very tongue-and-cheek manner asks "*Kya Papaji ke bare me?" and then, p*illow fight starts.

Phase 4: In the fourth phase, the TVC shows Aamir sitting with his friend who requests Aamir to ask his wife to play the match on TV. To this, Aamir replies that Indian wives do so much for their husbands and the men are so selfish that they can't even let their wives watch the TV. Then, Gul Panag tells the viewers that Aamir is saying so because of Tata Sky Plus which lets him record the live match and play it whenever desired.

Thus, it can be said that

- Tata sky in order to create awareness among the viewers about Tata Sky plus chose the Aamir-Gul duo to portray the tale of a typical Indian couple.
- The ads had the wit and power of a powerful brand ambassador, aamir khan, which make them very sharp and appealing to the general public.

Print Ad of Tata Sky Plus

Digital Strategy

There were 4 drivers to the online plan.

1. Rich media & video advertising that showcased the Pause, Record, Rewind function. Video formed a key component of the plan given the nature of the product. The campaign used the top portals (Yahoo, Rediff, MSN) for reach, integrating advertising into video sections, banners with videos on rollover, rich media banners with user interactivity, etc.

2. Innovations for launch impact: Homepage takeover on MSN and Sync Banners on Yahoo were some of the innovations used.
3. Sites reaching out to the High Networth Individuals (audience): Finance & News sites targeting the upwardly mobile audience such as BBC, Moneycontrol, etc.
4. Search generated a high volume of clicks, 25% of the overall campaign, and video ads formed a significant part of the mix.

Figure 1 shows one of the banner ads of Tata Sky Plus.

Figure 1: *Banner Ad of Tata Sky Plus*

While the focus was on Pause, Record and Rewind Live TV, two distinct routes were created.

1. Different concepts were created based on situations in people's lives when they would need to pause/record or rewind their favourite show e.g., boss calling, husband and wife fight over which serial to watch, missing your favourite dialogue, missing the stock update, going out with your family, etc.
2. Customized communications were also created based on the website where the product was being advertised. For instance, on cricket, a different banner was run as compared to entertainment and finance.

Result

With 157 Million impressions delivered and a campaign average CTR of 0.4%, this was one of the most successful digital campaigns for Tata Sky. The Video ad units generated 4-8 times the CTR (click through rate) of standard units. The Rich Media units had above average interaction rates. Overall the campaign delivered twice as many clicks as estimated with significant user interaction.

Reference: http://www.media2win.com/

Case Study

COCA COLA'S 'OPEN HAPPINESS' CAMPAIGN

The year 2009 saw Coca-Cola's long-time brand endorser, Aamir Khan 'Opening' happiness for the brand in India (Open Happiness being the global creative thought adopted by the brand a while ago). Aamir Khan, who has been endorsing Coca-Cola or Coke for over a decade, was seen as a messenger of optimism in the campaign, where a bottle of Coke brought people together in their joy. Taking the message further, is the Bollywood actor, Imran Khan, who joined his uncle, Aamir Khan as an endorser for Coca-Cola in 2010. The brand's objective remains the same - to reinforce its role as a cheerful friend. However, the younger Khan's association with Coke is a step towards getting the brand closer and more identifiable to teenagers.

Creative Agency: McCann Erickson

Creative Team: Prasoon Joshi, Tirtha Ghosh and Ashish Chakravarty

Production House: Freshwater Films (directed by Dibakar Banerjee)

Phase 1: The 'Shadow' Commercial

Storyboard of the Ad: The film opens with the protagonist (Imran Khan) who has just shifted in a new apartment. After putting down a heavy box and wiping the sweat off his brow, he notices a shadow being cast from the adjoining flat of a person working on a laptop. The person's shadow disappears for a moment and Imran hears the sound of opening of the Coke bottle. The shadow of the Coke bottle is put down in front of the laptop. Imran quickly looks around, grabs a lamp in his room and sets it so that the light falls just next to the shadows being cast from the adjoining flat. In an exciting sequence of shadow-play (flapping bird, dog and a straw), Imran tries to get close to the Coke bottle.

Suddenly the other person turns off the light and the shadow from the adjoining flat disappears. Worried, Imran rushes out of his apartment and into the balcony to realize that the shadow actually belonged to a pretty girl who too had rushed out and is now extending the Coke bottle towards him.

Speaking about the commercial, Prasoon Joshi, Executive Chairman, Regional Creative Director, Asia Pacific, McCann Erickson Pvt. Ltd said, "The new campaign is indeed very different from what we have done in the past. We have tried to use exciting elements of shadow puppetry and play to showcase how strangers connect over a bottle of Coca-Cola. It's about bringing people closer, building connect and breaking ice between strangers. It's a beautiful story in an ordinary day of our cosmopolitan life, where a boy in his new apartment enacts trying to reach out and sip out from a 'shadow' of a Coca-Cola bottle, using various elements of shadow-play (flapping bird, dog and a straw). The entire campaign has been executed beautifully and we are sure that everyone will find it appealing."

The new communication took the 'Open Happiness' theme to the next level, by building spontaneous human connections and sharing joys even with strangers. A new punch line, *'Coke khule toh baat chale'* (Coke opens up possibilities), was arrived at to further this thought.

Commercial First Released on: Mobile phones and online media

In an attempt to forge deeper connections with its young consumers, the 'Shadow' commercial was first released digitally, a medium that is a phenomenal trend these days. An exclusive preview of the TV commercial of the new campaign was uploaded on the microsite at cokeshadow.in, as a part of the teaser campaign. Users got a first-hand experience of viewing it online and on their mobile handsets and had the option of rating the TVC. They also had the option of sharing it with their friends through social networking sites such as Twitter and Facebook. The web link also enabled users to download the theme music as a ringtone and share it with their friends.

According to Anuj Kumar, Executive Director (South Asia) Affle, "This is the first time in India's advertising history that a company has launched its brand campaign first on mobile phones and digital space before releasing it in mass media."

Adding further, Anand Singh, Director-Marketing, Coca-Cola India, said, "The new Shadow campaign was first released using the digital platform in order to directly tap today's young consumer, who likes to the first to try out new products and offers. Additionally, the campaign was also made available through SMS and Blue-casting. This unique approach will certainly generate a buzz around the new Coca-Cola campaign by offering the target audience a sneak preview of the commercial and create a viral effect thereof."

The campaign was downloaded and previewed by over 300,000 consumers and had over 90,000 referrals online.

Phase 2: The 'Invisible Bottle' Commercial

The commercial, titled 'Invisible Bottle', features Imran Khan and Kalki Koechlin of DevD fame. It is a hot day in Mumbai, and the ad takes off from there. A jam packed bus, Imran Khan a college going teen is stuck between a few people and finally settles his glance on Kalki. The bus stops, it's hot and Kalki looks at a Coke poster outside, pretends to pick it up from the poster, open it and gestures to ask Imran if he would like a sip. He nods happily and pretends to take the Coke bottle from her hand. He sips the drink up in one quick gulp and turns his hand over as to say, I'm sorry, there's nothing left. Kalki looks angry, she makes a face and looks away. Just then, the charming Imran, pulls out an actual Coke bottle from his bag. As the two exchange sweet glances, the film concludes on the thought, *'Coke khule toh baat chale'*.

"The latest communication is based on the spontaneous human connections between people, particularly those who are unlike each other", says Prasoon Joshi. "Through the lovable device of the invisible bottle, brand Coca-Cola breaks the ice of social distance between a boy and a girl and brings them together." He also adds that the new campaign with Imran Khan is more youthful, playful and fun in nature.

The campaign was supported with mass media, as well as in-store and on-ground activities around youth hangout areas and colleges across various cities. Digital media, particularly social networking sites, were also leveraged to generate interaction with the brand.

References

http://www.coca-colaindia.com/

http://www.afaqs.com/

Advertising Glossary

A

Account Executive: A professional who represents the advertising agency to its clients. An account executive is the link between the ad agency and the organisation hiring the agency.

Account: The term account refers to the client/employer of the ad agency - a business entity, organisation or a corporate that employs the advertising agency.

Ad Testing: Any of a variety of methods used to qualitatively or quantitatively evaluate the effectiveness of an advertisement. Pre-testing involves showing different ad prototypes to groups to determine which is the most effective. Post-testing typically involves interviewing readers to determine how many remember seeing a particular ad, if they read it, and what they remember about it.

Advertiser: An advertiser could be an individual or an organisation, who wants to communicate with a target audience. The communication is about the products and services offered by the advertiser.

Advertising Agency: Advertising agency is a marketing service firm that assists its clients in planning, preparing, implementing and evaluating various activities of advertising campaign.

Advertising Appeal: An advertising appeal refers to the approach used by an advertiser to attract the attention or interest of consumers and/or influence their feelings towards the product, service or cause. Examples of advertising appeals are rational appeals, humour appeal, fear appeal, etc.

Advertising Budget: Advertising budget is the quantitative expression of future plan of advertising activities in monetary terms. It shows the total amount to be spent on advertising and its allocation among different advertising activities so that advertising objectives can be achieved in a specific period of time.

Advertising Campaign: A series of advertisement messages that share a single idea and theme which make up an integrated marketing communication.

Advertising Copy: An ad is made up of different elements and advertising copy refers to the textual matter or the written word in an advertisement.

Advertising Creativity: The ability to generate fresh, unique and appropriate ideas that can be used as solutions to communication problems.

Advertising Media: Advertising media are the vehicles for carrying the message of an advertiser to the prospects. They convey the ad message to the target audience. The most commonly used media are newspapers, magazines, radio, TV and outdoors.

Advertising Plan: An explicit outline of what goals an advertising campaign should achieve, how to accomplish those goals, and how to determine whether or not the campaign was successful in obtaining those goals.

Advertising Research: Research conducted to improve the efficacy of advertising. It may focus on a specific ad or campaign, or may be directed at a more general understanding of how advertising works or how consumers use the information in advertising. It can entail a variety of research approaches, including psychological, sociological, economic, and other perspectives.

Advertising: Any paid form of non-personal presentation and promotion of goods, services and ideas by an identified sponsor.

Advertorial: A paid advertisement that presents information in an editorial format, often with large amounts of text, rather than large photos typically used for display ads.

Advocacy Advertising: Advertising that is concerned with the propagation of ideas and elucidation of social issues of public importance in a manner that supports the position and interest of the sponsor.

Affordable Method: A method of determining the budget for advertising and promotion where all other budget areas are covered and remaining money is available for allocation.

Agency Commission: The agency's fee for designing and placing advertisements. Historically, this was calculated as 15 percent of the amount spent to purchase space or time in the various media used for the advertising. In recent years the commission has, in many cases, become negotiable, and may even be based on some measure of the campaign's success.

AIDA: AIDA is one of a number of models that analyse the customers' journey from ignorance of a product/service to its purchase. AIDA is an acronym for attention, interest, desire, action.

Aided Recall: A research method frequently used to determine what consumers remember about an advertisement that they have seen or heard.

Art Director: An employee who develops concepts, directs vendors and creates layouts and artwork that combine images and words to deliver the message of the client.

Attractiveness: A source characteristic that makes him or her appealing to a message recipient. Source attractiveness can be based on similarity, familiarity, or likability.

Audience: The number of people or households exposed to a vehicle, without regard to whether they actually saw or heard the material conveyed by that vehicle.

Average Frequency: The number of times the average household reached by a media schedule is exposed to a media vehicle over a specified period.

B

Banner Ad: Banners or banner ads are the most commonly used forms of online advertising. Banners of varied forms are used to carry the ad message at strategic positions on a website.

Behaviouristic Segmentation: A method of segmenting a market by dividing customers into groups based on their usage, loyalties, or buying responses to a product or service.

Benefit Segmentation: A method of segmenting markets on the basis of the major benefits consumers seek in a product or service.

Billboards: Billboards are widely used large sized outdoor signs that carry the advertising message on a mega scale. Billboards are able to catch the attention of passersby and other traffic due to their heightened visibility.

Billings: Total amount charged to clients, including the agency commission, media costs, production costs, etc.

Bleed Pages: Magazine advertisements where the printed area extends to the edge of the page, eliminating any white margin or border around the ad.

Body Copy: The main text portion of a print ad.

Boutique: An agency that provides a limited service, such as one that does creative work but does not provide media planning, research, etc. Usually, this refers to a relatively small company.

Brand Loyalty: Preference by a consumer for a particular brand that results in continual purchase of it.

Brochure: A tool that carries the advertising message.

C

Cable Television: A form of television where signals are carried to households by wire rather than through the airwaves.

Campaign Theme: The central message or idea that is communicated in all advertising and other promotional activities.

Carryover Effect: A delayed or lagged effect whereby the impact of advertising on sales can occur during a subsequent time period.

Cause Related Marketing: Advertising in which companies link with charities or non profit organisations as contributing sponsors, for improving/maintaining their image.

Celebrity Endorser: A celebrity endorser is defined as any individual who enjoys public recognition and who uses this recognition on behalf of a consumer good by appearing with it in an advertisement.

Channel: The method or medium by which communication travels from a source or sender to a receiver.

Circulation: Circulation of a print publication refers to the average number of copies distributed.

Classified Advertising: Advertising that runs in newspapers and magazines that generally contains text only and is arranged under subheadings according to the product, service or offering. Employment and real estate ads are major forms of classified advertising.

Click-through rate (CTR): CTR refers to the number of times visitors to a site click on an ad.

Clients: The organisations with the products, services, or causes to be marketed and for which advertising agencies and other marketing promotional firms provide services.

Clutter: The non-program material that appears in a broadcast environment, including commercials, promotional messages for shows, public service announcements, etc.

Commercial Advertising: Advertising that involves commercial interests rather than advocating a social or political cause.

Commercial: A commercial refers to an audio or visual advertisement that carries the advertiser's message through a range of media such as radio, television etc. Commercials are shown in between television programs and serve the purpose of informing, educating and creating an interest in the advertised brand.

Communication Objectives: Goals that an organisation seeks to achieve through its promotional program in terms of communication effects such as creating awareness, knowledge, attitudes, preference or purchase intentions.

Communication: Communication can be summarized as the transmission of a message from a sender to a receiver in an understandable manner. Communication may take several forms-oral, written, though visuals etc.

Comparative Advertising: The practice of either directly or indirectly naming one or more competitors in an advertising message and usually making a comparison on one or more specific attributes or characteristics.

Competitive Parity Method: A method of setting the advertising and promotion budget based on matching the advertising expenditures with that of competitors.

Continuity: Scheduling advertisements to appear at regular intervals over a period of time.

Cooperative Advertising: Retail advertising that is paid partly or fully by a manufacturer; two or more manufacturers cooperating in a single advertisement.

Copy Testing: Research to determine an ad's effectiveness, based on consumer responses to the ad.

Copywriter: A copywriter is a person who is responsible for transforming ideas into words, writing the body copy for advertisements etc.

Copywriting: Copywriting in print is the activity of putting words to paper, particularly those contained in the main body of the text (the main arguments and appeals used), headlines and sub-heads. In broadcast, the copywriter is a script writer who develops the scenario or script to be used in radio or television medium. Writing a jingle, that is, the lyrics for music may also be involved.

Corporate Advertising: Advertising designed to promote overall awareness of a company or enhance its image among target audience.

Cost Per Thousand (CPM): The cost to reach 1,000 units of audience, households or individuals, for advertising. CPM is used as a measure of efficiency among media and media schedules.

Coverage: A measure of the potential audience that might receive an advertising message through a media vehicle.

Creative Boutique: An advertising agency that specializes in and provides only services related to the creative aspects of advertising.

Creative Strategy: A determination of what an advertising message will say or communicate to a target audience.

Credibility: The extent to which a source is perceived as having knowledge, skill or experience relevant to a communication topic and can be trusted to give an unbiased opinion or information on the issue.

D

DAGMAR: DAGMAR is an acronym for Defining Advertising Goals for Measured Advertising Results. The concept was given by Russell H. Colley. The DAGMAR approach defines an advertising goal as a specific communication task to be accomplished among a defined audience, in a given period of time.

Decoding: The process by which a message recipient transforms and interprets a message.

Demographic Segmentation: A method of segmenting a market based on the demographic characteristics of consumers.

E

Effective Reach: A measure of the percentage of a media vehicle's audience reached at each effective frequency increment.

Emotional Appeal: Advertising messages that appeal to consumer's feelings and emotions.

Encoding: The process of putting thoughts, ideas or information into a symbolic form.

Ethics: Moral principles and values that govern the actions and decisions of an individual or group.

Eye Tracking: A method for following the movement of a person's eye as he or she views an ad or commercial. Eye tracking is used for determining which portions or sections of an ad attract a viewer's attention and/or interest.

F

Fear Appeals: An advertising message that creates anxiety in a receiver by showing negative consequences that can result from engaging in (or not engaging in) a particular behaviour.

Feedback: Part of the message recipient's response that is communicated back to the sender.

Flighting: A media schedule that involves more advertising at certain times and less advertising during other time periods.

Frequency: Frequency refers to the average number of times different households or individuals are reached by a medium in a given period of time.

Full-service Agency: An agency that handles all aspects of the advertising process, including planning, design, production, and placement.

G

Geographic Segmentation: A method of segmenting a market on the basis of different geographic units or areas.

Gross Audience: The audiences of all vehicles or media in a campaign, combined. Some or much of the gross audience may actually represent duplicated audience.

Gross Impressions: Total number of unduplicated people or households represented by a given media schedule.

Gross Rating Points (GRPs): Reach times average frequency. This is a measure of the advertising weight delivered by a vehicle or vehicles within a given time period.

H

Headline: An informative or benefit-oriented statement, usually in large type, intended to quickly attract a reader's attention and create interest in reading the copy.

Hiatus: A period during a campaign when an advertiser's schedule is suspended for a time, after which it resumes.

Hierarchy-of-Effects Model: A model of the process in which it is assumed that a consumer must pass through a sequence of steps from initial awareness to eventual action.

Hit: The number of times that a specific component of a website is requested.

Horizontal Cooperative Advertising: A cooperative advertising arrangement where advertising is sponsored by a group of retailers or other organisations providing products or services to the market.

I

Illustrating: Illustrating means the use of pictures and photographs including visual contents, colours, art work and identification marks (company logo, trademark, etc.). Such decisions are a crucial part of print advertising.

Impact: Impact refers to the qualitative value of an exposure through a given medium.

Infomercials: Television commercials that are very long, ranging from several minutes to an hour. Infomercials are designed to provide consumers with detailed information about a product or service.

In-house Agency: An advertising agency owned and operated by an advertiser, which handles the advertiser's account.

Inquiries: Consumer response to a company's advertising or other promotional activities, such as coupons. Used for measuring the effectiveness of some promotions.

Integrated Marketing Communication (IMC): A management concept that is designed to make all aspects of marketing communication (e.g., advertising, sales promotion, public relations, and direct marketing) work together as a unified force, rather than permitting each to work in isolation.

Interactive Media: A variety of media that allows the consumer to interact with the source of the message, actively receiving information, responding to questions, etc.

Internet: A worldwide means of exchanging information and communicating through a series of interconnected computers.

J

Jingle: A jingle refers to a musical piece of advertising message that is played on the radio or television and are meant to catch the attention of listeners. Jingles should be catchy, short and likeable in order to create a lasting impression.

L

Layout: The layout is the plan that indicates where the component parts of the ad - headline, body copy, illustrations, and other elements of a print ad are to be arranged and positioned on the page.

Local Advertising: Advertising done by companies within the limited geographic area where they do business.

Logotype (logo): A brand name, publication title, or the like, presented in a special lettering style or typeface and used in the manner of a trademark.

M

Mailing List: A type of database containing names and addresses of present and/or potential customers who can be reached through a direct mail campaign.

Market Segmentation: The process of dividing a market into distinct groups that have common needs and will respond similarly to a marketing action.

Marketing Communication: Marketing communications are the means by which firms attempt to inform, persuade and remind consumers, directly or indirectly, about the products and brands that they sell. The marketing communications mix consists of various elements – advertising, sales promotion, personal selling, public relations and publicity. Advertising is a very important element of the marketing communications mix.

Marketing Mix: Marketing mix represents the total marketing programme of a firm. It involves decisions with regard to product, price, place and promotion. These four elements constitute the core of a firm's marketing efforts and are called as the 4 P's of marketing.

Mascot: Mascots refer to any fictitious character, person or animal used to represent a brand and communicate about the brand and its offerings to the consumers. Mascots are used as communication channels between the consumer and the product.

Mass Media: Nonpersonal channels of communication that allow a message to be sent to many individuals at one time.

Media Buying Services: Independent companies that specialize in the buying of media time.

Media Planning: Media Planning refers to the process of selecting media time and space to disseminate advertising messages in order to accomplish advertising and marketing objectives of an organisation. The basic goal of a media plan is to find out that combination of media which enables the advertiser to communicate the message in the most effective manner at lowest cost.

Media Vehicle: The specific programme, publication or promotional piece used to carry an advertising message.

Message: A communication containing information or meaning that a source wants to convey to a receiver.

Moral Appeals: Moral appeals are those appeals to the audience that appeal to their sense of right and wrong. They are often used to exhort people to support social causes, such as cleaner environment, adult literacy, equal rights for women, consumer protection, and aid to the disadvantaged.

N

Noise: External factors that create unplanned distortion or interference in the communication process.

O

Objective and Task Method: A build-up approach to budget setting, involving determining advertising objectives, determining strategies and tasks required to attain these objectives and estimating the costs associated with these strategies and tasks.

One-Sided Message: Communications in which only positive attributes or benefits of a product or service are presented.

Online Advertising: Online advertising is a form of promotion that uses the internet and the World Wide Web for the purpose of delivering marketing messages to attract customers.

P

People Meter: A broadcast ratings measurement device that records individual audience members who are present during a program.

Percentage Charges: The mark-ups charged by advertising agencies for services provided to clients.

Percent-of-Sales Method: Method of determining the advertising budget based on an analysis of past sales, as well as a forecast for future sales.

Perception: The process by which an individual receives, selects, organizes, and interprets information to create a meaningful picture of the world.

Personal Selling: Face-to-face communication in which the seller attempts to assist and/or persuade prospective buyers to purchase the company's product or service or to act upon an idea.

Point-of-Purchase (POP) Displays: Advertising display material located at the retail store, usually placed in an area where payment is made, such as a check-out counter.

Pop-ups: Advertisement windows on the internet usually larger than a banner ad and smaller than a full screen.

Post-testing: Testing the effects of an ad after it has appeared in the media.

Primacy Effect: A theory which says that the first information presented in a message will be the most likely to be remembered.

Product Placement: A form of advertising and promotion in which products are placed in television shows and/or movies to gain exposure.

Promotion: The coordination of all seller-initiated efforts to set up channels of information and persuasion to sell goods and services or to promote an idea.

Promotional Mix: The tools used to accomplish an organisation's communication objectives. The promotional mix has many elements – advertising, personal selling, sales promotion, publicity and public relations.

Psychographic Segmentation: Dividing the product market on the basis of personality and/or lifestyles.

Public Service Advertising: Public Service Advertising refers to those advertising efforts which are done as a part of social responsibility by such entities as advertising agencies, Government, NGO's as well as other business organisations. The main objective behind Public Service Advertising is to spread social consciousness among the masses and promote important social issues which generally go unnoticed.

Publicity: Communications regarding an organisation, product, service, or idea that is not directly paid for or run under identified sponsorship.

Puffery: Advertising and other promotions that praise the item to be sold using subjective opinions, superlatives, or exaggerations, stating no specific facts.

Pulsing: The use of advertising in regular intervals, as opposed to seasonal patterns.

Pupillometrics: A method of advertising research in which a study is conducted on the relationship between a viewer's pupil dilation and the interest factor of visual stimuli.

R

Rational Appeals: Advertising appeals that focus on the practical, functional, or utilitarian need for a product or service and emphasize features, benefits or reasons for owning or using the brand.

Reach: Reach is the percentage of media audience exposed at least once to the advertiser's message during a specific time frame.

Recall Tests: Advertising effectiveness tests designed to measure advertising recall.

Receiver: The person(s) with whom the sender of the message shares thought or information.

Recency Effect: The theory that arguments presented at the end of the message are considered to be stronger and are therefore, more likely to be remembered.

Reminder Advertising: Advertising designed to keep the name of the product or brand in the mind of the receiver.

Response Hierarchy Models: Response hierarchy models of marketing communications concentrate on consumer's specific responses to communications. A number of models have been developed to explain how consumers may pass through various stages in eliciting some behaviour.

Response: The set of reactions the receiver has after seeing, hearing, or reading a message.

S

Selective Attention: A perceptual process in which consumers choose to attend to some stimuli and not others.

Selective Perception: The perceptual process involving the filtering or screening of exposure, attention, comprehension, and retention.

Selective Retention: The perceptual process whereby consumers remember some information but not all.

Self-regulation: The practice followed by the advertising industry of regulating and controlling advertising to remain within the ethical limits and thus, avoiding interference by outside agencies such as the government.

Shock Advertising: Advertising in which marketers use nudity, sexual suggestiveness, or other startling images to get consumers' attention.

Slogan: An adverting campaign often carries a slogan which is a combination of catchy and memorable words that represent the company's message and often identifies the brand.

Source: The sender (person, group or organisation) of the message.

Speciality Advertising: An advertising, sales promotion, and other motivational communications that employ useful articles of merchandise imprinted with an advertiser's name, message, or logo.

Split Run Test: An advertising effectiveness measure in which different versions of an ad are run in alternative copies of the same newspaper and/or magazine.

Storyboard: In case of a television ad, the storyboard represents the various stages of the commercial from start to finish.

Support Media: The media used to support or reinforce messages sent to target markets through other more "dominant" and/or more traditional media.

Surrogate Advertising: Surrogate advertising can be defined as the strategy used by manufacturers and advertisers to promote a product in the guise of another, when the advertisement of the former is banned by the law of the land.

T

Target Market: The target market for a product can be defined as the group of people or market segment(s) to which the marketer wants to sell a product.

Target Rating Points (TRPs): The number of persons in the primary target audience that the media buy will reach, and the number of times.

Teaser Advertising: An ad designed to create curiosity and build excitement and interest in a product or brand without showing it.

Trade Advertising: Advertising targeted to wholesalers and retailers.

Traditional Media: Commonly thought of media that have been employed for years. These include radio, television and newspaper advertising.

Traffic: Traffic refers to the number of visitors that come to the website.

Transit Advertising: Advertising targeted to target audiences exposed to commercial transportation facilities, including buses, taxis, trolleys, airplanes and subways.

Two-sided Message: A message in which both good and bad points about a product or claim are presented.

U

Unaided recall: A research method in which a respondent is given no assistance in answering questions regarding a specific advertisement.

Unique Selling Proposition: An advertising strategy that focuses on a product or service attribute that is distinctive to a particular brand and offers an important benefit to the customer.

V

Vehicle: A specific channel or publication for carrying the advertising message to a target audience. For example, if the medium is magazines, the vehicle could be Femina magazine.

Vertical Cooperative Advertising: A cooperative arrangement under which a manufacturer pays for a portion of the advertising that a retailer runs to promote the manufacturer's product and its availability in the retailer's place of business.

Voiceover (VO): A message on the screen in a television commercial that is narrated or described by the narrator who is not visible. Voice over is the voice behind an ad.

W

Website: Virtual location on World Wide Web (WWW), containing several subject or company related web pages and data files accessible through a browser.

Y

Yellow Pages: A telephone directory providing names of companies that provide specific products and/or services.

Z

Zapping: The use of a remote control device to change channels and switch away from the channels.

Zipping: Fast-forwarding through commercials during the playback of a programme that is previously recorded.